ALSO BY R. W. APPLE JR.

Apple's Europe

APPLE'S AMERICA

APPLE'S AMERICA

THE DISCRIMINATING TRAVELER'S GUIDE
TO 40 GREAT CITIES IN
THE UNITED STATES AND CANADA

for George Bill

R. W. APPLE JR.

with thanks for many good Houston's meals

Johnny Apple

NORTH POINT PRESS

A DIVISION OF FARRAR, STRAUS AND GIROUX

NEW YORK

North Point Press
A division of Farrar, Straus and Giroux
19 Union Square West, New York 10003

Distributed in Canada by Douglas & McIntyre Ltd.
Printed in the United States of America
First edition, 2005

Library of Congress Cataloging-in-Publication Data
Apple, R. W. (Raymond Walter), 1934–
Apple's America : the discriminating traveler's guide to 40 great cities in the United States and Canada / R. W. Apple Jr.— 1st ed.
p. cm.
Includes index.
ISBN-13: 978-0-86547-685-1
ISBN-10: 0-86547-685-3 (alk. paper)
1. United States—Guidebooks. 2. Canada—Guidebooks. 3. Cities and towns—United States—Guidebooks. 4. Cities and towns—Canada—Guidebooks. I. Title.

E158.A599 2005
917.304'931—dc22

2004057589

Designed by Jonathan D. Lippincott

www.fsgbooks.com

10 9 8 7 6 5 4 3 2 1

for Betsey, *sine qua non*

CONTENTS

INTRODUCTION

This book grew out of a series of monthly articles written for *The New York Times*, beginning in 1997 and ending in 2000. Like so much of my work, that series grew, in turn, out of a suggestion made by my wife, Betsey. Shortly after the 1996 campaign ended, and with it, or so I believed, my coverage of American politics, I was casting about for a new topic to add to my established repertoire of food, travel, and arts pieces.

The phone rang, and the voice at the other end, that of a semi-forgotten acquaintance, asked a series of questions about Minneapolis (or was it Milwaukee?), in anticipation of a business trip. Is there anything interesting to do there? Any music? Museums? History? Any good restaurants? Hotels? What's the place really like?

People had been coming to me with queries like that for many years, I suppose because they thought I must have learned something of value in the course of four decades crisscrossing the continent in professional pursuit of politicians and other quarry. I could usually give at least a sketchy answer because all that travel had indeed taught me useful lessons. In the days before cell phones and cable news channels, covering presidential campaigns was a lot like being in the army: brief islands of drama surrounded by seas of ennui. So journalists in search of diversion, supported by expense accounts approved by indulgent editors, found and frequented good restaurants around the country. Never a feckless eater, I enthusiastically played this game from the time of my maiden campaign voyage, following Nelson Rockefeller out to Oregon in 1964, when I first tasted the fabulous Pacific salmon at the Benson on Broadway in Portland. Time permitting, and a few times when it really didn't, I also indulged my other interests—exploring Chicago's pioneering skyscrapers, taking in a ball game here and there, prowling the corridors of Boston's museums, and spending the odd evening at the opera (for me, the highlight of George McGovern's campaign was Anja Silja, unforgettable as Lulu in San Francisco).

After listening to me playing Baedeker for the umpteenth time, for the man headed for Minneapolis or Milwaukee, Betsey said, "You ought to write all that stuff down." Well-drilled and occasionally well-behaved husband that I am, I did as she said—at modest length at first, beginning with Cleveland, near which I grew up, and at greater length later, finishing with Honolulu, the American fantasy city par excellence.

Before I began, I had been to most cities in America at least once, and to the important ones as many as fifteen or twenty times. Nonetheless, I revisited each of the cities I decided to write about, most of the time with Betsey, who drove dozens of rental cars, shared hundreds of meals, and visited countless historical sites. When people asked her how she spent her time, she took to replying, good-naturedly, "Driving Mr. Daisy."

How did I choose where to go? The twenty biggest cities in the United States, to start with, except for New York. Since the *Times* is based in New York, it runs articles about the city every day and felt no need of another from me, especially since the conceit of the series was to provide guidance for travelers based mostly in and near New York. I could have written a New York chapter especially for this book, of course, but it took E. B. White an entire volume, however slim, to describe what he called the city's "steady, irresistible charm," and I had no desire to go head-to-head with the master. So with my apologies, dear reader, you will have to read of the metropolis elsewhere.

What you *will* encounter here, in addition to cities like Miami and Seattle and Houston that you might have expected, are plenty of smaller towns that I have always found interesting because of their historical importance (Charleston, Louisville) or unique culture (New Orleans, Santa Fe). I include Hampton Roads and Tampa Bay, which are bodies of water, obviously, not cities, but which draw the urban areas surrounding them into metropolitan entities that function much like cities. And I include three great Canadian cities because they are close to the United States border and because I have had a love affair with our northern neighbor since taking boyhood fishing trips there.

Had I set out on my travels in a muckraking frame of mind, a rather different kind of book would no doubt have resulted. It might have focused in part on the federal government's dire neglect of American cities, during the Reagan administration in particular, and some of the many consequences thereof. But my intent was different: to celebrate assets that would give pleasure to the traveler, rather than to bemoan liabilities.

If I found plenty of dilapidation and discouragement, I also found things that surprised me and things to admire almost everywhere I went. Buildings by Henry Hobson Richardson, Louis Sullivan, and Frank Lloyd Wright, for example, remind visitors to Buffalo—who may have thought about the place only when the Bills got to the Super Bowl—that it was once a major economic and political center. Houston has a superlative opera company and one of the nation's finest new museums, the Menil Collection. Vancouver has the best collection of Asian restaurants in North America, in my estimation at least.

Once upon a time, only New York, San Francisco, and New Orleans attracted visitors because of the quality of their restaurants. But now, to the unending delight of a gourmand like myself, a case can be made for an eating trip to Chicago or Seattle or a dozen other cities. Seldom do I have to resort to my hard-to-ruin road meal of the bad old days—shrimp cocktail, strip steak medium rare, baked potato, apple pie. Few are the American cities today where you can't find worthwhile wine lists.

Mostly missing here, you'll see, is any discussion of bars or nightclubs. My daughter, Catherine Collins—my stepdaughter, actually, but we both find that word inappropriately harsh—says I couldn't talk my way past a red rope if my life were at stake. True enough, though I used to wangle my way in to hear Teddy Wilson or Mabel Mercer. To me, moreover, one bar is the same as another. I readily admit that I get jumpy in them after a martini or two—that's an unfashionably traditional gin martini, eight-to-one, if you please, with an olive or a twist, no chocolate and no cranberry juice.

For the book, I re-revisited many of my forty cities, followed their triumphs and travails in newspapers, in magazines and on the Internet, and then recast the original articles to bring them up to date. Some cities seemed to require more description, some less. I have stayed in nearly all the hotels and eaten in nearly all the restaurants recommended here; I have tried to avoid retailing others' judgments as my own. But restaurants are even more subject to change than most things in life, and a place that served me good meals may serve you bad ones. Some may have closed since press time.

In an era of headlong technological innovation, upheavals in trade and commerce, and changing patterns of migration, American cities have had a tough time of it during the last few decades. Manufacturing jobs have moved south and overseas, leaving parts of Detroit and Philadelphia desolate. Phoenix and San Diego have grown rapidly, thanks to their climates and appeal as leisure centers. Seattle and Boston and, more surprisingly, Pittsburgh have reinvented themselves as high-tech capitals. Without trying very hard, Miami has become a kind of offshore capital of Latin America, attracting migrants and part-time residents from all over that continent. And by trafficking in a kind of sin that most people find more naughty than truly reprehensible, Las Vegas has thrived as a bright, magical—if transparently ersatz—oasis in the desert.

Other cities have developed other strategies for rejuvenation. In some, universities have provided the required energy. In many others, notably Philadelphia, the arts have done so, and museums have taken on functions in civic life they never had before. With new buildings designed by the most celebrated architects of our day, the Andeos and Calatravas, the Gehrys and Hadids, museums have become not only places for the display of fine art but also foci of civic pride, educational centers, settings for gala social events, and, above all, lures for tourists with open wallets.

New museums and performing arts centers have also helped in the inner cities' ongoing competition with suburbs, exurbs, and "rim cities," providing experiences at the center that the periphery cannot. New ballparks, football stadia, and arenas built in or near aging downtowns have achieved one of Jane Jacobs's most treasured goals: urban streets thronged with people after business hours. Camden Yards, built in an appealingly nostalgic vernacular, brings thousands into the very heart of Baltimore, and MCI Arena has engendered a pulsating new business, hotel, and restaurant district in Washington.

I owe thanks to many people for their unstinting help over the long period of this book's gestation, not least to colleagues at the *Times*. Two executive editors, Joseph Lelyveld and Howell Raines, allowed me the time and money to range across our continent, without which I could not possibly have undertaken such a project. I am grateful to them and to Wendy Sclight, who edited the original articles, somehow managing, with nary a grumble, to find adequate space for them even when they grew longer. Susan Chira found a way for me to adapt the articles, whose copyright belongs to the *Times*.

The research assistance of Catherine Collins would have been invaluable in any event; since she is a much-loved member of the family, it was also immensely gratifying. She unearthed many fascinating nuggets and caught many instances where events had overtaken my original texts. She knows how much I appreciate her hard work, which she undertook although fully occupied with her own television documentary projects. My wife, Betsey, not only suggested the project, helped shape the choice of cities, and traveled with me on most of my reporting trips but also read every word before it first saw print, unfailingly improving my initial drafts. For going on twenty-five years now, she has been my indispensable partner in everything I do, a treasure truly beyond price.

For me, one of the great joys of *Apple's America* has been the fast friendship I have formed with its editor, the delightful and redoubtable Elisabeth Sifton. Blessed with good humor as well as consistently good judgment, always stocked with tasty morsels of gossip as well as arcane bits of information, she turned hard work into pure pleasure.

Literally hundreds of people helped me get my bearings as I moved from city to city. To list them all here would be tedious, but it would be niggardly not to express my appreciation to those who gave special aid. In Atlanta, Colin Campbell, Jimmy Carter; in Austin, Molly Ivins, James S. Fishkin, Patricia Sharpe, the late George Christian; in Baltimore, Paul S. Sarbanes, Raymond A. Mason, Marty Katz, Tony Foreman; in Boston, David Greenway, Anthony Lewis, Margaret Marshall, Caroline Taylor, Jasper White; in Buffalo, Tim Russert; in Charleston, Joseph P. Riley Jr., Jane Pinckney Hanahan.

In Chicago, William Rice, Newton N. Minow, Barbara Pittman, Jovan Trboyevic, Ward Just, Magda Krance; in Cincinnati, Chuck Martin; in Cleveland, Linda and Fred Griffith, Sidmon J. Kaplan; in Dallas, Paula Lambert, Patricia Perini, Harry McPherson, Dotty Griffith, Robert S. Strauss, Jim Lehrer, Raymond Nasher; in Detroit, Charles Eisendrath, Robert H. Giles, Robert Pisor; in Honolulu, Sam Choy, Jay Fidell, Samuel P. King, Joyce Matsumoto; in Houston, Robert and Mimi Del Grande, Edward P. Djerejian.

In Kansas City, Marc F. Wilson, Calvin Trillin; in Las Vegas, Sig Rogich, Steve Wynn; in Los Angeles, David Shaw, Sean Daniel, Barry Munitz, Tom Warner, Wolfgang Puck, the late Phyllis Jenkins; in Louisville, Henry Bessire, Daniel D. Maye, Susan Riegler; in Miami, Hodding Carter III, Ricardo Suarez, Norman Van Aken, Bonnie Clearwater; in Milwaukee, James Gramentine, Jack L. Goodsitt, Sandy D'Amato, the late Henry S. Reuss; in Minneapolis and St. Paul, Walter F. Mondale, John W. Milton.

In Montreal, Morley Safer, James MacGuire; in Nashville, John Egerton, John Siegenthaler, Karyn Frist, Joe Ledbetter; in New Orleans, Julia Reed, Lolis Eric Elie, Paul C. P. McIlhenny, Paul Fabry, Ella Brennan; in Hampton Roads, Peter Mark, Hunter B. Andrews, Robert C. Wilburn; in Philadelphia, Joseph H. Kluger, Rick Nichols, Arlen Specter, Anne d'Harnoncourt, Ruth Hirshey; in Phoenix, John McCain, Barbara Fenzl, Cheryl Alters Jamison; in Pittsburgh, Ted Smyth, Max King, Thomas Sokolowski.

In Portland, Steve McCarthy; in Providence, Frederick Lippitt, the late J. Carter Brown, Nancy Barr; in San Diego, Samuel Popkin, James L. Bowers, Neil Morgan; in San Francisco, Bob Long, Roberta Klugman, the late Herb Caen, Alice Waters, Stan Bromley, Willie L. Brown Jr.; in Santa Fe, Tom

Margittai, Barbara Buhler Lynes, Elizabeth Martin, Susan Conway and Patrick Oliphant, Joyce Idema; in Savannah, Ashby Angell, Elizabeth Terry; in Seattle, Shelby Scates, Phyllis Hayes, Jon Rowley, Speight Jenkins, Michael Kinsley; in St. Louis, Gerald Boyd, Danny Meyer, Tony Bommarito.

In Tampa Bay, Eugene Patterson, David E. Rosenbaum, Chris Sherman; in Toronto, Alan Sullivan, Alan Gotlieb; in Vancouver, Tom Rowe, Vicky Gabereau, John Nichol, Mike Harcourt, Nathan Fong, Christopher Gaze; in Washington, Roger Kennedy.

APPLE'S AMERICA

⫸ BOSTON

Boston is one of the oldest American cities, a repository of our national past, yet it has shown an extraordinary capacity to look to the future and reinvent itself when needed.

In days of yore, Boston traded and manufactured. Now it manages money and capitalizes on the technology developed in its laboratories. Finance and science fueled New England's surge in the 1990s, and when they hit hard times, so did metropolitan Boston's economy. Between 2001, when employment peaked, and the spring of 2003, Massachusetts lost nearly 5 percent of its jobs, mostly in Boston and its satellite cities.

But the worm is turning again. The city has lived through this cycle a dozen times in the past; bust follows boom, and then boom follows bust. The one constant has been ideas: Boston ideas have washed across the United States and around the world for more than two centuries. Actually, there is a second constant: the accent, as distinctive as those of Brooklyn and New Orleans. Hear a man say "farm"—"fahm"—in that special nasal way, and you know where he's from. The sound of "a brick-throated bullfrog," Ford Madox Ford called it.

The Pilgrims put down roots at nearby Plymouth in the seventeenth century, followed closely by the Puritans in Boston itself, where the first governor of the Massachusetts Bay Colony, John Winthrop, enforced a stern moral code. In the eighteenth century, Boston seethed with revolution and justly claimed for itself the resonant title Cradle of American Independence. There can be very few cities in the country with as much to offer those who are intrigued by the past.

Dockside at the Charlestown Navy Yard, you can board "Old

Ironsides," the frigate *Constitution*, commissioned in 1797 and never decommissioned. You can visit the Old South Meeting House, a Colonial gem, built in 1729, with a sounding board hung above the pulpit, where Samuel Adams roused five thousand Bostonians against the tyrant in London and precipitated the Boston Tea Party. You can see Faneuil Hall, built in 1742 and still used occasionally for political meetings, with its grasshopper weather vane. And you can stand beside the Old State House, where five protestors, including a black man, Crispus Attucks, were killed by Redcoats in the Boston Massacre of 1770.

Boston loves its culture, with reason. The Asian collection at the Museum of Fine Arts has no peer in the Western Hemisphere. After twenty-eight years under the baton of Seiji Ozawa, born in China to Japanese parents, the Boston Symphony Orchestra, traditionally one of the top five ensembles in the United States, welcomed Cincinnati-born James Levine as its music director in 2004—the first American to hold that position. The inimitable Boston Pops flourishes as it did when Arthur Fiedler and then John Williams conducted it. And the whole glorious panoply of American architecture, from Bulfinch to Richardson to I. M. Pei, is on display here.

Boston loves its sports, too. In fact, it has often been said that only three things count here: sports, politics, and revenge. The basketball Celtics, who have never recovered from the loss of the formidable Larry Bird when he retired in 1992, are nevertheless beloved. Having ended eighty-six years of futility by sweeping the 2004 World Series (take that, Bambino!), the baseball Red Sox stand first in the hearts of Bostonians. They play in Fenway Park, a wonderful old bandbox, as idiosyncratically shaped as the city itself. (The football Patriots, who won the Super Bowl in 2002 and again in 2004, to the astonishment of a city inured to sporting tribulation, play not in Boston but in Foxboro, halfway to Providence.)

Boston is that increasing rarity in the United States, a truly superb walking town. Compact and convenient, a mosaic of distinctive neighborhoods, it is a baby London. Right at its heart lie the Boston Common and the Public Garden, twin parks that are made for strolling. Swan boats, propelled by paddles turned by pedals, cruise the garden's pond, familiar to all as the setting for Robert McCloskey's children's classic *Make Way for Ducklings*.

For decades, Boston's fearsome Brahmin aristocrats, members of the city's oldest families, ran everything. Cabots spoke only to Lowells, as the doggerel says, and Lowells spoke only to God. (Or is it the other way around? Authorities disagree.) Then the Irish fought their way to power. Gradually, the two worlds—the world of John P. Marquand's *Late George Apley* and the world of Boss Martin Lomasney, celebrated in Edwin O'Connor's *Last Hurrah*—came to terms with each other and learned to co-exist. Senator Edward M. Kennedy carries the flag of his brothers, of House Speaker Tip O'Neill, and of Mayor James Michael Curley—Boston Irish politicians, all—while William F. Weld, governor of Massachusetts from 1991 to 1997, walks in the patrician footsteps of two presidential Adamses (from nearby Quincy) and two senatorial Henry Cabot Lodges. And now, mirabile dictu, the three-term mayor is an Italian American (Thomas M. Menino) and the governor (Mitt Romney) is a Mormon with Utah roots.

William Lloyd Garrison, foremost of the abolitionists, made his first anti-slavery speech in Park Street Church in 1829, and Robert Gould Shaw helped to raise a black regiment in Boston to fight in the Civil War. Memorialized in a sculpture on Beacon Hill by Augustus Saint-Gaudens, the 54th Massachusetts Regiment staged a heroic but suicidal charge at Fort Wagner, South Carolina, depicted in the movie *Glory*. But the city's tolerance was dented in the twentieth century. Opposition to the court-ordered busing of students in the interest of racial balance led to riots and controversy, with the city's intellectuals, many of whose children attended private schools, pitted against the clannish, less affluent Irish Americans of South Boston.

For decades, though no longer, Yankee hostility to other tribes was obvious, with the haughty Somerset Club a preeminent symbol of that. During the Civil War, the club was a stronghold of the Bostonians who sympathized with the Confederacy, known as Copperheads, and it is enshrined in Boston lore that they closed the club's windows whenever Robert Gould Shaw walked past. Until recently, even eminent Irish Catholics were unwelcome as members.

In the nineteenth century, Bostonians developed a reputation for blue-nosed narrow-mindedness—"Banned in Boston!" promoters used to say when they wanted to tout a naughty book or a risqué play—and for smugness in general. A guest at a White House party once told Franklin D. Roosevelt, "I'm from Boston." He replied, "You'll never get over it."

In 1857, Oliver Wendell Holmes Sr. wrote that Boston, or more precisely the State House atop Beacon Hill, was "the hub of the solar system." People still call their city the Hub today, but they use the term self-mockingly. They also call it Beantown, after their beloved baked beans, which gives them something in common with the inhabitants of Florence, another historic city, who call themselves "mangiafagioli"—bean-eaters.

Boston patriots led the way to American independence, dumping chests of English tea into the waters of the colonies' most important harbor to protest royal taxes. Paul Revere, silversmith and midnight rider, and John Hancock, president of the Continental Congress, were Bostonians. The history-changing battles of Lexington and Concord and Bunker Hill were fought on the periphery of the city.

American legal tradition also owes much to Boston. The Supreme Judicial Court of Massachusetts, founded in 1692 and thus predating the United States Supreme Court, has sat without interruption longer than any other court in the Western world.

In the early days, Boston lived by the sea, its trade built upon cod. That humble fish, though increasingly scarce, is still a favorite on local dinner tables, and a wooden replica, the Sacred Cod, hangs in the chamber of the House of Representatives in the State House (just as the Lord Chancellor in Britain sits on a sack of wool as a reminder of the source of England's early wealth). When the British market dried up, Boston opened trade routes to the East, bringing porcelain, spices, and silks to the young United States in its rakish clipper ships. And when steel-hulled ships made clippers obsolete, the city turned to manufacturing; Boston money and management built the mills in the smaller cities nearby, like Lowell.

The manufacturing profits funded Boston's great educational and cultural institutions. Henry Lee Higginson came home from the Civil War, established the Boston Symphony

Orchestra, and gave the Boston Museum of Fine Arts a Roger van der Weyden painting to which it still accords a place of honor. Harvard University, founded in 1636, across the Charles River in Cambridge, flourished anew. Throughout the nineteenth century, Boston was the nation's intellectual locomotive.

The city and its suburbs were filled with writers whose names still resound: Ralph Waldo Emerson, Henry David Thoreau, Margaret Fuller and the other Transcendentalists, the poet Henry Wadsworth Longfellow, the historian Francis Parkman, the psychologist William James, the educational reformer Horace Mann, the philosopher George Santayana, and the novelist William Dean Howells, editor of *The Atlantic Monthly*.

They have their modern-day successors in scholars and writers like John Kenneth Galbraith and Henry Louis Gates Jr. Houghton Mifflin, the Beacon Press, and *The Atlantic* carry on the city's long publishing tradition. WGBH, Boston's public television station, produces much of the best fare on PBS, including *The American Experience* and *Frontline*, and it helped to change the eating habits of a nation with Julia Child's pioneering cooking programs.

Boston and its suburbs are home to countless colleges and universities: peerless Harvard, the oldest institution of higher education in the United States, whose law, medical, divinity, public health, and business schools educate many of the nation's leaders-to-be; the Massachusetts Institute of Technology, which is one of the world's great science and engineering schools; Wellesley College, Hillary Rodham Clinton's alma mater; Tufts and Brandeis Universities; Boston College; Boston University; and Northeastern University. The Boston Latin School, founded April 23, 1635, is the nation's oldest public school. Eminent hospitals, such as Massachusetts General and Brigham and Women's, draw patients from everywhere, and high-technology businesses cluster around almost every exit on Route 128, the semicircular highway that skirts the city.

For almost half a century, from the 1920s to the 1960s, Boston slumbered contentedly, subsisting largely, it seemed, on memories. But the presidency of John F. Kennedy, starting in 1961, focused national and world attention on the city once again. (Kennedy's presidential library is housed in a building designed by I. M. Pei in Dorchester, south of the city center.) Equally important, a mayor named John Collins and a redevelopment genius named Edward Logue began to reshape the place at the same time. They cleared out the malodorous neighborhood around Scollay Square, famous for the stripteases at the Old Howard, installing a new government center there. The nearby Quincy Market was turned into a chic shopping precinct by the architect Benjamin Thompson, incorporating the raucous old eating house called Durgin-Park, famous for roast rib of beef and Indian pudding. In and near Copley Square, new office towers were built for the Prudential and John Hancock insurance companies, helping to revive that neighborhood.

For a time in the 1990s, average rents exceeded those in Manhattan and San Francisco, and hotel rooms were as scarce as downtown parking meters. But real estate softened, and so did tourism. Economic frustration focused on The Big Dig, an enormous enterprise begun in the 1980s and designed to bury the city's unsightly main north-south highway deep beneath the ground. The project was supposed to cost $2.5 billion, but after fifteen years, the bill had risen to $14.5 billion, and the highway was still not finished. The completion date slipped to 2005 or 2006.

Still, the new highway and other improvements to the transportation network prompted public and private planners to press ahead with ambitious projects around the harbor, especially in South Boston—"Southie" to generations of proud, insular Irish Americans. These include hotels; housing; retail blocks; a sinuous, $140 million, glass-clad office tower for Manulife Financial; and a vaulted, $700 million convention center.

But to return to the arts. Boston has a downtown commercial theater district, where many an aspiring Broadway show has had its kinks ironed out (or not). The city's theatrical life has long centered, however, across the Charles River in Cambridge, where the gifted, turbulent Robert Brustein founded and for twenty-two years directed the American Repertory Theater (ART), an unfailing source of new dramatic ideas. Cherry Jones, one of the joys of the American stage, honed her talents playing classic roles under Brustein's aegis. The ART's artistic director as of 2004 is Robert Woodruff, who made his name in regional theater, especially in northern and southern California, at first with the plays of Sam Shepard but more recently with radical takes on Shakespeare, Chekhov, and Brecht. In 2001 Mikko Nissinen stepped into Robert Marks's shoes at the Boston Ballet, New England's first professional repertory ballet company, and won quick plaudits for what *The Boston Globe* called a daring, energetic season.

Opera is a less happy story. For decades, Sarah Caldwell, who founded the Opera Company of Boston in 1957, kept it going, innovative if unstable, with bailing wire and duct tape. She also championed the music of Russian modernists like Rodion Shchedrin and Alfred Schnittke. But the Caldwell era collapsed in a heap of recriminations over questionable financial practices in 1990, and the Boston Lyric Opera, now headed by Leon Major, a Canadian, is a more modest proposition, with only three productions a year, after flirting briefly with four.

The Boston Symphony Orchestra (BSO) has always been Boston's performing arts favorite. In winter this superb ensemble plays in Symphony Hall—which need not take a back seat, aesthetically or acoustically, even to the Musikverein in Vienna—and in summer it plays in the Music Shed at Tanglewood, in the Berkshire Hills of western Massachusetts. Ozawa, lithe and balletic, who was praised for musicianship by many but condemned for stodgy programs by many others, led it for twenty-eight years, longer even than the Russian Serge Koussevitzky or the Frenchman Charles Munch, two of his noble predecessors. The stocky, more restrained Levine— "Jimmy" to everyone in the musical world—built a great orchestra and a shining reputation for himself at the Metropolitan Opera. Getting him was considered a great coup for Boston, and Bernard Holland, a tough critic, found his conducting style as compelling as ever in an early outing here.

If music played on original instruments has struggled elsewhere, it has scored success after success in Boston, through the Handel and Haydn Society, the Boston Baroque, and the Boston Camarata. Then there is the Boston Pops, a group made up mostly of BSO players that performs light music; it is as much admired across the country, through its recordings and its PBS broadcasts, as in Boston. And a rich musical life revolves around the New England Conservatory of Music.

The Museum of Fine Arts stands first among Boston's many museums. Its great Japanese collection, worth a visit all by itself, was greatly amplified in the 1890s by a Harvard scholar of Japanese culture, Ernest Fenollosa, the brilliant son of a Spanish musician who had settled in Salem, Massachusetts. The European and American pictures stem from many sources; in addition to Higginson's van der Weyden, *St. Luke Painting the Virgin*, possibly the most important Flemish painting in America, they include what may be Gauguin's masterpiece, *Where Did We Come From? What Are We? Where Are We Going?*, Copley's portrait of Paul Revere (much of whose silver the museum also shows) as the epitome of the republican craftsman, and Gilbert Stuart's iconic portrait of George Washington.

The MFA's director, Malcolm Rogers, has recently subjected the museum to what the critic Ada Louise Huxtable called "a seismic shake-up," which will climax in 2008 with the completion of an expansion from 531,000 to 677,000 square feet. The British architect Norman Foster conceived the plan for the new building, whose most important element is a glass-and-steel atrium similar to the one he designed to cover the Great Court at the British Museum in London.

In 2006, it is hoped, the smaller, funkier Institute of Contemporary Art will move into quarters on the revivified waterfront in South Boston. Designed by a relatively little-known New York wife-and-husband team, Elizabeth Diller and Ricardo Scofidio, the building was hailed by Huxtable in *The Wall Street Journal* as "essentially a viewing box, inside and out, for art and the harbor, making a seamless experience of both."

The Isabella Stewart Gardner Museum is to the Museum of Fine Arts as the Frick is to the Metropolitan Museum of Art in New York. Built in 1903 in the style of a Venetian palazzo by a wealthy widow known as "Mrs. Jack," it is filled with treasures she chose with the help of Bernard Berenson, including a smashing late Titian, *The Rape of Europa*; fascinating canvases by Giotto, Martini, and Raphael; a Sargent portrait of Mrs. Gardner herself, in a then-daring black gown; but no longer, alas, *The Concert*, a tranquil little Vermeer that was stolen in a daring 1990 heist.

Harvard University administers a dozen museums, notably the Fogg, which would be the premier collection in most cities, and the Sackler, with a fine array of Asian art. The Busch-Reisinger is my favorite, with a first-rate collection of German Expressionists, including Klee, Beckmann, and Nolde.

Boston and its environs have buildings by leading modernists, including half a dozen prime works by the omnipresent I. M. Pei and landmark structures by Eero Saarinen (the MIT Chapel) and Le Corbusier (the Carpenter Center for the Visual Arts at Harvard, his only United States building). The clapboard Paul Revere House, in the North End, and the Parson Capen House, in Topsfield, are among the few seventeenth-century buildings left in America. Charles Bulfinch, the nation's first professional architect, designed the State House, one of Boston's finest late-eighteenth-century buildings, with an imposing Palladian facade and a dome covered with gold leaf. And in Copley Square the Boston Public Library, a sedate beaux arts structure of 1888–95, by Charles F. McKim of McKim, Mead & White, found a superbly compatible if stylistically contrasting addition at the hand of Philip Johnson in 1972.

But it is Henry Hobson Richardson, high priest of Romanesque Revival, an important precursor of the modern era, who best epitomizes Boston architecture. For the Harvard Yard, where "at certain hours of the day," in Henry James's words, "a thousand undergraduates, with books under their arm and youth in their step, flit from one school to another," he built Sever Hall and Austin Hall, both shy of his best. On residential Brattle Street nearby stands one of the handsomest of his Shingle-style buildings, Stoughton House. His masterpiece, one of the triumphs of the nineteenth century, is Trinity Church, Boston, built for Phillips Brooks in 1876, whose rusticated stone is as burly and forceful as the architect himself. Its interior glows, on sunny days, with light refracted through John LaFarge's celebrated stained-glass windows.

The whole area on and at the foot of Beacon Hill is packed with lovely, ruddy, brick townhouses, a few of them with purple windows that have changed color because of an excess of manganese oxide in the glass. The area is one of the nation's splendid architectural ensembles. Behind the sandstone facade of 10½ Beacon Street stands the Boston Athenaeum, a distinguished private library, which holds George Washington's personal book collection. Tucked away off a side street is Louisburg Square, my favorite space in the city. A handsome rectangle of nineteenth-century houses, it has sheltered some of Boston's literary lions—Howells at No. 4 and the novelist Louisa May Alcott at No. 10—along with other people of taste. (My much-loved great-aunt Marguerite A. Barton first showed me the wonders of old Boston; she never lived on Louisburg Square, but she would have fit right in.)

WHERE TO STAY

Boston Harbor Hotel, 70 Rowes Wharf, (617) 439-7000. On the waterfront, a few steps from the city's financial district, this place offers arresting harbor views, especially wonderful to see from your room at sunrise. It offers a water taxi to Logan Airport, which lets you bypass snarls in the tunnels. Rowes Wharf, the hotel's restaurant, specializes in modern New England cooking, with the best brunch in town on Sundays.

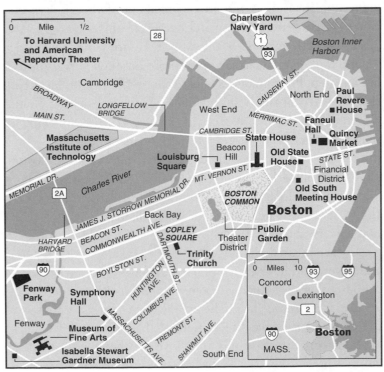

Charles Hotel in Harvard Square, 1 Bennett Street, Cambridge, (617) 864-1200. Great for old grads, visiting lecturers, and proud parents. (Is there any other kind, when the young-uns get into Harvard or MIT?) The 375 bedrooms, mostly on the snug side, have a lean, Quakery feel, with quilts and Colonial-style furniture. Chilly reception. Jody Adams's Rialto restaurant can falter, but most nights the Mediterranean fare scores.

Eliot Suites Hotel, 370 Commonwealth Avenue, (617) 267-1607. This is a find, a fairly priced neo-Georgian hotel built in 1925 and discerningly renovated not long ago. Tucked into patrician Back Bay, it is convenient for shopping along nearby Newbury Street. Many of the seventy-nine suites have kitchens, and Clio, a restaurant with the innovative cuisine of Ken Oringer (great sea urchin dishes), and the new Uni sashimi bar await downstairs.

Four Seasons, 200 Boylston Street, (617) 338-4400. Overlooking the Boston Common and Public Garden, with the State House dome just beyond, this one gets an A for location—and for everything else: attentive service, with jolly, efficient doormen; large, handsome bedrooms (including one, to which I was once upgraded, with a grand piano); one of Boston's very best restaurants (see below), lush lobby flowers; and a fifty-foot indoor pool.

WHERE TO EAT

Aujourd'hui, Four Seasons (see above). The first time I took Julia Child out to eat, I asked her where she wanted to go; it was her town. She chose Aujourd'hui. Like Julia, it epitomizes unaffected style and charm. The kitchen produces Americanized haute cuisine that lets the quality of the ingredients shine through, and some think it Boston's premier restaurant. "*Très chic, très cher*," says *Boston Magazine*, which pretty well sums it up.

Blue Ginger, 583 Washington Street, Wellesley, (781) 283-5790. So much fusion cooking is so bad that it's a joy to taste that of Ming Tsai, a Food Network star though still only in his thirties, who grew up in his family's Chinese restaurant in Ohio, then went to Yale. Try his crab cake with kaffir lime, and you'll think Baltimore and Bangkok at the same time, or the shu mai dumplings stuffed with foie gras and shiitakes in caramelized onion broth. No one in the country quite matches Tsai's virtuosity in this idiom.

East Coast Grill, 1271 Cambridge Street, Cambridge, (617) 491-6568. Author, grillmeister, and hot-sauce maven Chris Schlesinger serves barbecue in several regional styles. Waygood raw bar, reasonable prices, good sides but no side.

Hamersley's, 553 Tremont Street, (617) 423-2700. That's Gordon Hamersley in the Red Sox cap at the range, and his winter menu delivers genuine cold-weather cheer. To the superb roast chicken, he adds items like seared foie gras with prunes and armagnac, choucroute with smoked bacon, sausage and quail, and slow-cooked Vermont pig with endive, all accompanied by Mrs. Hamersley's sagely chosen wines. My local HQ.

Legal Seafoods, 26 Park Square, (617) 426-4444; and other locations. Don't go to Legal for fancy cooking; go because Roger Berkowitz buys the best fish and shellfish and tests it for freshness and purity. The oysters and clams on the half shell are nonpareil; the clam chowder is Boston's best, rich but not thick; and oh, the fried clams!

Locke-Ober, 3 Winter Place, (617) 542-1340. Lydia Shire has done the near-impossible, dragging this clubby, old-fashioned Brahmin dining experience into the twenty-first century. The mahogany bar shines, as does the food—notably lighter versions of classics like JFK's Lobster Stew, a Lucullan fantasy of cream, sherry, butter, and shellfish.

Oleana, 134 Hampshire Street, Cambridge, (617) 661-0505. Seattle-born, Paris-trained Ana Sortun is Norwegian American, but it is the food of the Mediterranean, especially Turkey, that she prepares with such flair at her cozy restaurant. Try the bean and walnut pâté and the kunefe, an addictive dessert of puff pastry, cheese, pistachios, nutmeg, sugar, and rose water. Go on, try them. You'll soon be another Sortun convert.

Summer Shack, 10 Scotia Street, (617) 867-9955. There's not much that Jasper White, a jovial giant of a chef from New Jersey, doesn't know about New England seafood. He offers a rotating selection of a dozen kinds of oysters daily, from all points of the Northeastern coast, Prince Edward Island to Connecticut. His lobsters should not be missed, either, whether simply steamed or pan-roasted with chervil, chives, and bourbon.

Les Zygomates, 129 South Street, (617) 542-5108. This is the kind of wine bar every town needs, a jazzy meeting place for young and old, rich and just getting by. Ian Just, the chef, learned his craft at the Paris mother house of Les Zyg, and his plats du jour warm the heart (and other parts). The name, fittingly, refers to the muscles that make you smile.

IIII➡ PROVIDENCE

Lord Bryce, the English commentator on trans-Atlantic matters, suggested that Providence might become the first American city-state. That never happened, but the city's name is embedded in the state's official title, Rhode Island and Providence Plantations, and the two are hard to separate.

Neither is big. The state, covering only 1,214 square miles, is the nation's smallest; a particularly bumptious Texas governor once suggested that his state could wear Rhode Island as a watch fob. The city, founded by Roger Williams in 1636 as a refuge for religious dissenters, is an urban pipsqueak, with only 173,618 inhabitants, although 1,188,613 people live in the two-state metropolitan area. Situated at the head of Narraganset Bay, this spreads from Rhode Island into Massachusetts.

Providence revels in its patrician heritage. For nearly two centuries, the Five Families—Browns, Metcalfs, Goddards, Lippitts, and Chafees—have played prominent roles in the city's life. (Today, Lincoln Chafee is one of Rhode Island's two United States senators, a Republican from an overwhelmingly Democratic state.) No city has a snootier social redoubt than the Hope Club, where even the servants seem extravagantly well mannered, and no city has a finer collection of Colonial and Federal houses than those on the "mile of history," Benefit Street between Church and Transit Streets.

The arts are well supported. Since 1964, Providence has had one of the nation's leading regional theaters, the Trinity Repertory Company, whose artistic director, Oskar Eustis, commissioned the Pulitzer Prize–winning *Angels in America* from Tony Kushner. The museum at the Rhode Island School of Design houses an art collection of comprehensible size but global reach. Among its treasures are superb examples of furniture by several of the great Newport cabinetmakers, including Job Townsend and his son-in-law John Goddard.

But the city also has a less noble face. Since early times, it has been a school for scandal. Cotton Mather, that stiff-necked old Massachusetts Puritan, called Rhode Island "the sewer of New England," and George Washington accused it of "impolitic, unjust—and one might add, without much impropriety—scandalous conduct." In 1904, the muckraker Lincoln Steffens wrote in *McClure's Magazine* that "Rhode Island is a state for sale, cheap." In the last several decades, the careers of two governors, a chief justice, and a prominent congressman have been marred by lofty inattention to the ethical niceties.

Which brings us to Buddy, more formally known as Vincent A. Cianci Jr. Shrewd, gregarious, and hard as nails, a tireless promoter and reshaper of Providence, Cianci has been in and out of the mayor's office, and in and out of jail, since 1974. He is a folk hero in "Rogues' Island," a burly lover of marinara sauce and red wine. Cianci was convicted in 1984 of roughing up a man he suspected of sleeping with his estranged wife; witnesses said he stubbed out a cigarette in the eye of his victim, a wealthy contractor, and beat him with an ashtray and a log. He served five years' probation, working as a radio talk-show host, and swept back into office in 1991, only to be sentenced in December 2002 to sixty-four months in federal prison in a bribery scandal. "He's a crook," one voter confided to me, "but I'd vote for him again."

Perhaps Roger Williams's sermons on tolerance have echoed down the generations. A. J. Liebling, who began his journalistic career here, said this about Providence: "There was nothing you could do about anything, but then nothing was so bad that you felt a burning urge to do anything about it."

In 1793, the Industrial Revolution came to North America in Pawtucket, just north of Providence, when Samuel Slater reproduced from memory Richard Arkwright's water-powered spinning frame, on which he had worked in England. The restored Slater's Mill, a humble frame building, looks more like a farm shed than an industrial landmark. But vast riches flowed from the mills that grew out of Slater's invention, not least into the pockets of the Brown family, the descendants of the Reverend Chad Browne, who came to Providence in 1638 with his wife and eight-year-old son, John, "for reasons of conscience." One of his great-great-grandsons, Joseph Brown, designed the First Baptist Meeting House, a harmonious Georgian structure with a 185-foot steeple, built in 1774. He modeled the church, which houses the nation's oldest Baptist congregation, after a design in James Gibbs's *Book of Architecture*, published in London in 1728. The austere interior, dominated by an eighteenth-century Waterford chandelier, is surprisingly spacious. It was built to hold 1,200 people, at a time when the whole colony numbered only 4,321!

Joseph Brown had three brothers, John, Nicholas, and Moses; the four were known as Josey, Johnny, Nicky, and Mosey. All were astute businessmen who manufactured pig iron and spermaceti candles; some grew ever richer in the Triangle Trade, which linked New England, the West Indies, and West Africa in the traffic of molasses, rum, and slaves.

The Browns invested in the mills that grew out of Slater's innovation, in turnpikes and in banking and insurance. They traded with the Orient. They were the main early patrons of Rhode Island College, later Brown University, the seventh such institution founded in the colonies, in 1764. (Irony of ironies, it was the first to choose an African American as president, Ruth J. Simmons, in 2000.) They also built themselves a palace.

John Quincy Adams described the Browns' three-story brick house, which stands on the corner of Benefit and Power Streets, as "the most magnificent and elegant private mansion that I have ever seen on this continent." It is equally ravishing today, the showpiece of eighteenth-century Providence architecture. The aesthetic ideals of the Enlightenment, balance and symmetry, are writ large on the house's facade: a chimney at each corner, a balustrade around the roof and another over the entrance porch, a Palladian window in the center. Inside, too: a broad central hall, with a grand staircase at the rear, flanked by paired rooms. The rich decoration includes swags, pilasters, medallions, and scroll pediments.

Another grand house with family connections, the Nightingale-Brown House, dating from 1792, houses the John

Nicholas Brown Center for the Study of American Civilization at Brown University. Browns lived in it for five generations. Unlike the John Brown house across the street, redone decades ago, the Nightingale-Brown House reopened only in 1993, and it still looks "a bit anesthetized by restoration," as the interior designer Mark Hampton once observed. Time and daily use will doubtless remedy that.

The twenty-four-room wooden structure is notable not only for its clapboard exterior painted a milky yellow, with a Palladian window and white quoins, but also for its interiors: pine-paneled dining room, library in crimson damask, parlor in green, and a foyer lined with some of the most covetable wallpaper in America. Printed from woodblocks made in France in the 1840s by Zuber, it depicts West Point, Niagara Falls, and other nineteenth-century American vistas.

Twentieth-century family members included the late J. Carter Brown, director of the National Gallery of Art in Washington, a patrician populist who pioneered blockbuster exhibitions, helping to redefine the modern museum. His father, John Nicholas Brown, was dubbed the richest boy in the world while at Harvard. The Browns paid for the Nightingale-Brown House restoration by selling a Goddard secretary at Christie's, where it brought $11 million, a world record for a work of art other than a painting.

Providence produced many rich men, including Senator Nelson Aldrich, nicknamed "the General Manager of the United States" and described by Geoffrey Wolff in his novel *Providence* as "a grocer-to-plutocrat Anglican who knew how to lay down a bribe and take one up." His daughter married John D. Rockefeller Jr., and they named one of their sons Nelson Aldrich Rockefeller. Henry Lippitt, a textile magnate who sold to both sides during the Civil War, was another wealthy local who went into politics, serving a term as governor. His palazzo on top of College Hill, begun in 1862, stayed in the family until 1981, and it was never "improved" by remodeling. What you see today is the authentic excess of Lincoln-era design, all but shouting its costliness: a powerful brick structure filled with painted ceilings, inlaid floors, gold leaf, marble, tiger maple, mirrors, and etched glass. It makes the head reel.

But that was as nothing compared to what went on in Newport, thirty-five miles south, toward the sea. It had been a major colonial seaport in its own right, as attested by a number of its buildings: the lovely Hunter House, with more fine Goddard furniture; Colony House (1739), and the Touro Synagogue (1759–63). The oldest synagogue in America, it has a pristine Classical interior, dominated by a dozen white Ionic columns, symbolizing the tribes of Israel.

Then, at the turn of the last century, when the fiendish income tax had yet to be invented, Newport became the world capital of conspicuous consumption. Sugar, coal, and shipping barons spent millions on "cottages"—houses of Babylonian opulence they occupied for two summer months a year. They raced lordly sloops called J-boats and fed caviar to their dogs. Oliver Hazard Perry Belmont of Belcourt Castle ordered evening clothes for his horses. When the journalist Bill Bryson reached Newport on the cross-country trip that he recorded in his book *The Lost Continent*, he was stunned by the Breakers, the most opulent of them all, designed in 1893 by Richard Morris Hunt for Cornelius Vanderbilt in the style of a sixteenth-century Genovese palace. Bryson called it "a mountain with windows."

McKim, Mead & White, the storied New York firm, had a hand in several Newport cottages and also designed Providence's grandest public building, the State House (1895–1901), whose marble dome is the second largest of its kind in the world, after St. Peter's in Rome. But for me, the best of Providence is smaller in scale, and the best way to see it is on foot.

You can walk through the old neighborhoods, along streets with names full of optimism: Benevolent, Benefit, Hope, Harmony, Concord, Justice. Or head for the West Side and Federal Hill, the heart of a community that a quarter century ago included 20 percent of all the Italian Americans in the country. Follow the red, white, and green stripe down the middle of Atwells Avenue, the main drag, to atmospheric shops like Venda Ravioli, at 265 Atwells, and Gasbarro's, at 361, which has one of the nation's best stocks of Italian wines.

You can visit museums, too. Providence's star cultural turn, I think, is the collection at the School of Design, which includes such gems as the largest wooden Buddha outside Japan, brilliant Japanese textiles and prints shown in rotation, four Copley paintings, a roomful of Impressionists and Post-Impressionists, one of the very best of Lyonel Feininger's Gelmeroda paintings, and a gripping pair of canvases by the great Cuban painter Wilfredo Lam. And then there are five examples, no less, of the magnificent workmanship of Goddard and Townsend, the nonpareil Newport cabinetmakers of the eighteenth century. With characteristic seashell reliefs, they are, in the memorable words of a British critic, "as sensible, well made and unpretentious as the prose of Benjamin Franklin."

Not too long ago, Providence had as many problems as New Haven; today, thanks mainly to Buddy Cianci, it's on the move. You can walk on the Riverwalk, through the rejuvenated downtown area, where the paved-over Woonasquatucket, Moshassuck, and Providence Rivers have been uncovered, redirected, and landscaped. Though several of the city's banks have been merged into out-of-state behemoths, some of its industries have withered, and its newspapers have been sold to Texans, there is a palpable spirit of revival in the air. The waterfront sparkles anew, and a 150-store, $460 million mall now stands in the shadow of the State House.

You may even hit it lucky and witness one of the weekend Water Fire evenings. On those, forty or more bonfires, built in braziers by volunteers led by Barnaby Evans, a local artist, blaze from dusk to midnight on the rivers, with the primal force of a tribal ritual. And if the fires aren't burning, something interesting will likely be on at the Trinity Repertory Company's Lederer Theater, or the Providence Performing Arts Center, where megamusicals like *Miss Saigon* and *The Phantom of the Opera* play. One recent Rep season included productions of Shakespeare (*The Merry Wives of Windsor*), O'Neill (*A Moon for the Misbegotten*), and David Auburn (*Proof*).

WHERE TO STAY

Westin, 1 West Exchange Street, (401) 598-8000. This twenty-five-floor postmodern tower, a major feature on the city's skyline, moved Providence into the hotel big leagues. Completed in 1994, it offers an airy lobby in the shape of a two-story rotunda, a health spa, 363 rooms decorated with prints of Providence streetscapes, and a popular seafood restaurant called Agora. Linked to the nearby Convention Center.

Providence Biltmore, 11 Dorrance Street, Kennedy Plaza, (401) 421-0700. A penthouse-to-wine-cellar renovation in 1996 did wonders for this old-timer, designed in 1922 by Warren & Wetmore, architects of Grand Central Station in New York. The 291 rooms, reached by a glass elevator, are larger than most, with couches and work areas. Choose the Westin for its New World zip, the Biltmore for its Old World sophistication.

Providence Hotel, 311 Westminster Street, (401) 861-8000. With eighty rooms slotted into a pair of nineteenth-century buildings, this elegant establishment opened in 2004 in the Arts and Entertainment District. Its owner, a prominent antique dealer, has filled it with his wares and tasteful reproductions. A bonus is L'Epicureo, perhaps the best of the city's Italian restaurants, relocated from its original site on Atwells Avenue.

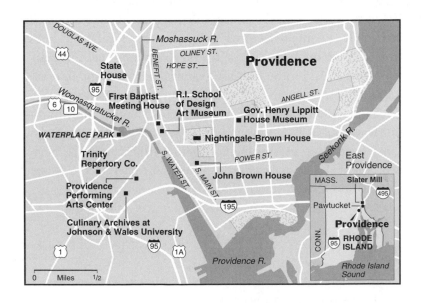

WHERE TO EAT

Al Forno, 577 South Main Street, (401) 273-9760. Al Forno has built a regional and national reputation on virtuoso grilling over a wood fire, and the herbed chicken, lamb, and steak are superb. George Germon and Johanne Killeen also turn out smoky, tissue-thin pizza, brittle as a poppadum, topped with tomatoes and cheeses, and luscious orange crepes filled with lemon ice cream. No reservations; constantly crowded; good-natured if harried service.

Aunt Carrie's, 1240 Ocean Road, Narragansett, (401) 783-7930. The shore dinner is the grandest Rhode Island culinary tradition. In the screened seaside dining room at Aunt Carrie's, a 1940s throwback where waitresses wear white uniforms, the shore dinner includes chowder, steamer clams, clam cakes (deep-fried fritters, actually), sole, brown bread, corn on the cob, lobster, and Indian pudding. Sometimes the cooking falters, but not the nostalgia.

New Rivers, 7 Steeple Street, (401) 751-0350. Tucked into a pair of storefronts, this hunter-green dining room holds exactly forty people. No ego elephantiasis here; Bruce Tillinghast, the sure-handed chef, a former art student, has made New Rivers a model of taste, restraint, and warmth. Try the sweet little bay scallops, if they are in season, or an Asian-influenced dish like clams and mussels cooked in lemongrass broth with bok choy, or something rustic like a Delmonico steak with ramps (wild leeks) from West Virginia.

Pot au Feu, 44 Custom House Street, (401) 273-8953. Formal upstairs, casual downstairs, Pot au Feu has had its ups and downs. But Bob Burke, restaurateur-raconteur, a fourth-generation Rhode Islander, faithfully tends the flame of traditional French cooking. What better to brighten a gloomy New England eve than an exemplary omelet, a perfect steak frites or a steaming pot-au-feu, that most restorative of dishes?

Mills Tavern, 101 North Main Street, (401) 272-3331. Jaime D'Oliveira's relaxed, rollicking restaurant, with Michael Lofaro Jr., an alumnus of Quest in New York, now in the open kitchen, has been a smash hit since day one. The food is like this: figs stuffed with gorgonzola, served with salty ham; cod roasted in a wood-burning oven, topped with mildly spiced crabmeat, resting on a bed of cleverly reinvented succotash; rabbit stew, accented with salty olives and sweet prunes, on a tangle of pappardelle. Multidimensional food, never precious.

⬛⬛⬛➡ BUFFALO

Like a dowager in decline, Buffalo still has good bones to remind people of her more prosperous and glamorous days.

Take Delaware Avenue, one of several fine boulevards radiating from downtown, laid out in 1800 by Joseph Ellicott, a brother of Andrew Ellicott, Pierre L'Enfant's chief surveyor in the planning of Washington. Baronial manors line it, like the Williams-Butler Mansion at the corner of North Street—an urban version by Stanford White of the huge "cottages" his firm designed for the Vanderbilts in Newport and the Hudson Valley.

Late in the nineteenth century, when such houses were built, and early in the twentieth, when architects of genius like Frank Lloyd Wright worked here, Buffalo was a city of burly self-confidence and substantial riches, drawn from the great factories and steel mills on its periphery. Grain elevators (a Buffalo invention) towered over its waterfront along Lake Erie. An outpost of the East and a gateway to the West, it was a vital transportation hub, profiting from its privileged position at the point where communication lines from New York City—the Erie Canal, which opened in 1825, and later the New York Central Railroad—reached the Great Lakes.

The designer of the monumental Art Deco City Hall (1927), John J. Wade, said that it "expresses primarily the masculinity, power and purposeful energy of an industrial community." So it does, with reliefs of toiling workers above columns resembling gigantic Roman fasces. It also memorializes, in statues at the facade's corners, the two presidents who came from Buffalo, Millard Fillmore and Grover Cleveland. Neither ever quite made the first team. Of Fillmore, Harry S Truman, a noteworthy successor, said derisively: "At a time when we needed a strong man, we got a man who swayed with the slightest breeze. About all he ever accomplished as President, he sent Commodore Perry to open up Japan to the West, but that didn't help much as far as preventing the Civil War was concerned."

Theodore Roosevelt, a wholly different character, took the presidential oath of office at the apogee of Buffalo's power in 1901, after William McKinley was assassinated while visiting the Pan-American Exposition here. Only the Parthenon-like headquarters of the Buffalo and Erie County Historical Society remains from the dozens of buildings built for the exposition, which was spectacularly lighted by electricity generated at Niagara Falls, then newly harnessed. Some in Buffalo speak of "the curse of McKinley," giving credence to the civic myth that the city's slide from eighth largest in the country to fifty-ninth began with the assassination.

The city has changed swiftly in the last half century. Most of the mills have closed; the children and grandchildren of the blue-collar workers who manned them are mostly white-collar workers (if they haven't fled to cities like Charlotte and Phoenix). The state of New York is the largest employer, and the State University of New York at Buffalo, with two campuses, is another big one. With a population of 292,648 in 2000 (down from 328,123 in 1990), Buffalo remains the state's second largest city, but it is dwarfed by New York City's 8 million. And then there is the snow: Rochester gets more of it in most years, Buffalonians protest, but Buffalo gets the jokes.

Bethlehem Steel once employed 22,000 workers in suburban Lackawanna; now it is bankrupt, and its retirees face reduced pensions and health benefits. With unemployment high, more young and middle-aged people are moving to the Sun Belt. "It's sad the South is plucking all the talent from the Northeast," said Timothy J. Dwan, a local judge.

Fighting back, the city has sought to link itself across Lake Ontario with its neighbor Toronto, in a giant, binational metropolitan area. Toronto has not been very keen on this, yet Ontario's trade with New York State, much of it with the Buffalo area, amounted to nearly $50 billion in 2000, and three-quarters of the audience of some Buffalo television stations is Canadian.

Thriving medical technology, aerospace, and automotive parts industries have helped. But high taxes have hurt—*Kiplinger's Personal Finance* found in 1998 that Buffalo residents were the most highly taxed in the nation—and so has the disgrace of John J. Rigas and his family, whose Adelphia Communications was seen for a time as the city's potential economic savior. Accused of looting their cable television company, Rigas and his son Timothy were found guilty of conspiracy, securities fraud, and bank fraud in July 2004.

Yet Buffalo remains a tightly knit, family-oriented, heavily Roman Catholic community, a rich ethnic stew of Polish, Irish, Italian, and German Americans. It is fiercely proud of its hockey Sabres and football Bills (even though they lost four straight Super Bowls in the early 1990s), as well as Ani DiFranco, the punky pop star who runs her own record company in the city. Buffalo stands apart, less homogenized than many American cities. It eats hamburgers with the rest of us, but also Ted's charcoal-grilled hot dogs and Wardynski's kielbasa, Perry's ice cream and of course Buffalo chicken wings.

Every block or so has its tavern, with a fish fry on Friday night, and people tend to identify themselves by their parish. Ask them where they live, and they answer, St. Monica's, or Holy Family, or St. Stanislaus.

Opportunities have been missed. Largely cut off from Lake Erie by expressways and industrial jungles, Buffalo took far less advantage of the water's scenic and recreational potential than Chicago did with its parks, piers, and beaches along Lake Michigan. But now a move is afoot to focus attention on, and attract tourists to, the lake and the Niagara River, which inspired the city's name (French explorers called the place *beau fleuve*, or beautiful river, which metamorphosed into "Buffalo"). Mayor Anthony M. Masiello, once a local basketball hero, said: "The City of Buffalo grew up from its waterfront. We need to reconnect with our waterfront in order to grow again."

Tim Russert, a native son and the anchor of *Meet the Press* on NBC, is Buffalo's booster in chief. He boasts about the Bills, when they're winning, about the city's five lovely parks designed by Frederick Law Olmsted, and about the accomplishments of people like Peter J. Crotty, the state and local Democratic leader who helped make John F. Kennedy president and Robert F. Kennedy a senator. Crotty lived all his adult life in the same simple South Buffalo house, a self-taught scholar of Latin who liked to read the *Aeneid* in his basement library.

Culturally, Buffalo owes a huge debt to the discerning eye and open wallet of a Woolworth heir named Seymour H. Knox, universally known as Shorty. Thanks largely to him, the Albright-Knox Art Gallery houses one of the nation's best collections of modern art. It has two buildings, a Greek Revival temple whose design derives from that of the Erechtheum on the Acropolis, with caryatids carved by no less than Augustus Saint-Gaudens, and a sleek International Style addition by Gordon Bunshaft of Skidmore, Owings & Merrill, a Buffalo native famous for the sleek Lever House on Park Avenue in New York City.

The Albright-Knox's holdings date back to the Cycladic era, but it excels in European and American painting of this century. Mark Rothko and Jackson Pollock are represented, along with Max Beckmann and Henri Matisse, whose quickly brushed *Glimpse of Notre-Dame in the Late Afternoon* is one of my favorites. Other museums can match such canvases, but only Buffalo has a roomful of the jagged, vividly colored pictures of the reclusive Clyfford Still, who gave the Albright-Knox no fewer than thirty-one works.

Buffalo has an even longer history of architectural distinction than Chicago; you could do worse than take it as a textbook for a course in modern American buildings. Henry Hobson Richardson, the great forerunner of the modern movement, built his first neo-Romanesque building here. It is an enormous mental hospital, later called the Buffalo Psychiatric Center, with a pair of rusticated, châteaulike sandstone towers at its center. Pavilions are linked to them and to one another by curving passageways that can be sealed off in the event of fire or other disturbance—an early example of form following function. Even in its shabby state today, this is a building of real magnificence, awaiting restoration.

Next in the pantheon comes Louis Sullivan, who is also significantly represented in Buffalo. With his partner, Dankmar Adler, he designed the Guaranty Building, the first skyscraper entitled, in my view, to be called a masterpiece. With the Wainwright Building in St. Louis, it is one of only two surviving Sullivan towers, and it would have been lost were it not for the labors of the late Senator Daniel Patrick Moynihan. Completed in 1896, it looks as fresh as the day after tomorrow. The frame is steel, but every square inch of the exterior is covered with Sullivan's foliate ornamentation, executed in ocher terra-cotta so that the building "reads" from a distance as stone. The filigree reaches a climax at the corners atop the thirteen-story structure, which is capped with a row of oculi and a flat overhanging roof. Inside, much of the vibrant decor has been preserved—the intricate metalwork of the elevator cages, door handles, and balusters; the mosaics, the crisp lighting fixtures, and an exquisite stained-glass skylight. How could anyone have thought of tearing it down?

Sullivan's protégé and onetime draftsman Frank Lloyd Wright left a distinctive architectural mark on Buffalo: five houses, all still standing. But his greatest Buffalo project, the Larkin administration building, a brutish, almost unadorned structure finished in 1906, was demolished only forty-four years later. It had the stark geometric power of the Old Spanish churches in Santa Fe and Taos, and its soaring atrium, central if rudimentary air-conditioning system, and metal office furniture were decades ahead of their time. Today, it is universally considered one of the landmarks in modern industrial architecture (along with the equally massive AEG building by Peter Behrens in Berlin).

Wright's residential work in the Buffalo area was commissioned by people connected with the Larkin Company, then a flourishing mail-order firm. The William R. Heath house, built for a Larkin vice president, strikes me as forbiddingly fortresslike, especially when compared with the Robie House in Chicago, for which it was a kind of prototype. No such criticism can be leveled at Wright's houses in the Parkside section, near the Buffalo Zoo (a rather cramped place which nonetheless boasts an animated group of gorillas and spectacular snow leopards). The Walter V. Davidson House, commissioned by a junior Larkin executive, shows what Wright could do on a relatively limited budget, using stucco instead of brick or stone and clear instead of stained glass. For the nearby Darwin D. Martin complex (1907), now being restored at a cost of $23 million after long periods of neglect, the sky was obviously the financial limit. The main house is a large, splendidly horizontal affair, with terraces, elongated urns, deeply overhanging roofs, and interior spaces that flow seamlessly into one another; it is the best example of the Prairie Style outside the Midwest. A pergola is to be rebuilt, along with a carriage house and conservatory, linking the main house to other buildings—a trim little gardener's cottage and the subtly cruciform George Barton house, which was built for Darwin Martin's sister and her husband, who, like Martin, worked for Larkin.

Martin was also connected, through his marriage to a sister of the writer and philosopher Elbert Hubbard, to Hubbard's Roycroft community at East Aurora, half an hour east of Buffalo. This was a semi-utopian Arts and Crafts colony that for a time rivaled Gustav Stickley as a producer of furniture, metalwork, and other decorative arts. The handsome Roycroft Inn, built to house visitors to the community, has been faithfully restored, down to the last carpet and table lamp, and it is once again operating as a hotel.

Of the buildings erected in Buffalo in the last seventy-five years, the most influential by far is the Kleinhans Music Hall (1940), designed by the father-and-son team of Eliel and Eero Saarinen. It harks back to the elder Saarinen's Romantic Revival buildings in Finland, like the Helsinki railway station, and, especially in the airy interior, looks forward to the younger Saarinen's sweeping curves in the TWA building at Kennedy Airport in New York City and the terminal at Dulles Airport in Washington. The acoustics approach perfection.

The Buffalo Philharmonic Orchestra, the main tenant in the Kleinhans hall, has recently skated along the edge of bankruptcy; its players even advertised, a few years back, for another city to adopt it. That was quite a comedown for an ensemble whose music directors have included Josef Krips, William Steinberg, Julius Rudel, and the composer Lukas Foss, a champion of innovative programs. But JoAnn Falletta, who began her tenure in 1999, has lifted the orchestra's spirits. One of only three women leading major American orchestras, she has been called one of the stars of her generation.

The local theater scene has much to recommend it. Residents and visitors alike can see first-run musicals, dance and pop concerts at Shea's Performing Arts Center, which is built around an ornate old movie palace. For roughly half the year, Buffalo can also profit from the excellent Shaw Festival at bucolic Niagara-on-the-Lake in nearby Ontario, which mounts world-class productions of GBS classics like *Major Barbara* as well as works by his eminent contemporaries, including John Galsworthy and Harley Granville-Barker.

A prime attraction for visitors to the Buffalo area is, of course, Niagara Falls, half an hour north by freeway. The world has been beating a path to the falls for more than two centuries; Joseph Bonaparte, Napoleon's nephew, took his bride there in 1803. These days, 8 to 10 million visitors a year come to watch billions of gallons of gray-green water crash spectacularly over a precipice that extends for 3,600 feet, in two parts—the American Falls on the United States side and the Horsehoe Falls on the Canadian side. Some are impressed, some aren't. Henry James called the falls "the most beautiful object in the world," but Oscar Wilde dismissed them as "the second most disappointing experience of American married life." The point is, both made the trip, and so should you, if you get as close as Buffalo.

The newest game in town is the $750 million Niagara Fallsview Casino Resort, in Ontario, a Las Vegas look-alike with 368 rooms, a 1,500-seat theater, five restaurants, a spa, unlimited opportunities to lose your money, and, of course, a view of the cataracts. Other views can be had from the Skylon, a tower on the Canadian side; from the Maid of the Mist, a boat that bobs in the spray beneath the falls, and from the Cave of the Winds walk along the base of the cliffs. But for my money the best vantage point is Queen Victoria Park, also on the Canadian side, where you can stroll in bountiful, immaculate gardens opposite the falls. They look close enough to reach out and get your finger wet.

Hyatt Regency, 2 Fountain Plaza, Pearl and Huron Streets, (716) 856-1234. In the thick of things downtown, only a few blocks from theaters and restaurants, this is a little bit scruffy by the usual Hyatt standards. But it is a useful piece of urban recycling, combining a modern glass atrium, something of a Hyatt hallmark, with a building dating from 1923. Three bars and two restaurants generate a fair amount of hubbub.

Mansion on Delaware Avenue, 414 Delaware Avenue, (716) 886-3300. This splendid, 135-year-old house was turned into a twenty-eight-room hotel a few years ago. Although reservations can be hard to get, it's worth trying; these are the best accom-

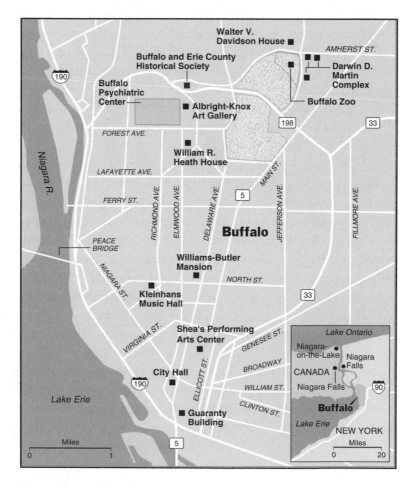

modations in town. "Butlers" (aka bellhops) will drop you at nearby restaurants free of charge.

Marriott, 1340 Millersport Highway, Amherst, (716) 689-6900. Location, location, location—in this case only a few minutes from the airport, right on the way to Niagara Falls and not too far from downtown Buffalo. The recently renovated 356 rooms and suites are cookie-cutter specials. Welcome features are a year-round indoor-outdoor pool and a courtyard garden fairly overflowing with summer blooms.

WHERE TO EAT

Anchor Bar, 1047 Main Street, (716) 886-8920. Frank and Teressa's Anchor Bar remains unchanged, a dingy neighborhood tavern where most of the food is forgettable, but the chicken wings, invented here, are immortal. Well, almost. They deep-fry them on command, a minimum of ten to an order, which is plenty for a snack for two. Pay your $5.65 and marvel at the habit-forming qualities of these chubby chicken chunks nestling in a puddle of hot sauce, with celery sticks and Roquefort dressing on the side.

Hutch's, 1375 Delaware Avenue, near Gates Circle, (716) 885-0074. Every Friday and Saturday night, they run two hundred or more people through this bubbling bistro, with paper table coverings and Thonet chairs, and everyone eats well. The rib-eye steak rubbed with garlic, stuffed poblano chilies, dark-hued french fries, oysters, and tuna are all exemplary. There is swift service from waiters in long white aprons, and check out the rock-bottom wine prices.

Ming Teh, 126 Niagara Boulevard, Fort Erie, Ontario, (905) 871-7971. Across the Peace Bridge from Buffalo, Ming Teh serves Beijing, Cantonese, and Sichuan dishes. Gaudily ugly outside, quietly modern inside, it faces the swift-flowing Niagara River, where you can watch the speedboats dart past on summer evenings. Our pickled Sichuan cabbage soup with pork, tangy steamed vegetarian dumplings, and chewy dry-fried beef strips with ginger and garlic were all subtle and complex. Sweet but disorganized service.

Schwabl's, 789 Center Road, West Seneca, (716) 674-9821. Schwabl's makes one of America's great sandwiches—beef sliced thinly from a steamship round when you order it, piled on a sliced hard roll studded with caraway seeds and pretzel salt, moistened with natural juices and perked up, if you like, with a smear of horseradish and a Molson's. It's called beef on weck (short for *kümmelweck*), and it's worth the drive from downtown Buffalo, or Toronto, for that matter. The family has been in the business since 1837.

Tsunami, 1141 Kenmore Avenue, (716) 447-7915. Michael Andrzejewski is as close as Buffalo comes to a celebrity chef, and rightly so. Formerly at Oliver's, he has gone in a different direction at Tsunami (Japanese for "tidal wave"). Here, he features Asian dishes like sashimi and dim sum, and sprightly Asian-influenced items like kaffir lime grilled prawns, lotus-steamed haddock, and tandoori duck with pomegranate sauce. Yum.

IIII➤ PHILADELPHIA

Philadelphia is a city on second base, wondering if it will ever make it all the way home.

The old Philadelphia, which lived on manufacturing and banking and lawyering, ran out of steam at least a half century ago. In the new century the city is betting a billion dollars that a newly aggressive Philadelphia can prosper on history and culture and tourism, that people will come here not merely for the obligatory visit to the Liberty Bell with the kids but for several days of meetings, music, art, shopping, and good food.

An unmistakable energy has taken hold in Center City, as the locals call downtown Philadelphia. Without losing its manners, the city has begun to bounce. Walnut Street's sidewalks are crowded at 10 p.m. A Democrat, Ed Rendell, a husky former mayor, now Pennsylvania's governor, gets credit for jump-starting the transformation. John F. Street, the current man at City Hall, has moved things along, yet the work is still far from done. "You can see signs of a real renaissance in important parts of the city," said Senator Arlen Specter, who served as Philadelphia's district attorney before heading to Washington. "But don't delude yourself. Fifteen blocks from the center, enormous problems remain."

Philadelphia was America's original convention city, beginning with the Continental Congress in 1774, which produced the Declaration of Independence two years later. In 1948, three political parties met there, the Democrats to choose Harry S Truman, the Republicans to nominate Thomas E. Dewey, and the Progressives to settle upon Henry A. Wallace. A lot has happened since then, most of it bad. Philadelphia lost many of its defining institutions, including *The Saturday Evening Post*, once the nation's leading magazine; the *Bulletin*, a venerable evening newspaper; the Pennsylvania Railroad, one of the first great routes to the West; John Wanamaker's department store, a mass-merchandising pioneer; and the Philadelphia Athletics, who made baseball history under Connie Mack. It had a surly white mayor, Frank Rizzo, whose confrontational approach to blacks was typified by the nightstick he famously tucked into his cummerbund one night, and a star-crossed black mayor, W. Wilson Goode, who dropped a firebomb on the headquarters of a radical group in his own city in 1985. In 1976 an outbreak of a mysterious respiratory disease killed thirty-four members of the American Legion attending a meeting here.

An important step toward recovery was the opening of a new convention center in 1993. Then, in 1996, 548,000 people came to see a Cézanne exhibition at the Museum of Art, many of them suburbanites who hadn't been downtown in years, others from New York, Washington, and farther afield. Local leaders realized there was big money in culture. Broad Street got a face-lift and a new name, the Avenue of the Arts, and in 2001 a $245 million Regional Performing Arts Center opened there, designed by Rafael Viñoly of New York in emulation of Paxton's glittering 1851 Crystal Palace in London.

Thousands of hotel rooms have been added in the metropolitan area in recent years, with two hotels and several restaurants taking over banks. The metaphor is almost too apt. The much-admired PSFS building (the letters stand for Philadelphia Savings Fund Society, though few remember that) is now a Loews hotel, with all its architectural glories miraculously intact, including a polished black granite base that bends around a corner. Designed by William Lescaze and George Howe in 1932, it was the first International Style skyscraper built in the United States, just at the end of the Art Deco era. And the old Girard Trust Company, a little Ionic temple with a perfect dome, designed in blindingly white Georgia marble by the great Stanford White, has become a Ritz-Carlton.

Philadelphia used to concentrate on food that filled big men up fast: cheese steaks, hoagies, soft pretzels, L. D. Bassett's world-class ice cream, scrapple (a Pennsylvania Dutch blend of cornmeal and unmentionable pig parts), sticky buns, and pepper pot soup (a potent brew of honeycomb tripe and hot chilies). Most of the traditional fare can still be found at the Reading Terminal Market (often sold there by Mennonite women in white gauze caps) or in South Philadelphia, Rocky's rough-hewn domain.

But now the city is a playground for foodies, with heroically hip restaurants opening every month. These are no storefront improvisations; Neil Stein, who started it all with a place called Striped Bass, opened five worldly spots at a cost of $10 million before going bust.

Rick Nichols, who has watched the city's travails for years from various posts at *The Philadelphia Inquirer*, warned me to leave my rose-tinted glasses at home. "The fate of Philadelphia really hangs in the balance," he said. "Can we live off this culture-dining-service boom, or do we need more lunch-bucket jobs to keep the whole thing going?"

Look carefully on the side streets downtown and you will see vacant shops and even a few vacant buildings. The region's retail nexus is not there but out in the suburbs at King of Prussia, in a megamall where Hermès and Neiman Marcus and other chic merchants court the carriage trade. Jobs have fled the city, too, as companies like Bell Atlantic and CoreStates Financial have closed or shrunk their Philadelphia offices because of mergers.

After far too many years at the dank, rat-infested Veterans Stadium, the football Eagles got a bright new stadium in 2003 and the baseball Phillies got a smart new home in 2004. But the vaunted Disney Quest is just another hole in the ground, its financing having collapsed. Mayor Rendell was devastated; the project had so excited him that he told an English visitor, "To call it virtual reality is to call Michelangelo a house painter."

William P. Hankowsky, Philadelphia's industrial development czar, acknowledged frankly that "you have two contradictory phenomena here at the same time: Center City is booming, with people moving back downtown, while the population as a whole is still in decline." With some exceptions, like Chestnut Hill, the northern, western, and southern parts of Philadelphia are worn and worried. Between 1990 and 2000, the city lost 4.3 percent of its population; of the ten largest cities in the United States, only Detroit and Philadelphia shrank, and Philadelphia shrank more. But the tri-state metropolitan area, the nation's sixth biggest, which includes parts of New Jersey and Delaware, grew 5 percent during the same period, reaching 6,188,463.

"Cheering against the home team is a time-honored tradition in Philadelphia," wrote the social historian E. Digby Baltzell some years ago. For whatever reason, a Philadelphia-born comedian of minimal talent, W. C. Fields, has been allowed to fasten a joke to the city like a limpet. Asked what he wanted on his gravestone, the great man is said to have replied, "On the whole, I'd rather be in Philadelphia." That one-liner has been repeated ad nauseam. Yet this has always been a richly endowed city, full of distinctive neighborhoods, a center of artistic and intellectual life since the days of Benjamin Franklin and the Peales, much loved by those who live here. The population is less transient than in most other large American cities; Philadelphians may flee to the suburbs, but most of them go no farther. Whether they call it Philadelphia or Philly, a nickname liked by some and loathed by others, whether they are Rocky Balboas or Frankie Avalons from gritty, Italian American South Philadelphia or Tracy Lords from the rich, pastoral Main Line, they are loyalists.

The Philadelphia story started with that redoubtable Quaker William Penn, founder of the colony he named Pennsylvania, after his father. He laid out the city's grid in 1682. It was he, not some adman, who named it the City of Brotherly Love, and he who gave it many of its appealing characteristics: broad streets and vast parks, religious tolerance and closely knit families and respect for education. (Temple, Villanova, Haverford, Swarthmore, Bryn Mawr, and Drexel, as well as the University of Pennsylvania, with its celebrated Wharton School of Business, carry on that tradition.)

As usual, Mark Twain got the picture. In Boston, he said, people ask, "What does he know?" In New York they ask, "How much does he make?" In Philadelphia, the crucial question is, "Who were his parents?" Some of the city's families can be frosty and self-satisfied, their lives consecrated to the First Troop Philadelphia City Cavalry, the Merion Cricket Club, and the Union League Club, whose brownstone building bears a plaque celebrating its loyalty to the North in the Civil War. Many live in the western suburbs known as the Main Line because a rail line links them on a route running west to Paoli. Generations of college students learned a mnemonic aid to help them find their way home: "Old maids never wed and have babies," for Overbrook, Merion, Narberth, Wynnewood, Ardmore, Haverford, and Bryn Mawr.

But of course Philadelphia is not all socialites, Quakers, and Italian Americans, and even if the current gamble succeeds, it will never be a mere tourist target. Anne d'Harnoncourt, director of the Museum of Art, New York–bred but devotedly Philadelphian by adoption, calls this "a city full of nooks and niches." It is not just Rittenhouse Square, the traditional center of patrician Philadelphia, bounded by mismatched buildings that give it visual vigor, used every day by dogs and bums and Frisbee-tossing adolescents and pram-pushing nannies and students from the nearby Curtis Institute of Music, and celebrated for its vitality by no less than Jane Jacobs. Philadelphia is also the home of an old and eminent black community, which has produced national leaders like A. Leon Higginbotham Jr., a towering presence on the federal appeals bench from 1977 to 1993; former congressman William Gray, who later led the United Negro College Fund; and William Coleman, a former transportation secretary.

And it is a river town. The Delaware River makes Philadelphia a port, and the smaller Schuylkill (pronounced SKOO-kul) is an urban delight, especially when filled with sculls and eight-oared shells from the venerable rowing clubs along its bank. Grace Kelly's father and brother, both named Jack, rowed there and won national and international titles.

The tide of the Revolution flowed through and around Philadelphia, which in the late eighteenth century was America's leading city. Washington crossed the Delaware just north of here, lost to the Redcoats at Germantown and spent the severe winter of 1777–78 at Valley Forge. But it is in the Old City, in the blocks south of Walnut Street between Second and Sixth, that the drama of those astounding years comes to life. Perhaps, as its promoters say, it is "The Most Historic Square Mile in America," and now it has a high-tech visitors' center so cleverly done that it makes our national past vivid for kids. Few visitors miss the Liberty Bell in its new $12.9 million home, or Independence Hall, where both the Declaration of Independence and the Constitution, those two extraordinary products of Enlightenment genius, were debated and finally approved. The fabric of the venerable buildings has been mended as often as an old sock, but even the history-averse are stirred.

Benjamin Franklin was a dominant figure in the life of Philadelphia and the young United States, so it seems fitting that he is buried nearby, across the street from the Free Quaker Meeting House. His grave is strewn with coins tossed by tourists mindful of his maxim "A penny saved is a penny earned"; the site of his house is marked by a steel frame devised by Robert Venturi, a "skeleton" of the original and far more evocative than a mere reconstruction.

Many of the red-brick houses where Washington and Madison and the others lived during the 1790s, when Philadelphia was the nation's capital, still stand on the cobbled streets, shaded by plane trees, south of the Independence National Historic Park. At Christ Church on Second Street, you can sit in the very pews where the Founding Fathers sat (Washington used Pew 58). Its six-sided, 209-foot steeple, finished in 1754, was the tallest structure in America for more than a century. Influenced by the designs of Gibbs and Wren in London, the church is remarkable for its broad expanses of clear glass.

Some idea of Philadelphia's wealth in the late eighteenth century may be gained from Georgian mansions like Cliveden (1767), which is in suburban Germantown, and Mount Pleasant (1762), which is in Fairmount Park, the biggest urban reserve in America. Cliveden, seat of the Chew family, contains chairs and a sofa built by Thomas Affleck, one of the greatest of American furniture makers.

After the federal government left for Washington in 1800, Philadelphia never again enjoyed the same eminence. But it built as if it did. That was the doing mainly of Nicholas Biddle, then the city's social, cultural, and financial star, and the founder of its most notable dynasty. He returned from a trip to Athens in 1806 with this in his diary: "The two great truths in the world are the Bible and Grecian architecture." Soon the city was awash in Greek Revival temples, from the Philadelphia

Water Works (1819) along the Schuylkill to Biddle's own magnificent house, Andalusia (1836), high above the west bank of the Delaware River, with an enormous, six-column-wide portico by Thomas U. Walter. The Second Bank of the United States (1819–24), designed by William Strickland, parts of which literally copied the Parthenon, is the masterpiece of the genre. In this grand white marble building, Biddle, the bank's president, fought with Henry Clay against Andrew Jackson for control of the nation's monetary supply, and lost.

Philadelphia clung to its taste for monumentality. A climax was reached in the exuberant Second Empire City Hall (1872–1901), a hulking, multi-pavilioned whopper of a building topped by a statue of the city's founder, William Penn. The creation of Alexander Milne Calder, Penn stands up there in a broad-brimmed hat, all of thirty-seven feet tall.

Benjamin Franklin Parkway, the city's ceremonial boulevard, used to be a Calder-to-Calder-to-Calder triple play. From City Hall, it leads to Logan Circle, which was modeled after the Place de la Concorde in Paris; the fountain in the center is by AM's son Alexander Stirling Calder. A bold red stabile by AS's son Alexander Calder used to stand at the far end of the parkway, at the top of the steps leading up to the Greek Revival facade of the Museum of Art. It is gone now, but plans are afoot to build a Calder Museum nearby, designed by the Japanese Tadao Audo, if sufficient funds can be raised.

(Some Philadelphia arts potentates would like to move the dazzling Barnes collection from its home in suburban Merion, where relatively few manage to see it, to the same neighborhood. But the proposed move, like everything about Albert C. Barnes and the works of art he collected, including rustic furniture and ironwork as well as paintings, is mired in legal and aesthetic dispute. No one can say for sure where the stupendous Cézannes, Renoirs, and Matisses that people travel thousands of miles to see will finally come to rest, or when.)

The transitional figure in Philadelphia architecture was Frank Furness, whose taste for the exotic is evident in the Pennsylvania Academy of the Fine Arts, built in 1871–76. His enthusiasm for certain kinds of foliate decoration communicated itself to a young draftsman in his office named Louis Sullivan, who returned to his native Chicago and became a pioneer of modernism. Then, in the twentieth century, Philadelphia had two great architects: Louis I. Kahn, whose Richards laboratories at Penn (1960–64) turn the unavoidable technological folderol into crisp design elements, prefiguring the Pompidou Center in Paris, and Venturi, the father of Pop architecture. For me at least, the local buildings by Frank Lloyd Wright (a synagogue in Elkins Park) and Helmut Jahn (the Liberty Place skyscrapers) are much less successful.

The Museum of Art and the Philadelphia Orchestra are both ranked among the top five or six institutions of their kind in the nation. Founded in 1900, the orchestra is world-famous; under Eugene Ormandy and Leopold Stokowski it introduced many great twentieth-century works to American audiences, including Stravinsky's *Rite of Spring* in 1922. Joseph H. Kluger, the orchestra's president, said that recent programs of relatively modern music had reduced the worryingly high average age of its audiences and provided "an idea we can build on."

For years, the orchestra was housed in the Academy of Music, a charming opera house built in 1857 whose acoustics are poor for symphonic music. In December 2001, after a gala centennial concert and tours of Europe, Asia, and the United States, it moved into its new home at the Kimmel Arts Center. The move was not without dissention: The old Academy may be the city's most beloved building, and neither the Pew nor Annenberg foundations, the city's cultural mainstays, contributed to the new center's cost. The cello-shaped hall where the Philadelphians now play has been widely praised for its beauty but was also criticized for colorless, bass-free sound until adjustments were made. The masterly Christoph Eschenbach, the orchestra's seventh and current music director, is coping nicely. His account of Messiaen's thunderous *Turangalîla* symphony had critics doing cartwheels.

The changeover conferred at least one unarguable benefit on the city by opening more room and time at the Academy for the Philadelphia Opera, which has made considerable progress under Robert B. Driver, despite a difficult economic climate in recent years, and the Pennsylvania Ballet. Across from the

Academy is the Wilma Theater, designed by Hugh Hardy and named for an imagined female sister of William Shakespeare. Two Czech-born directors, Blanka and Jiri Zizka, have presented plays there by David Gow, Tom Stoppard, and many others, including Arthur Miller's new *Resurrection Blues*, in productions that are often controversial but seldom dull.

The vast, honey-colored Museum of Art looks as if it had been there for seven hundred years, not seventy. (An annex in an Art Deco building across the street will provide 100,000 square feet of badly needed additional space.) The museum's holdings are enormous, ranging from period rooms (including one by the great Scottish designer Robert Adam) to impressive arrays of armor and Oriental art. Its old masters include lavish gifts from John G. Johnson, a Philadelphia lawyer who argued a record 168 times before the Supreme Court. Johnson's van Eyck and Giovanni di Paolo are outshone, for me, by his majestic Rogier van der Weyden diptych of the Crucifixion with the Virgin and St. John the Evangelist—a real "pilgrimage piece," to use the phrase of my friend Earl A. Powell III, the present director of the National Gallery in Washington. Van der Weyden shows the austere figures against red hangings, the Virgin crumpling in grief, the edges of Christ's loincloth lifted by a mysterious force. It is the museum's saddest painting and one of the greatest in the United States.

In another part of the building are assembled the exciting, before-their-time collections of Louise and Walter Arensberg and of A. E. Gallatin, notably including Brancusis, Mirós, and Duchamp's once-scandalous *Nude Descending a Staircase* (1912). Of course, the museum also prides itself on its paintings by local artists, and it would be a mistake to miss Thomas Eakins's *Concert Singer*. A far greater Eakins painting, *The Gross Clinic* (1875), hangs at Jefferson Medical College, and others are at St. Charles Borromeo Seminary in Overbrook, where the Philadelphia painter often sought solace on Sunday afternoons.

In fact, art is omnipresent in Philadelphia. The Pennsylvania Academy of the Fine Arts boasts a fine early American collection, including superb works by Gilbert Stuart, Winslow Homer, and all the Peales. The University of Pennsylvania's museum houses golden treasures from the ancient Sumerian city of Ur and much else. And the Rosenbach Museum and Library contains rare books and manuscripts accumulated by Dr. A.S.W. Rosenbach, a scholarly, piratical dealer who helped build Washington's Folger Library and the Huntington Library near Los Angeles.

WHERE TO STAY

Four Seasons, 1 Logan Square, (215) 963-1500. The opulent, flower-filled lobby tells the story: no expense has been spared here. But as one hotel executive says, "The mahogany and marble are the easy parts." The hard part is building an attentive, kindly staff, and the Four Seasons succeeds superbly on that count, too. The Fountain dining room is the peer of any restaurant in town, and bedrooms offer every modern amenity.

Loews, 1200 Market Street, (215) 627-1200. A tip of the Apple hat to the Tisch family, which converted the landmark PSFS building into a hotel of ravishing Art Deco beauty. The old vault doors and silvery sans-serif signs have been used to great graphic effect in the lobby, amid rosewood and etched glass. The 583 bedrooms murmur "Hollywood, 1930," with a chaise longue in every one; the library holds vintage books.

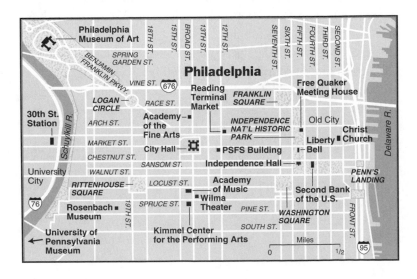

Rittenhouse, 210 West Rittenhouse Square, (215) 546-9000. The harsh zigzag facade does little for the harmony of the urban environment, though it gives the 128 guest rooms leafy views. Otherwise, the Rittenhouse is hard to fault, with a central location, an invitingly cool lobby, and bedrooms swimming with space. The service is charming.

WHERE TO EAT

Fork, 306 Market Street, (215) 625-9425. With bare floors, an open kitchen, and a fixation on freshness worthy of Alice Waters, this is a good place for lunch on a tour of the Colonial shrines. Enjoy the satisfyingly rustic chicken-mushroom-barley soup, a fishy or meaty salad, and the chocolate cake with banana gelato, plus a beer from the long list.

Lacroix, in the Rittenhouse Hotel (see above), (215) 790-2533. Jean-Marie Lacroix, a warmhearted veteran, cooks with a youngster's zest and imagination. At his new place, opened in 2002 and now perhaps the best table in Philadelphia, the cliché-free food and modern decor make Le Bec-Fin on Walnut Street, the city's longtime French champ, feel a little tired. The treetop view, the intense, deeply colored pheasant consommé with truffles, the luscious veal breast with braised leeks, and the immaculately kept cheeses will make you sing.

¡Pasión!, 211 South Fifteenth Street, (215) 875-9895. For my money, Guillermo Pernot's nuevo Latino cooking is among the most exciting in Philadelphia right now. A superlative chili-laced ceviche of Chilean sea bass and seaweed, presented in a scallop shell, is served with broad smiles in a tented room full of palms and bright fabrics. Likewise, an Argentine mixed grill, a Haitian empanada, and the very best Chilean wines.

Morimoto, 723 Chestnut Street, (215) 413-9070. Pyrotechnic design by Karim Rashid—lighting that changes colors, undulating wood ceiling—and pyrotechnic cuisine by Masaharu Morimoto, ex–Iron Chef, ex-Nobu. Ten-hour-braised pork belly with hot rice porridge is Japanese comfort food at its best; rock-shrimp tempura with sparky chili and miso aioli and smoky eel steamed in a bamboo leaf also star. Or go for an omakase (chef's choice) menu. Stephen Starr, the city's restaurant pooh-bah, is the moneyman.

Pat's King of Steaks, Ninth and Passyunk Streets, (215) 468-1546. This is the real deal: it gave the world the Philly cheese steak—thinly sliced, quickly grilled beef, slapped onto an Italian roll, slathered with Cheez Whiz, topped with grilled onions. You eat at a plastic table, right there on the street. It's silly, sloppy, and, in its own way, sublime.

Striped Bass, 1500 Walnut Street, (215) 732-4444. The lofty ceilings and the marble columns of this erstwhile banking hall, built in 1927, always put me in a mellow mood, as do the Fortuny lighting fixtures and the nifty metal fish hanging overhead. The new owner, Stephen Starr (who else?), saved it from bankruptcy and brought in Alfred Portale, from Manhattan's Gotham Bar & Grill, as consultant chef. Early hits: striped bass ceviche, roast lobster with rhubarb lemon butter, grilled halibut with morels.

Susanna Foo, 1512 Walnut Street, (215) 545-2666. Born in Mongolia, Sue Foo, as the local Asian grocers like to call her, is equally at home with Asian and European culinary traditions. In a dining room full of orchids and Asian art, she serves a trio of dumplings (shrimp, duck, lobster), each in a deliciously different wrapper, and dares to pair fish in a tangy sauce with sweet rice. Five-spice Pennsylvania venison is another hit.

⫸ BALTIMORE

Cal Ripken embodied the very best of Baltimore: steadfast, hardworking, blue-collar. The Orioles' nonpareil, long-serving infielder (1981–2001), who broke Lou Gehrig's supposedly unbreakable record for consecutive games played, was the latest in a line of homegrown heroes to become national figures. A local boy of an earlier era, Francis Scott Key, born up the road near Frederick, witnessed the bombardment of Fort McHenry at the entrance to Baltimore's harbor in 1814 from a British man-of-war and wrote the stirring verse that, set to music, became famous as "The Star-Spangled Banner."

You can visit the homes of other icons: Edgar Allan Poe, whose quotable raven has been adopted as a mascot by the city's National Football League team; Babe Ruth, the fun-loving saloonkeeper's son whom sportswriters enthroned as the Sultan of Swat; and Henry Louis Mencken, author, iconoclast, and closet sentimentalist, whose three-story townhouse on Union Square, with the locally obligatory front stoop, bears the words "To please my ghost, forgive some sinner and wink your eye at some homely girl."

But by 1999, when Martin O'Malley was elected mayor at the age of thirty-six, things were grim. Baltimore, a city of 630,000 persons, led the nation in drug abuse, with 60,000 addicts. People here were killing each other at almost five times the rate of New Yorkers. More than 40,000 abandoned buildings disfigured the streets.

Since then, progress has undeniably been made. The city's neighborhoods are somewhat safer. The Ravens bathed a sport-obsessed populace in a glow of purple by winning the Super

Bowl in 2001. In the first nine months of 2002, while many areas were losing jobs, Baltimore and its suburbs added 40,000. Construction cranes have been busy on projects like a better Baltimore Visitor Center; the Hippodrome Performing Arts Center, created at a cost of $63 million out of the old Hippodrome theater and two adjacent banks; an expansion of the National Aquarium; and the new Reginald F. Lewis Museum of Maryland African-American History and Culture.

Baltimore continues as one of the nation's busiest deep-water ports, a status it has enjoyed for more than two hundred years. It remains a leader in roll-on, roll-off auto imports and several other categories. It has become a thriving financial center, the home of brokerage and mutual fund companies like T. Rowe Price, Deutsche Bank Alex. Brown, and Legg Mason. And McCormick & Co., the world's biggest spice merchant, maintains its headquarters in suburban Sparks, Maryland.

Yet terrible things keep happening, calling into question the one-word slogan "Believe" that you see emblazoned on billboards, buses, T-shirts, and almost everywhere else. In October 2002, Angela Dawson, thirty-six, a true believer in Baltimore's anti-drug crusade, burned to death with five of her children in their row house in a fire apparently set by a drug dealer as an act of retribution. The next month, six police officers were gunned down in eight days.

Baltimore has a cherished history of tolerance. Maryland, the state it dominates, was the only one of the thirteen original colonies founded by Roman Catholics, and the first Catholic cathedral in the United States still stands here. At the intersection of South and North, the city has had a distinguished black community for more than a century. The widely read newspaper *The Afro-American* is published here, and it was here that the pioneering Justice Thurgood Marshall of the Supreme Court grew up.

Civic leaders have worked hard to preserve the civil relations among ethnic groups that have long graced Baltimore. Senator Paul S. Sarbanes told me, "This is not a hard-edged city, which is why it works." In the Cross Street Market late on a Saturday afternoon, blacks, Greeks, Italians, Jews, and Irishmen eat crabs, drink beer, talk Ravens, talk Orioles, and, of course, talk lacrosse, the graceful sport at which Marylanders have excelled for many decades.

The joys of "Bawlmer," as its natives call it, have been extolled recently in Anne Tyler's novels and in the movies of Barry Levinson, who explored to great comic effect the raffish world of the siding salesman, and John Waters, poet laureate of beehive hairdos, who once described Baltimore as "a gloriously decrepit, inexplicably charming city." Not nearly so well-known outside the Middle Atlantic region are the people whose wealth, taste, and civic commitment have made Baltimore a longtime cultural center of consequence—people named Walters and Cone, Peabody and Pratt and Johns Hopkins.

The Baltimore Symphony Orchestra was brought to international prominence by its former director, David Zinman, who was replaced in 1999 by Yuri Temirkanov, the music director of the St. Petersburg Philharmonic Orchestra. He fit almost as snugly into the Baltimore scene, a critic wrote, as its famous row houses. With their sound newly burnished, the Baltimoreans play in the $15 million Joseph Meyerhoff Symphony Hall, designed by Pietro Belluschi and built in 1982 of bronze-colored brick, with an oval auditorium holding 2,460 people. Even if you can't hear a concert, try to see the building as you head to the Baltimore Art Museum and a date with the Cone sisters.

They were a remarkable pair, Dr. Claribel and Miss Etta Cone, two independent-minded, well-to-do spinsters from nineteenth-century Baltimore who fell in love with avant-garde French art under the influence of their friend Gertrude Stein, the writer and collector. Beginning in 1898, they bought widely and wisely, and in the end they donated their paintings, including one of the world's greatest collections of works by Matisse (and a significant group of Picassos as well) to the museum in their hometown. Eight completely redesigned galleries, opened in 2001, afford a look at more than one hundred paintings, sculptures, and works on paper, as well as material about the sisters' lives. Two of Matisse's most significant pictures are here, the big, bold, Cézanne-influenced *Blue Nude* of 1907, which hung in the Armory Show of 1913 in Manhattan, and the much more abstract, frame-filling *Pink Nude*, done twenty-eight years later; so are interiors and portraits, including *The Woman in a Turban*.

Elsewhere in the museum, whose main block was designed by John Russell Pope in 1929, are fine collections of old masters and of French nineteenth-century art, as well as a suite of seven rooms from old Maryland houses.

Just north of the museum stands the extensive main campus of The Johns Hopkins University, named for the man who gave the money for it. A wealthy Baltimore merchant who began in the grocery business and branched out into shipping, banking, and insurance, he helped to build this major institution from scratch. It was the very first American research university (opened 1876) and is still one of the best, and its medical school has long been considered top-notch. The city's largest employer, Hopkins is the home base of the nation's preeminent research group on HIV and AIDS, under Dr. Robert Gallo.

Homewood, an exceptionally beautiful red-brick Federal mansion (1801–6), sits atop a knoll on the eastern edge of the Johns Hopkins campus, with a slender portico facing Charles Street, the city's main north-south corridor. Like Monticello, it is relatively small; two "hyphens" connect flanking pavilions to the central part of the structure. It was built by Charles Carroll of Carrollton, Maryland, a wealthy landowner and signer of the Declaration of Independence, as a residence for his son, Charles Jr., who was its architect. A painstaking restoration was completed in 1987, and today the richly decorated interior, clearly influenced by the Scot Robert Adam, looks as it did almost two hundred years ago. The delicate fanlight windows, plaster cornices and fireplace surrounds are all remarkable. Only one other house in Maryland can touch it: the 1774–76 Hammond-Harwood House in the capital, Annapolis, which has perhaps the most beautiful doorway in America.

Chesapeake Bay, America's largest estuary, made Baltimore's first trading fortunes and gave it an early reputation as the nation's "gastronomic metropolis," to use Oliver Wendell Holmes Sr.'s phrase. He and others came to eat canvasback ducks, terrapin, striped bass (here called rockfish), and soft-shelled crabs at restaurants like the lamented Miller Brothers. The first two comestibles have almost disappeared and the third is endangered, but Baltimore remains Crab City, as devoted to its blue swimmers as Dallas is to steak.

The definitive crab cake—the finest on earth—is made at Faidley's Seafood in the Lexington Market, which was established in 1782. Local gourmands swear the best steamed crabs in town (a weighty judgment, that) are served at the Costas Inn in Dundalk, where the huge Sparrows Point mill spews out smoke and hot-rolled steel. Spice-slathered crabs are dumped unceremoniously in front of you to attack with mallet and pick. The last time I made this gustatory pilgrimage, I finished happily—with stinging lips, fingers smeared with reddish gunk, and a tumulus of shell rising before me.

But I digress, as I tend to do when eating is involved. To return to economic history, Baltimore throughout the nineteenth century pursued commercial interests in the West, to which it was linked first by turnpike, then by canal, and finally by railroad. America's first chartered rail line was the Baltimore & Ohio, which made its initial regularly scheduled run from the Mount Clare Station to Ellicott City, Maryland, on May 24, 1830. The first telegraph message was sent to the same station from the Capitol in Washington on May 24, 1844, by the device's inventor, Samuel F. B. Morse.

The station has been turned into the nation's largest railroad museum, with more than 120 pieces of rolling stock on display in an old roundhouse and outside—steam and diesel locomotives along with tenders, cabooses, diners, boxcars, and tank cars. An 1838 Nova Scotia directors' car looks like a stagecoach mounted on trucks, which is exactly what it was, and a huge HO-gauge model railroad is a paradise for children (and their fathers and grandfathers, many wearing engineer's caps). Regrettably, a snowstorm in February 2003 caused extensive damage to the building and its contents that took $30 million and more than a year to repair.

Railroads meant speed. They meant thousands upon thousands of jobs to Baltimore, and they meant riches for men like William T. Walters and his son Henry, collectors who first started exhibiting in 1874 and eventually bequeathed to the city their 22,000 works of art. Born in 1934 and reborn in 2001 after a three-year renovation, the Walters Art Gallery greets visitors with a dramatic four-story glass-walled atrium. Its collections range widely, from paintings to armor to manuscripts, but its renown was made by classical objects like seven magnificent second-story A.D. Roman marble sarcophagi, one of which shows "A Procession of Bacchus to India" with remarkable liveliness. There is also an extraordinary Etruscan ivory box, crowned by a striding, winged sphinx. New galleries were added in 1991 in the Hackerman House to hold a major collection of Asian art, including bronzes, sculpture, scrolls, screens, and what may well be the finest vase in existence in the Chinese monochrome "peach bloom" glaze.

The Walters is a major feature of the neighborhood around Mount Vernon Place, once the city's flossiest residential district, where Henry James found "a perfect felicity" of life. Also there or nearby are the Washington Monument, a colossal 120-foot column by the great Federal-era architect Robert Mills; the Peabody Conservatory, one of the nation's leading music schools; and the Enoch Pratt Free Library, founded in 1886.

Across the street from the library stands the Basilica of the Assumption, the cathedral built by John Carroll, the first Roman Catholic bishop (later archbishop) of the United States, and his architect, Benjamin Henry Latrobe. It is one of our best nineteenth-century buildings. The facade is neoclassical, with a double Ionic portico, but the interior is a study in geometric complexity. The rotunda beneath the great dome traces a circle within an octagon within a square.

Lovers of ecclesiastical architecture will also find in Baltimore an excellent red-brick church built by Richard Upjohn in 1854–56, Old St. Paul's, an Italianate structure that bears no stylistic resemblance to his Gothic Revival Trinity Church in lower Manahattan. St. Paul's has stained-glass windows by the two great American masters of the form, Louis Comfort Tiffany and John La Farge. Lovely Lane Methodist Church, the "mother church" of American Methodism, is a striking neo-Romanesque work in rusticated granite, dominated by a massive square bell tower with a conical roof, built in 1887 by Stanford White.

Late-twentieth-century urban renewal, which vandalized so many American cities, brought downtown Baltimore back from the dead in a mere quarter century. This is America's bootstrap city: still plagued with urban ills, struggling to get a handle on the twin terrors of poverty and crime, but blessed all the same with two vividly rejuvenated neighborhoods at its core.

One is mostly for locals: a thirty-three-acre mixed-use project called Charles Center, which is anchored by the Morris A. Mechanic Theater, a rugged, rough-hewn concrete building (designed by John M. Johansen) that is suspended from bold concrete piers. The other is mostly for the tourists who now visit the city in T-shirted, Nike'd droves: the Inner Harbor, a complex of office buildings, parks, shops, hotels, restaurants, and other attractions, which replaced acres of rotting docks, slums, and warehouses along the waterfront. Its centerpiece is the truly fabulous National Aquarium, where stingrays, electric eels, octopuses, frolicking dolphins, minute tropical fish, and giant sharks are displayed in tanks holding hundreds of thousands of gallons of water.

The Inner Harbor is also the site of the relatively new but intentionally old-fashioned home of the Orioles, Camden Yards, whose success has prompted several other cities to abandon big, barny stadiums for cozier, fan-friendly ballparks, and an innovative new stadium for the Ravens, just to the south, which made its debut for the 1998 season.

Two improbable mayors presided over Baltimore's renewal. One was William Donald Schaefer (1971–87), a gifted if sometimes grouchy populist who promoted himself and his city with equal zeal. The other was Kurt L. Schmoke (1987–1999), a quiet, studious onetime Rhodes scholar, seemingly rattled by nothing, part of a notable new generation of coalition-building black leaders but eventually stymied by the city's protracted epidemic of violent crime.

WHERE TO STAY

The Harbor Court Hotel, 550 Light Street, (410) 234-0550. This hotel rules the roost in Baltimore, and has for quite some time. It's the closest thing the city has to a Ritz or Four Seasons, with an accommodating staff. Though the exterior is bland and blocky and the location a bit inconvenient, the bedrooms, some with four-posters and parquet floors, are all one could ask, as are the marble bathrooms. The place looks as if Ralph Lauren had been the interior decorator.

Renaissance Harborplace, 202 East Pratt Street, (410) 547-1200. This is the pick of the big convention and tourist hotels clustered on the north (Aquarium) side of the Inner Harbor. It is well managed, the decor is peppy, and the lobby is always animated. A skywalk links the hotel to the Harborplace shopping and noshing pavilions. But it's a monster (12 stories, 622 rooms), and you may feel there like part of a thundering herd.

Tremont Hotel, 8 East Pleasant Street, (410) 576-1200. If peace, quiet, and residential intimacy are your choices, the pert

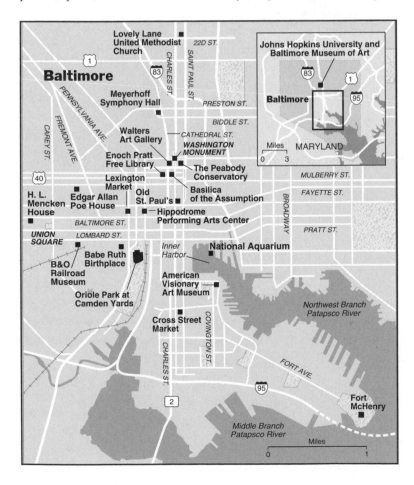

little Tremont, with sixty suites, each with mini-kitchen, may suit you fine. A converted 1960s apartment building, it feels much more European than American, and it has the best service in town, including a concierge who knows his city cold.

The Inn at Henderson's Wharf, 1000 Fell Street, (410) 522-7777. Here is another offbeat winner, about a mile from the Inner Harbor, to which it is linked by water taxi. In the Fells Point district, the center of Baltimore's nightlife, the building began in the mid-nineteenth century as a tobacco warehouse, but it has been invitingly restored. The waterfront location and the garden are pluses; the skimpy continental breakfast a minus.

WHERE TO EAT

Charleston, 1000 Lancaster Street, (410) 332-7373. The prince and princess of Baltimore restauration are Tony Foreman and his wife, Cindy Wolf. He is a grape nut, a buddy of the famous wine critic Robert Parker, and the business brains behind not only this downtown restaurant but also the Petit Louis Bistro, up north. She is as assured in the style of New Orleans (shrimp with grits, tasso, and andouille) as in that of the Low Country (duck with beans and rice). Their cheeses are selected, matured, and served with discrimination and care.

Hampton's, Harbor Court Hotel, 550 Light Street, (410) 347-9744. Calm and elegant, this is one of the restaurants that helped to revolutionize hotel dining in the United States in the 1990s. One dish that I tried, lamb cooked in three ways—roasted leg, sautéed chop, and spicy merguez sausage—bore comparison to a similar dish at Lucas-Carton, Alain Senderens's three-star shrine in Paris. Avocado soup with lobster quenelles makes a luscious starter. Excellent wine list, including scarce "boutique" labels from California.

Helmand, 806 North Charles Street, (410) 752-0311. An ethnic treasure, this upmarket Afghan place is run by Qayum Karzai, brother of Afghanistan's head of state, no less. Its kaddo (sautéed pumpkin) and chopan (charcoaled rack of lamb) make it *vaut le voyage*.

Marconi's, you have to understand, has been at 106 West Saratoga Street—(410) 727-9522—more or less forever. My late mother-in-law remembered eating there not long after World War I. Though unfeelingly modernized, the narrow dining room is a culinary time capsule, with courtly waiters, Belle Époque dishes like lobster Cardinale, and the thick lamb chops loved by Mencken and my wife, Betsey. Also good dry martinis, better fried eggplant, and the fudgiest chocolate sundae I know of.

Pierpoint, 1822 Aliceanna Street, Fells Point, (410) 675-2080. Like a good athlete, this restaurant plays within itself: no over-reaching, no showboating. The chef and proprietor Nancy Longo can speak a lot of culinary languages, from down-home Chesapeake Bay (Maryland tomato-crab soup and Eastern Shore Silver Queen corn chowder) to Manhattan eclectic (bar-becued New York duck egg rolls). I would travel a long way just for her smoked Maryland crab cakes, a perfect blend of inno-vation and tradition, sweet and aromatic, served with brussels sprouts coleslaw. Since 1989.

Women's Industrial Exchange, 333 North Charles Street, (410) 685-4388. Another survivor, this one serves near-perfect chicken salad, tomato aspic, deviled eggs, and cupcakes: sim-ple, delicious WASP luncheon food from the Eisenhower era.

⫸ WASHINGTON

Like Brasília, Canberra, and many other created capitals, by which I mean cities custom-built as seats of government, Washington has been bad-mouthed from the very beginning. Thomas Jefferson, obviously not foreseeing the day when he would gaze in perpetuity from his marble tempietto at the Tidal Basin, called the city "that Indian swamp in the wilderness." Charles Dickens, who described Washington as "the city of magnificent intentions," complained about "spacious avenues that begin in nothing and lead nowhere." John F. Kennedy remarked that the capital was "a city of Northern charm and Southern efficiency." Ever enigmatic, Dylan Thomas thought that Washington was not a city at all but an abstraction.

Complaints that there are two Americas, one inside the Beltway surrounding Washington and one outside, often reach deafening proportions. It is hard to say who is held in the lowest esteem by the average Janes and Joes who live outside Interstate 495: politicians, journalists who write and talk about them, or lawyers and lobbyists who seek to influence them. Anyway, all of them are thought to be terminally out of touch. Henry James observed in 1907 that "Washington talks about herself and about almost nothing else." Insularity is nothing new in the capital, nor is obsession. One of James's literary heirs, the novelist Ward Just, observed in 1997 in *Echo House* that in Washington "Life flourishes on flat surfaces, desks, conference tables, lecterns and dinner tables: an indoor world."

Of course. This is still the hometown of the largest enterprise on earth, the United States government. And even when the murder rate soared, when nobody bothered to plow the snow or pick up the trash, when the schools couldn't open because the courts said the buildings were unsafe, when the infamous mayor Marion Barry went to jail on a drug rap, when lead turned up in the city's drinking water—even then Americans flocked to Washington. To most visitors, the local news in the nation's capital is irrelevant. They come not to listen to some tiresome Claghorn on Capitol Hill or to tut-tut at the mean streets where the city's poor live, not to count the manifold ways in which the government falls short of the Founding Fathers' ideals, but to pay homage to the ideals themselves, to keep the ideals alive, and to imbue their children with them. This is why Washington is thronged several times each year with family groups, looking slightly confused, maps in hand, taking in the American dream.

If Washington sometimes seems like the world capital of philistinism, hypocrisy, and self-importance, it is also gifted with a seductive grandeur. Even cynics feel a stir at seeing Lincoln up there in his thronelike marble chair, where Daniel Chester French put him in 1922, or when they walk up the awesomely broad steps of the Supreme Court, whose very name embodies an absolute primacy rare in modern life. Much of Washington's appeal resides in its being at the nexus of American power. Although the attacks of September 11, 2001, put a dent in the Pentagon and the myth of the nation's omnipotence, and led to the erection of raw concrete barricades around most of Washington's public buildings, which sometimes make one feel as if the nation's leaders are cowering from their enemies, the old machismo survives in places like the Palm Restaurant, where pols, lobbyists, journalists, and apparatchiks gather to swap rumors, gossip about the Redskins, listen to the jokes of Tommy Jacomo, the boss, and devour martinis, steaks, and lobsters.

Washington is centered on the Capitol, sited on Jenkins Hill by a grumpy French military engineer named Pierre Charles L'Enfant in 1790. He laid out a city of boulevards that drew inspiration from Paris, with four quadrants meeting at the Capitol—numbered streets running north and south from it, and lettered streets running east and west. But the straight, splendid avenues that run on the diagonal give Washington much of its scale and dignity. L'Enfant was right to think that

Capitol Hill was "a pedestal waiting for a monument." The men who governed the young American republic thought of themselves as the political progeny of the ancient Greeks and Romans, so they filled their new city on the Potomac with pillars and porticoes. But only the Capitol—first a much smaller building, finished in 1826, and then expanded—has a 9-million-pound cast-iron dome, completed in the midst of the Civil War. Congress meets in this building, the Senate in the north wing and the House of Representatives in the south wing. Its original sandstone came from Virginia quarries owned by George Washington.

North of the Capitol stands Union Station, designed by the great Chicago architect Daniel H. Burnham in 1908 and restored to all its magnificence in 1988 by another Chicagoan, Harry Weese, with busy shops and restaurants enlivening the concourse. (Weese, who died in 1998, also designed the Washington Metro with arched and coffered ceilings that lend the stations the noble air of Roman vaults.)

Because of laws restricting the height of buildings, plus two centuries of zealous preservation of green spaces, Washington has an airier, less congested feeling than many cities. On a fine spring day, with the cherry, pear, dogwood, and redbud trees in bloom, with the immaculate white buildings gleaming in the sun, it can take your breath away. If you happen to be there on such a day, do yourself a favor and walk west from Union Station to an undervisited treasure, the Pension Building (1881), now known as the National Building Museum. The city's most stunning room is its immense central court, as long as a football field and pierced by eight brick Corinthian columns the size of redwoods, each seventy-six feet high and twenty-five feet around—bigger than the pillars of the ancient temple at Baalbek in Lebanon.

The Capitol is also one of the city's great outdoor stages. Gala concerts are held there on patriotic holidays and presidents take the oath of office there every four Januarys.

A long, grassy rectangle, the Mall stretches westward from the Capitol, flanked by museums. At the far end stands another great stage, the Lincoln Memorial, where crowds often rally on behalf of the poor and the oppressed. For members of my generation, it will forever be linked with the March on Washington of 1963, at which the Reverend Dr. Martin Luther King Jr., addressing a throng of more than a quarter of a million, promised his people in unforgettably eloquent terms that one day they would be "free at last."

Three monuments stand between the Capitol and the Lincoln Memorial: the immense obelisk memorializing George Washington; Maya Lin's stirringly simple Vietnam Memorial, a gash in the green lawns that recalls the wound opened by that wretched war; and the more conventional, less rapturously received World War II monument, dedicated in 2004, which consists of two curving arcs of pillars, fifty-six in all, flanking a pool.

Off to the north of the Mall, across another stretch of lawn that is known because of its shape as the Ellipse, are the extensive grounds of the White House, where presidents live and make their often-fateful decisions. There you can see Ulysses S. Grant's chandeliers in the East Room; Harry S Truman's balcony; Gilbert Stuart's famous portrait of Washington, which Dolley Madison herself snatched from the fire set by the British during the War of 1812; and even, perhaps, network correspondents doing their stand-uppers on the lawn.

On or near the Mall are repositories of American and world history: the National Archives, home of the Declaration of Independence, the Constitution, the Bill of Rights, and the Emancipation Proclamation; the Library of Congress, the world's largest with a collection approaching 100 million items, including a Gutenberg Bible, Charlie Chaplin movies, a vast trove of cookbooks, 3.5 million pieces of sheet music and five Stradivarius violins; the National Portrait Gallery; the National Air and Space Museum; the National Museum of Natural History, and the National Museum of American History, an attic stuffed with items as big as a 280-ton locomotive and as small as a postage stamp, including Julia Child's kitchen and the Star-Spangled Banner itself.

Many of these museums (all free) are parts of the Smithsonian Institution, the legacy of an Englishman named James Smithson, who died in 1829, leaving his fortune to a city he had never visited to found an organization "for the increase and diffusion of knowledge among men." It has grown into the largest museum complex in the world. Together the museums may sometimes become mere entries on a list, in danger of turning into the yadda yadda of a visit to Washington. But anywhere else, any one of them would be deemed remarkable.

The glory of Washington's cultural life is its art museums. Our young capital lacks Rome's lengthy history, Paris's sophistication, and London's royal traditions, but it can compete on equal terms with those cities, and with New York and Berlin, in the immense richness of the paintings and sculpture, drawings and prints assembled here over many decades. I particularly like the Freer Gallery, devoted to Asian art, and especially its Peacock Room, flamboyantly decorated in blue and gold by James Abbott McNeill Whistler, whom the museum's founder, the Detroit industrialist Charles Lang Freer, saw as a vital link between the aesthetics of East and West. The compact, scintillating Phillips Collection, once a private mansion, holds Renoir's masterpiece *Luncheon of the Boating Party* and important groups by two of my favorite moderns, Klee and Rothko.

But who would want to miss the Corcoran, with its splendid Hudson River School canvases? Who does not eagerly await the reopening, in 2006, of the Smithsonian American Art Museum, with its Hassams and Hoppers? Or the exquisite pre-Columbian relics housed in Philip Johnson's deliciously refined little pavilion at Dumbarton Oaks in Georgetown? At Dumbarton Oaks, which is owned by Harvard University, you earn bonuses—the Byzantine collection housed in the Federal-style mansion (where groundwork was laid for the United Nations), and the romantic gardens, designed in the 1920s by Beatrix Ferrand, a legendary American landscape architect.

At the summit, of course, stands the National Gallery of Art, endowed by people of unimaginable wealth like Andrew Mellon and his children, Chester Dale, and Joseph Widener, and built into a world-class institution by a succession of directors including John Walker, J. Carter Brown, and the incumbent, Earl A. Powell III, a refreshingly unstuffy soul who is known to almost everyone as Rusty. (Powell is a member of the Williams College mafia, one of many museum directors who studied there.)

The gallery has two buildings. The first was designed in 1941 by John Russell Pope, whose pared-down neoclassical style left a deep mark on Washington through the Jefferson

Memorial, Constitution Hall, and other landmarks. The second is the work of I. M. Pei (1978), a pair of cleanly articulated triangles that house offices, galleries, and a vast atrium where Alexander Calder's huge final mobile twists lazily overhead. Inside hang the only Leonardo da Vinci painting in America, a portrait of Ginevra de Benci; Raphael's *Alba Madonna*, van Eyck's *Annunciation*, Vermeer's *Girl with the Red Hat*—all iconic pictures familiar from a thousand posters and a million postcards—and dozens of other Renaissance and Impressionist gems. Outside is a delightful new sculpture garden.

Pei's is one of the city's few significant modern buildings. Beyond it there is only a relatively minor library by Mies van der Rohe, supposedly recycled from the plans for a Bacardi factory designed for Havana but never built. The troubled new National Museum of the American Indian is more notable for its artifacts than its architecture. But the area boasts two of the nation's handsomest airports, Dulles by Eero Saarinen and Reagan by Cesar Pelli, both across the Potomac in Virginia, and the Corcoran Gallery is soon to have a dramatic new 140,000-square-foot wing by Frank Gehry.

The Kennedy Center (1971), designed by Edward Durrell Stone, is a performing arts triumph and an architectural dud (although it is planning an expansion by the Uruguayan-born star Rafael Viñoly). Leonard Slatkin, its elfin music director, who came from St. Louis, has raised the National Symphony to a new level, and Plácido Domingo has done the same for the Washington Opera, though neither yet stands among the nation's best. Varied theater offerings and film programs find venues at Kennedy Center; an inspired innovation is the nightly free concerts before the main events, designed to attract people who could not afford tickets, and underwritten by the center's former chairman, James A. Johnson, and his wife, Maxine Isaacs.

There is music and theater all over town. Institutions as diverse as Dumbarton Oaks, the Library of Congress, the National Gallery, and the Corcoran all stage first-rate chamber concerts. Experimental and more conventional theaters abound, including the Arena Stage, founded by Zelda Fichandler in 1950 (it has three stages, in fact), a leading repertory company that sends a good number of productions to New York and has developed outstanding actors like Robert Prosky. Surprisingly, Washington is mad for the Bard. It supports not one but two Shakespearean stages—the Shakespeare Theater and the replica Elizabethan theater that is part of the 250,000-volume Folger Shakespeare Library, built in 1932 with Standard Oil millions.

Once proudly called "Chocolate City," 70 percent African American, with a flourishing black commercial and artistic tradition of which Duke Ellington was a notable product, Washington now has fewer blacks, more Asian and Hispanic residents, and a prosperous white minority. (The metropolitan area has 5.4 million people, the city 572,000—60 percent black, 7.9 percent Hispanic, and 2.7 percent Asian.) It is still a hard town for some people: those who live in crack-infested neighborhoods, those who sleep in Lafayette Park, near the White House, and those who find the pressure of loneliness too much to bear. One of Washington's poignant monuments, popularly known as *Grief*, is a memorial by Augustus Saint-Gaudens to Clover Adams in Rock Creek Cemetery. Married to Henry Adams—a widely known writer himself, a grandson of John Quincy Adams and a great-grandson of John Adams—she committed suicide. But it is a town of possibilities, too. Georgetown University, President Clinton's alma mater, has emerged under two recent presidents, Timothy S. Healy and Leo O'Donovan, as the nation's top Catholic university. Howard University is one of the nation's oldest and best historically black colleges. And Gallaudet is a world leader in the education of the deaf.

Small pleasures as well as large thrills abound in the city. Try a walk or a horseback ride in Rock Creek Park, Washington's bosky answer to the Bois de Boulogne, which separates Washington from Georgetown; a stop at the spectacularly restored United States Botanic Garden's Palm House, near the Capitol; a visit to the little-noted Churchill statue near Lutyens's monumental British Embassy, or a quiet hour examining Cass Gilbert's Supreme Court Building (1935). I enjoy looking at the Iowa cornstalks that replace acanthus leaves in the "Corinthian" capitals, and at the sculptured portraits on the pediment, including one of the immodest Gilbert himself.

Different people are drawn to different things: the National Zoo, perhaps, despite its recent tribulations; the wonderful Arboretum in the far northeast; the Pentagon and the many other military installations; the National Cathedral and the National Shrine of the Immaculate Conception; and the city's various residential neighborhoods. Adams-Morgan is one of the funkiest and Cleveland Park one of the pleasantest, with roomy frame houses that in the days before air-conditioning used to be refuges from the summer heat downtown. Many of the city's rich live in grand spreads on Woodland Drive and in the not very well-known Kalorama neighborhood.

But nothing quite matches Georgetown, a modest little river port to the west of Washington before all the grandees came to town and now an ideal inner-city enclave, leafy and full of red-brick survivors of the Federal period, but also old wooden buildings, intricate remnants from the Victorian era, a few modern houses tucked in here and there, and a big French-style mansion where the late Katharine Graham of *The Washington Post* lived.

You will best savor Georgetown's flavor and tempo by wandering at random along its narrow streets, past Dumbarton Oaks, to be sure, and Tudor Place, built in 1794 by Dr. William Thornton, the original architect of the Capitol, for Martha Washington's granddaughter Martha Parke Custis and her husband, Thomas Peter. But stroll as well down N Street NW, past John F. Kennedy's onetime house at 3307, perhaps, and one of the most beautiful doorways anywhere at 2812, and lovely Cox Row from 3327 to 3339.

WHERE TO STAY

Four Seasons, 2800 Pennsylvania Avenue NW, (202) 342-0444. A nondescript brick box on the outside, a festival of fine fabrics and fresh flowers on the inside, this is Washington's premier hotel. Its location on the brink of Georgetown and the air of discreet seclusion will cost you dearly, but you won't feel cheated. You can witness political power breakfasts in the Seasons restaurant, or eat a delicious dinner there yourself.

Willard Intercontinental, 1401 Pennsylvania Avenue NW, (202) 628-9100. Designed by Henry J. Hardenbergh, the architect of the Plaza Hotel in Manhattan, this grand beaux arts pile has stood tall between the White House and Capitol Hill since 1908. It has a spectacularly opulent lobby, brilliantly restored, and rooms of varying dimensions, occupied by the rich, the famous, and the not quite. High-powered law offices are nearby.

Jefferson, 16th and M Street NW, (202) 347-2200. Understated, private, calm, and clublike, this sixty-eight-room gem is European in conception and style. Robert Rubin, the Treasury secretary, lived in one of its suites during his six years in the Clinton cabinet. Flawless service, and there are few better places for a civilized drink after work.

WHERE TO EAT

Ben's Chili Bowl, 1213 U Street NW, (202) 667-0909. Founded in 1958, when it stood amid clubs that gave U Street the nickname "Black Broadway." Ben Ali's kids run the place now, but they still serve his firm half-smoke sausage, browned on the grill, tucked into a bun, painted with mustard, and topped with thick, peppery chili. Unwieldy perhaps, but unbeatable, it brings people like Bill Cosby (and me) back again and again.

Citronelle, in the Latham Hotel, 3000 M Street NW, (202) 625-2150. Michel Richard was trained as a pâtissier by the great Paris caterer Gaston Lenôtre, went on to fame and fortune in Los Angeles, and now wows Washington. His witty food is marked by concentrated flavors (summery basil aspic, impossibly velvety cauliflower puree), and he likes to reinvent the commonplace. His onion soup is a puree of onions over a savory cheesecake, and his deconstructed vitello tonnato is a napoleon of raw tuna and poached veal.

Equinox, 818 Connecticut Avenue NW, (202) 331-8118. After long stints in local kitchens, Todd Gray set up shop on his own a block from the White House and quickly emerged as the city's most assiduous forager for ingredients. You can count on him for the fattest chickens, the ripest tomatoes, the most delicate spring lamb, and the sweetest corn from the Delmarva Peninsula—all prepared in his clean, lean, intelligent style.

Inn at Little Washington, Main and Middle Streets, Washington, Va., (540) 675-3800. Self-taught, Patrick O'Connell applies modern French technique to Virginia ingredients like oysters, shad roe, and country ham, with world-beating results. Reinhardt Lynch has molded one of the country's best, most pampering waitstaffs from a group of youngsters who, like the inn, dwell in the lee of the Blue Ridge, about ninety minutes west of Washington. Hire a car and driver for the trip, or stay in a pasha-worthy bedroom.

Kinkead's, 2000 Pennsylvania Avenue NW, (202) 296-7700. Confession: this is our local, where my wife, Betsey, and I eat at least once a month when we're home. The mammoth iced shellfish platters always delight Betsey, and no one, anywhere, serves better fried clams than Bob Kinkead, whose talent was honed in his native New England. The menu zooms giddily but confidently from Asian-style whole bass to salmon in dill-scented Scandinavian-style broth. The wine list is equally catholic, and Hilton Felton provides subtle piano jazz downstairs.

Obelisk, 2029 P Street NW, (202) 872-1180. Peter Pastan isn't Italian, but his sensibility is. Every day he offers a market-based menu with several choices at each stage, always full of fresh, unaffected goodness. He has a fondness for offbeat mollusks like cockles and periwinkles and for game birds. Served in a slim little room with crisp blond decor, his dishes are complemented by outstanding Italian wines and knee-buckling grappas.

Zaytinya, 701 Ninth Street NW, (202) 638-0800. José Andrés— a graduate of Ferran Adria's trendsetting kitchen at El Bulli, north of Barcelona—has been Washington's most influential chef for a decade. Having celebrated tapas and the food of Latin America in his first two restaurants, he turned to Greece, Turkey, and Lebanon for Zaytinya's menu. Happy, noisy crowds lap up the minty raw beef, zucchini-cheese patties, and spanakopita.

⫸ PITTSBURGH

One fine day in 1999, wreckers toppled six smokestacks along the Monongahela River. Once part of a huge coke works but long idle, they were the last vestiges of Big Steel left within the Pittsburgh city limits. Mills that once employed tens of thousands of workers and produced a third of the world's steel had vanished like ghosts at dawn, and Iron City, aka Steeltown U.S.A., was no more.

Pittsburgh bounced back with surprising speed from the grueling loss of most of its heavy industry. In a display of gritty urban pride, new downtown buildings went up to symbolize the city's post-industrial renaissance—two stadia readily accessible from downtown (one for baseball, one for football), a theater designed by Michael Graves, and a glittering $331 million riverfront convention center by Rafael Viñoly with an upswept roof shaped like a catenary curve. Building on the base provided by three big universities with 45,000 students, Pittsburgh forged a surprising new economic identity as a high-tech center and as a regional medical capital.

But all the while, trouble was brewing. Although the metropolitan area remained one of the nation's twenty-five largest, with 2,358,695 people in the millennial census, the population of the city itself continued to dwindle—from 604,332 in 1960 to 334,563 in 2000—and its tax base shrank. Unable to tap the wealth of the blossoming suburbs, Pittsburgh borrowed and borrowed, until debt payments consumed 20 percent of its annual budgets. City services were slashed, the Pennsylvania state legislature officially declared Pittsburgh distressed, Standard & Poor's classified its bonds as junk, and the ugly word "insolvency" began to be whispered in local banks and boardrooms. By 2004, a crisis was at hand, comparable to the one that propelled New York City to the brink of bankruptcy in 1975 before the federal government stepped in to guarantee $1.65 million in emergency loans.

"Some of the problems are my fault," longtime mayor Tom Murphy told a reporter from *USA Today*. "Some of it goes back twenty years. We kept pushing our problems into the future, and now the future is here." The situation was worsened by the national economic downturn in the new century, as some promising technology-based start-ups folded and others cut back. But Pittsburgh retains the headquarters of blue-chip companies including Alcoa, H. J. Heinz, USX (formerly U.S. Steel), PPG Industries, and the Mellon and PNC banks. Downtown office towers are full, though two department stores, Lazarus and Lord & Taylor, pulled out.

Cultural institutions were pummeled as well. In seven years beginning in 1997, under the exciting, Latvian-born Mariss Jansons, one of the many young conductors who have emerged recently from the Baltic countries, the century-old Pittsburgh Symphony Orchestra—led in the past by such notables as Fritz Reiner, William Steinberg, and Lorin Maazel—has reached new heights. The *Evening Standard* in London called it "one of the finest orchestras on the planet." It boldly opened one recent season not with never-fail Beethoven or Brahms but with Schoenberg's immense, romantic, seldom-heard *Gurrelieder*, sung by two superstars, the Canadian tenor Ben Heppner and the American mezzo-soprano Jennifer Larmore, among others. But the stock market ravaged the orchestra's endowment, contributions fell off, and morale suffered. "If Pittsburgh wants to have a great orchestra, it needs to help us out," Gideon Toeplitz, the managing director, said not long before announcing his resignation. Now it must also replace Jansons, who is taking up prestigious posts in Munich and Amsterdam.

As in other Rust Belt cities like Cleveland and Detroit, the jury is still out on job creation. Pittsburgh's population is as old as those in some Sun Belt retirement cities, while many talented young people leave in search of economic opportunity elsewhere. But for those who stay or move here, the amenities are many. Leafy, close-in suburbs like Shadyside and Squirrel Hill. A low crime rate. Good schools. Moderate housing and living costs. Extensive parks. A terrific zoo. Three identical suspension bridges, all painted an identical primrose yellow, crossing the Allegheny River side by side. Three substantial universities: Carnegie Mellon, strong in science and technology; Duquesne, known for its liberal arts and law faculties; and the University of Pittsburgh, a medical powerhouse where some of the pioneering liver transplants were carried out.

Pittsburgh has its own vernacular. "Redd" means clean, as in "redd off the table," and "youns" is the plural of "you." It has a certain innocence as well. Maybe the city is provincial, as some people complain, but it also lacks the edgy aggression of many larger places. This was, after all, the hometown of Fred Rogers, the kids' sweet-natured friend Mr. Rogers, whose program was made at WQED, the nation's first public television station.

Pittsburgh glories, as ever, in its magnificent site at the "Forks of the Ohio," scouted by George Washington for the British in 1753. The city lies within the Appalachian Mountains, where the Allegheny River joins the Monongahela to form the broad Ohio. Ernie Pyle wrote once that it was a place of "hills, mountains, cliffs, valleys and rivers, up and down, around and around, in betwixt," better suited to goats than to people. A pair of antique funiculars, called inclines, slide up and down the steep face of Mount Washington, across the water from the skyscrapers packed into downtown Pittsburgh at the very tip of the Golden Triangle.

You arrive in Pittsburgh from the west, where the airport is situated, by way of the Fort Pitt Tunnel. One minute you are cruising along amid wooded hills, the next you are in the half-mile-long tube, and then suddenly you emerge onto a bridge. Dead in front of you is Pittsburgh's skyline, a dramatic, unexpected, exhilarating sight, akin to spying the towers of New York or San Francisco from a steamship in the days before the dawn of jet travel. But of course the approach did not always look so impressive. Not by a long shot.

In its heyday as the self-described Workshop of the World, Pittsburgh was an inferno. A half century ago, the rivers teemed with tugs and barges, and the mills poured brown and green ooze into the water and black and gray soot into the skies, so much so that streetlights were often kept on all day long. One week in 1948, thirty people were killed by smog in the grimy little riverside borough of Donora (where the baseball hall-of-famer Stan Musial grew up).

"Blackest place I ever saw," said the nineteenth-century English novelist Anthony Trollope, and he knew grim industrial landscapes at home. But Pittsburgh produced steel in prodigious quantities. At the end of World War II, U.S. Steel, the first billion-dollar corporation in history when it was formed in 1901, made twice as much steel as the entire Soviet Union. Set against that, the leaders of the time asked, what was a little pollution? Pittsburgh also produced enormous fortunes for men like Andrew Carnegie, an immigrant from Scotland who built a steel empire; Henry Clay Frick, the king of coke, the baked coal essential to making steel, who was first an aide and then a rival to Carnegie; and Andrew W. Mellon, the banker who grew rich financing the new industrial magnates.

Mellon money built the National Gallery in Washington, and by the time Andrew Mellon's son, Paul, died at the age of ninety-one in 1991, he had given it more than a thousand pictures, including two van Goghs and twelve Winslow Homers in a final bequest, as well as $75 million. Frick money built New York's finest small art museum. Carnegie money built libraries around the world. Only fractions of the families' wealth stayed in Pittsburgh, though their names still grace monuments, buildings, parks, streets, and museums here.

To work in the mills, peasants came from all over Europe. A sign from one Carnegie plant, preserved in the excellent (if clumsily named) John Heinz Pittsburgh Regional History Center, warned of danger in English, Italian, Hungarian, Slovak, and Serbo-Croatian. (My great-grandfather was one of the hardy spirits who crossed the Atlantic to work in Pittsburgh.) Myths grew up about industrial Bunyans like Joe Magarac, a Hungarian who could derail a locomotive with his little finger, and Steve Mestrovic, a Serb who could twist a 500-pound steel bar into a pretzel. In real life, the tough river towns where the immigrants settled produced more than their share of sports heroes, notably pro football quarterbacks like Johnny Unitas, Joe Montana, Jim Kelly, Joe Namath, and Dan Marino.

Pittsburgh quickly became a battleground between labor and capital. In the notorious Homestead strike of 1892, Pinkerton detectives employed by Frick clashed with workers; twenty people were killed, three hundred wounded, and the Amalgamated Association of Iron and Steel Workers was crushed. Industry won the battle, though decades later labor won the war.

Blacks streamed into Pittsburgh as well. *The Pittsburgh Courier* was for years the nation's leading African American newspaper, and the city produced a seemingly endless procession of jazz stars, from Billy Strayhorn to Mary Lou Williams to Erroll Garner. Before the integration of big-league baseball, the Pittsburgh Crawfords and Homestead Grays flourished on the black circuit with top players like Josh Gibson and the inimitable Satchel Paige. Sports still loom large, as befits the city's Joe Six-Pack image. Legends live on, like the Pirates infielder Bill Mazeroski's improbable last-of-the-ninth home run to beat the Yankees, 10–9, in the seventh game of the 1960 World Series, and Steeler running back Franco Harris's "immaculate reception" of Terry Bradshaw's deflected last-minute pass in a crucial playoff game in 1972.

Pittsburgh is rediscovering its significant architectural heritage and urging visitors to do the same. The region has two of the most celebrated American buildings, Henry Hobson Richardson's Allegheny County Courthouse and Jail, in Pittsburgh, and Frank Lloyd Wright's wonderful cantilevered country villa, Fallingwater, seventy-two miles to the southeast. Built in 1937 for the Pittsburgh department store magnate Edgar Kaufmann, Fallingwater juts boldly over a waterfall on Bear Run Creek. An icon of the modern style, it has been called "the greatest house ever built in the United States," but harsh weather over the years caused it to crack and sag, necessitating $11.5 million in repairs, beginning in 2002. The courthouse— a massive, masculine castle-like structure of rough-hewn granite with a 325-foot tower—is connected to the jail by a bridge like the Bridge of Sighs that links the Doge's Palace and the jail in Venice; the *voussoirs*, or blocks, that form the main entrance, one of Richardson's Romanesque arches, are eight feet long.

If Richardson whets your appetite for more good buildings, walk down Grant Street. On the way you will see the Union Trust Building (1915), with a breathtaking stack of nine balconies, crowned by a round stained-glass skylight, and a froth of terra-cotta turrets, pinnacles, and balustrades; the Koppers Building (1929), in an urbane Art Deco style; and the USX Building (1970), a bold tower in Cor-Ten steel, which oxidizes to red-brown. The USX Building is an advertisement for the company that built it, better known as U.S. Steel. So is the former Alcoa Building (1953), nearby on Sixth Avenue, whose skin is made of preformed aluminum panels; and the glass-faced PPG Place (1984), on Fourth Avenue, which was built by a corporation formerly called Pittsburgh Plate Glass.

No one has done more for Pittsburgh, especially the arts in Pittsburgh, than the Heinzes, purveyors to the world of 57 Varieties—actually more like 5,700. It was H. J. Heinz II, known as Jack (the last Heinz to actively run his famous company), who had the idea that cultural resources could aid in fostering the economic revival here. He bought four abandoned movie theaters downtown and helped to turn them into the Cultural District, anchored by Heinz Hall, home of the symphony. The new home of the Pittsburgh Public Theater, across the street from Heinz Hall, opened in 1999 with the world premiere of a play by August Wilson, a Pittsburgh native. Designed by Michael Graves, with a copper cowl giving its facade a distinctive look, it has a Heinz connection, too. It was partly financed by friends of, and named for, Anthony J. F. O'Reilly, the H. J. Heinz Company's charismatic Irish-born former chairman.

Another Frick art museum, a country cousin of the New York showplace, exhibits the collection of Henry Clay Frick's daughter, Helen; its highlights are a magisterial Rubens portrait and works by the Sienese masters Duccio and Sassetta. But the heaviest cultural hitters in town, in addition to the symphony, are the Carnegie and Warhol museums. The Carnegie complex, in Oakland, east of downtown, includes a museum of natural history, renowned for its dinosaur collection, and the art museum, which is headquarters for the influential Carnegie International exhibitions, held every three to five years, most recently in 2004. Since its beginning, the art museum has concentrated principally on art of the nineteenth and twentieth centuries—"the old masters of tomorrow," as Carnegie himself put it. Paintings, sculpture, and decorative arts are mingled to good effect in the permanent collection's galleries. Take, for instance, the room devoted to the Arts and Crafts movement, where furniture by C.F.A. Voysey and Harvey Ellis and copperware by W.A.S. Benson keeps company with two Pre-Raphaelite canvases by Edward Burne-Jones. First-rate pictures by Cézanne, Kirchner, and Degas (a smashing portrait of the engineer Henri Rouart) lie ahead, as well as an intriguing group of early American abstractions by Burgoyne Diller, George L. K. Morris, and Stanton Macdonald-Wright.

Over at the hip, innovative Andy Warhol Museum—"the posthumous home of the King of Pop," as someone called it—installed in an old seven-story building renovated by the New York architect Richard Gluckman, you are greeted by a big cobalt-blue self-portrait of the artist, wide-eyed, spiky-haired.

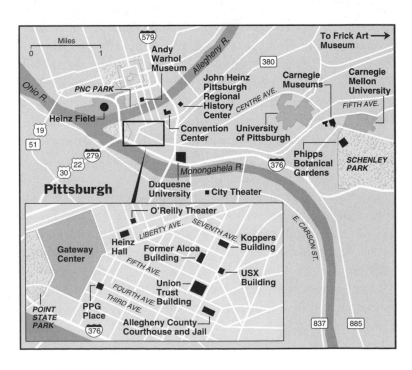

The building is filled with Warhol's collections (milk glass, shoes of famous people); Warhol's wallpaper (I was taken by the pink-and-yellow cow pattern); Warhol's films and Warhol's portraits of Mao, Liz, and Mick. A Pittsburgh native whose parents came from the Carpathian Mountains in central Europe, Warhol once wrote: "You live in your dream America that you've custommade from art and schmaltz and emotions just as much as you live in your real one."

Pittsburgh has taken slowly to the museum. "It's a sober city, very Presbyterian," says Thomas Sokolowski, the museum's director almost since it opened in 1994.

WHERE TO STAY

Pittsburgh Hilton, Gateway Center, (412) 391-4600. In a city that woefully lacks a top-drawer hotel, the Hilton is blessed with the three cardinal virtues: location, location, and location. Overlooking the junction of the Allegheny and Monongahela, with 711 modern rooms, it is a convention hotel par excellence, with all the pluses and minuses that go with that. The crisp, modern upper-floor accommodations are the most desirable.

Renaissance Pittsburgh, 107 Sixth Street, (412) 562-1200. Constructed in 1906 as the Fulton Building by Henry Phipps, Carnegie's partner, and renovated in 2001, this hotel is smack in the middle of the Cultural District. A spectacular twenty-ton glass-and-iron dome caps the spacious lobby, and a grand marble staircase leads up to the meeting rooms.

Sunnyledge, 5124 Fifth Avenue, Shadyside, (412) 683-5014. Oakland once had a pair of fine big hotels, the Schenley and Webster Hall. Both are long gone, alas, but this eight-room redbrick inn provides a classy refuge for visitors to the universities and museums. All mod cons: minibars, cable television, Jacuzzis, hair dryers, Frette linens.

Omni William Penn, 530 William Penn Place, (412) 281-7100. Henry Clay Frick built this beaux arts pile to house his business friends when they came to town. After countless face-lifts, the old girl is handsome enough, with enormous crystal chandeliers in the Palm Court. But the service can be disheartening, with desultory delivery of baggage and messages. Today's nabobs send their visitors to the veddy private Duquesne Club.

WHERE TO EAT

Bona Terra, 908 Main Street, Sharpsburg, (412) 781-8210. Douglass Dick searches out seasonal produce at local farmers' markets for his fledgling bistro near the Allegheny River northeast of town, and he adds seafood flown in daily from North Carolina. Intriguing combinations abound: osso buco with pureed chestnuts, shrimp and grilled peaches with lemon verbena beurre blanc. Sarah Billingsley of the *Pittsburgh Post-Gazette* terms the food "pleasurable and invigorating, like a long back rub." BYOB, at least for now.

Cafe Allegro, 51 South Twelfth Street, (412) 481-7788. The food is a bit uneven at this relaxed spot just off post-industrial Carson Street, next to the South Side Market House, built in 1915. One night, a veal chop was juicy and sweet seared scallops were nicely mated with a tangy tangerine reduction, but dry smoked trout and overcooked soft-shell crabs disappointed. A rich crème brûlée with orange peel made up for the shortcomings.

Casbah, 229 South Highland Avenue, Shadyside, (412) 661-5656. This sultry, sand-colored souk with faux-Fortuny lamps is the lead restaurant of an entrepreneurial duo who call themselves Big Burrito Inc. The menu ranges across the Mediterranean: pastas, aromatic tagines from Morocco, fearlessly fiery merguez sausage from Tunisia, a dense lamb ragout with couscous. The flavors are as emphatic as a smack in the chops.

La Cucina Flegrea, 2114 Murray Avenue, Squirrel Hill, (412) 521-2082. The tiny room is plain and windowless, but the minute you walk in, you know you're in the right place. It smells

Italian, not Italian American. Anna Fevola comes from a village north of Naples, and her cooking has that unadorned clarity of flavor we all long for. Order the grilled sausage, with charred edges, served beneath a blanket of bitter rapini. BYOB.

Tessaro's, 4601 Liberty Avenue, Bloomfield, (412) 682-6809. You're tired of beurre blanc and balsamic vinegar and waiters named Clyde. You need a joint with no attitude. In Pittsburgh, Tessaro's fills the bill perfectly: an old blue-collar bar and grill with Sam Adams on draft, decadently juicy half-pound burgers cooked over hardwood coals, and plenty of good cheer. No french fries, no dessert, no reservations, just sensational meat.

⫸ MONTREAL

In Paris, the familiar eight-sided red street signs say STOP, and the Académie Française, guardian of linguistic purity, utters not a peep of complaint. But in Montreal, where these matters are deemed crucial to cultural identity, the signs say ARRÊT. The proud old Queen Elizabeth Hotel, which dates from Canada's days as a dominion, is now Le Reine Elizabeth, never mind what the chatelaine of Buckingham Palace calls herself. In a fit of "linguistic cleansing," as the late Mordecai Richler termed it, the authorities judged the word "hamburger" impure and replaced it, officially at least, with hamburgeois. They even tried unsuccessfully to force a local stonecutter to take down his sign; it was bilingual, OK, but the Hebrew letters were larger than the French ones.

All of this opera bouffe has a serious side, of course. It is a manifestation of the deep-seated frustration and resentment that many Quebec Francophones feel toward Canada's top-heavy Anglophone majority, which once monopolized Montreal's economy. That there was widespread discrimination until fairly recently is beyond dispute; for many years English-speaking clerks in some smart shops shunned French-speaking customers.

Twice near the end of the twentieth century, hard feelings pushed Quebec close to separation from Canada, with potentially severe consequences for Montreal. The rancorous debate about sovereignty subsided and the separatist Parti Québécois lost power in 2003, but it retains a strong voice in Parliament. *Je me souviens*, provincial license plates say, "I remember," as if warning that past slights will one day be avenged.

Although some of Montreal's big corporations and many English-speaking residents fled in the 1980s, it has built a new economy. Drug, aerospace, and software companies are flourishing, lured by a multilingual workforce and an energetic, cosmopolitan way of life. The world's second largest French-speaking city, Montreal is delightfully "foreign," almost Parisian in ambience. Yet under its skin, says Morley Safer, the Canadian-born CBS correspondent, it is a lot like New York, which no one would say about Toronto.

In summer, when the sun shines bright for a few precious weeks, the people of Montreal spill into parks and sidewalk cafés and onto boats in the broad St. Lawrence River, which lies at their doorstep. A jazz festival, which celebrated its twenty-fifth anniversary in 2004, attracts 1.7 million enthusiasts a year, and there are festivals as well of bikes and jokes, film and hot-air balloons. Dragon boat races, fireworks competitions, a kite-flying derby, a Beer Mundial, and the Carifiesta help to pack the calendar from May to August.

In winter, when up to twelve feet of snow sometimes falls on the city, Montrealers move underground into a well-lighted maze of passages that connect a half dozen downtown malls, thirty movie theaters, and eight hotels. People shrug off storms, like one that knocked out power to 1.4 million households in 1998, and after a few days the good times roll on.

Brian Moore, the Ulster-born novelist who once worked in Montreal as a reporter, always remembered something that caught his eye on his first trip in from the airport. It summed up the city for him: a shop called the Notre-Dame-de-Grâce Kosher Meat Market. Drive or walk up Boulevard St.-Laurent, which climbs from the Old Port toward the distant Laurentian Mountains, and you will witness a parade of nationalities on the sidewalks, in the shops, and in the restaurants of this food-mad city. People call the boulevard "the Main," and in theory it separates the French east side of town from the English west side. But the barrier is porous, and the Main itself is polyglot. You will hear Chinese, Vietnamese, and Malay spoken at the bottom, and then, higher up, especially between Roy and Duluth Streets, Thai, Russian, Hungarian, Ukrainian, and Portuguese.

A couple of blocks over, and you're on Rue St.-Urbain, the main stem of Duddy Kravitz's not entirely fictional world. It's no longer quite as Richler described it in his 1959 novel *The Apprenticeship of Duddy Kravitz*, with a cigar store, grocery store, and fruit man on each corner. The Jews have moved on and up, and some, like the Bronfmans, who made their millions in whiskey, are now leading citizens of the wider world. New immigrants have taken their place and experienced what it is like, as Mr. Cohen told the rapscallion Duddy, to "land in this country with three words of English and 50 cents in your pocket."

Not many Americans know it and few U.S. schools teach it, but Montreal played a fascinating if minor role in the American Revolution. The rebellious colonists hoped to enlist Canadians in their fight against Britain, and in November 1775, seven months after the battles of Lexington and Concord, General Richard Montgomery captured Montreal without much of a struggle, forcing the British governor of Quebec, Major General Guy Carleton, to withdraw.

Presumably to vent their political passions, American troops defaced a bust of King George III that stood in the Place d'Armes. (A statue of Paul de Chomedey, Sieur de Maisonneuve, founder of Montreal, stands there today.) In April 1776, envoys sent by Congress, headed by Benjamin Franklin, took up temporary residence in Montreal. But even after he was reinforced by troops led by Benedict Arnold, Montgomery was unable to drive Carleton from Quebec City, and Franklin and company headed back south in 1777. The house where the Americans lived and worked in Montreal, known as Château Ramezay, has been preserved as a memorial. It is one of the hundreds of handsome gray sandstone buildings that make Vieux Montréal such an attractive eighteenth- and nineteenth-century neighborhood.

First stop: the brilliantly conceived museum at Pointe-à-Callière, where Montreal began four hundred years ago. Built over extensive excavations, which are open to visitors, it mounts changing shows on the city's history and boasts a bilingual multimedia show that is not only informative but also witty, à la Monty Python. Don't miss the viewpoint on the museum tower, where you can scan the skyline and the site of the Expo '67 World's Fair. A financial flop, the fair left behind Buckminster Fuller's biggest dome, built as the United States exhibit, now the Biosphere, an environmental display; the French pavilion, now the Montreal Casino; and Habitat, Moshe Safdie's futuristic modular apartment block, a sensation at the time and popular with its tenants ever since.

Stroll down Rue St.-Paul, a cobblestone street, to taste more of Old Montreal, both good and bad. Concentrate on the stout, honest architecture of the buildings and try to ignore the cheesy souvenir shops that fill most of them. Among the highlights are the spruced-up Marche Bonsecours, with a tin dome; Place Jacques-Cartier, filled with tubs of geraniums in summer; and the Hôtel de Ville, or City Hall, where the rabble-rousing Charles de Gaulle ended a 1967 speech with the words "*Vive le Québec libre!*" ("Long live free Quebec!").

The nearby Place d'Armes, which for centuries was the city's focal point, stands near the heart of the old financial district. Around it cluster the imposing neoclassical office of the Bank of Montreal; the Art Deco Aldred Building (1929), inspired by Rockefeller Center, then under construction; and the extraordinary Notre Dame Basilica, a Gothic Revival whoop-de-do in red, gold, white, and lots of sky blue that seats 3,800 worshippers. The pop diva Celine Dion, a Quebec girl, was married in a gala ceremony in the basilica, which looks like a set for a Cecil B. DeMille movie executed by A.W.N. Pugin, the designer who decorated London's Houses of Parliament in a vividly polychromatic "Gothic" style.

If the church has dubious aesthetics, it has excellent acoustics. My wife, Betsey, and I had the good fortune to hear a concert there by the Montreal Symphony Orchestra, conducted by the Swiss-born Charles Dutoit, its music director for twenty-five years, who resigned in a huff in 2002 after the musicians' union publicly accused him of abusive and autocratic behavior. Whatever his style, Maestro Dutoit made the orchestra the most admired in Canada, while also serving as music director of major ensembles in Paris and Tokyo. It has appeared in Europe, Asia, and Latin America, and it plays annually at Carnegie Hall.

Some in Montreal wonder whether Dutoit's successor, Kent Nagano, a Japanese American with heavy responsibilities elsewhere, will measure up when he takes over in 2006.

Another of the city's major institutions, the Montreal Canadiens—adored winners of no fewer than twenty-four Stanley Cups, far more than any other team in hockey—also encountered trouble in the new century, on and off the ice. Saddled with punishing taxes on their new arena, the Molson Center (nickname: the Keg), the Canadiens started missing the playoffs for the first time since the early 1920s. Finally, unthinkably, the Molson brewery shocked Canada by selling a controlling interest in the team—Jean Beliveau's team, Boom-Boom Geoffrion's team, Rocket Richard's team—to an American businessman, George Gillett.

Quebecois are different. They smoke more and divorce more than other Canadians. They are forbidden, unlike other Canadians, to turn right on red. But isolation enriches their cultural life, in a way. In most of Canada television programming comes principally from the United States, but in Quebec 70 percent is Canadian-produced. French Canadian theater and French Canadian literature prosper.

The leading English theater in Montreal, the Centaur, is housed in the creatively adapted old stock exchange. Gordon McCall, the artistic director, has mounted several Irish and American works, including *The Crucible* by Arthur Miller, but he is perhaps best known for assaulting the language barrier by presenting, in English translation, a play by Michel Tremblay, the best and best-known of French Canadian playwrights, whose work is usually shown at the outstanding French-language Rideau Vert Theater. McCall's production traveled across Canada, to Washington, D.C., and to Ireland.

Montreal's performing arts hub is the Place des Arts, a complex of five theaters and concert halls, begun at a time of growing French cultural awareness in the 1960s. It includes the Montreal Contemporary Arts Museum, which concentrates on Canadian and particularly Quebec artists, and the all-purpose 2,982-seat Salle Wilfrid Pelletier. This is home base for the symphony, the lively Montreal Opera, which collaborates with companies throughout the hemisphere, and Les Grands Ballets

Canadiens, founded in 1958 by Ludmilla Chiriaeff, who more or less single-handedly created a lively dance scene in Montreal. It has been led since 1999 by Gradimir Pankov, a noted Latvian-born dancer.

The Montreal troupe best known abroad is the Cirque du Soleil, which has grown from modest origins—a pooling of talents by street performers in 1984—into a global phenomenon, seen by more than 40 million people. Its boss, Guy Laliberté, once a fire-eater, is now a millionaire. A circus without animals, but not without genius, it has resident companies in Las Vegas and at Disney World in Florida, as well as units touring in North America, Europe, and Japan. Montreal's well-developed taste for the surreal and avant-garde lights up the Cirque's performances everywhere.

To get a good picture of what Montreal has been up to recently, stand on the little platform on Rue Cathcart, with your back to I. M. Pei's Place Ville-Marie, which helped establish the new, revitalized downtown when it opened in 1962. You will be looking up Avenue McGill College toward McGill, perhaps Canada's premier university. The avenue scrambles up the steep flank of the wooded hill for which Montreal is named, Mount Royal, which was landscaped by the American master Frederick Law Olmsted. Most of Canada's best postmodern architects have been employed by the builders of the shimmering skyscrapers on either side of the avenue. Peter Rose, of whom more in a moment, helped design the rose-and-pale-blue Montreal Trust building at No. 1500.

At the top of Avenue McGill College, just before the university gates, you will reach Rue Sherbrooke, Montreal's Fifth Avenue, which is lined with hotels, antiques shops, and fashion outlets, many of which sell Canada's fine furs. Here, in the so-called Golden Square Mile, lived the Britons, most of them Scots, who controlled three-quarters of Canada's wealth at the turn of the last century. Now the McCord Museum, a historical collection with fine Indian artifacts, and the Museum of Fine Arts are leading residents. The art museum's newest building houses both the comprehensive special exhibitions in which it specializes plus its international collections—portraits by Memling and Rembrandt, a pair of riveting grisailles by Mantegna, and a string of excellent modern pictures by Picasso, Feininger, and Léger, among others. A millennial merger with the Museum of Decorative Arts added a prestigious collection of twentieth-century decorative art.

Typical of the ambitious temporary shows was *Cosmos: From Romanticism to the Avant-Garde* (1999), which traced artists' conceptions of, and reactions to, far corners of our world and universe. One saw Goya looking at balloons, Moran at Yellowstone, Church at icebergs, van Gogh at the sun and stars, Calder at the solar system, along with Malevich, Kupka, Delauney, Kiefer, and Balla, all seeking to answer the unanswerable.

The visual delights of metropolitan Montreal, a port 994 miles from the Atlantic Ocean with 3.5 million people, run on and on. Paramount among them, I think, is the Canadian Center for Architecture a few blocks away, designed by Peter Rose and financed by Phyllis Lambert, a Bronfman heiress. It may well be the best of its kind anywhere. Its exhibitions (Carlo Scarpa, when I was last there), and exhibitions elsewhere to which it lends, are enriched by a collection of a quarter million books, prints, models, and photos. Fifteen minutes to the northeast, finally, is Montreal's fabulous Botanic Garden, exceeded in size only by the Kew Gardens in London. Extensive greenhouses, including a wonderful array of "economic plants"—did you know strychnine grew in Burma?—give way to annuals, perennials, and acres of trees, including Canada's birches, spruces, and, of course, maples.

When beauty pales, you can visit the notably ugly Olympic Stadium nearby, which has the additional virtue of a retractable roof that no longer retracts. No wonder the Expos, who played there, were the Flying Dutchmen of the baseball world, playing some home games in Puerto Rico before agreeing to move to Washington in 2005. But hey, your greenback is worth $1.30 in Montreal. Who cares about the stadium?

WHERE TO STAY

Bonaventure Hilton, 1 Place Bonaventure, (514) 878-2332. The hotel sits atop a soulless exhibition complex in the city center, but once you take the express elevator to the three top floors, that seems irrelevant. There, a lobby decorated with Japanese screens and bonsai awaits you, plus an outdoor pool you can enter from indoors in winter, and a two-acre garden with waterfall.

Loews Hôtel Vogue, 1425 Rue de la Montagne, (514) 285-5555. A stylish, low-key hotel, rather European in style, hides behind a pink facade across from Ogilvy, the carriage-trade department store, and down the street from the Museum of Fine Arts. The bathrooms boast whirlpool tubs, and L'Opéra, the snug lobby bar, welcomes one and all.

Hôtel Place D'Armes, 701 Côte de la Place d'Armes, (514) 842-1887. Installed in an 1870 office block of golden stone, with a cheery, wood-floored, high-ceilinged lobby, this forty-eight-room property is one of the best of Montreal's raft of appealing new boutique hotels. Many rooms offer views of the square, the basilica, and nearby Vieux Montreal.

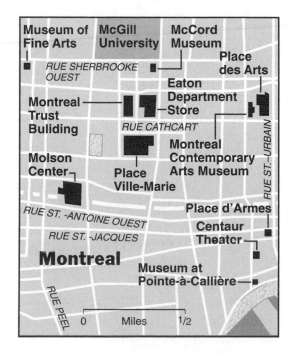

Ritz-Carlton, 1228 Rue Sherbrooke Ouest, (514) 842-4212. Montreal's grandest hotel, smack in the middle of the Square Mile, is an Edwardian dowager, built in 1912. Expensively updated, it still has a few frumpy rooms. Brass elevator doors in the lobby, tea served in china cups, Boudin oils, and proper keys, not plastic key cards, are welcome touches. Elizabeth Taylor was once married here, but lots of places can say that.

WHERE TO EAT

Area, 1429 Rue Amherst, (514) 890-6691. This trendy, thirty-eight-seat restaurant, draped in gauzy white curtains, lives up to its motto—"intelligent fusion." Dishes like foie gras with sherry-poached apricots and sweetbreads in a gingerbread crust succeed here because innovation is tempered with classical discipline and never permitted to run amok.

Au Pied De Cochon, 536 Rue Duluth, (514) 281-1114. When the continent's cooking professionals convened in Montreal a few years back, Martin Picard's new place was their haunt of choice. During the winter, pig is king, from crisp cracklings served in a paper cone to andouillettes and pigs' feet. Good use is made of an old wood-fired oven. When summer comes, the emphasis switches to fish from lakes, rivers, and ocean.

L'Express, 3927 Rue St.-Denis, (514) 845-5333. A sliver of a room where the buzz never stops. With marble tables, mirrored walls, and checkerboard tiles, it convincingly evokes 1930s Paris. The food is up to snuff, too: pot-au-feu with marrow bones, calf's liver with tarragon, onglet with good frites, and floating island worthy of grand-mère.

Schwartz's, 3895 Boulevard St.-Laurent, (514) 842-4813. Officially the Delicatessen Hébraïque de Montréal, Schwartz's is the size of a diner, and just as chic. Its raison d'être is smoked meat, a dry-cured Montreal beef similar to pastrami. Piled high onto mustard-smeared rye, it makes a delectable sandwich. The cholesterol-averse will wince.

Toque, 900 Jean-Paul-Riopelle, (514) 499-2084. Unlike the critics, who raved, the New York public failed to embrace Normand LaPrise's Manhattan venture, Cena, so it closed. In Montreal he rules the roost in dining rooms bathed in primary colors, where he serves inventive dishes based on adroit combinations of carefully chosen local products. The spice-glazed eel with green beans, the maple-lacquered quail, and the caramelized fig tart made me sigh with delight. The service is as good as the food: young, savvy, and jolly.

ⅢⅢ➤ TORONTO

Toronto the Good, people used to call it, with a sneer; it was so pious and proper that a man had trouble buying an aspirin on Sunday. It was a plain-vanilla town, "a nest of British-thinking, British-acting people," as a local writer said, who threw up their hands in horror at anything vaguely exotic. Now Toronto calls itself "the world within a city." With 4.7 million people, Greater Toronto is Canada's largest metropolitan area and one of North America's ten largest. Nearly half of its people were born someplace else, often a long way away—China and India and Africa and the Caribbean. In addition to English and French, the official languages, you hear a lot of Cantonese, Italian, Tamil, Portuguese, and Spanish on the city's streets.

One in five residents of Toronto proper—a total of 516,635 among a population of 2.5 million—came to Canada during the 1990s, arriving in hard times as well as good. Today Toronto is a city of immigrants without many slums, without much poverty, and without daily gridlock. It is lively but seldom frenetic, a metropolis with clean air and healthy downtown neighborhoods—in short, a city that works. Its citizens are proud of their way of life. So the SARS outbreak early in 2003, which cost the city an estimated $500 million in lost revenues from tourism, came as a stunning (if temporary) surprise.

Jane Jacobs, the Pennsylvania-born author of *The Death and Life of Great American Cities* (1961), who made "urban renewal" and "bulldozer" into dirty words, is Toronto's guardian angel and perhaps its most distinguished resident. Born in 1916, she has lived in Canada since 1968, fighting expressways and reveling in the city's bustle and diversity. You can sense her spirit wherever you go. Toronto finds room for old things that other cities throw away. When the soaring, three-block-long Eaton Center shopping mall was built, an updated version of Paxton's Crystal Palace, the plans were revised so as to save the small but historic Church of the Holy Trinity. The Hockey Hall of Fame, which celebrates Canada's national game with tributes to Bobby Orr and Gordie Howe and a replica of the Montreal Canadiens' dressing room, is tucked into a bank building dating from 1885; the Stanley Cup is displayed beneath the stained-glass dome of the old lobby.

Most recently, a Dickensian factory district comprising forty-four distilleries and other buildings, once the heart of the Hiram Walker empire, has been transformed into the Distillery Historic District. Peppy crowds mill through shops, galleries, cafés, and first-class eating houses like Patrick Riley's Perigee. Declining neighborhoods are recycled as well. Spadina Avenue (pronounced spa-DYE-na) used to be one of Toronto's Chinatowns. (There are at least three at the moment.) Now a thriving Vietnamese community calls it home. The bounteous Kensington Market, originally Jewish, has become a stew of eastern European, Portuguese, Indian, and Caribbean ingredients. Once dowdy Victorian houses in the Yorkville section, north of downtown, have been dolled up and turned into super-chic restaurants, boutiques, and art galleries. And when the century-old cast-iron streetlamps on Palmerston Boulevard were threatened with destruction, people in the neighborhood rose up in protest and finally saved them.

This is not to suggest for a moment that Toronto shuns the modern. City Hall is housed in a pair of curved towers designed by the great Finnish architect Viljo Revell in 1965. BCE Place incorporates several old buildings under a graceful glass-and-steel galleria designed by the Spanish trailblazer Santiago Calatrava. In an innovation that other cities have started to copy, the street signs downtown are illuminated from within at night. The Toronto Dominion Bank Tower is Ludwig Mies van der Rohe's tallest skyscraper, if by no means his best, and the CN Tower is the tallest freestanding structure in the world at 1,815 feet 5 inches. Buildings by Daniel Libeskind and Frank Gehry, a native son, are in the works.

A French trading post, Fort Rouillé, founded in 1750, stood

at the site of Toronto until the fall of New France. In 1788, the new British rulers bought the land occupied today by metropolitan Toronto, and five years later John Graves Simcoe established a military garrison that he called York, after the Duke of York, the soldier son of George III. It grew slowly. By the time American troops raided it twice during the War of 1812, it was popularly known as "Muddy York," because the swampy land on which it was built regularly turned roads into quagmires.

The town began to swell with immigrants at the end of the Napoleonic Wars, and in 1834 it was renamed Toronto, a Mohawk word meaning "meeting place." But power was concentrated in the hands of a few wealthy men of privilege with links to Britain, a group known as the Family Compact. Despite a short-lived rebellion in 1824, led by a radical Scot, William Lyon Mackensie, they dominated the city until the middle of the twentieth century, fastening upon it a moralistic Anglo-Saxon culture and an unshakable reputation as Dullsville.

During the Depression, puritanism deteriorated into intolerance. Anti-Semitic riots broke out, Chinese immigration was banned, and blacks suffered the sting of fierce racism. But all of that waned after World War II when a second great wave of newcomers inundated the city. Toronto became one of the fastest-growing cities in the world, and its economy expanded rapidly to provide jobs for almost all of them. Today it is Canada's financial dynamo.

Thanks to the St. Lawrence Seaway and to its naturally protected harbor on Lake Ontario, shielded by offshore islands, Toronto is a major port. It has an important stock exchange, powerful banks, and big insurance companies. The English-language services of the Canadian Broadcasting Company are based here, along with the country's two dominant national newspapers—the venerable *Globe and Mail* and the upstart *National Post*. Toronto sits at the center of the "Golden Horseshoe," where most Canadian manufacturing is based, along the lake from Oshawa to Hamilton. Greater Toronto is North America's second largest center of automaking, employing 90,000 people. Food and beverage industries, with 40,000 employees, electrical and electronic manufacturing, with 39,000, and printing and publishing, with 38,000, are other economic mainstays.

Impressed by the city's efficiency, the actor Peter Ustinov once called it "New York run by the Swiss." People in Toronto proudly repeat that aphorism, but it captures only one aspect of the city's multifaceted character. Toronto is equally notable for its cultural life. It is the third most active theater town in the English-speaking world, after New York and London. Audiences are so dependable that the impresario David Mirvish sank $26 million into building the Princess of Wales Theater, with Frank Stella murals, to house *Miss Saigon*. The Second City theater has nurtured Canadian-born comedic talents like Dan Aykroyd, Mike Myers, and John Candy. Martin Bragg guides CanStage, the Canadian Stage Company, the nation's largest contemporary theater ensemble, which produces English and American plays from Shakespeare to Tennessee Williams, Stephen Sondheim, *Ain't Misbehavin'*, and *Urinetown*. More significantly, it stages the work of well-known Canadian playwrights like Carol Shields (*Thirteen Hands*) and others less famous. Two of North America's premier theater festivals, focused on Shakespeare at Stratford and on Shaw at Niagara-on-the-Lake, are less than two hours away by car. One weekend a few years back, theater buffs had a choice between *Romeo and Juliet* or *Camelot* at Stratford and *Mrs. Warren's Profession* or *The Chocolate Soldier* (a musical take on *Arms and the Man*) at Niagara-on-the-Lake. *The Importance of Being Earnest* was at the Princess of Wales in town, and *The House of Martin Guerre* was at CanStage.

Filmmakers flock to Hollywood North, as they call Toronto, to make pictures like *Chicago*, *Queer as Folk*, *The Long Kiss Good Night*, and Ron Howard's *Cinderella Man* because labor is cheap and the city's streetscapes have successfully doubled for almost everywhere—Chicago, Vienna, Tokyo, Tehran. In 2002, $1.16 billion worth of motion pictures and television films were shot in the city, providing 28,000 jobs; stars like Michael Douglas and Renée Zellweger have come to know Toronto very well.

And every September, the city becomes more than the back lot of Los Angeles when it stages the party-hearty Toronto International Film Festival, a rival to Cannes.

Many of the city's arts institutions, like their counterparts in the United States, are building new facilities (in Toronto's case, partly with government money), while struggling to raise adequate funds for their operations. The Toronto Symphony Orchestra, which plays in the acoustically enhanced Roy Thomson Hall, designed by Canada's premier architect, Arthur Erickson, has teetered repeatedly on the brink of bankruptcy. The Canadian Opera Company is much stronger. Its staging of Puccini's *Turandot* a few years ago, conducted by the young Italian Marco Armiliato, bore little resemblance to the Metropolitan Opera's lavish Franco Zeffirelli spectacle, but worked equally well, using clever projections in lieu of backdrops and several wheeled scaffolds as props, with the Emperor, the Son of Heaven, perched atop the tallest one.

Now the company is finally to have its own house. Designed by Jack Diamond—born in South Africa, a protégé of Louis I. Kahn, with a worldwide practice based in Toronto—it will stand at one of the city's busiest intersections, Queen Street and University Avenue. With a four-story wall of glass out front and a traditional 2,000-seat horseshoe-shaped auditorium inside, it will house the celebrated National Ballet of Canada, a versatile ensemble headed by the noted choreographer James Kudelka, as well as opera. Named the Four Seasons Center for the Performing Arts in honor of its major benefactor, the Toronto-based hotel chain, the house will open in 2006 with Canada's first staging of Wagner's *Ring of the Nibelungen*, conducted by the company's general director, Richard Bradshaw, an Englishman. Each of the four operas in the cycle is assigned to a different director, and two Canadian singers with international reputations will sing major roles—Adrianne Pieczonka as Sieglinde and Frances Ginzer as Brünnhilde.

Pride of place among Toronto's main museums goes to the Royal Ontario, which in 1984 completed a thoroughgoing renovation of its handsome main structure, built in 1914. Now it is at work on a $200 million expansion masterminded by Daniel Libeskind which includes six new galleries enclosed by interlocking prismatic crystal forms. The decorative arts collections are excellent, as are the scientific displays, but the showstopper is the T. T. Tsui Galleries of Chinese Art. These include the only Ming tomb in the West, fine Qing monochromes, and superb collections of tomb retinues, replicas of people and animals buried with the dead. My own favorite is a tiny Tang figure of a female polo player, her head and that of her horse dramatically twisted with exertion.

Across the street is the Gardiner Museum of Ceramics, whose collections include pre-Columbian pottery, Renaissance pieces from Urbino, Deruta, and Gubbio, English pieces from several eras, and a wonderful array of Commedia dell'Arte figures from all over Europe. It, too, is expanding, by adding a commodious third floor. The Meissen collection is huge: a monkey band, made in 1749 to ridicule Dresden's court orchestra; seven pieces from the "swan service" that belonged to Heinrich von Brühl, who headed the factory; and a fierce white eagle, beak open, eye peeled, modeled by J. G. Kirchner.

The Art Gallery of Ontario is known for its Henry Moores, more than three hundred in all, capped by eighteen large, primal-looking plaster originals that stand in a top-lighted gallery like the bleached bones of a defunct race of giants. Downstairs are old masters and several fine modern works by Naum Gabo, Natalia Gontcharova, and the Italian futurist Gino Severini. With the help of Gehry, who grew up in its Grange Park neighborhood, the art gallery hopes to transform itself into something grander. He has designed a major renovation including a frontal promenade covered by a tilted, 60-foot-high glass window the length of two football fields. The project aims to make the museum less austere and to provide space for two thousand pieces from the eclectic collection of the publishing magnate Ken Thomson. But it has run into opposition from residents, contributors, and the media.

At the Bata Shoe Museum, you can jump into pop culture with both feet. There you can inspect Dutch wooden shoes; Indian moccasins; shoes for Chinese bound feet; Viviers; Ferragamos; a pair of pink pumps that belonged to Diana, Princess of Wales; Elton John's zebra-striped platform shoes; and Elizabeth Taylor's silver, stiletto-heeled sandals.

If you have an hour or two left over, drive out to the wonderful zoo, where three young Sumatran tigers and a perfectly terrifying Komodo dragon from Indonesia await you.

WHERE TO STAY

Four Seasons, 21 Avenue Road, (416) 964-0411, is the chain's
flagship, with nearly flawless service and a perfect location in
the heart of the chic Yorkville shopping district, just a few steps
from the Royal Ontario Museum. Truffles, one of two exceptionally good restaurants, serves classic French cuisine and great
wines in a grand dining room. Among the many grace notes are
fresh flowers in the guest rooms and afternoon tea in the lobby.

Le Germain, 30 Mercer Street, (416) 345-9500, Toronto's hot
boutique hotel of the moment, is a glass, metal and blond-wood
essay in postmodern design. Subdued colors and Frette sheets
help soften the hard edges, as do sprightly tulip and cloud images by James Lahey, a local photographer. The brothers Guy
and Michael Rubino oversee the rustic Italian fare served at the
hotel's trattoria, Luce (as in light, not as in Henry).

Sutton Place, 955 Bay Street, (416) 924-9221. This hotel is a
longtime favorite of film and stage stars, and also a hangout for
lobbyists working the Ontario legislature nearby. Built in 1967

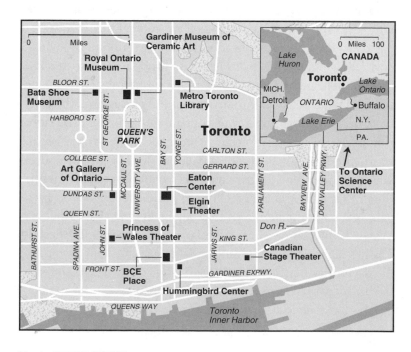

and renovated in 1998, 33 stories tall, it has 230 bedrooms and 64 suites. The public rooms are formal and Frenchified; the bedrooms run more to chintz.

Windsor Arms, 18 St. Thomas Street, (416) 971-9666. Built in the 1920s, renovated in the 1990s, this mannerly establishment has the sensibility the new Toronto cries out for. With only two rooms and twenty-six suites to look after, the staff delivers service of truly exceptional quality—willing, winsome, and personal. Bunyanesque beds with Frette sheets and bathrooms with whirlpools and heated floors may tempt you to hibernate.

WHERE TO EAT

Avalon, 270 Adelaide Street West, (416) 979-9918. Since 1995, Chris McDonald has been thrilling diners with forceful flavors. In an intimate, ivory-walled room, he pleases the aristocrat in you with limpid consommés of duck and beef with truffles, while also appealing to your earthy side with wild boar, luscious duck rillettes, and crispy-outside, creamy-inside calves' brains. Try the taleggio cheese from down the pike in Stratford, too.

Canoe, 66 Wellington Street West, (416) 364-0054, perched on the fifty-fourth floor of a Mies-designed skyscraper with sweeping views of the lake, features Canadian products: salmon smoked over maplewood, Prince Edward Island oysters, lobster bisque. Chef Anthony Walsh pairs tender Ontario pheasant with spaetzle and roasts Yukon caribou to perfection, conserving its juicy richness. Cocktail-hour drinks good, too.

Chiado, 864 College Street West, (416) 538-1910. Toronto has North America's largest Portuguese community, and this sunny spot serves the food it loves—fresh fish (bass, swordfish), flown in daily from the Algarve or the Azores and grilled with care, and of course salt cod, often roasted in olive oil. Garlic accents many dishes, including cataplana, a savory fish stew. Prime Portuguese wines, including more than sixty ports.

Jamie Kennedy Wine Bar, 9 Church Street, (416) 362-1957. Kennedy's star has been shining in Toronto for twenty years, first at one place, then at another. His new digs are constantly mobbed, not surprising given the rock-bottom prices and the quality of his trademark dishes, like unctuous, winy braised oxtails and crisp Yukon Gold fries. First-rate wines—lots of half bottles—no reservations, and inconsistent service.

Lai Wah Heen, in the Metropolitan Hotel, 108 Chestnut Street, (416) 977-9899, serves the best dim sum in Toronto, maybe the best in North America, including sweet, delicate pea-sprout dumplings, in a room full of wood and black marble. The inexhaustibly creative Terence Chan makes his own smoky-spicy XO sauce. No carts here; you mark your choices on a printed checklist. Drink white peony or jasmine tea.

North 44, 2537 Yonge Street, (416) 487-4897. Glamour is the name of the game at this ultramodern restaurant, named for the city's latitude—glamour in the decor, the clientele, and the food. Mark McEwan's loin of venison, pappardelle with sage-braised rabbit, and rum-glazed banana soufflé reflect tremendous technical expertise. Wines primarily from the New World, including the Niagara Frontier and the Okanagan Valley, Canada's best.

Susur, 601 King Street, (416) 603-2205. Ponytailed Susur Lee is Toronto's über-chef, a magician with foie gras—hot, cold, spiced, jellied, terrined—equally adept in Eastern and European cooking. He shops every morning, searching for rare ingredients like lily bulb to incorporate in seven-course tasting menus, with the most substantial dish (say, a rack of lamb with mango-mint-chili salsa) served first, not next to last. A smash at Lotus, his first Toronto restaurant, then at Singapore's Club Chinois, Lee wows 'em again here.

⯈ HAMPTON ROADS

Hampton Roads, the great natural harbor where the James River and several lesser streams meet Chesapeake Bay, has had a balcony seat for history. It was into these waters that Captain John Smith and his companions sailed in 1607 after their first landfall at Cape Henry, on their way to establish Jamestown. It was near here that the French admiral François de Grasse turned back a British relief fleet in 1781 and sealed the fate of Lord Cornwallis's troops at Yorktown. Here Commodore Perry set sail for his epic voyage to Japan in 1853, here the *Monitor* fought the *Merrimac*, heralding the age of the ironclad that revolutionized naval warfare, and here the American invasion force set out for North Africa in November 1942. American warships have been in Newport News for many generations, and the powerful Atlantic Fleet is headquartered in Norfolk.

But until recently, much of Tidewater, as the locals call the region around the Roads, was a backwater. The writer William Styron grew up in Tidewater, and in his early novel *Lie Down in Darkness* (1951) he wrote of "the low, sorrowful beauty of tideland streams winding through marshes full of small, darting, frightened noises and glistening and dead silent at noon, except for a whistle, far off, and a distant rumble on the rails." You still find such places, bypassed by twenty-first-century turbulence. One is the little county seat of Surry, across the river from Jamestown, where a Confederate memorial bears the bittersweet inscription "Our Heroes." Life there is lived legato.

Such isolated spots are no longer typical, however. Hampton Roads—for our purposes, the cities of Portsmouth, Norfolk, Virginia Beach, Hampton, and Newport News, plus the nearby towns of Jamestown, Yorktown, and Williamsburg—has long since overtaken Richmond, Virginia's state capital, as a metropolitan area. Its population now exceeds 1.6 million, a fifth of the state's total, and Virginia Beach, of all places, is the Old Dominion's largest city, with 425,000 people.

On a long weekend in the area, my wife, Betsey, and I were flabbergasted by the transformation. As a schoolgirl fifty years ago, she took the train to Buckroe Beach in Hampton on swimming trips, and as a draftee forty-five years ago I was based at sleepy Fort Monroe, nearby, writing speeches for General Bruce Clarke, one of the lions of the Battle of the Bulge, and sometimes for General Maxwell Taylor, a D-Day hero. What happened? I asked my brother-in-law St. George Pinckney, a Richmond man to his core.

"The foreigners and other come-heres did it," he said evenly. "In the last twenty-five years, Europeans at the NATO headquarters in Norfolk, people at the military bases, civilians from all over the country whose companies moved them into the area—they all helped to break through the crust of insularity. In Richmond, we never had that."

Benign weather also helped to attract people to the region. Norfolk may not quite be the Sun Belt, but snow is only slightly more common in Hampton Roads than Russian submarines.

The U.S. armed forces remain the economic prime mover, despite a lot of recent diversification. People here work in a Ford assembly plant and a Budweiser brewery, for the mail-order queen Lillian Vernon and Pat Robertson's Christian Broadcasting Network. But one in every four workers in Hampton Roads—like Los Angeles County, it is politically subdivided but economically united—takes home a paycheck from Uncle Sam, and total defense spending here in 1997 totaled $6.92 billion. In terms of active-duty personnel, seven of the nation's sixty largest military installations are to be found in Hampton Roads.

The Army has Fort Eustis, its transport center, and Fort Monroe, the only moated installation in active use, where Jefferson Davis was imprisoned after the Civil War. The Air Force has Langley Air Force Base, the oldest active air base in the country. Near that is America's first civilian aeronautics laboratory, Langley Research Center, established in 1917, now a part of NASA, where pioneering astronauts learned the Right Stuff for the Mercury and Apollo space shots.

Norfolk is the Navy town par excellence. Along its western flank rise the fearsome gray superstructures of aircraft carriers, cruisers, and other vessels—fighting machines catching their breath between missions. Naval Station Norfolk is the largest in the world, home to a hundred major ships and thirty-six aircraft squadrons. More than 85,000 people in uniform and nearly 28,000 civilians toil for the Navy in Norfolk itself, in Virginia Beach and elsewhere in Hampton Roads.

But Norfolk is no longer the brawling liberty town of World War II and the early postwar years. Main Street, a young man we met there told us, "used to be nothing but bars, cathouses, tattoo parlors, and more bars." Now it is lined with gleaming modern buildings, including hotels, a world trade center, and bank towers, as well as Nauticus, a Disneyesque maritime museum. Most surprisingly, perhaps, Norfolk's metamorphosis has included its emergence as a cultural center of note, with the Chrysler Museum of Art and Virginia Opera in the vanguard. Both rank among the outstanding institutions of their size in the South and, for that matter, the nation.

It was Walter P. Chrysler Jr., son of the founder of the Chrysler Corporation, who enabled Norfolk to join the late-twentieth-century revolution in which museums have helped to power the revival of struggling cities. Married to a Norfolk native, he lifted a provincial collection into the elite ranks in 1971 with the gift of thirty thousand objects that "any museum in the world would kill for," as John Russell wrote in *The New York Times*. In 1989, the museum was deftly enlarged, modernized, and reorganized by the Washington architects George Hartman and Warren Cox. One set of galleries houses a resplendent collection of Art Nouveau furniture by Majorelle and Colonna, accompanied by Tiffany and Gallé accessories; another contains a feast of glass, unmatched on this continent except in the glass-making towns of Toledo, Ohio, and Corning, New York. Case after case is filled with Favrile vases and Tiffany lamps, dozens of major pieces of Lalique, Steuben, and Wiener Werkstätte glass, Sandwich glass, Amberina and Murano glass. Elsewhere, an elaborate parcel-gilt silver cup in the shape of a pineapple, made in London in 1610, testifies to the sophistication of the civilization the Jamestown settlers abandoned for a rude life in the Virginia wilderness.

In the picture galleries, my eye was caught by a precise profile portrait of a man in a red turban attributed to Domenico Veneziano, Piero della Francesca's teacher, whose surviving works are exceedingly rare; Georges de La Tour's pensive St. Philip; a brassy, recumbent blonde, *Mlle. Monna Lils*, by the Dutch modernist Kees van Dongen; and a mural by Thomas Hart Benton, painted for the original Whitney Museum of American Art in New York, which exemplifies the breakneck pace of modern life.

The Virginia Opera has had but one general director in its thirty-year existence, the Brooklyn-born conductor Peter Mark, who was trained as a violist. He has put it on the musical map in three areas, actually—the Virginia suburbs of Washington, Richmond, and the company's principal residence at the Harrison Theater in Norfolk, a smart postmodern conversion (by the Boston architect Graham Gund) of a seedy former USO theater and wrestling arena, completed for less than $10 million in 1993. Mr. Mark has given important early breaks to singers as important as Renée Fleming, and two dozen of his alumni are on the roster of the Metropolitan Opera. The company has done *Don Pasquale* as a spaghetti western, no less, and it has presented acclaimed premieres of several works by Mr. Mark's wife, the Scottish American composer Thea Musgrave, most recently her eighth opera, *Simón Bolívar*, in January 1995. "Coming here was like picking up a live wire," he said. "In New York and L.A., people take things for granted. Here, people who want a better life for their children know they have to roll up their sleeves and create it."

The eighty-year-old Virginia Symphony Orchestra, which plays for the opera's performances, has begun to burnish its reputation under its young conductor, JoAnn Falletta, a winner of the Toscanini, Stokowski, and Bruno Walter awards. In recent years it has pleased big-city critics with performances at Carnegie Hall and at the Kennedy Center in Washington, and it records, especially music by American composers.

Norfolk is a very old city, and quite a few handprints of history have survived the free-swinging wrecker's ball. Among the most notable are three grouped close together downtown: St. Paul's Episcopal Church (1739), shaded by towering magnolias, which has a Revolutionary cannonball lodged in its south wall; the Federal-style Moses Myers House, built in 1793 by the city's first Jewish family, who brought with them from New York portraits by Gilbert Stuart and Thomas Sully, which still hang in the house; and the gray-and-white Old Norfolk Academy (1840), designed in a rigorous Greek Revival style by Thomas U. Walter, who added the House and Senate wings and the cast-iron dome to the United States Capitol.

Another of Walter's local buildings, the domed Old City Hall, was turned into a Napoleonic mausoleum for General Douglas MacArthur, a tomb almost as grandiose as his ego. No fan of his, I gave it a pass and instead visited the Scope Arena (1972), a soaring, saucerlike dome of interlocking concrete triangles, supported by massive buttresses outside. The work of the Italian Pier Luigi Nervi, this is engineering as art.

You have to climb into a car to see the three seventeenth-century brick buildings that lie beyond the city's perimeter. So far as I know, they are the only survivors of their kind in the United States: the simple story-and-a-half Adam Thoroughgood House in Virginia Beach (circa 1680), named for a man who came to Virginia as an indentured servant and made a fortune in tobacco; Bacon's Castle (1665), near Surry, a two-story Jacobean manor house with a pair of triple chimneys and curvilinear gables; and the cherry-pink St. Luke's Church (1632), near Smithfield, a Gothic-style gem with the stone buttresses, pediment, crockets and finials of the old-country models faithfully copied in brick.

If you come to Hampton Roads in springtime, you will encounter an intoxicating array of flowering shrubs and trees along most streets—Bradford pears, wisteria, camellias, magnolias, and azaleas. The gaudiest show is at the Norfolk Botanical Gardens, created by the Works Progress Administration in 1938.

A ten-minute trip north via the Hampton Roads Bridge-Tunnel takes you to Hampton, the oldest continuous English-speaking community in America. Fort Monroe, "the Gibraltar of the Chesapeake," stands on an adjacent point overlooking the Roads; it was once the largest fortress in America, and has been continuously garrisoned since 1823. Burned twice, in the War of 1812 and the Civil War, the old town itself has little to show for its long history, with the exceptions of Hampton University, founded in 1868 as Hampton Institute to educate freed slaves, and St. John's Church, the oldest Anglican parish in the Western Hemisphere, dating from 1610. The present church dates "only" from 1728, but its silver communion plate, made in England in 1618, is still in use weekly.

Newport News, west of Hampton, is more of a nineteenth-century phenomenon. Collis P. Huntington, the railroad baron, chose it in 1867 as the eastern terminus of his new Chesapeake & Ohio Railroad, with which he linked his rail lines in the West to the Atlantic. He also established the gigantic Newport News Shipbuilding and Drydock Company, still the nation's biggest.

It was Collis's son Archer who contributed to the city the institution you're most likely to visit there, the Mariners' Museum. It has superb collections of ship models, from six inches to six feet long; ship's figureheads, including a 3,200-pound eagle from the USS *Lancaster*, built in 1881; and artifacts from the *Titanic*.

Farther up the Peninsula of Virginia, as the tongue of land between the James and York Rivers is known, two towns witnessed the beginning and end of Britain's colonial experience in America. Yorktown is not nearly so interesting a battlefield as Gettysburg or Antietam, and the re-created Jamestown Settlement has something of the theme park about it. But the site of the original village includes the broken tower of the settlers' fourth church, finished in 1647, which stands today amid lacy dogwoods—"God's perfect trees," as Betsey calls them.

We spent much of our time gazing at the surrounding swamp where the settlers struggled to survive, now inhabited most visibly by herons. In the museum nearby, we found the simple list of the 104 settlers who stayed in 1607 and the 50 among them who died within six months unexpectedly moving. It was fascinating, too, to put some flesh on the cardboard figure of John Smith, the colony's gutsy, imperious leader. Long before he reached the American wilderness, it turns out, he had fought in

Hungary, been taken in captivity to Turkey, been sold into slavery in Russia, killed his master, escaped, and made his way home to Britain. I guess he must have sailed for Virginia to inject a little excitement into a humdrum life.

I have saved for last the area's tourist magnet, Colonial Williamsburg, the reconstituted capital of Colonial Virginia, the city familiar to Patrick Henry and George Washington, which was called back into existence by the vision of W.A.R. Godwin, a local Episcopalian rector in the 1920s, and the untold millions of John D. Rockefeller Jr. There is no more need to describe it than to describe the Statue of Liberty. Although total attendance is down in recent years, I have never tired of the restored Governor's Palace, with its formal gardens, or the George Wythe House, which belonged to Jefferson's law teacher, or the elegant Christopher Wren Building at the College of William and Mary, the oldest academic building in continuous use in the country. When Betsey and I went to a midday prayer service at Bruton Parish Church, we sat in a box pew that belonged to St. George Tucker, whose descendant, another St. George Tucker, christened her. Fond of continuity, these Virginians.

Of course, it's the ensemble that counts in Williamsburg—shops, taverns, craftspeople—plus a pair of amazing museums. One houses Abby Aldrich Rockefeller's innovative collection of American folk art; the other, designed by Kevin Roche and named for DeWitt Wallace, a cofounder of *Reader's Digest*, houses a world-class decorative arts collection.

WHERE TO STAY

Colonial Houses, 302 East Francis Street, Williamsburg, (757) 565-8440. This is Williamsburg's best-kept secret. It's hard to imagine a more charming place to spend a night or weekend than in one of the eighteenth-century houses or taverns in the colonial capital, with authentically creaking floors, time-worn antiques, working fireplaces, and modern plumbing. Ours, once occupied by Cary Grant, came with a quartet of well-mannered sheep grazing across the lane.

Marriott Waterside, 235 East Main Street, Norfolk, (757) 627-4200. An unusually well-managed chain hotel, Norfolk's best, with fascinating views over the ship-filled harbor from rooms on the upper stories. Right in the middle of the downtown area, near the Waterside Marketplace, close to freeways. The 405 rooms are bright and immaculate, if hardly luxurious.

Page House Inn, 323 Fairfax Avenue, Norfolk, (757) 625-5033. Four rooms, two suites, in a superbly refurbished Georgian Revival brick mansion, built in 1898, with the leafy streets of the Ghent district on the doorstep. This urban, urbane bed-and-breakfast is so close to the Chrysler Museum of Art that you could come back in mid-visit to rest your feet for an hour.

Williamsburg Inn, 136 East Francis Street, Williamsburg, (757) 229-1000. The region's premier hotel, owned by Colonial Williamsburg, is sedate and costly. Bedrooms and bathrooms were enlarged in a meticulous restoration completed in 2002. The decor is agreeably old-fashioned, with quilted sateen bedspreads, swag curtains, and flowered wallpaper, but the electronic

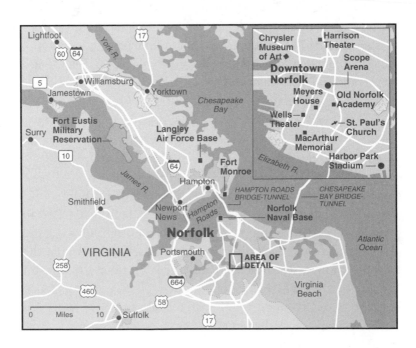

gear and air-conditioning are up-to-the-minute and the sheets and towels are lush. Old South breakfasts.

WHERE TO EAT

Blue Talon Bistro, Prince George Street, Williamsburg, (757) 476-2583. Among his peers, David Everett has long been considered one of the South's standout chefs. Now, from a formal dining room overlooking a suburban golf course, he has moved into town with a casual menu featuring French comfort food like pot-au-feu and coq au vin alongside American standbys like mac and cheese and potpies. Virginia ham and crabmeat also make appearances.

Lucky Star, 1608 Pleasure House Road, Virginia Beach, (757) 363-8410. A congenial spot, this, filled with 1940s flea-market finds. Butch Butt, once a fisherman, knows where to find the best seasonal raw materials—"If the fish was any fresher you'd have to spank it," one local says. His partner, Amy Brandt, cooks it simply and skillfully. Highlights: prime soft-shell crabs, from the Atlantic, not the Bay; cherrystone clams from their place of origin, Cherrystone Creek on the Eastern Shore; and wild rockfish.

Pierce's Pitt Bar-B-Que, 447 East Rochambeau Drive, Lightfoot, (757) 565-2955. You won't miss it on the highway near Williamsburg, not with its orange-and-red Day-Glo paint job. Pierce's is expanding again, but the pitmaster sticks to tradition: succulent ribs and pork shoulder, slow-cooked over oak and hickory logs. Pitt? A sign painter's mistake that stuck.

Surrey House, Route 31, Surry, (757) 294-3389. A 1950s roadhouse near the James River ferry serving authentic, unadorned regional food: peanut soup, proper crab cakes, country ham cured down the road by S. Wallace Edwards & Sons, and lemon chess pie with a featherweight crust. Wanda, the waitress, has the sweetest smile and softest voice this side of heaven.

Todd Jurich's Bistro, 150 West Main Street, Suite 100, Norfolk, (757) 622-3210. Norfolk's standout restaurant was recently installed in handsome new quarters. Jurich is a wizard with Eastern Shore shellfish; try his juicy, mouthwateringly plump fried oysters, the giant prawn curry, or the potato-crusted crab cakes with creole mayo. The wine list is exemplary and the prices are reasonable.

⯈ CHARLESTON

You can't say this about very many cities, but you can certainly say it about Charleston: one man has changed its destiny. His name is Joseph P. Riley Jr. As Charleston's mayor since 1975, he has halted the city's long decline, which lasted for a hundred years after the Civil War, turning it from a proud but rotting relic into a model modern city. And after twenty-eight years on the job, in an era of pervasive skepticism about politicians, he won an eighth term in 2003, without a runoff. Even the cabbies believe in him. One old-timer told me, "I'd bet my life that he's never stolen a dollar or cheated a soul."

Mayor Riley had help, of course: from a business community galvanized into action when the ninety-five-year-old Charleston Naval Base was closed in 1996; from a devoted band of preservationist volunteers determined to restore the beauties of antebellum Charleston; from an unconventional police chief, Reuben Greenberg, a black Jew with two degrees from Berkeley whose Deep South brand of tough love slashed the crime rate and forged better race relations; and from Gian Carlo Menotti, who rejuvenated the city's cultural life when he established an American version of his Spoleto arts festival here.

The mayor has also been helped by history. Tourists, more than 4 million a year, flock to Charleston to trace its footprints in the jasmine-scented streets and aristocratic houses, many owned by outsiders who too seldom use them. They admire the porches (called piazzas) positioned to catch ocean breezes, the Mediterranean interplay of light and shade, and the gardens full of boxwood, old roses, and brick paths. The one made by

Emily Whaley, a blossom-filled plot at 58 Church Street, measures only thirty by a hundred feet. "Early to bed," she advised, "early to rise, work like hell and fertilize."

There is so much left from yesterday and the day before: the box pews at St. Michael's Episcopal Church, finished in 1761, where George Washington and Robert E. Lee both came to pray, and its noble white steeple, a near-replica of the one at St. Martin's-in-the-Fields in London (it may have been designed by the same architect, James Gibbs). The rice planters' Italianate and Greek Revival mansions along the Battery, looking out toward the point where, as the natives like to say, the Ashley River meets the Cooper to form the Atlantic Ocean. The ruined Fort Sumter, across the bay toward which Confederate gunners under the grandiloquently named General Pierre Gustave Toutant Beauregard directed the first shots of the Civil War on April 12, 1861. The restored midget submarine *Hunley*.

Some of the visitors buy baskets, made from dried sweetgrass, sold by elderly African American women with soft Sea Island accents at the corner of Broad and Meeting Streets. Others buy antiques. Everyone tucks into the Dixie cooking, unashamedly rich and sweet, of chefs like Louis Osteen, formerly downtown, now up the coast at Pawley's Island. His down-home fried peach pie with butter pecan ice cream can make you forget Escoffier's pêches Melba.

There is plenty of revenue in the city's romantic old buildings, which Charleston was once "too poor to paint, too proud to whitewash," and in its oh-so-courtly Southern ways, which year after year win Charleston the number-one position on the list of Most Mannerly Cities in America compiled by Marjabelle Young Stewart, a leading etiquette expert.

This is a small, peninsular city, with only 96,000 people, though the metropolitan area has several times that. Wise travelers come in spring and fall, for Spoleto and the house and garden tours, avoiding the suffocating days of summer. But Charleston seldom seems crowded or hurried in any season. Life ambles along with all the urgency of a drawl. It was ever thus. Toward the end of *Gone With the Wind*, Rhett Butler tells Scarlet, "I'm going back to dignity and grace. I'm going back to Charleston, where I belong." The scale is human. The streets are clean, free of graffiti and litter; motorists, except for the occasional surly outsider, rarely honk their horns. You can stroll down Ropemaker's Lane or Price's Alley, leaving the twenty-first century far behind, yet this is a living community, not a museum like Williamsburg.

I suppose that at this point I should declare an interest, as the British like to say. My wife's maiden name was Betsey Pinckney, and she comes from the storied clan that more or less invented Charleston. Two of her forebears signed the Constitution; one of them, Charles Pinckney, later served as minister to Spain; the other, Charles Cotesworth Pinckney, a second cousin, was named envoy to France and ran unsuccessfully as the Federalist nominee for president (twice) and for vice president. Charles Cotesworth's brother, Thomas, served as minister to England. All three of them fought in the Revolutionary War.

They say that Charlestonians are like the Chinese, in that they eat rice and worship their ancestors, and I admit that the Pinckney-tude of Charleston used to get my goat: Pinckney Street, Pinckney Island, and Castle Pinckney, and graveyards full of Pinckneys. Betsey once rode in a carriage pulled by a horse named Charles Cotesworth Pinckney. But Eliza Lucas Pinckney won me over. Born in Antigua, the daughter of a colonial governor, she married Charles Pinckney (Carolina's first native-born lawyer, not to be confused with the signer) in 1744. She bore three children (including Charles Cotesworth and Thomas), compiled one of the first colonial recipe books, and took over the management of several large plantations, where she taught slaves to read and write. Most important, she introduced the cultivation of indigo to the state—a crop so valuable to the British textile industry for dyes that it made South Carolina a favored child of the mother country.

Like many settlers, the Pinckneys came from England via the Caribbean. Others came directly from Britain and France. These last were mostly Huguenots, French Calvinists, and their tradition lives on in names like Manigault and Huger (pronounced you-GEE). The planters who lived along the sluggish low-country rivers maintained ties to Britain for generations. In 1715, Palladio's treatise on classical architectural styles was first published in England, and thirty years later John Drayton built a porticoed plantation house on the Ashley River whose Tuscan and Ionic columns come directly from Palladio's pages. Drayton Hall still stands; alone among the great houses in its neighborhood, it was spared by General Sherman's soldiers because, it is said, the owner had his slaves tell the federal troops that the house was being used as a smallpox hospital. Never converted to central heating or electric lights and painted only twice, the interior of the house retains its elaborate original architectural details and elegant plaster moldings and ceilings.

But it is Middleton Place, marvelous Middleton, that always lures us out of the city and up the Ashley on fine days. Its manor house is a ruin; only one small flanking building survives, and it has been much altered. Never mind. It is filled with family portraits by Benjamin West, valuable silver, eighteenth-century beds with posts carved to resemble rice stalks, and other furniture from the workshop of Thomas Elfe, Charleston's most noted cabinetmaker. Bookshelves and tables hold rare first editions by Catesby and Audubon, who came here to draw the ospreys and egrets that still nest in local marshes. (While in South Carolina, Audubon formed a friendship with Joel Poinsett, an erudite Charleston-born diplomat, who brought the Christmas plant named for him to this country from Mexico.)

Henry Middleton began to plot his classical gardens in 1741. Now grown to mellow maturity, they are anchored by a pair of lakes shaped like a butterfly's open wings, which lie below a series of scalloped terraces. On another part of the plantation a flock of sheep grazes quietly. A pathway leads beneath arching camellia bushes that carpet it in pink in early March. And everywhere there are stupendous trees—gums, magnolias, crape myrtles and a mighty oak, a marker on an Indian trail long before Columbus reached America. The oak has reached a circumference of 30 feet and a spread of 145. It took a hundred slaves ten years to lay out the parterres, the terraces, the canals, and the rest of the rigorously geometric design. To my mind they created the greatest garden that we have inherited from colonial America.

Slavery and its legacy, white supremacy, hung over Charleston like a pall for generations. When the French author Simone de Beauvoir came to Charleston in 1947, she was bewitched by the place, especially the Spanish moss, exulting in her journal that "it is the color of smoke, the color of amber and twilight," but not by the plantations. "Creating those private Edens, which are as extravagant as the Alhambra," she commented, "required the vast wealth of planters and the hell of slavery. The delicate petals of the azaleas and camellias are stained with blood."

Between 1700 and 1775, the peak years of the slave trade, 40 percent of the Africans brought to America in chains passed through Charleston. Ever since, blacks have formed a big part of the city's population. DuBose Heyward's 1925 novel *Porgy*, transformed by George Gershwin into the folk opera *Porgy and Bess* in 1935, portrayed the lives of some of the poorest of them, who lived on Church Street in the dependencies of houses on Cabbage Row, or Catfish Row, as Heyward renamed it. The city's blacks gave another gift to Broadway, the kinetic dock workers' dance that was transformed into the Charleston for *Runnin' Wild*, a 1923 hit.

Happily, Charleston has moved well beyond its darkest days, and in casting off the shroud of white supremacy it has gradually begun to remember and to acknowledge the black role in its history. It took time; not until July 1, 2000, and not until after a boycott led by the NAACP, did the state haul down the Confederate flag from the dome of the capitol in Columbia.

The College of Charleston's Avery Research Center delves into the African American past, maintaining collections of manuscripts and papers, including records of the 54th Massachusetts Regiment, the black unit that mounted the heroic assault on Fort Wagner depicted in the film *Glory*. That Civil War battle, in which the 54th's commander, Robert Gould Shaw, lost his life, is fully described at the wonderful Charleston Museum.

But the process is just beginning. Important moments of black history remain submerged. The plaque at the Emanuel African Methodist Episcopal Church on Calhoun Street says simply, "Founded 1818, closed 1822, reopened 1865." What heartbreak lurks behind that simple word "closed"! The church was closed because it had been burned down by a white mob in revenge for the actions of Denmark Vesey, a parishioner who tried to foment an early slave uprising.

Mayor Riley told me that economic opportunity had provided the key to a dramatic improvement in race relations. "You make the table bigger," he said when we met in his office, which was piled high with files, newspapers, and official documents. "You don't tell some people that they have to leave. We've made progress in housing, in police work, in guaranteeing the full participation of all our citizens in the affairs of the city council. But you can never relax. In a diverse society like this, there are always a lot of opportunities for misunderstanding, so you have to be sure that new bridges are built and old ones are maintained."

Riley has pioneered "scatter-site" public housing in an effort to combat the ghetto mentality. He passed ordinances banning T-shirt shops, neon, and tour buses in the historic district and hotels on the waterfront, lest the very element that brings visitors to Charleston, its charm, be submerged in tourist tattiness. He has built things that appeal to locals and visitors, rich and poor, like a Waterfront Park and a minor-league ballpark.

What sets Riley apart from run-of-the-mill mayors is a passion for his work. He is—dare I use the word in this cynical era?—a true visionary, and it is his vision of a city reborn that has carried him and Charleston through nightmares like Hurricane Hugo in 1989, which damaged 90 percent of the city's roofs and made a shambles of businesses.

The closing of the naval base in 1996, Mr. Riley said soon after it happened, "was like death, because no one had ever imagined life in Charleston without the Navy." The city's longtime congressman L. Mendel Rivers had poured Pentagon dollars into the city for decades; his slogan was, "Rivers Delivers." Yet the city not only survived the blow but surged ahead. The Charleston Regional Development Alliance has more than replaced the 22,500 lost Navy jobs, attracting capital investments of more than $2.8 billion to the area. The goal is "not more jobs but better jobs," in knowledge-based sectors like information technology and medical research, said David T. Ginn, the alliance president. About 140 new companies have arrived in the last seven years, a third of them foreign, lured by the climate, the mostly nonunion labor force, and the booming port. Charleston, quaint little Charleston, is now the largest container port in the South and second only to New York on the East Coast. Plans are afoot to make it much bigger by building a new terminal on part of the old naval base, but conservationists, who blocked an earlier plan to build on Daniel Island, may succeed in blocking the new project, too.

Meanwhile the restoration of Old Charleston continues apace. One recent beneficiary is the Fireproof Building, designed in 1826 by Robert Mills as a records office. A draftsman for Jefferson at Monticello, Mills became South Carolina's greatest architect, building courthouses and churches, including the First Baptist on Church Street in Charleston, in a severe Classical Revival style. (The Treasury and the Washington Monument in Washington are his designs, too.) A favorite of mine in the same style, though not by Mills, is the Hibernian Hall on Meeting Street, a chaste white structure with a gilded harp above the door, across from the Fireproof Building. It was designed by Thomas U. Walter, who also went on to greater architectural glory in Washington, designing the dome of the Capitol. Since the years after the Civil War the hall has been the site, on the third Thursday in January, of the annual St. Cecilia Ball, Charleston's oldest, most exclusive social function. "Exclusive" in Charleston means just that. The right to attend is inherited. A favorite local put-down, Betsey's cousin Jane Hanahan told us, is to say of someone, "He doesn't go to the ball." To which Betsey's irreverent brother Tom replied merrily, "It's all that's left, with the House of Lords gone."

Portraits of the ancestors of today's ballgoers can be seen at the Gibbes Museum of Art, whose collection includes important works by the likes of Samuel F. B. Morse, Gilbert Stuart, and Thomas Sully. The gem of the collection is an unforgettable image of John C. Calhoun, South Carolina's combative champion of states' rights, by Rembrandt Peale.

But the real monuments to the men and women who built Charleston are their houses, no fewer than 3,500 of them built before 1860. Two that should not be missed are the Nathaniel Russell House, with an oval staircase that vaults upward with no visible means of support, and the Heyward-Washington House, whose pine floors and cypress paneling date from 1772. Its unmatched collection of Charleston furniture includes a chest-on-chest-on-chest, one of only three in existence. Try to peek at the Sword Gates at 32 Legare Street, too, and at the elegant Miles Brewton House, with a two-story portico.

When you have had your fill of houses, there are plays at the Dock Street Theater, where the Charleston Stage Company presents 120 performances a year, and at the Footlight Players' intimate 240-seat house. Though it has had financial difficulties lately, the Charleston Symphony, for which Mayor Riley dreams of building a proper hall one day, has attracted soloists of the caliber of Itzhak Perlman and Sherrill Milnes in the past.

It is only at festival time, however, that the city comes fully alive culturally. The Spoleto Festival, accompanied by its "fringe," known as Piccolo Spoleto, fills halls and churches for seventeen days in late May and early June each year with theatrical, operatic, orchestral, and dance performances. Among the highlights in 2004 were performances of the spectacular eighteen-hour Chinese opera *The Peony Pavilion* and appearances by Mikhail Baryshnikov. In late September comes the Mojo Arts Festival, an exuberant celebration of African American and Caribbean art, with a rich array of jazz, gospel, theater, and storytelling.

WHERE TO STAY

Charleston Place, 205 Meeting Street, (843) 724-8410. With a prime location, two top-flight restaurants, and an indoor-outdoor rooftop pool, this 450-room sister ship of Venice's Cipriani easily tops the roster of Charleston hotels. The bustling lobby, dominated by a huge white Murano chandelier, is the city's crossroads. But too many little things misfire: front-desk phones sometimes go unanswered after twenty-five rings, for example.

Planters Inn, 112 North Market Street, (843) 722-2345. Nothing but nothing is more characteristic of Charleston than the piazza or veranda overlooking a brick-paved, palmetto-shaded courtyard. The Planters Inn has both, plus high-ceilinged rooms, many of them with four-poster beds, and a warmly welcoming attitude at the reception desk.

Wentworth Mansion, 149 Wentworth Street, (843) 853-1886, was built by a cotton merchant in the Gilded Age and looks it. Crystal chandeliers, tile and marble floors, carved paneling, and

Tiffany-style windows give the place an air of tasteful opulence. Each of the twenty-one rooms has a CD player, a big-screen television, a fireplace, and lots of antiques; the suites are seignorial. Sweeping views from the rooftop cupola.

WHERE TO EAT

Cypress, 167 East Bay Street, (843) 727-0111. When you walk in, you can see chef Craig Diehl at work in his show kitchen and five thousand bottles of wine waiting along the glass-faced north wall. The Asian-influenced food fulfills expectations thus aroused, particularly shrimp crusted with benne (sesame) seeds, fried in tempura batter and spiked with chili oil, and tea-smoked duck with cilantro-lime grits, a cross-cultural triumph.

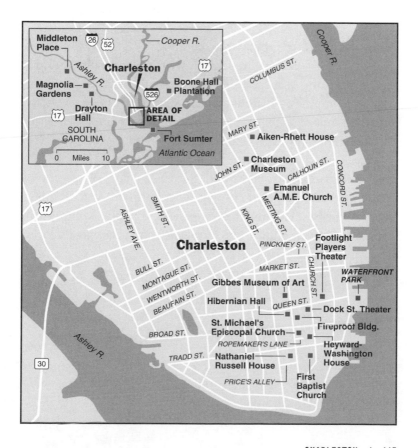

Hominy Grill, 207 Rutledge Avenue, (843) 937-0930, is as unpretentious as they come—a former barbershop with clapboard walls and butcher paper on the tables—but everyone in town knows how good and fairly priced it is. One morning not too long ago, two pickups and a Rolls-Royce were parked outside. Try chef Robert Stehling's wonderful shrimp on cheese grits or toasted banana bread for brunch, his pimento cheese sandwich with arugula (!) for lunch, and his unbeatable buttermilk pie any old time.

McCrady's, 2 Unity Alley, (843) 577-0025, has a tavernlike decor, but there's nothing proletarian about Michael Kramer's cooking. A young Californian, he likes to tool around town on a canary-yellow Italian racing bike and to formulate richly flavored New American dishes like pan-roasted scallops with melted leeks and truffle butter, and roast chicken on parsnip puree. The wine list, strong on Rhônes, is well thought out.

Peninsula Grill, Planters Inn (see above), (843) 723-0700. A cosmopolitan, subtly lighted room with velvet walls, the grill serves brilliantly seasoned, hard-to-resist dishes like chef Bob Carter's sumptuous Carolina quail stuffed with pecan cornbread. Smiling service, superb wines, and memorable five-layer coconut cake more than seal the deal.

39 Rue De Jean, 39 John Street, (843) 722-8881. A soupçon of Paris in an artsy, up-and-coming neighborhood, with familiar brasserie dishes like mussels steamed in white wine, steak frites, and braised rabbit. The raw seafood platter, mostly local, is first-rate.

⫸ ATLANTA

This is a city without a historic core, a city in constant evolution—a Deep South version, you might say, of Los Angeles. Of course, it does have a past, a real one as well as the one that Margaret Mitchell so vividly imagined in *Gone With the Wind*. A decisive Civil War battle was fought over this ground, and the momentous civil rights movement of the 1960s had its principal headquarters here. That most American of products Coca-Cola was invented here. But Atlanta, a city in a hurry, keeps putting its past behind it.

If it were not for the Cyclorama depicting the fighting of 1864 and the superlative Atlanta History Center, with its evocations of the great newspaper editor Henry W. Grady, the golfer Bobby Jones, and, yes, William Tecumseh Sherman, who burned the city down, a visitor might easily come here and miss Atlanta's past altogether. After all, Atlanta is the dynamic, business-minded, if economically stressed, capital of the New South, proud to have played host to the 1996 Olympic Games, pleased to promote itself as "The World's Next Great City" and not just another vestige of the Old South. Southern in manners and language, Southern in values, yes, but not Faulkner-Southern. "Atlanta had never been a true Old Southern city, like Savannah or Charleston or Richmond, where wealth had originated with the land," Tom Wolfe wrote in his novel *A Man in Full* in 1998. "Atlanta was an offspring of the railroad business. It had been created from scratch barely 150 years ago, and people had been making money there on the hustle ever since."

Quite so. Atlanta, or rather the Atlanta region, has been one of the global capitals of New Money, much of it made in real estate. It went to build the trophy houses in the ritzy residential area along West Pace's Ferry Road in Buckhead, near the History Center, and to buy the BMWs and Land Rovers that clog the lots around Buckhead's many shopping centers, and to pay for the food and drink in the neighborhood's glossy restaurants. But the pace slowed after the millennium, even more drastically in Atlanta than in most of the country. As Atlanta-based companies like Coke, Home Depot, and Delta Air Lines bled jobs—61,800 between October 2001 and October 2002, more than any other city in the country—some of the bloom faded on Buckhead's roses.

Other neighborhoods have suffered, too. Downtown is bustling by day, much less so at night; people work there but don't play there; and Centennial Olympic Park, created for the 1996 games, did not pull it together the way the city fathers had hoped. The economic downturn has led to lower hotel and office-building occupancy rates. As for midtown, it is struggling to extend its comeback as a pleasant place to live, as is the poorer and shabbier, mostly African American south side of town. In Virginia-Highlands, a walkable neighborhood of bars, boutiques, and bookshops, and in close-in Inman Park, Atlanta still flaunts its charm, especially in spring, when dogwood blossoms brighten the streets.

A compact, relatively small city of 425,000, Atlanta retains enough vibrancy to continue luring hordes of people from other parts of the country. Most of them have settled in the hinterland. To get a true picture, you must focus not on the city alone but on the unruly seventeen-county sprawl that has spread ever outward from it, with no mountains or seacoast in the way, across Cobb and DeKalb, Gwinnett and Forsyth and Cherokee and a dozen other counties. It is now home to 4,250,000 people, and the Atlanta Chamber of Commerce expects that number to top 5 million by 2012.

Three of the nation's ten fastest-growing counties lie within commuting range of Atlanta, and their exploding populations have helped make Georgia the tenth largest state. But with growth, with prosperity, with the shady trees and tidy yards of the suburbs have come problems: higher taxes to pay for infrastructure, air and water pollution, and nerve-shattering three-hour drives to and from work. Drivers endure the country's longest average commute—a 34-mile round-trip every working day, often snarled by gridlock.

The Sierra Club calls Atlanta the most sprawl-threatened large city in the United States; an official of the American Farmland Trust termed it "the poster child for sprawl." Stung by those descriptions, the state government is working on tactics to bring greater order to the region, through organizations such as the Georgia Regional Transportation Authority, created at the urging of then-governor Roy Barnes in 1999.

How much the sprawl bothers you depends on where you sit. My friend Colin Campbell, a newspaper columnist, lives in midtown and wishes more suburbanites would move there. It still has a slightly hollowed-out feeling, he said. But our host at lunch one day, former mayor Sam Massell, now known as the unofficial mayor of Buckhead, which houses 15 percent of Atlanta's population and pays 45 percent of its taxes, said the only alternative to more sprawl was more smog and traffic jams in the city.

Originally, Atlanta was called Terminus, but that was a misnomer. It has always been about linkage. It came into being as the place where the railroads from the strategic ports of Mobile and Charleston and Savannah met the line running south from Chattanooga, which is what made it such a strategic objective in the Civil War. Atlanta later became the southeastern hub of the highway system, where Interstates 20, 75, and 85 meet. The hub of the airline network, too. Even on your way to heaven, southerners used to say, you have to change planes in Atlanta. Atlanta's airport pioneered instrument approaches and air traffic control, and today it is the busiest in the world, measured by the number of passengers passing through it, with an estimated 79 million in 2003.

Several generations of visionaries have made possible the city's rise from the ashes of defeat. They thoroughly disproved the prophecy of a Union soldier, Private First Class Theodore Upson, who wrote in his diary after the battle of Atlanta in September 1864: "We have wholly destroyed Atlanta. I don't think that any people will want to live there now." Henry Grady was the first to see the future clearly. As the editor of *The Atlanta Constitution,* he argued after the Civil War that the salvation of his ruined city, state, and region lay in attracting Northern investment to a "New South," a phrase he coined. In a famous speech in New York in 1886, he assured the New England Society that Southerners had accepted the outcome of the war and bore the North no ill will.

His vision of good race relations—"sunshine everywhere and all the time," as he put it—was never realized in his lifetime. The South remained the nation's economic stepchild, and Atlanta's history was marred by spasms of violence, including the 1906 race riots, in which whites attacked blacks, and the 1913 lynching of Leo Frank, a Jew from Brooklyn. Anti-Semitism reared its head more recently in the 1958 bombing of a synagogue.

When the federal government ceased enforcing black rights, Jim Crow laws brought on segregation in restaurants, hotels, and other public places. Blacks were denied the vote. But they built successful parallel institutions, including churches, newspapers, radio stations, banks, insurance companies, and two of the nation's best predominantly African American colleges, Morehouse for men and Spelman for women. Between the world wars, Auburn Avenue ("Sweet Auburn") became a mecca for blacks.

The great visionary of the civil rights movement, of course, was the Reverend Dr. Martin Luther King Jr., born in a clapboard and shingle house that still stands on Auburn Avenue, not far from Ebenezer Baptist Church, where Dr. King and his father preached. He won the Nobel Peace Prize in 1964, at the age of thirty-five, the youngest person ever to do so. He is buried in a marble tomb in a reflecting pool at the Martin Luther King Jr. Center for Nonviolent Social Change, also on Auburn.

Across the street at a National Park Visitors Center the still photographs of Birmingham and Selma by Charles Moore and James Karales evoke that era of accomplishment and strife. But the genius of the place lies in the films of Dr. King delivering his eloquent speeches, in that prophetic voice mingling calm, cultivation, and steely determination. I heard many of them in person as a young reporter, and like many of my generation I can recite bits of several from memory—"Free at last! Free at last! Thank God Almighty, we are free at last"—but neither my wife, Betsey, nor I was prepared for the powerful waves of emotion that washed over us as we listened. Atlanta offers no experience to match it, and not many other cities do either.

Dr. King had important coworkers, including Jesse Jackson and Andrew Young, later a member of Congress, ambassador to the United Nations, and mayor of Atlanta. A large black middle class helped lend stability to the city when others, potential rivals for Southern leadership, fell apart. Mayors William B. Hartsfield and Ivan Allen pronounced their city "Too Busy to Hate," and Ralph McGill preached moderation in his column in the *Constitution*. Shirley Franklin, the current mayor, is also an African American, confronting the gulf between Atlanta's haves and its have-nots like her predecessors.

Coca-Cola, Atlanta's first great international business, was built by Robert W. Woodruff, who took a tonic developed in 1886 by Dr. John Stith Pemberton, a local chemist, and peddled it around the globe. Woodruff philanthropies, large and small, are inescapable in Atlanta. The World of Coca-Cola, a self-aggrandizing corporate museum where the Coke is free but the admission isn't, has attracted more than 10 million visitors since opening in 1990. (A newer, bigger version is under construction.) The last time I stopped by, a blinking electronic sign informed passersby that more than 6 trillion 39 billion bottles have been sold. So the news a few years ago that the company was changing CEOs and eliminating 6,000 jobs worldwide, including 2,500 in Atlanta, hit the city like a tornado.

Today, the city's leading citizen is former president Jimmy Carter, much more admired out of office than in, who builds houses for Habitat for Humanity, lectures, writes books, and travels the world with his wife, Rosalynn, promoting peace and working to eradicate disease and ease hunger. He won the Nobel Peace Prize in 2002.

Carter has a rival in Ted Turner, the voluble entrepreneur who turned an underpowered UHF television station into a superstation that is viewed across the country. He invented CNN, based in downtown Atlanta, which has become the world's channel of choice when big news is breaking. He made the Atlanta Braves, winners of thirteen consecutive division titles (if only one World Series) under the imperturbable Bobby

Cox, into one of the nation's most successful sports franchises. He married (and split from) Jane Fonda. He gave $1 billion to the United Nations. And he owns 1.6 million acres of ranch land, more than any other American.

But then, entrepreneurial Atlanta is full of success stories, from Delta Air Lines to Home Depot and UPS. Over the years, it has built up important institutions like the national Centers for Disease Control and Prevention, Georgia Tech, and Emory University, a superb liberal arts school less well-known than Tech, perhaps because it lacks the Ramblin' Wrecks' sports legends. Emory's well-regarded Michael C. Carlos Art Museum was renovated and expanded by the postmodernist Michael Graves in 1993. The Robert W. Woodruff Library snared the immense Danowski poetry collection—sixty thousand volumes and tens of thousands of other items related to twentieth-century poetry—early in 2004. At a stroke, it made Emory a world center for literary research.

Atlanta boasts tourist attractions like the zoo, with a winsome pair of pandas, Lun Lun and Yang Yang, two of only nine in the country, and the Stone Mountain Monument, a kind of Confederate version of Mount Rushmore, out to the east of the city. Soon it will have a 5-million-gallon aquarium, funded in part by a $200 million contribution from Bernie Marcus, one of the founders of Home Depot.

I must not forget the Art Deco–style Varsity, the nation's largest drive-in, where they move the customers through at double time, all day every day. And I must mention a curiosity of Atlanta nomenclature: there are thirty-two streets, lanes, drives, circles, and roads named Peachtree in the metropolitan area.

Culturally speaking, Atlanta remains a stripling, and it has suffered two important losses in recent years. Ned Rifkin, the director of the High Museum of Art, left in 2000, complaining of a chronic dearth of arts financing, both public and private. (He's now at the Smithsonian, in Washington.) Harriet Sanford, director of the Fulton County Arts Council, left to take a similar position in Charlotte, North Carolina—"a place," she said, "that has a different level of appreciation for the arts." Georgia ranked forty-sixth in the nation in 2002 in per capita cultural giving. Yet Atlanta likes to think of itself as a much more important city than Charlotte and as a legitimate rival to Houston. So it was not surprising that the *Journal-Constitution* ran an editorial chastising both business and local governments for failing to commit the big bucks needed to move the city into the artistic big leagues.

But better days have dawned for the Atlanta Symphony Orchestra, the largest performing arts organization in the Southeast, with a budget of $25 million and an endowment of some $70 million. Founded in 1945 as a youth orchestra but really created, to a considerable degree, by the noted choral conductor Robert Shaw, its director from 1966 to 1987, the orchestra struggled during the 1990s. In 2000, the symphony named Robert Spano, the then thirty-eight-year-old leader of the Brooklyn Philharmonic, to succeed the departing Yoel Levi. A highly touted young American, he had been mentioned as a possibility for a half dozen other orchestras, some of them bigger. At the same time, Donald Runnicles, the Scottish-born, German-trained music director of the San Francisco Opera, was named principal guest conductor. Since then, the orchestra's recordings have won several Grammy Awards, and it has announced ambitious plans for a new $240 million home to be designed by the Spanish master Santiago Calatrava.

For many years, the Metropolitan Opera came to Atlanta every year on tour. When the visits ended in 1987, the Atlanta Opera, which had begun as an amateur outfit, transformed itself to fill the void. Starting, in the words of William Fred Scott, its artistic director, with "somebody who answered the phone and a sextet of well-meaning ladies in station wagons," it has grown into a company with an annual budget of almost $5 million. Almost 50,000 people attend its productions most years. This "meteoric growth," the British magazine *Opera Now* said, is "creating noises everywhere." In 2004 the company moved into the newly renovated 4,599-seat Boisfeuillet Jones Civic Center, which will make possible four performances of each of five operas, but some opera lovers, me included, will miss the glorious 4,514-seat Fox Theater, an Art Deco movie palace that retains its "Thousand and One Nights" decor.

If any Atlanta arts organization embraces the whole city, black and white, urban and suburban, it is the Alliance Theater

Company, a repertory group based at the Woodruff Arts Center. Its founder, Kenny Leon, who left in 2001, must have been one of the few artistic directors around who stood outside after some performances, greeting the audience members like a parish priest. Leon cast African American actors and actresses in traditionally white roles in *A Christmas Carol* and *Medea,* which featured the *Cosby* star Phylicia Rashad. "I think controversy is probably my middle name," Leon said on the CBS News program *Sunday Morning* a few years ago, "not because I want to be controversial but because I want to ask questions that will make us better human beings. I think the theater can be a place where we can come and realize that we all bleed the same blood, we all walk the same way, and we all want the same things."

Replaced at the Alliance by Susan V. Booth, a freelance director who had headed new play development at the top-drawer Goodman Theater in Chicago, Leon has launched a new African American theater company called True Colors into a sea of economic tribulations. Eventually, he hopes, it will be based in Washington as well as Atlanta. His first Broadway production, *A Raisin in the Sun,* won two Tony Awards in 2004.

As befits a city whose main business for the last century has been building itself, most of Atlanta's architecture is developer architecture. The city's most important homegrown architect in the postwar period was John Portman, himself a developer, who built most of the postmodern towers that define downtown Atlanta, including the vast Peachtree Center, the Atlanta Merchandise Mart, and the seventy-story Westin Peachtree Plaza Hotel. He is best remembered for the Hyatt Regency Hotel, for which he adapted and expanded the atrium lobby used in nineteenth-century hotels like the Brown Palace in Denver. The Hyatt's twenty-two-story skylit courtyard, with bedrooms opening onto cantilevered balconies hung with vines and with transparent, twinkling "bubble" elevators whisking awed guests to their floors, was copied all across the United States soon after it opened in 1967.

Philip Johnson and John Burgee contributed a pair of skyscrapers in the late 1980s, the more successful of the two forming an anchor for the midtown neighborhood. Called the IBM Tower, it is a neo-Gothic campanile, refined in its ornament and satisfying in its proportions. A few other notable buildings are scattered here and there, including a series of elegant mansions designed in the 1920s and '30s by Philip T. Shutze, a gifted classicist who took his stylistic cue from the best Regency and Federal models. Sadly, the clumsy McMansions that have joined them along the wealthy wooded byways of Buckhead in the last two decades have none of Shutze's finesse. Meant to resemble Venetian palazzos, Georgian country seats, Tuscan villas, or French châteaus, they succeed only in looking hugely expensive. A scroll pediment here and a Palladian window there don't cut it.

At the moment, only one leading modernist can be seen at the peak of his game in Atlanta, and that is Richard Meier, whose High Museum (1983), clad in dazzlingly white porcelain-enameled steel panels, resembles a space station that has settled gently onto the greensward along Peachtree Street. A big, colorful Calder mobile (a lunar explorer?) sits alongside it, and a series of curving ramps lead into and through the exhibition spaces. More than 450,000 people visit the building each year. When the new symphony hall is completed, Meier will be joined by Calatrava and after that by Renzo Piano, who has been commissioned to design a three-building addition to the High itself. Meier was not even considered for that job, although he won worldwide acclaim for the Getty Center in Los Angeles; the addition, said Michael E. Shapiro, the new High Museum director, "will make Richard's part look even better." One can only hope so.

The High's collection is skimpy in spots but has significant strengths, including the spectacular Virginia Carroll Crawford collection of nineteenth- and twentieth-century American furniture and decorative arts (several Herter Brothers pieces are of special note) and idiosyncratic objects made by Howard Finster of Summerville, Georgia, a well-known outsider artist.

I especially like the way in which pictures or other objects have been set in unlikely juxtapositions: a Rothko next to a Martin Johnson Heade, one abstract, one not, but both divided into three horizontal bands; an old Yoruba door from West Africa next to a door painted in New Orleans by a black artist named Herbert Singleton, born in 1945; children as seen by three portraitists, Mary Cassatt, Samuel F. B. Morse, and George Bellows. The pedagogy is not heavy-handed, but the lessons are there for those who seek them.

WHERE TO STAY

Ritz-Carlton Buckhead, 3434 Peachtree Road NE, (404) 237-2700. Set in a sterile suburban sea of shopping malls and office towers, the Ritz nonetheless conveys a feeling of graceful luxury. The public rooms are lush; the bedrooms benefit from thick carpets and thicker towels, but you may wonder why faxes take so long to reach you. The dining room (see below) has been a superstar since it opened in 1984.

Four Seasons, 75 14th Street, (404) 881-9898. Strategically positioned between Buckhead and downtown, only a few steps from the High Museum of Art and the Woodruff Arts Center, this opulent property occupies the bottom twenty floors of a postmodern high-rise. Offices and condominiums take up the top floors. Corridors and bedrooms are bright and amply proportioned, and room-service breakfasts are delectable.

Ritz-Carlton Downtown, 181 Peachtree Street NE, (404) 659-0400. The Buckhead property is the chain's flagship, but this "other" Ritz clearly ranks as the best hotel in downtown Atlanta. Acres of marble, fine Oriental rugs, a seventeenth-century Flemish tapestry, and an eighteenth-century chandelier lend the lobby all the luxury anyone could ask for, although the overall feeling is a little bit institutional. Some rooms have four-posters.

WHERE TO EAT

Bacchanalia, 1198 Howell Mill Road, (404) 365-0410. Installed in a former slaughterhouse west of downtown, Bacchanalia expends every effort to track down prime raw materials: Niman Ranch pork, lamb, and beef; cherry-red Ahi tuna from Hawaii; cheeses from not only Italy, France, and Britain but also North Carolina, California, and New York. Stunning Meyer lemon soufflé for dessert, great California cabernets.

Bluepointe, 3455 Peachtree Road, (404) 237-9070. At the moment, this is ground zero for Hotlanta, a bold blend of primary colors, hard edges, and waitstaff in black Mandarin tunics. The fusion food is terrifyingly good-looking on the plate and packed with flavor. Try the Thai chicken and coconut soup, or the peanut-crusted grouper atop bitter choy sum greens. Better service and much less frenzy at lunch than at dinner.

Brasserie Le Coze, 3393 Peachtree Road, (404) 266-1440. A cousin of Le Bernardin in New York, this is a true brasserie, with white tile floors and Lipp-like mosaics between tall pier mirrors. Parisian dishes (onion tart, roast skate) and Franco-American specials (salads, roast lamb on olive bread with garlic mayonnaise) are both terrific. Perfect for a lunch break during a shop-till-you-drop day at Lenox Square.

Dining Room at Ritz-Carlton Buckhead, 3434 Peachtree Road, (404) 237-2700. The United States is full of synthetically sophisticated Continental restaurants, but this is the real thing:

immaculate service, counter-snob wine advice, fresh new Oriental decor, and fine fusion cuisine (e.g., conch salad with soba) from Bruno Menard, a Frenchman late of Osaka. Save room for the wicked tart made with Cuban chocolate.

Joël, 3290 Northside Parkway, (404) 233-3500. The draw at this unpretentious new place is the lean, mean, flavor-packed cuisine fashioned by the brilliant Joel Antunes, whose London restaurant, Les Saveurs, earned two Michelin stars. If available, try his lamb loin in puff pastry, potently flavored with coriander, curry, and basil. Divine.

Seeger's, 111 West Pace's Ferry Road, (404) 846-9779. Gunther Seeger introduced world-class cooking to Atlanta, and he continues to push out its margins at his small, understated restaurant in Buckhead. His kitchen is bigger than his dining room; his style is intellectual. One example: a fillet of sea bass, marinated in sake, covered with a Japanese cherry leaf. You may wonder whether you deserve such refinement.

Watershed, 406 West Ponce De Leon Avenue, Decatur, (404) 378-4900. Scott Peacock, protégé and companion of Edna Lewis, the high priestess of Southern cooking, holds her banner aloft in his delightful little restaurant, once a suburban gas station. Try the already legendary Tuesday-night roast chicken, salmon croquettes, pecan tart, or pimento cheese sandwich; this is lip-smacking country food, made with finesse.

⏵ SAVANNAH

The genius of Savannah resides in its contradictions. Here is a city of 132,000 souls that is Cartesian in the logic of its layout. A grid of broad streets covers two square miles, punctuated by twenty-one squares, each with a statue, fountain, or gazebo. Yet the rectilinear regularity never palls, because the streets and parks are shaded by magnificent live oaks hung with garlands of Spanish moss. Could anything possibly be less Cartesian than Spanish moss, with its sultry, inescapable whiff of decadence?

Here is a city whose people, rich and poor, are so steeped in good manners—in the smile, the soft word, the easy humor of the Old South—that truck drivers wave at pedestrians as they pass. Yet there is nothing low-key or mannerly about Savannah's horticultural trademark, the azalea, whose Technicolor floral eruptions each spring couldn't be brasher.

How lucky Savannah is! Lucky in its founder, General James Oglethorpe, a practical idealist and as such a kind of contradiction himself, who came here in 1733 from England to found a new colony for English settlers. Lucky in its escape from pillage during the Civil War, when General Sherman, who had sown such havoc on his march to the sea, rode unopposed into town and wired Abraham Lincoln on December 22, 1864, "I beg to present to you as a Christmas gift the City of Savannah, with 150 heavy guns and plenty of ammunition, and also about 25,000 bales of cotton." Lucky in its bad luck as well. A century of postbellum poverty—not really poverty, I suppose, more a lack of prosperity—made it hard for the greedy to redevelop the charm out of the city in the dread name of progress.

Now the question is whether Savannah can survive its latest

stroke of good fortune, John Berendt's vivid portrait of the city's glories and eccentricities in *Midnight in the Garden of Good and Evil*, which local people refer to simply as "the book." Published in 1994, it has sold 3.3 million copies to date, and it spent longer on the best-seller lists than any previous work of nonfiction. The visitors and retirees who have flocked to Savannah in Berendt's wake have changed the place, of course. It still lies "off the beaten track, en route to nowhere but itself," to borrow his phrases, but the sound of the streets is no longer "an overarching hush." After his book was published, overnight stays by tourists more than tripled to 10.5 million a year.

Savannah, which lies eighteen miles upriver from the Atlantic, is now the fifth largest port in the United States. A spacious convention center opened in 2000 and served as the media headquarters for the G-8 global summit on nearby Sea Island in June 2004. Long-vacant storefronts along Broughton Street have started to fill up, and the *Savannah Morning News* has added a regional business section to its Sunday editions. Distribution centers for chains like Wal-Mart and Home Depot have been built, along with plants for Gulfstream Aerospace, which makes business jets, and several big paper producers. The efficient airport may be the best of its modest size in the nation.

More than 19,500 soldiers are stationed at nearby Fort Stewart, home of the Third Infantry Division (Mechanized), and at Hunter Army Airfield, even closer, from which the Third and other units are dispatched to flash points around the world, including Iraq. Together, the two form the largest military complex east of the Mississippi, and a significant portion of their $730 million annual payroll wends its way into Savannah.

Little by little, the city is joining the New South of Atlanta and Charlotte. But when my wife, Betsey, and I returned to Savannah for our first post-Berendt visit, the city seemed as sweetly seductive as ever, its beauty unblemished by newfound fame and fortune. It is a bit provincial, self-absorbed but not self-satisfied, and there is something loosey-goosey about a place that calls its minor-league baseball team the Sand Gnats. Like New Orleans and Charleston, Savannah dances to languid rhythms. In the humidity of high summer, the mood becomes even drowsier, as residents retreat to their jasmine-scented gardens.

Throughout its history, Savannah has been a cosmopolitan place, as befits a seaport. Besides its original English settlers, the city attracted Irish Catholics and Huguenots, Germans and Sephardic Jews, and, despite the influence of Oglethorpe's anti-slavery views, enslaved African Americans. The Sea Islands off the Georgia coast preserve their semi-indigenous black culture, where many speak Gullah, a patois that lies somewhere between English and West African dialects. Many place and family names are African. A slave rebellion erupted in 1803 at Ebo Landing, named for the Ibo people of Nigeria.

Savannah itself is exceptionally rich in African American history. Two buildings bear witness to a struggle for dignity that has been waged for two centuries. The First African Baptist Church (1788), which claims to be the oldest continuously active black church in North America, has loose floorboards beneath which runaway slaves once cowered. Across town stands the unadorned little Second African Baptist Church (1802), where General Sherman read out the Emancipation Proclamation and promised newly freed slaves "40 acres and a mule." Almost a century later, the Reverend Dr. Martin Luther King Jr. preached an "I Have a Dream" sermon there prefiguring his historic speech in Washington.

In 1738, only five years after Oglethorpe founded the last of the original thirteen colonies, Jews began coming here, and descendants of some of them, including Sheftalls and Minises, remain prominent in Savannah's economic and cultural life. Temple Mickve Israel, built in 1876 and the only Gothic Revival synagogue in the United States, has cast-iron cluster pillars, a fine Spanish chandelier, and glowing stained glass.

Savannah's ambitious symphony orchestra went under in 2003, unable to pay a $1.3 million debt, but the city maintains a spring Shakespeare festival in Forsyth Park that is now almost two decades old, and a once-sleepy spring music festival has evolved into a fifteen-day marathon of jazz, zydeco, Beethoven, Gershwin, gospel, and Southern rock. The influence of the 6,000-student College of Art and Design is seen in the numerous painters, potters, and other craftspeople who came to study, stayed on in Savannah, and flourished.

Savannah is also home to the Telfair Museum of Art, the

oldest art museum in the South, with heroic statues of five artistic eminences from the Old World—Rembrandt, Phidias, Michelangelo, Raphael, and Rubens—standing sentinel over its Corinthian porch. The collection is an extremely mixed bag: lots of gloomy nineteenth-century Germanic kitsch, redeemed by a first-rate group of American Impressionists (Childe Hassam in particular) and Realists (George Bellows, George Luks, and Robert Henri, the latter represented by a radiant Velázquez-like portrait of a young woman in a scarlet gown, *La Madrilena*).

A daring expansion called the Jepson Center, designed by the Canadian Moshe Safdie and destined to house twentieth- and twenty-first-century art and traveling shows, is scheduled to open late in 2005. During the design process, tomorrow in the person of Safdie clashed with yesterday in the form of the local establishment. The original plan for an all-glass facade was denied a "certificate of appropriateness"—how very, very Savannah!—and the architect was forced to reduce the glazed expanse. Many in the city doubt that the revised addition will measure up to the present palazzolike building, one of the legacies of William Jay, a young Englishman (1792–1837) who came to Savannah and in a span of a few years gave the city the best collection of Regency buildings in the United States.

Jay's masterpiece is the Owens-Thomas House, also owned by the Telfair. Suggestive of the Regency villas of his native Bath, with a warm stucco exterior and walled parterre garden, and of Sir John Soane's London townhouse, it has a cast-iron veranda on the south side, the first use of that material for architectural purposes in the United States. Inside, a dramatic, intricate staircase rises from the ground floor to a landing, then splits and doubles back to the second floor. The dining room details are immaculate: a pair of beautifully curved doors, a plaster cornice of anthemia, and a Greek-key cutout, high on one wall, filled with amber glass that allows sunlight to penetrate into the room. There are no windows in the north wall; my wife's cousin, Ashby Angell, told us that in the nineteenth century, people thought malaria was caused by a miasma from the river to the north.

My favorite Jay building is the William Scarborough House, built for one of the owners of the *Savannah*, the first steamship to cross the Atlantic. It has been altered over the years, but it retains its muscular Classical facade, and its impressive two-story faux-marble entrance hall, supported by four stout Doric columns and topped by a sky-blue barrel vault. The building now houses the Ships of the Sea Maritime Museum, which displays marine models (including a riveting miniature *Titanic*), scrimshaw, figureheads, navigational equipment, and other things nautical and nice. One of the displays is a nineteenth-century ceramic cat, of a type placed in the windows of brothels in European port cities. I learned an etymological lesson, to wit: if the cat's eyes were green, that meant come in; if they were red, that meant the house was full or the police were nearby; and if the cat's back was turned, the house was closed. From this, it is suggested, comes the term "cathouse."

You can—you should—drench yourself in good architecture in Savannah. Close to the Savannah River, near where Oglethorpe lived, is the Customs House, whose columns are crowned with tobacco leaves instead of the more traditional acanthus. Fifteen miles down the river and very near the sea stands the rugged, moated Fort Pulaski, planned after the War of 1812 revealed how shaky America's coastal defenses were. It took eighteen years (1829–47) and 25 million bricks to build, but as a Confederate stronghold it fell in 1862 after only thirty hours of Union bombardment. The presumed invulnerability of its heavy masonry was utterly demolished by ten new guns that fired rifled projectiles instead of standard cannonballs. They changed the course of warfare forever.

In addition to Jay's houses, at least two others command attention: the Davenport House Museum, a Federal gem (1820) with a lemon-yellow entrance hall punctuated by a pair of slim Ionic pillars supporting a graceful arch, and the Gothic Revival Green-Meldrim House (1850), where Sherman stayed, notable for its iron verandas and, inside, its exuberant plaster ornament. There are now more than a thousand restored houses, many with the side porches that low-country folk call "piazzas," some antebellum, some Victorian, some made of distinctive "Savannah gray" brick, which is actually pinkish brown. Some were restored by the owners, others rescued from decay by the pioneering efforts of the Historic Savannah Foundation, an organization of volunteers, mostly women, which started in 1955 at the Davenport House, which had deteriorated into a seedy tenement.

You sense the city's genteel traditions in antique shops like Alex Raskin, James Morton, and DeLoach, and at the very fine E. Shaver, a twelve-room treasury of books and maps. But the restored neighborhoods are also alive with the sights and sounds of modern life—a woman of classical profile pruning her oleanders, a baby crying, a cook frying chicken at a window—and that makes them genuine. A lyrical place, Savannah produced some lyrical sons and daughters. You can see the graves of two of them at Bonaventure Cemetery, not far from downtown but otherworldly all the same: the songwriter Johnny Mercer ("Nov. 18, 1909–June 25, 1976 . . . And the Angels Sing") and the poet Conrad Aiken ("Aug. 5, 1889–Aug. 17, 1973 . . . Cosmos Mariner Destination Unknown").

WHERE TO STAY

Ballastone Inn, 14 East Oglethorpe Avenue, (912) 236-1484, maintains its antebellum refinement. Once a bordello, the Ballastone was built in 1838 and named for the stones carried in ships' holds for stability. It blends the old (love seats, marble-top tables and framed engravings from *Harper's*) with the new (color televisions and VCRs).

Hyatt Regency, 2 West Bay Street, (912) 238-1234, is the best in-town hotel. Its location is ideal: on the riverfront, within walking distance of the historic district. From many of the well-kept modern rooms you can watch ships from Oslo and other distant ports creep upstream to dock. The valet parking crew must be the speediest anywhere.

Gastonian, 220 East Gaston Street, (912) 232-2869. This is perhaps the best bed-and-breakfast in a city full of good ones, good enough to make it into the picky Relais and Châteaux group. Two refined 1868 houses in the Italianate style, furnished with period antiques, bedrooms with working fireplaces; only a somewhat remote location is a minus.

Westin Savannah Harbor Resort, 1 Resort Drive, (912) 201-2000. This 403-room newcomer, located on Hutchinson Island, across the river from downtown Savannah and adjacent to the convention center, offers it all: an eighteen-hole golf course designed by Sam Snead, two pools, three tennis courts, and super-comfortable beds. The historic district on the other riverbank is a few minutes away by fast water taxi.

WHERE TO EAT

Elizabeth on 37th, 105 East Thirty-seventh Street, (912) 236-5547, housed in a stately Greek Revival manse, is the creation of Elizabeth Terry, whose credo is simple: "I do comfort food. One shouldn't be embarrassed about that." These days, others do it for her, with little falloff in quality. Winners include smoky

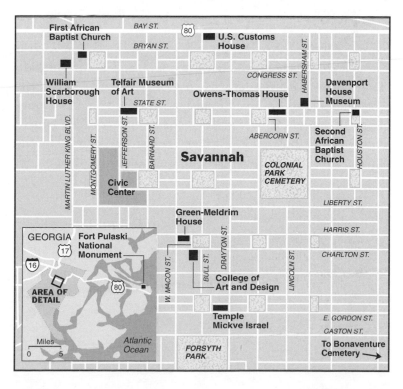

shrimp with red-eye gravy and grouper with peanut sauce and cucumbers. Kind, knowing service and carefully chosen wines.

Lady & Sons, 311 West Congress Street, (912) 233-2600, serves a lunch to make calorie-counters weep: tumblers of minty, syrup-sweet iced tea; scrumptious cheese biscuits, offered again and again by cheerful waiters; creamy crab soup laced, I think, with sherry-pepper sauce; and chicken potpie with a puff-pastry crust. Paula Deen, the lady in question, also does tasty salads for people with more character than I.

Mrs. Wilkes's Dining Room, 107 West Jones Street, (912) 232-5997, is a survivor from another age. Brimming bowls of food are delivered to common tables and left for emptying. Pork chops, a gazillion vegetables, and banana pudding for lunch, maybe, all authentically prepared. But breakfast is best, with scrambled eggs, country ham, bacon, three kinds of sausage, grits, and fine, flaky biscuits. Mrs. W. presided in her plain little domain, ever the monosyllabic matriarch, until her death at ninety-five in 2002.

Sapphire Grill, 110 West Julian Street, (912) 443-9962. Chris Nason, who used to cook at Bistro Savannah, turns out judiciously seasoned dishes at this cool, edgy boîte, like meltingly tender buttermilk-marinated calamari with a lime and coriander pesto. His crunchy-crisp fried green tomatoes set a benchmark for flavor. But be forewarned: the night we stopped by, the din was awful and the lights so dim we couldn't read the menu.

⫸ TAMPA BAY

Once upon a time, when there were more orange groves than golf courses in Florida, Tampa Bay was surrounded by a series of distinct communities: ethnic Tampa, white-bread St. Petersburg with its Midwestern retirees, laid-back Bradenton and Clearwater, and arty, cosmopolitan Sarasota, about forty miles down the Gulf Coast, where the Ringling Bros. and Barnum & Bailey Circus spent the winter. "We never went to St. Petersburg, ever," recalled my *New York Times* colleague David E. Rosenbaum, who grew up in Tampa during the 1940s and 1950s. "We had the port and the unions and Latins, and they had the beaches and tourists and shuffleboard."

Now, in fact if not law, it's one big metropolitan area, laced together with bridges and freeways. People watch the same television stations and root for the same professional sports teams. Many of them send their children to the booming, multicampus University of South Florida. They shop at the same enormous malls, like the Citrus Park Town Center, only recently a pasture, which drew upward of 100,000 cars on opening day in 1999.

On road maps, this entity of more than 2.5 million people doesn't exist. Only the old place names are there. But everyone calls it Tampa Bay, and it is a prototypical example of the Sun Belt's explosive growth. Orders go out to Iraq and Afghanistan from McDill Air Force Base, headquarters of the Central Command. Subdivisions sprawl under the postcard-blue skies. The economy thrives. Cultural venues and sports facilities multiply.

Even baseball spring training, a seasonal ritual in Florida for decades, is attracting new interest, thanks to home-run derbies and the sprucing up of some of the ballparks where the big leaguers strut their stuff. No fewer than six teams train in the area, including the Yankees, whose main owner, George Steinbrenner, is a Tampa tycoon. They play their preseason games at the modestly named Legends Field (address: 1 Steinbrenner Drive).

Hernando de Soto, historians think, was Tampa Bay's first tourist, landing near modern Bradenton in 1539 and lingering there briefly before heading west on a fruitless search for jewels and gold that ended with his death on the banks of the Mississippi River in 1542. Not much happened for the three centuries after that, until Henry B. Plant built a railroad linking the Tampa Bay area to the rest of America in 1883. In 1891 he added the astonishing 500-room Tampa Bay Hotel, built in an eccentric Moorish style, with keyhole-shaped windows, thirteen silvery minarets topped with golden crescents, and a peacock park, very nearly making good on his pledge to "turn this sandheap into the Champs-Élysées." With Tampa the staging point for the American forces dispatched to Cuba in the summer of 1898 at the outbreak of the Spanish-American War, Army and Navy officers (including Lieutenant Colonel Theodore Roosevelt) sat on the hotel's veranda in rocking chairs, sipping champagne or iced tea, awaiting orders. The expeditionary force sailed away in June, and the hotel never recaptured those days of glory; it closed in 1930. But the building survives as a monument to the man who built the Gulf Coast, used by a city museum and the University of Tampa.

St. Petersburg blossomed, too, southeast of Tampa on the other side of the bay, once a railroad was extended to it in 1888, by luring white-collar refugees from the cruel winters and high taxes in Ohio, Michigan, and Indiana. It was shaped by determined newspaper editors who came from the Midwest: W. L. Straub of *The St. Petersburg Times*, who in the early years of the twentieth century opposed industrialization of the city's waterfront, and his visionary successor, Nelson Poynter, a crusader for civil rights and clean government.

Three art museums have opened along the waterfront in recent years, lending a new dimension to the city and contributing to a regional surge of cultural development. Oldest is the Museum of Fine Arts, whose twenty galleries house a small but inclusive collection. Its highlights include an aggressively scarlet *Poppy* by Georgia O'Keeffe; a subtle Lely portrait of Nell Gwyn, the actress mistress of King Charles II; a shimmering Monet from the Parliament series, *Effect of Fog*; and a supremely 1920s portrait of Mr. and Mrs. Chester Dale, benefactors of the National Gallery in Washington, by Guy Pène du Bois.

Down the street, improbably sited next to a pleasure boat marina, is the world's largest collection of paintings and drawings by the flamboyant Catalan Surrealist Salvador Dalí. There are plenty of melting watches and a telephone shaped like a lobster, the kinds of images that made Dalí's fame, but the four immense so-called "masterworks" are the star attractions. The best of them, *The Discovery of America by Christopher Columbus*, pays homage to the explorer, to Dalí's idol, Velázquez, and especially to Dalí's wife and muse, Gala.

The third of the trio, the Florida International Museum, housed in a former Maas Brothers department store, is not so much a museum as a 20,000-square-foot hall for hire. It has no collection of its own, relying instead on a succession of special shows—Romanov treasures, artifacts of the Incas, and a celebration of Diana, Princess of Wales.

Not to be outdone, the Tampa Museum of Art commissioned the architect Rafael Viñoly (whose convention center in Pittsburgh and concert hall in Philadelphia have won critical plaudits) to design a new building. Scheduled to open in 2006, it will have a dramatically glass-sheathed double-height grand lobby facing out toward the Hillsborough River.

But to get to the best museum in the region, perhaps the best in Florida, you have to drive south across the thrilling Sunshine Skyway Bridge spanning the mouth of Tampa Bay. Opened in 1987 (and patterned after the much shorter Brotonne Bridge across the Seine near Rouen), it is supported by a single central web of cables, not two parallel sets, and they are painted bright yellow. Many consider it the most impressive span built in this country since the Golden Gate Bridge.

Five or six miles south of it you come to Sarasota, and the John and Mable Ringling Museum of Art, part of a bayfront cluster of Italianate buildings, with gleaming white rooftop statues. Inside the spectacle continues. A circus man, Ringling had little taste for understatement. He sought to stun with art as he stunned under the Big Top, so he bought pictures by Baroque masters like Rubens and Pietro da Cortona during the 1920s and 1930s when their exuberance was out of fashion. Today they anchor a collection of rare originality, recently rehung to excellent effect despite a tight financial situation. It ranges from Guercino and Titian to Piero di Cosimo's *Building of a Palace* and an early, full-length Velázquez portrait of Philip IV. The high point, almost certainly, is the set of four immense tapestry cartoons by Rubens, purchased in 1926 from the Duke of Westminster and exhibited in a 40-foot-high gallery. A circus museum is also part of the Ringling complex.

Sarasota is a busy performing arts center. Every February and March its opera company stages four productions, and it does not confine itself to warhorses. Under Victor DeRenzi, its longtime artistic director and principal conductor, it mounted *May Night*, a little-known folkloric piece by Rimsky-Korsakov, based on a Gogol story, in 1999, and another rarity, *Il Corsaro*, as part of its continuing Verdi cycle in 2004. Astonishingly for a city of only 55,000, Sarasota supports an Equity theater company with two theaters, associated with a drama school. Shaw, Wilder, Sheridan, Coward, Odets, Sherwood, Alfred Uhry, Neil Simon, Herb Gardiner, and Steve Martin have been among the recent offerings at the Asolo Theater, thanks to Howard J. Millman, the longtime producing artistic director.

Each June the city stages a well-regarded chamber music festival, and all year long the Van Wezel Performing Arts Hall, painted an unsettling shade of purple, presents a parade of visiting musicians. The Czech Philharmonic, the Guarneri String Quartet, Willie Nelson, Bobby Short, Bernadette Peters, and big Broadway musicals have all paid calls. In fact the whole area is on a performing arts roll—with Ruth Eckerd Hall in Clearwater, the Mahaffey Theater in St. Petersburg, and the huge Tampa Bay Performing Arts Center in Tampa full to overflowing with music and drama. On a single night not long ago the local music fan could hear Gordon Lightfoot, Tony Bennett, the Rolling Stones, or the Vienna Boys' Choir. And that is without reckoning with the Florida Orchestra, which plays a seven-month season in several halls under the music directorship of Stefan Sanderling, a promising young German conductor. The orchestra administers to the Bay the prescribed monthly doses of Mozart, Mahler, and Beethoven, but it has also made time for works by Hovhaness, Korngold, Shostakovich, Shulamit Ran, and William Schuman.

In many ways bigger has proved to be better for Tampa Bay. Start with the Tampa airport, which must be the nation's best. Opened in 1972, its main terminal is linked to four remote buildings housing the gates by fast automated trains that run above ground, up in the sunshine, not buried in some dingy tunnel. Bright, close in, with plenty of elevators, escalators, and easily understood signs, TPA ought to be cloned nationwide.

Along with the climate—the sun is said to shine 361 days a year—the airport has helped to attract all kinds of businesses, including the Home Shopping Network, Verizon, and back-office operations for big financial institutions, as well as biotechnology and other high-technology companies. ("High tech in the mangroves," a local booster calls them.) It has also brought tourists, who head west to fifty miles of beaches along the Gulf of Mexico and east to Busch Gardens, the popular offshoot of the local Budweiser brewery.

You can take your wild animals in Tampa with or without roller coasters. For the purist there is the Lowry Park Zoo, where you can see a Sumatran tiger, a rare Florida panther, and a rarer Indian rhinoceros. It also specializes in the rehabilitation of the manatee, an endangered species of huge, cowlike marine creatures. Only 2,500 remain in the wild.

Busch Gardens is bigger and brassier. It has four roller coasters, which flip and plunge and twist and climb until you think you've left your insides in another time zone, and bumper cars called Ubanga-Banga. (Geddit?) Its theme is Africa, more or less, but no one is too rigorous about it, so you will see koalas from Australia and elephants from India and flamingos from Chile. The "Nairobi" train station looks like South Africa, not Kenya, and the dolphin show inexplicably takes place in a mock-up of landlocked Timbuktu. But I doubt there are many places on this continent to rival the hundreds of antelopes and other animals that roam more or less freely on Busch Gardens' realistic simulation of the Serengeti Plain. Many are rarities seldom encountered in Africa: greater kudus and blesboks, elands and addaxes, sable antelopes and magnificent roan antelopes, bred at the park. Hokey the rides may be, but the young staff members care a lot about the animals.

A good sequel is the growing Florida Aquarium in downtown Tampa, an $84 million shell-shaped extravaganza in green glass whose tanks contain exhibits of aquatic life on Florida's coral reefs, in its oceanic depths and in its streams and mangrove swamps—everything from menacing sharks to playful river otters to darting rainbow parrotfish. Flora, not fauna, is the lure at Sarasota's Marie Selby Gardens, known for its orchids.

Not everyone is crazy about Tampa Bay's coming of age. St. Petersburg, in particular, worries about losing its identity. Politicians and taxpayers there complain that out-of-town visitors often mistakenly assume they are in Tampa, like the reporters who came for the vice presidential debate in 1996 and the sportswriters who come to cover the Tampa Bay Devil Rays baseball team at the slope-domed Tropicana Field in St. Petersburg.

Tampa has also lost something of value in the rush toward tomorrow. The mystery writer John D. MacDonald wrote about it in his Travis McGee novel *Bright Orange for the Shroud*. "They've opened up the center of the city into a more spacious characterlessness," he complained, "and more and more they are converting Ybor City into fake New Orleans." The gloriously grumpy MacDonald somewhat overstated the case. If the postmodern skyscrapers of downtown Tampa lack architectural distinction, it is less sterile than many late-blooming cities, and the bankers and lawyers have to work somewhere, don't they? But Ybor City, where Hispanic tobacco workers and Italian immigrants once lived, has indeed turned into an ersatz French Quarter, loaded with wrought-iron balconies and chockablock with bars. On far too many Friday and Saturday nights, the young and the rowdy own it.

If Tampa has lost most of its cigar factories, it has kept some of its authentic Latin flavor. To taste that, visit La Teresita at

3248 West Columbus Drive, a long-serving Cuban American restaurant with green oilcloth on the tables, nestled amid shabby stores selling guava turnovers and Cuban sandwiches, not far from the airport. Go for Sunday lunch if you can, eat the Capdevila family's wonderful black beans and yellow rice, with vinegary roast pork on the side, and drink a café con leche. (I did; it cost $8.81 with tax and tip.) The clientele is young and old, rich and poor, Anglo and Latin. Rednecks mingle with blue rinses; girls in communion dresses joke with sisters wearing skimpy crop-tops.

Nor has St. Petersburg (named by a pioneer developer for his Russian hometown) lost its Midwestern blandness. It remains a low-key place, represented by politicians like C. W. Bill Young, chairman of the all-powerful House Appropriations Committee, who has been the congressman from Florida's 10th District since 1970—a conservative, of course, but not the kind who goes out of his way to punch you in the eye.

If you linger a while in the vicinity of Fourth Avenue North and Fifth Street, you will see institutions that cater to the city's geriatric population: the St. Petersburg Chess Club; the St. Petersburg Lawn Bowling Club, founded in 1926; and the proudly self-proclaimed "World's Largest Shuffleboard and Duplicate Bridge Club," on the shore of Mirror Lake.

WHERE TO STAY

Don CeSar Beach Resort, 3400 Gulf Boulevard, St. Pete Beach, (727) 360-1881. Discerningly restored a few years ago, this peachy-pink neo-Moorish palace, built in 1928, offers a fine beach, a spa, tennis courts, two pools, superlative fishing, and 232 handsome guest rooms. If Scott and Zelda Fitzgerald stayed there, as everyone says, they knew the locale as St. Petersburg Beach; local lawmakers, no poets, later clipped off two syllables in the interest of brevity.

Grand Hyatt Tampa Bay, 2900 Bay Port Drive, Tampa, (813) 874-1234. Facing Tampa Bay, surrounded by flora and fountains, this crisply up-to-date fourteen-story, four-hundred-room hotel stands a head taller than the average Hyatt. Oystercatchers, named after a bivalve-loving local bird, serves tasty regional seafood.

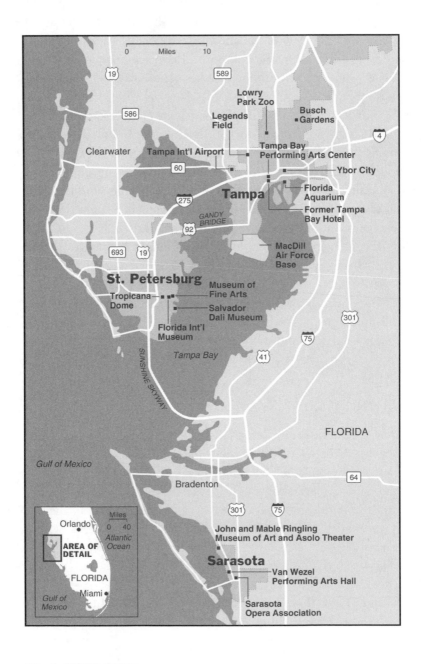

Renaissance Vinoy Resort, 501 Fifth Avenue NE, St. Petersburg, (727) 894-1000. On the bayfront downtown, the Vinoy is another reborn 1920s relic—flamingo pink on the outside, ornate inside, with stenciled pecky cypress beams in the lobby. Its 360 luxury rooms, plus pools, tennis courts, steam bath, and croquet lawn, attract the affluent.

Ritz-Carlton, 1111 Ritz-Carlton Drive, Sarasota, (941) 309-2000. This downtown high-rise caused a major stir in sedate Sarasota when it opened in 2001, and seasoned Ritz clients will not be disappointed by its wood-paneled bar and its marble-clad bathrooms. But it's a ten-minute drive to the hotel's beach club on Lido Key across Sarasota Bay. Devotees of sugar sand might prefer the *Resort at Longboat Key Club*, 301 Gulf of Mexico Drive, Longboat Key, (941) 383-8821, right on the Gulf of Mexico. Across Sarasota Bay from Ringlingville, it emphasizes sports, with forty-five championship golf holes and thirty-eight top-flight tennis courts.

WHERE TO EAT

Beach Bistro, 6600 Gulf Drive, Holmes Beach, Anna Maria Island, (941) 778-6444. Four good reasons to visit this out-of-the-way spot midway between Tampa and Sarasota: (1) remarkable smoked salmon, imported weekly from J. Willy Krauch, an artisanal smoker in Tangier, Nova Scotia; (2) perfectly cooked grouper, the local fish of choice; (3) a bountiful wine list, including Australia's prized Grange and five vintages of Château Pichon-Longueville; (4) fabulous Gulf sunsets. As elsewhere in this area, there is a regrettable tendency to litter the plate with superfluous garnishes.

Bern's, 1208 South Howard Avenue, Tampa, (813) 251-2421. Bern Laxer, the founder of this bunkerlike steakhouse, died in 2002. His son, David, has cut the encyclopedic wine list from 2,500 pages to 179 (with Château Latour back to 1920). He has also toned down the bordello decor, bought new china and cutlery, and added new starters, new sides, new sauces, and much more fish. The steaks remain stupendous.

Mise en Place, 442 West Kennedy Boulevard, Tampa, (813) 254-5373. Marty Blitz pioneered modern American cooking in the region, and his restaurant remains a local leader. Tasty house-made charcuterie epitomizes the ambition and technical savvy of the kitchen, and I admired the mustard-crusted rack of lamb, served on a hillock of cheddar grits and moistened with bourbon shallot demi-glace. The room is suave, service less so.

SideBern's, 2208 West Morrison Avenue, Tampa, (813) 258-2233. Bern's still packs them in, but the sizzle has shifted to SideBern's, its young sibling. There Jeannie Pierola, a gifted chef of eclectic bent, sets off fireworks with Westernized dim sum, like duck buns with vinegar syrup and shellfish dumplings with tamarind butter; seared red snapper from the Gulf with harissa, and (homage to the old guard) a dynamic duet of short ribs and hanger steak.

Ted Peters Smoked Fish, 1350 Pasadena Avenue South, St. Petersburg (727) 381-7931. This is the place, a local foodie told me, that he'd take Calvin Trillin to if he ever came to St. Petersburg. Since 1950, not long after the founder pulled into town from Olean, New York, this roadside shack has dished up definitive versions of local delicacies like smoked mackerel and gray mullet and a tangy fish spread that tastes great on saltines.

Fred's, 1917 South Osprey Avenue, Sarasota, (941) 364-5811. A welcoming bistro in Southside Village, whose neighbors include sophisticated wine and food shops, Fred's serves comfort food (chicken potpie with a puffed crust) and more innovative but never pretentious plates like crisp sea bass in a subtle smoked-tomato broth. Chris Sherman of the St. Pete *Times* vouches for the espresso flan. Noisy as a brass band on weekends.

⫸ MIAMI

South Florida's sprawling, polyglot metropolis, so familiar to us all as the backdrop for *Miami Vice*, for the bitter tug-of-war over the Cuban lad Elián González, and for numberless photo shoots of bikini-clad models, is rapidly developing into a major arts center. In fact, it may already have the richest cultural life of any city in the Southeast. Just by itself, the southern end of Miami Beach has the largest assemblage of Art Deco buildings in the country, the home auditorium of a ballet company that upholds the Balanchine tradition as well as any, and the most comprehensive collection of early modern design in the world.

All over Miami-Dade County—in Miami, North Miami, Miami Beach, Coconut Grove, and places betwixt and between—there are attractions for the mind as well as the senses. Big-time contemporary art collectors are filling huge spaces with their private holdings. Don and Mera Rubell, for example, house six thousand edgy works, including Cindy Shermans, Keith Harings, and David Salles, in an old Drug Enforcement Administration warehouse in the seedy Wynwood section of Miami. Art Basel Miami Beach has become one of the country's liveliest annual art shows. Other ambitious new projects are afoot, too, including a $334 million performing arts center, the largest built in this country since the Kennedy Center in Washington. Its backers maintain that it "will transform Miami into the cultural capital of the Americas," no less.

That would be quite a transformation. *Baywatch* blondes, gangsters, Eurotrash, drag queens, nouveau riche extravagance, fleets of white stretch limos, mindless hours of sun worship, and the murder of Gianni Versace have combined to give Miami an unenviable reputation. The hanging chads in the dubious election of 2000 didn't help much, either. Many people would swear that a sentence containing the words "art" and "Miami" must be a typographical error.

The comedian Lenny Bruce once derided South Florida as the place where neon comes to retire. Norman Van Aken, the area's most gifted chef, redresses the balance with a more upbeat epigrammatic comment. "Miami," he says, "is where the future comes for tryouts." Hip, carefree and crowded with lithe, lovely, fashionable people, if also cursed with widespread poverty, Miami rocks to a Hispano-Caribbean beat, with ample supplies left over for export to the rest of the country. This is Gloria Estefan's town, at least part of the time, and Ricky Martin's and J.Lo's and Enrique Iglesias's. Foreign-born, largely Latin-born residents account for a majority of the county's total population of 2.3 million people—51.4 percent, the largest such proportion of any county in the United States.

Many Latin American immigrants move quickly into Miami's middle class and even into the ranks of the wealthy, but not all of them make it. Miami has drug problems, racial tensions, and a higher percentage of poor people than any other American city of 250,000 or more.

Still, the city has become a Caribbean transportation, banking, and commerce hub, and wealthy businessmen from Venezuela, Colombia, and elsewhere maintain Miami homes, shuttling in and out. A long-standing local joke says that Miami is no longer the southernmost city in the United States but the northernmost city in Latin America.

Calle Ocho, Eighth Street, the bustling main street of Little Havana, is the heartland of Hispanic Miami. At the corner of Southwest Thirteenth Avenue stands a stark memorial to those killed in the bungled Bay of Pigs landings, marked with an eternal flame and a Spanish inscription recalling the fiasco of April 17, 1961. Miami's last two mayors have both been Cuban Americans—Joe Carollo, who noisily supported Elián González's local relatives in their fight against sending him back to Cuba, as Washington wanted, and Manny Diaz, a lawyer who argued their case in court.

The agora of the city's (and nation's) Cuban American community is a mirrored barn of a restaurant called the Versailles, where the politicos and almost everyone else who matters season their gossip with arroz con pollo and rocket-fuel shots of café cortado. After midnight, the scene shifts to the Latin American Cafeteria, with an excited crowd joyously gesturing, jabbering, and chowing down. It is the mecca for lovers of the delectable grilled Cubano sandwich, stuffed with pork, ham, and cheese.

But the city's Venezuelans congregate in Doral, a suburb, and one seven-block strip of Collins Avenue in Miami Beach, formerly the home of Jewish retirees, has been revitalized with businesses representing a half dozen South American countries, including a Brazilian martial arts studio, a Peruvian seafood restaurant, and an Argentine grocery.

Miami is a new city peopled almost entirely by men and women who were born elsewhere. Many are refugees from icy Northern winters; many more are refugees from politically or economically repressed parts of the Caribbean—mainly from Cuba and other Spanish-speaking countries, of course, but also boat people from Haiti, which means that Creole is widely spoken. Many of these heterogeneous newcomers are trying hard to grow together ethnically and politically, commercially and culturally. "You could have the same demographics in New York or Los Angeles, and it wouldn't mix," said Bonnie Clearwater, director of the ambitious Museum of Contemporary Art in North Miami, who has lived in all three cities. "But here, for some reason, it does."

To see how life used to be lived in the old Miami, you could do worse than begin at Vizcaya, the lavish winter home of James Deering, an International Harvester tycoon who between 1914 and 1916 caused there to arise on the steamy shores of Biscayne Bay a grand faux-Renaissance villa, complete with pipe organ. Like William Randolph Hearst, Deering plundered Europe for his New World showplace, taking a gate from a Pisani palace and a tinted plaster ceiling from the Rossi Palace, both in Venice. He clearly liked Venice a lot: his stone breakwater is shaped like a Venetian barge with obelisks perched upon it, and Venetian-style striped dock poles rise from the water near the landing.

Another dreamer, George Merrick, built Coral Gables

a decade later. He called it "The City Beautiful," a slogan that seems less far-fetched, even now, than most developers' coinages. The centerpiece is the romantic, Mediterranean-style Biltmore Hotel, newly restored and worth a visit even if you do not stay there; all around it, on streets mostly named for Spanish cities, are tile-roofed bungalows shaded by fig trees and live oaks. Coral Gables has its allusion to Venice, too: an enormous public swimming hole, the Venetian Pool, cut from a quarry and festooned with ferns, palms, and waterfalls.

The Art Deco district of South Beach has not only been preserved but also turned into the city's symbol. More than 650 buildings from the 1930s, centered on Ocean Drive, have been restored, many as hotels, and painted butterscotch, turquoise, mint green, coral, and teal. (Teal is Miami's color, whether we are talking about sport coats, the uniforms of the football Dolphins and the baseball Marlins, or the signs identifying towaway zones.) Hot-hot-hot for a time, then so very, very over, South Beach has regained its luster. The boldface names and wannabes are back. Clubs like Mynt, Crobar, and Rok Bar, cafés like Nexxt, and an endless parade of throwaway fashion boutiques pull in the big crowds.

If you're a day bird instead of a night owl, buy a guidebook or join a tour at the Art Deco Welcome Center at 1001 Ocean Drive. Among the choicest and best-restored buildings are the blue-and-white Park Central Hotel, at 640 Ocean Drive, by the prolific Henry Hohauser; the Clevelander, at 1020 Ocean, with a flying-saucer sculpture; and the Leslie, at 1244, lemon yellow with handsome fluted columns. The Cardozo, a fine Streamline Moderne building at 1300 Ocean, was re-renovated in 2001. Versace lived at 1114 Ocean, an atypical Mediterranean-style palace, and expired on its steps in July 1997. As you walk, notice the high jinks on the beach opposite: an architect manqué building a minutely detailed sand castle, complete with turrets and cannon; improbably fit men and women Rollerblading; beefcakes doing push-ups. Days, it's all about sand and sunblock.

The local tradition of extravagant architecture was perpetuated in the postwar years by Morris Lapidus, whose splashy, theatrical buildings, like the Hotel Fontainebleau (1954), outraged the critics of the day but found favor with their successors half a century later. Lapidus himself never wavered, entitling his memoirs *Too Much Is Not Enough*. He proudly called the Fontainebleau, whose interiors were painted in twenty-seven colors, "the world's most pretentious hotel," adding guilelessly, "I wanted people to walk in and drop dead."

Today the torch is carried by Arquitectonica, a Miami-based firm with a worldwide practice. Three condominiums on Brickell Avenue near downtown Miami—the Palace at 1541, the Imperial at 1627, and the Atlantis at 2025, with a red triangle on the roof—show the exuberant style to the best advantage: bright colors, skillful massing, and always some little geometrical trademark. In Miami Beach, the firm has built an award-winning parking garage at Sixth and Collins, with the openings between levels cleverly masked with bushes and vines that cut down on air pollution (and on the visual kind as well).

There is something slightly absurd about walking out of the brilliant sunlight of South Beach into the Wolfsonian collection a couple of blocks inland. Sadly, few people try to jump the cultural hurdle that divides the two; the Wolfsonian, whose name exemplifies a longing by the principal donor, Mitchell Wolfson Jr., to share the glory of Washington's Smithsonian, is too often empty. What a mistake that is! You begin the tour of this converted storage warehouse with the scintillating frontispiece from a theater in Norristown, Pennsylvania, and continue through items selected from a collection of 70,000 pieces. Modernist icons like Christopher Dresser and Josef Hoffmann and Victor Horta are represented, but so are obscure designers of household objects like radios and ephemera like posters, bond certificates, and newspaper ads.

Arata Isozaki, the Japanese mannerist who designed the Museum of Contemporary Art in Los Angeles in 1986, gave the Bass Art Museum in Miami Beach 21,000 square feet of additional space in 2002—a new wing of pure white rectangles raised on columns in a reflecting pool. Its eclectic permanent collection spans five centuries, from Botticelli's *Coronation of the Virgin with Saints* through noteworthy tapestries to modern design. The Bass forms one element in a new Miami Beach Cultural Park, near the oceanfront, along with a spectacular rehearsal facility for the local ballet company that has glass-walled, street-level studios (designed by Arquitectonica) and a regional library (by Robert A. M. Stern).

Bonnie Clearwater's Museum of Contemporary Art is housed in another standout local building, a simple, flexible structure by Charles Gwathmey, composed of cubes and cylinders. It shows works by rising stars around the world, recently including the young Frenchman Jean-Michel Othoniel (who designed an acclaimed new kiosk for the Palais Royal Métro station as a millennium project) and Laura Owens, a versatile Los Angeles painter and photographer.

The Miami City Ballet, with forty-eight full-time dancers and a 2005 budget of about $10 million, stages most of its performances at the Jackie Gleason Theater in Miami Beach. (The people in charge of nomenclature on the beach seem to be stuck in the 1960s; Arthur Godfrey Road crosses the island a few blocks to the north.) Assembled and trained by Edward Villella, who was one of George Balanchine's best dancers, the troupe is well-drilled, powerful, and utterly devoted to the master's vigorous neoclassical style. Many in New York long for such commitment from the New York City Ballet.

Down the street from Villella's Miami Beach headquarters, the New World Symphony, a training orchestra that draws promising musicians from around the world, performs regularly under the baton of the redoubtable Michael Tilson Thomas. The organization has commissioned Frank Gehry to design a new hall and broadcast center around the corner, to be called Soundspace. And across the water the Coconut Grove Playhouse, one of the nation's oldest regional theaters, founded in 1926, offers performances by marquee names like Lucy Arnaz and Theodore Bikel.

Both the ballet and the symphony are scheduled to move in 2006 into the Performing Arts Center of Greater Miami, designed by Cesar Pelli, in the heart of downtown Miami. It will include a 2,200-seat concert hall, a 2,480-seat ballet and opera house, and a small studio theater. (Another planned tenant, the Florida Philharmonic, collapsed in May 2003 and auctioned off its assets in 2004 after several attempts at reorganization foundered.) The city is counting heavily on the project to help breathe new life into a blighted and withering urban core. Another renewal project envisions the redevelopment of an abandoned twenty-nine-acre downtown plot to provide new homes for the Miami Museum of Science and the fledgling Miami Art Museum, specializing in art created since 1940, mainly in the Western Hemisphere, which has yet to celebrate its tenth birthday.

The main entrance to the Everglades National Park, a wonderland of saw grass prairies and mangroves that is fighting for its survival, lies only thirty-eight miles from downtown Miami. It can be explored on foot, by bicycle, by boat, and by tram.

Closer in, we come to a special, secret place. It is called the Kampong, and it was the home for decades of Dr. David Fairchild, the plant explorer who over four decades of work for the U.S. Department of Agriculture (1889–1928) brought blood oranges and cashews and durum wheat to North America. Unlike the public garden named for Fairchild, this one offers tours only by appointment, which is its joy (no crowds) and its curse (a chronic lack of money). The Kampong is planted with tropical fruit trees ranging from the key lime to the pomelo. On some trees, Larry Schokman, the director of horticulture, has made grafts that yield blossoms two or three times a year. He showed us one hybrid with one parent from Ghana and the other from Brazil.

Fairchild Tropical Gardens, not very far away, were heavily damaged in the hurricane of 1992. But the Kampong survived almost intact, with an amazing *Ficus bengalensis* at the entrance, 351 feet around, roots dangling in the air, and a long vista down to the sea, interrupted by a haunting lagoon.

WHERE TO STAY

Biltmore, 1200 Anastasia Avenue, Coral Gables, (305) 445-1926. A magnificently restored 1926 landmark, with a tower patterned after the Giralda in Seville, a two-story lobby with a stunning painted ceiling, a 17,000-square-foot swimming pool, a top drawer restaurant with a remarkable wine list, and comfortable rooms at relatively sane prices.

Delano, 1685 Collins Avenue, at Seventeenth Street, Miami Beach, (305) 672-2000, the hottest spot on South Beach, is Ian

Schrager's ethereal all-white fantasy, with a forest of unadorned columns in the airy lobby echoed by a forest of palms outside. Philippe Starck's bathrooms are handsome but not very practical. Giddy clientele, surreal pool.

Four Seasons, 1435 Brickell Avenue, (305) 358-3535. The latest word in downtown Miami, this stylish retreat shares its seventy-

story tower with condominiums. Most of the 221 guest rooms have window seats with panoramic views over Biscayne Bay, and there's lots of fun in the sun at three swimming pools. The spa covers 45,000 square feet, about the same area as a football field.

Mandarin Oriental, 500 Brickell Key Drive, (305) 913-8288. The first of the new luxury hotels in Miami, located on a residential island near downtown, the Mandarin was designed to appeal to the swarms of business travelers arriving from points south. With lavish bathrooms and knockout views, it appeals to tourists, too. Sleek surfaces and subtle lighting give the place a cool, unmistakably twenty-first-century feeling.

Ritz-Carlton South Beach, 1 Lincoln Road, Miami Beach, (786) 276-4000. "Directly on the ocean," as the old ads said, and just a few steps from the Lincoln Road mall. This, the third Ritz in the Miami area, was once the DiLido Hotel, an early Lapidus design; $20 million later, it is a cosmopolitan mini-resort with 375 rooms that resemble staterooms on a yacht. Artworks by Miró, Matta, and others are scattered throughout.

WHERE TO EAT

Azul, at the Mandarin Oriental, (305) 913-8254. There is no gainsaying the beauty of this place, with sparkling streams of water in the foyer and shellfish tucked into shining beds of ice inside. There is no doubt about the talent of Chef Michelle Bernstein, a onetime ballerina. But her complex Latino-Eurasian cooking walks a high wire; mostly it stays on (quail with pumpkin tempura, snapper with nuoc mam, mango slivers, and kim chee), but sometimes it falls off (chocolate-mole-painted foie gras with Italian cherries).

Blue Door, at the Delano, (305) 674-6400, stages South Beach follies, but it's quite a remarkable restaurant, too, especially when Claude Troisgros, the consultant chef, is there to cook his sautéed foie gras with starfruit and his jumbo ravioli filled with taro-root mousseline, nestling in a sea of wild-mushroom foam. Scion of the three-star Troisgros clan of Roanne, France, he once ran CT in Manhattan and now lives and cooks in Rio.

Joe's Stone Crab, 11 Washington Street, Miami Beach, (305) 673-0365, has been there forever—well, eighty-five years. It still serves delicious hash browns, tasty key lime pie (though the chief piemaker recently died), and the world's best stone-crab claws, with unforgettably sweet meat to dip into creamy mustard sauce. The shells, Damon Runyon once wrote, are "harder than a landlord's heart." Open mid-October to mid-May only.

Norman's, 21 Almeria Avenue, Coral Gables, (305) 446-6767. Norman Van Aken helped to create New World cuisine, an amalgam of France, Florida, and Latin America. At Norman's, perhaps Florida's best restaurant, he cooks dishes that sound hideously complicated but taste perfectly integrated, like rum-and-pepper-painted grouper with mango and habanero chili sauce. Curaçao-seared foie gras with French toast works, too.

Pacific Time, 915 Lincoln Road, Miami Beach, (305) 534-5979. Nothing could be less likely a few blocks from the Atlantic than a restaurant called Pacific Time. But there it is, and Jonathan Eismann continues to turn out mouthwatering Pacific Rim dishes. A few favorites: crab wontons; black grouper in delicate green curry with coconut broth; and a pair of winning sides, baby bok choy and sweet potato tempura puffs.

➤ NEW ORLEANS

Folks have their own way of doing things in the Big Easy. They always have. They work and play at their own languid pace, which led Tennessee Williams, a sometime resident, to rhapsodize about "those long rainy afternoons in New Orleans, when an hour isn't just an hour but a little piece of eternity dropped into your hands, and who knows what to do with it?"

They have their own music—not only jazz, which was more or less invented in Storyville, the red-light district long since replaced by a scruffy, drug-plagued housing project, but also zydeco, the stomping sound from the Cajun settlements west of NOLA, and the blues, in whose evolution New Orleans, along with other Mississippi Delta towns, played a big part.

They have their own drinks, seldom found elsewhere— sazeracs at the Fairmont, an old Huey Long haunt, sugary hurricanes at Pat O'Brien's on Bourbon Street, and Barq's root beer, which has lately become a national brand. They have their own sandwiches, like muffulettas and po' boys, their own sauces, like rémoulade and ravigote, derived from but not really that similar to the French originals, and idiosyncratic dishes like étouffées, which are seafood stews. They drink coffee heavily laced with chicory and eat sugared beignets with it rather than doughnuts.

They have their own accent, which at its ripest sounds a little bit like Brooklyn's and a lot like Savannah's; as rendered by its inhabitants, the name of their city is "New AWL-yuns."

They have their own legal system. Like all of Louisiana and unlike the other forty-nine states, they operate under the Napoleonic Code, a legacy from the days when the city was

Nouvelle Orléans, the pride of French North America. For the same reason, they live in parishes, not in counties.

They have their own way of burying the dead. Because the city was built on low-lying land, coffins placed underground had a nasty habit of bobbing to the surface during floods. So New Orleans cemeteries are filled with row after row of above ground mausoleums. "Cities of the Dead," these are called—every bit as spooky in the moonlight as in Anne Rice's novels.

They have their own odd place names. The streets that cross St. Charles Avenue (and its tram line) at the downtown end are named for Greek muses—Terpischore, Erato, Clio, and Euterpe. In the French Quarter every first-time visitor encounters and inevitably mispronounces Chartres Street (properly "Charters") and Burgundy ("Burr-GUN-dee"). You can still drive down Elysian Fields Avenue, yet another echo of New France, but unhappily, the streetcars no longer run to Desire.

Right from the start, New Orleans has been French, Spanish, black, and Catholic, standing apart from the Protestant, Anglo-Saxon American norm. Founded by Jean-Baptiste Le Moyne in 1718 on a bend in the Mississippi (hence the "Crescent City"), ruled by Spain and by France, it came under American control with the Louisiana Purchase of 1803. Its ways were already set. This is a Caribbean city, an exuberant, semitropical city, perhaps the most hedonistic city in the United States. You see more orgies (and more nuns) in New Orleans than anywhere else in the nation. Even more than Miami, it looks south, toward the volatility of Latin America.

A long time ago, that paragon among journalists A. J. Liebling described New Orleans as a cross between Port-au-Prince, Haiti, and Paterson, New Jersey. It reminds me of Marseille, with a culture marked by crime, corruption, humidity, poverty, and poor education on one hand, and a love of good food, good drink, and good times on the other. Its joie de vivre is well-nigh inexhaustible, and for all its raffishness and fine distinctions of class and caste, its people have an inborn sweetness that extends from Garden District matrons to garage mechanics.

From time to time New Orleans mayors have struggled against corruption. One who did so was an aristocrat named deLesseps S. Morrison Jr., known as "Chep," who held office during the 1950s. Later Ernest Morial and his son Marc had a go, and a new crusade has been launched by C. Ray Nagin, the first businessman mayor, who defeated Richard J. Pennington, the police superintendent, in 2003. Nagin told supporters on election night, "I don't have a Superman shirt under my suit," and graft remains endemic. In truth, the city seems to prefer its politics with a dash of Tabasco. There was always plenty of backing in New Orleans for Edwin W. Edwards, the smooth-talking Cajun governor of Louisiana who boasted that he would never be beaten unless he was "found in bed with a live boy or a dead girl." But after one trial that ended in a hung jury and another that produced an acquittal, Edwards was convicted of racketeering, conspiracy, and extortion in May 2000, and sentenced to ten years in jail.

Meanwhile, poverty persists, cheek by jowl with wealth, much of it inherited. A block or two from mansions with palm-shaded gardens stand crude unpainted bungalows fronting on crumbling streets, reminiscent more of the third world than of dot-com America. In 2000, according to Census Bureau figures, 28.4 percent of New Orleanians lived below the poverty line—an improvement, if not a very large one, on the 1995 figure, which was 33.6 percent, one in three. In a city three-quarters black, most of the poor are African American. Few are Asian. The 10,000 Vietnamese who in the 1970s and 1980s settled in a climate as hot and damp as the one they fled have prospered.

Although New Orleans ranks thirty-fifth among metropolitan areas in the United States, with a population of 1.35 million, the city itself is rather small, with 485,000 people. It is a very, very violent place. The FBI Uniform Crime Report for 2002 said that New Orleans had 258 murders that year, a rate of 53.3 per 100,000, compared with 43.5 for Detroit and 46.2 for Washington, D.C., often called the nation's homicide capital. (The rate for the country as a whole was 5.6.) While he still headed the police force, Richard Pennington, who is now police chief in Atlanta, told me that most of New Orleans' violent crime takes place in or around public housing and other poor neighborhoods. "We don't have very many black people preying on white tourists or on white residents," he insisted.

Once the South's largest city, the nation's fifth largest in

1860, New Orleans fell behind Houston in 1950 and has slipped further in the half century since. Although it has its share of new skyscrapers, it has been overtaken by Atlanta and Nashville and Charlotte, the economic capitals of the New South. The days when cotton was king have long since passed, and now the oil boom has expired as well. Most local banks are now branches of bigger banks in bigger cities. "Tourism has become not only the leading industry but the only industry," said Paul Fabry, the retired head of the local World Trade Center. "We are a colonial economy. We are left with low-paying jobs, mostly—taxi drivers, waiters, bellmen. The port? Well, the port is mostly about transferring bulk commodities from ships to barges and from barges to ships. We make about as much money from the port these days as the mailman does from the $500 check in his sack."

Fabry also detects reluctance on the part of able young people, black as well as white, to remain here. Still, for every Walter Isaacson, who moved north and became the editor of *Time* magazine, others move south, attracted by the climate, the cheap, easy living, and the good food. In the old days, writers like Tennessee Williams, William Faulkner, and Sherwood Anderson spent time in New Orleans. Anne Kearney, a prominent chef, arrived on vacation in 1991, just before Mardi Gras, "saw that the trees were green," and stayed for years.

Eating is a New Orleans obsession; the city has more overweight people for its size than any in America. This is where brunch was invented, by a certain Mme. Begue, who called it second breakfast. (One apparently wasn't enough for her clients.) Oysters Rockefeller were first served at Antoine's and bananas Foster were created at Brennan's, where you can still order them as the crowning glory to a modest breakfast of baked apple followed by a crawfish omelet.

Friends, meeting in the street, exchange thoughts about where to find the best red beans and rice on Monday, when that homely favorite is traditionally eaten. They go to Casamento's for oyster loaves, which are baguettes hollowed out and filled with fried oysters. To the Central Grocery for muffulettas, which are sandwiches of Italian cold cuts, cheese, and crushed olives on round rolls. To Felix's, where oysters are opened before your eyes and placed on a broad marble bar for your pleasure, innocent of plate. To the Camellia Grill, a glorified diner housed in a miniature Tara, for pecan-studded waffles in the morning and cheeseburgers at midnight. To Zachary's or Dooky Chase for gumbo. To the Café du Monde, day or night, for another coffee.

And they know why they eat what they do. I asked Paul C. P. McIlhenny, whose family firm has made Tabasco for generations, why he and his fellow townsmen liked chicory in their coffee. We were having a leisurely lunch at Galatoire's, the most traditional of all New Orleans restaurants, where the waiters sometimes call their customers, male or female, "cher" or "chère," for "dear." The chicory habit started during the Napoleonic Wars, he explained after a mouthful of oysters en brochette. The British blockaded French ports, so Parisians made do with the roasted and ground roots of endive, or chicorée in French. When the war ended, almost two centuries ago, the French went back to the real thing. "Here in New Orleans, we never got the message," he said.

"For us heritage is not something you see in the rearview mirror," commented Quint Davis, the producer and director of the annual Jazzfest. "It also shines brightly through the windshield." A big part of that heritage, of course, is Carnival, the explosion of parties, balls, and parades that swirls through New Orleans just before Lent, ending on Fat Tuesday, the day before the lean days begin. The rhinestones, tulle, and masks of Mardi Gras cost an immense amount of money—hundreds of thousands of dollars to stage one ball among dozens—and it is all paid for by private citizens, from all classes and races, and by the city. No corporate subsidies.

Originally the domain of the Creole upper crust, descended from the French and Spanish settlers, Mardi Gras has become everyone's property while remaining a tightly orchestrated social ritual. For the grandees, having one's daughter named queen of one of the "krewes," or clubs, ranks among life's great milestones. For simpler folk, the goal is green, gold, and purple fun. One krewe, Babylon, is made up mostly of physicians. Zulu is mostly black. Iris is for women only. Rex is the grandest. The king of Rex is automatically king of Carnival, and for more than a century he has been a business or civic leader who belonged to the old-guard Boston Club.

If you're not in New Orleans at showtime, you can get a sense of the thing at the Mardi Gras museum housed in the old Presbytère—one of the historic landmarks on Jackson Square, along with the Cabildo, the Pontalba Apartments, and St. Louis Cathedral, the oldest church in Louisiana, parts of which date to the 1720s. Recent parades are shown on videotape. Costumes and floats from years past are on display, along with plastic "go-cups" (so vital for portable booze) and "throws"—cheap beads and aluminum "doubloons" that float-riders toss to the crowds in response to the cry, "Throw me something, mister!"

You can also take the city's exuberant pulse every night of the year at jazz and blues haunts like Preservation Hall and the Funky Butt and all-purpose clubs like Tipitina's and the Maple Leaf. The action centers on Bourbon Street, the only street in the quarter where neon is permitted. New Orleans has no legal closing hour, and some nightspots are still throbbing when sanitation men arrive in the dirty white light of morning to sweep debris from the gutters.

The Mardi Gras collection is part of a trend that threatens to turn New Orleans into a museum town, of all things. The Old U.S. Mint, a stern gray Greek Revival temple (1855), now houses the Louisiana State Museum's small but choice collection of the Arts and Crafts pottery made early in the 1900s at Sophie Newcomb College for Women, as well as the New Orleans Jazz Collection, a must for any aficionado. There are photographs there of old jazzmen, letters testifying to the hard lives they lived, a map of Storyville "showing the principal sporting houses." Instruments, too: Johnny St. Cyr's banjo, Irving Fazola's clarinet, Bix Beiderbecke's cornet, the kazoo that Tony Spargo played in the Original Dixieland Jazz Band, and, in a place of honor, the trumpet Louis Armstrong learned on.

New Orleans has a small opera company and a symphony orchestra, the Louisiana Philharmonic, patched together more than a decade ago by the never-say-die musicians of the defunct New Orleans Symphony. But the city's most profound musical passions bubble up from the streets, into jazz and rhythm and blues, brass bands and zydeco, Cajun fiddling and gospel song. Armstrong, born a century ago, a graduate of a boys' reformatory, is the city's hero, with a park named for him. His global renown eclipsed that of any other American musician. Jelly Roll Morton, Buddy Bolden, and Sidney Bechet, also born in New Orleans, were other pioneers of jazz. Mahalia Jackson, the greatest of gospel singers, is the city's favorite musical daughter.

Why did so much music flower here? Lolis Eric Elie, a columnist for the New Orleans *Times-Picayune*, offered this: "The French in New Orleans had different conceptions about slavery than the English in the rest of the country. The French let the Africans keep their drums."

A famous battle was fought near New Orleans on January 8, 1815, when Andrew Jackson beat crack British troops under Major General Sir Edward Pakenham at Chalmette. This last battle of the War of 1812 cemented the American claim to the Mississippi and lifted the young nation's spirits. Ironically, the battle was fought, and General Pakenham died, after a peace treaty had been signed but before word of it reached the two armies.

The big military noise in New Orleans more recently has been the debut of the National D-Day Museum, situated here because of a remark Dwight D. Eisenhower made to a biographer, the late Stephen E. Ambrose, a professor at the University of New Orleans. The general asked Professor Ambrose whether he knew about Andrew Jackson Higgins, a hard-drinking, hard-driving boat builder who invented and then built thousands of flat-bottomed, ramp-fronted boats that ferried American troops onto enemy beaches in Italy, Normandy, and the Pacific. "That Higgins," Ike told Ambrose years after V-J Day, "was the man who won the war for us."

Now a new Higgins boat built by some of his 30,000 former employees sits in the atrium of a museum that attracted 175,000 people in its first three months. On the upper floors visitors can view a mockup of a D-Day glider landing, view hundreds of photographs, and listen to excerpts from thousands of interviews with survivors of the invasion.

Across the street, the Taylor Library (1888), the only building in the South by Henry Hobson Richardson, a Louisiana native, has been restored, and new buildings have been built adjacent to it. Together, they constitute the Ogden Museum of Southern Art, showing 1,500 pieces from the collection of Roger H. Ogden, a local businessman. It contains works by well-known American artists like Martin Johnson Heade and John James Audubon, among others, and some people most of us don't consider visual artists at all, like Eudora Welty, a talented photographer as well as a superior novelist.

Audubon, the great Haitian-born naturalist and painter, lived for a time in New Orleans, and he is remembered in the name of the Audubon Zoo, one of the city's real ornaments. It provides vivid glimpses of many animals, some of them rare: muscular jaguars with pale, menacing eyes; alligators cruising silently beneath slimy green waters, with only their eyes showing; tall, spindly, red-crowned cranes. Most are shown in natural settings, constrained by moats and not cages.

The zoo lies just outside the Garden District, the architectural showpiece of New Orleans—block after block of Greek Revival and Victorian houses built in the glamorous antebellum years when this was one of the richest cities in America. Especially interesting are the "Seven Sisters" on Coliseum Street, a series of elegant and fastidiously maintained houses built on speculation; the three-story house at 1410 Jackson Avenue, with forty-eight classical columns and 22,000 square feet of living space; and the grand mansion at 2343 Prytania Street. A beautiful cast-iron fence made to resemble cornstalks surrounds the Italianate house at 1448 Fourth Street.

Besides the blare of the Bourbon Street bars and the mule-drawn carriages queued at Jackson Square, the French Quarter, aka Le Vieux Carré, offers antique shops like Keil's on Royal Street, founded 1899, and Patrick Dunne's Lucullus on Chartres Street, which specializes in food-related items. But the best of the quarter lies downriver from Ursulines Avenue in the area called Faubourg Marigny. The Old Ursuline Convent, the oldest building in the Mississippi Valley, is just the kind of formal, symmetrical building you find in provincial French capitals; the nearby Gallier House, at 1118–32 Royal, has elegant cast-iron columns and a wonderful wrought-iron balcony.

Finally, the New Orleans Museum of Art merits a few hours of your time, for its glass collection, its Paul Storr silver, its three

Derains and three Mirós, and its fine Gilbert Stuart portrait of Major Peter Fort, who fought under Jackson at Chalmette. But nothing so gripped me as the Degas portrait of his sister-in-law and first cousin, Estelle Musson Degas. The French artist's mother was born in the city, and he came here to visit in 1872 and 1873, producing not only this fine picture but also the famous view of his uncle's cotton office, which now hangs at Pau, in southwestern France.

WHERE TO STAY

Audubon Cottages, 509 Dauphine Street, (504) 561-5858. You reserve these enchanting one- and two-bedroom cottages (reserve them early, if you hope to snag one) through the Hôtel

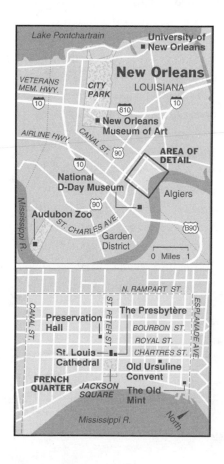

Maison de Ville, and you go there (727 Toulouse Street) to check in. Built in 1788, filled with antiques, the cottages encircle a small pool and lush gardens, set well back from the street. In the very heart of the turbulent French Quarter, all you can hear is the murmur of the wall fountains.

Ritz-Carlton, 921 Canal Street, (504) 524-1331. Along with the return of streetcars, this brave venture is designed to spark the rebirth of Canal Street, once the city's showpiece but now a seedy embarrassment. Installed in the terra-cotta building that formerly housed the Maison Blanche department store, the Ritz is hitting on all cylinders: flower-filled public spaces, ample guest rooms with superb bed linens, and service as competent and cheerful as any in America.

Soniat House, 1133 Chartres Street, (504) 522-0570. Every city covets an elegant small hotel like this one, but few cities have innkeepers like Rodney Smith, who has meticulously restored an exquisite old Creole house, built of soft pink brick, and filled it with handsome furniture from Europe and America. Goose-down pillows and Oriental rugs contribute to an air of civilized luxury. The calm, cool courtyard, an ideal setting for breakfast, has a lily pond.

Windsor Court, 300 Gravier Street, (504) 523-6000. For a decade and more, this hotel has set a standard of excellence for New Orleans: clubby, full of leather chairs and English pictures (Reynolds and Gainsborough, among others), featuring oversized rooms and suites, many with river views. Nice touches: dressing tables, televisions at the foot of beds. The Windsor Court has been named by glossy magazines as the nation's best hotel; it's good, but not quite that good.

WHERE TO EAT

August, 301 Tchoupitoulas Street, (504) 299-9777. John Besh used to run Artesia, a cottagey place across Lake Pontchartrain, where he served a miraculously perfumed kirsch sorbet. Now his wares are set out beneath glittering chandeliers in a historic Warehouse District building. He learned his trade well, in the Black Forest and Provence, and his food is better than ever. The tiny, soft-shelled buster crabs, fried to crisp perfection, are not to be missed, nor are the finfish (amberjack, sea bass, blackfish), which come in many glamorous guises. Imposing wine list.

Bayona, 440 Dauphine Street, (504) 525-4455. Susan Spicer, back in her kitchen, proposes a satisfying change from hackneyed New Orleans standards. Her understated, wide-ranging menu finds room for touches of Asia (shrimp with coriander) and Alsace (salmon and sauerkraut) as well as fresh regional ideas (pear and quail salad, duck breast with pepper jelly). The welcome is always warm in this nineteenth-century Creole cottage; try to eat in the lovely, well-lighted courtyard.

Commander's Palace, 1403 Washington Avenue, (504) 899-8221. This sky-blue mansion in the Garden District, named for Emile Commander, who built it in 1880, epitomizes the grand New Orleans style. It serves hundreds of meals a week, but the food seldom stumbles, thanks to Tory McPhail, the chef; and the service shines, thanks to Ella Brennan, doyenne of American restaurateurs. Try the explosively spicy shrimp Henican, turtle soup, and bread-pudding soufflé.

Emeril's, 800 Tchoupitoulas Street, (504) 528-9393. As those who watch Emeril Lagasse kick it up a notch on television might not suspect, he is a classicist at heart. I love the bold flavors of his andouille with homemade Worcestershire sauce and his shrimp in barbecue sauce with tiny rosemary biscuits. The banana cream pie, too. Julio Hernandez and, since his departure, Matt Lirette, have assembled the city's best wine list, with white Burgundies in profusion from growers like Leflaive, Coche-Dury, and Carillon.

Galatoire's, 209 Bourbon Street, (504) 525-2021. Tile floor, mirrors on the walls, ceiling fans, no reservations, waiters with attitude: the old order changeth not at Galatoire's, thank the Lord (despite the new dining rooms upstairs). The food at this century-old restaurant defines New Orleans: the spiciest shrimp rémoulade; the fattest soft-shells imaginable; the freshest pompano and red snapper, sautéed just so and topped with lump crabmeat; and the most potent sazeracs and Ramos gin fizzes.

Jacques-Imo's Cafe, 8324 Oak Street, (504) 861-0886. "All crunch and grease and garlic," is how *Gourmet* magazine described Austin Leslie's irresistibly peppery chicken. Chez Hélène, his Creole bistro, has been defunct for years, but Leslie fries birds at Jacques-Imo's, a chronically overcrowded uptown madhouse that also turns out A-list alligator sausage and eggplant with oyster dressing. You may wait an hour or more for a table, but you'll have a blast, guaranteed.

Uglesich, 1238 Baronne Street, (504) 523-8571. Tony Uglesich is of Croatian descent, like the Buiches of Tadich's in San Francisco, and he knows his seafood. He cooks in a crowded ramshackle bungalow in a crummy neighborhood. You order from him, taking his blunt advice if you're wise, eat a dozen or so raw oysters, and wait. The legendary crawfish étouffée and fried oyster po' boys are worth it; so are new dishes like shrimp and crab cakes with tomatillo sauce.

⚏⮕ NASHVILLE

I wouldn't know a Gibson from a Stratocaster. My favorite guitarists are Eddie Lang, Django Reinhardt, and Andrés Segovia, and none of them ever played at the Opry. That casts a long shadow, I suppose, over my qualifications as a guide to Music City, U.S.A., except that there is a lot more than picking and fiddling, a lot more than ballads of love and loss, in Nashville's past, present, and future—especially its future. Country music earns $2 billion a year, by some estimates, but local leaders have spent millions to play down the city's hillbilly image and emphasize its developing cosmopolitanism.

Like Charlotte, North Carolina; Jacksonville, Florida; and a number of other second-tier Southern cities, Nashville is acquiring big-time accoutrements. In Nashville's case, that includes the Titans of the National Football League. With a new $292 million stadium, a bruiser of a running back named Eddie George, and a fearsome, long-limbed defensive end named Jevon (the Freak) Kearse, the Titans went to the Super Bowl in 2000 and made the city swagger a little. Already in business or on the way are a zoo, an enormous new Country Music Hall of Fame, a megamall, a new library designed by Robert A. M. Stern, an arena to house the Nashville Predators of the National Hockey League, the ambitious Frist Center for the Visual Arts, and Schermerhorn Hall, a new home for the Nashville Symphony.

What interests me most about Nashville, though, is its often-neglected role as an agent of political and intellectual change.

It was from Nashville—or rather from the Hermitage, his home just east of town—that rugged old Andrew Jackson set off for Washington in 1829, having ousted the aristocratic John

Quincy Adams in the pivotal election of 1828. A frontiersman, a general, the first president from west of the Alleghenies, and the first self-made man to move into the White House, Jackson reshaped American democracy in the image of his own egalitarianism, fostering government by the masses instead of the propertied classes. The muddy boots of Jackson's followers spoiled the carpets at the post-inaugural party, and his opponents derided him as "some kind of border savage," in the words of Arthur M. Schlesinger Jr. But he proved them wrong, taking a more aggressive style of leadership to Washington and blazing a path for a tramontane political dynasty that included James K. Polk and Abraham Lincoln, a Kentuckian before he moved to Illinois.

A century later, in the early 1920s, a group of writers at Vanderbilt University, west of downtown Nashville, coalesced around a journal called *The Fugitive*. They railed against both the industrialization of the South and what they called the "moonlight and magnolia" distortion of true agrarian values. Allen Tate and John Crowe Ransom, important modern critics, were members of the group, and its star was Robert Penn Warren—poet, critic, novelist, playwright, essayist, and biographer. In 1946 Red Warren wrote perhaps the greatest of American political novels, *All the King's Men*, whose protagonist, Willie Stark, was a ringer for Huey P. Long, the populist governor of Louisiana, and he was the only person ever to win Pulitzer Prizes for both poetry and fiction.

Founded in 1872 and endowed by Cornelius Vanderbilt, Vanderbilt University has evolved from Methodist and regional origins into an institution of national repute with 10,000 students. Already among the twenty wealthiest colleges and universities in the nation, it has found a new champion in Martha R. Ingram, whose family controls Nashville-based Ingram Industries, one of the nation's dozen largest privately held companies. In 1998 Mrs. Ingram gave Vanderbilt $300 million in Ingram stock—at the time the second largest donation ever made to an American university—and the university may well be entering a bright new era.

Nashville's first white settlers hiked from Virginia through the Cumberland Gap, a natural opening in the Appalachian barrier near the point where Virginia, Tennessee, and Kentucky meet. They stopped several hundred miles west along the Cumberland River, which cuts through lovely limestone hills, and established Nashborough, as they first called it.

For many generations, Nashville's banks and insurance companies formed the basis of its prosperity. They gave Union Street a modest reputation as "the Wall Street of the South," but many of those firms have been sold in recent years to out-of-town interests, along with *The Tennessean*, long the city's dominant newspaper, and a number of important radio and television stations. Big hunks of Music Row now belong to foreign conglomerates like Bertelsmann of Germany. "Nashville used to be a home-owned, home-operated kind of city," said John Egerton, a social historian who has lived here for almost forty years. "But for a long time, it has had an aspiration to celebrity, and by this point it is clearly a city on the make. Now it's a money culture. But that's the New South."

As Tennessee's capital, Nashville remains a cockpit of political drama. Closely divided between the parties, Tennessee has produced prominent Democrats like Cordell Hull, Franklin D. Roosevelt's secretary of state; Senator Estes Kefauver, the 1956 vice presidential nominee; and Senators Albert Gore Sr. and Jr., the latter the 2000 presidential nominee (whose Yankee staff members learned more than they wanted to know about biscuits with cream gravy). It has also produced Republican senators like Howard H. Baker Jr. and Bill Frist, a Princeton- and Harvard-trained physician who became majority leader in 2003 and may seek the presidency in 2008.

In fact, though, health care is the growth industry in Middle Tennessee, the region anchored by Nashville. The city has a string of important hospitals, and it is the headquarters of HCA, the largest hospital management company in the country. HCA was founded by Senator Frist's father, and after many corporate tribulations Thomas F. Frist Jr., the senator's brother, returned home as chief executive to turn it around. The city's economy benefits as well from a Nissan factory at Smyrna and a Saturn factory at Spring Hill, both south of Nashville. Bridgestone/Firestone makes tires and Dell ships computers from Nashville plants. Since the early 1980s, this has been one of the boom towns of the South, growing more rapidly than any other city between Atlanta and Dallas.

The swells of Nashville live in Belle Meade, a suburb of enormous houses beneath lofty shade trees on even more enormous lawns. Guardians of garden-club gentility, politically conservative, they do not mix much with the denim-clad country crowd, and this is more and more their city. But the rhinestone cowboys ride on, a posse of musicians and would-be musicians, strumming their guitars almost everywhere—in rundown bars, on street corners, in legendary dives like Tootsie's Orchid Lounge and Robert's Western World. Robert Altman got it right in *Nashville*, his brilliant, Chaucerian film about the princes and princesses of country music, with egos the size of cathedrals, as well as its no-hopers.

The striking new Country Music Hall of Fame—all four stories and $37 million of it—teaches country-music philistines like me and my wife, Betsey, how much good stuff has flowed from Nashville into the American pop-culture mainstream. As a fan of Benny Goodman and Artie Shaw, I was intrigued to learn more about Bob Wills, who made "San Antonio Rose" popular and more or less invented the wonderfully rhythmic music called Western Swing. Apparently he never performed without a five-cent cigar in his mouth. I had not previously known that Lester Flatt and Earl Scruggs played the captivating banjo tune called "Foggy Mountain Breakdown" on the soundtrack of *Bonnie and Clyde*. And for sheer gaudy glory, what could possibly match Elvis Presley's "solid gold" Cadillac, an icon of American excess?

Longtime Nashville residents remember the days when Music Row consisted of ratty houses used as music publishers' headquarters. The Opry played in the pre-renovation Ryman Auditorium, whose roof sometimes leaked. Today's Grand Ole Opry House, at a riverside site on the edge of town, has a light board and sound system that would do credit to Las Vegas and more seats than the Metropolitan Opera House (4,400 versus 3,800). Nearby stand the kitschy Opryland Hotel and a sprawling mall called Opry Mills.

Its fans treat the Opry with tremendous seriousness, according it a place in their hearts alongside stock car racing and evangelical Christianity. An Opry performance feels a little like a secular church service. The audience is, in fact, seated in pews, not individual seats. Everyone listened raptly and respectfully the Saturday night we were there, munching popcorn and slurping Big Drinks, with none of the hubbub of a rock concert. Viewed from another perspective, this is vaudeville for hayseeds, with a carefully calibrated blend of corny jokes, spangly costumes, bottle blondes, and a surprising range of music— not just country and bluegrass, but also honky-tonk, western, rockabilly, gospel, and quasi-Cajun. The lyrics may be banal and the emotional range limited, but there are big voices on the stage, and the performers are unmistakably skilled. "You'd need a heart of steel not to like this stuff," said Betsey, charmed by Porter Wagoner, the gray-haired, gold-booted master of ceremonies, who joined the company forty-five years ago and helped to advance the career of a buxom thrush named Dolly Parton.

There are other art forms in Nashville, but sometimes you have to look hard for them. You might despair about the city's contemporary architecture if all you saw was its skyline, dominated by the Bell South Building. I thought it looked like a mooring mast for dirigibles. As usual, the word on the street was more apt: Nashville folk call it the Batcave or the Batman Building. My friend Joe Ledbetter, a Nashville businessman with broad interests, clued me in. The concrete bridge on the Natchez Trace Parkway south of town, he said, "is perhaps the most beautiful sight in all of Nashville." So it is: a single broad, handsome arch across a green valley, an engineering gem as graceful as the soaring Sunshine Skyway in Florida.

The same goes for pictures. Nashville's showplace is Cheekwood, a limestone mansion built in 1929 by Leslie Cheek, who made a bundle from Maxwell House Coffee (named for the Nashville hotel where Theodore Roosevelt supposedly proclaimed it "Good to the Last Drop"). While we admired the eighteenth-century English silver on display, some of it by Hester Bateman and Matthew Boulton, we found the paintings disappointing and the gardens, except for the boxwood hedges, battered by Nashville's remorseless midsummer heat.

But at Fisk University, in a far less leafy part of town, we came upon an unheralded trove of early American modernism.

Founded by missionaries and freedmen in 1866, only a year after Appomattox, Fisk may be the oldest historically black college in the country. A statue of W.E.B. DuBois, its most famous alumnus, stands on the campus. After the death of the trend-setting photographer and art dealer Alfred Stieglitz in 1946, his widow, Georgia O'Keeffe, divided his art collection five ways, giving most of it to big urban museums but sending 101 paintings to Fisk, where they hang today in a modest red-brick building. A few are by European masters, including Severini and Renoir and Signac. There is a caustic portrait of a dandy in pince-nez and his companion, swathed in pearls and furs, done by the German George Grosz in New York during World War II. But the treasures of the Fisk are American—large groups of works by Marsden Hartley, Arthur G. Dove, and Charles Demuth (especially a precise, curiously touching little watercolor of an eggplant and some bell peppers), and more than a dozen watercolors and drypoint etchings by John Marin, ranging from Venice to Manhattan to the Maine coast. It is a pity that no corporation or government body has yet stepped forward to underwrite improvements to the galleries at Fisk or to help publish a catalog of its holdings.

Perhaps one day the Stieglitz collection will be shown at the $45 million Frist Center, recently carved out of the old Nashville Post Office, a good-looking New Deal building guarded by stone eagles outside and decorated with graceful Art Deco aluminum screens inside. It gives Nashville 24,000 square feet of gallery space to house major traveling exhibitions that once passed the city by (illuminated manuscripts from Philadelphia, for example). "We're rather late to the party," said Chase W. Rynd, the center's first executive director. "Good art is very expensive these days, so we are concentrating our resources on the building, on education, and on holding prices down."

Nashville will hit another cultural milestone in 2006 with the opening of Schermerhorn Hall, named for the Nashville Symphony's longtime conductor, Kenneth Schermerhorn. The orchestra played in Carnegie Hall for the first time in its history in September 2000. Like pro football fans, more than a thousand local residents booked trips to New York to cheer their musicians in a program featuring the violin virtuoso Nadja Salerno-Sonnenberg.

Classical music seems somehow appropriate for a city that has so much classical architecture, notably old houses like the early nineteenth-century Belle Meade Plantation. This is the kind of Southern mansion, in the words of the cultural critic Roger G. Kennedy, that seems to be "sleeping away the centuries, its white columns composing a kind of cage to keep what lies within from being touched by time."

Andrew Jackson's Hermitage is another such house, set next to a garden ablaze with hollyhocks and crape myrtle in high summer. Its most impressive exterior feature is its portico, with six two-story wooden columns painted, then sprayed with sand to simulate stone. Inside, the furniture, though largely original, is outshone by the textiles and wallpapers, especially the remarkable scenes of Telemachus and Calypso in the foyer, printed in Paris in 1837.

Then there is the work of William Strickland, who came to Nashville from Philadelphia after designing the magnificent Second Bank of the United States there. Here, he produced the Downtown Presbyterian Church (1851), the nation's finest Egyptian Revival building, a taste of Thebes on the Cumberland, and the State Capitol (1859), finished by his son. And finally, Nashville's Parthenon, the only full-size replica in the world, an apparition built of wood and plaster in 1897, and then, twenty-five years later, when it had started to melt like ice cream in the sun, replaced with a copy in brownish concrete.

WHERE TO STAY

Hermitage Hotel, 231 Sixth Avenue North, (615) 244-3121. The legendary pool hustler Minnesota Fats ended his days here, and Dinah Shore began her career here with Francis Craig's orchestra. Under keen new ownership, the richly marbled lobby and the spacious guest rooms regained their beaux arts glory through a $17 million renovation in 2002. The Capitol Grille serves fine Southern specialties like cornbread-stuffed quail.

Loews Vanderbilt, 2100 West End Avenue, (615) 320-1700. A sparkling travertine lobby, a plugged-in young staff (including car parkers working their way through the university just across the street), and a convenient location more than compensate for run-of-the-mill rooms. Ruth's Chris Steak House caters to itinerant carnivores.

Opryland Hotel, 2800 Opryland Drive, (615) 889-1000. This is the capitol of the Kingdom of Schlock, a maze of 2,883 guest rooms, 15 restaurants, 27 shops, 600,000 square feet of meeting and exhibition space, 3 pools, and 9 acres of indoor gardens, hard by the Grand Ole Opry. Yogi Berra said he had to cross three time zones between the reception desk and his bed.

WHERE TO EAT

Loveless Cafe, 8400 Highway 100, (615) 646-9700. Local foodies complain that tourists have taken over and insist that the salty country ham is not quite as authentic as it once was. Per-

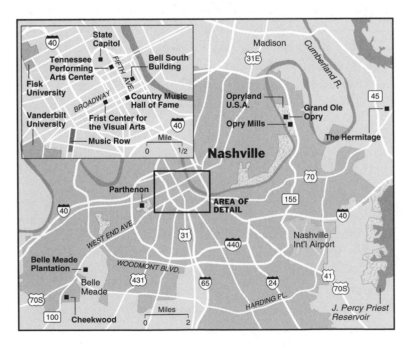

haps, but the fried chicken, scratch biscuits, homemade preserves, sweet shoepeg corn, and red-eye gravy still deliver down-home flavor. You eat at tables with red-checkered cloths, pampered by waitresses with personalities as sweet as sorghum.

Margot Cafe and Bar, 1017 Woodland Street, (615) 227-4668. From her open kitchen in a charmingly converted former garage in East Nashville, Margot McCormack sends out dishes with the fresh, fragrant simplicity of Tuscany and Provence. Only six apps and six mains nightly, but who needs a bedsheet menu when treats like a veal roulade stuffed with spinach and a touch of blue cheese are on offer? Great desserts.

Rotier's, 2413 Elliston Place, (615) 327-9892. This beloved hole-in-the-wall near Vanderbilt University has been serving things like chicken-gizzard dinners since 1945. Evelyn Rotier, who founded it with her late husband, still phones to check up every day. Meat-and-three (vegetables), fabulous lemon icebox pie, and truly exceptional grilled hamburgers, served on toast. Buttermilk is the drink of choice.

Sunset Grill, 2001 Belcourt Avenue, (615) 386-3663. A lot of music industry executives eat at this glossy, relaxed restaurant, with a good, mostly modestly priced wine list. Pastas, salads, stir-fries, and grills dominate Randy Rayburn's Cal-Tenn menu. The odd weirdness, like swordfish stuffed with Brie, is more than offset by goodies like shrimp with brisk roasted-cumin salsa and boffo butterscotch-habanero bread pudding.

Wild Boar, 2014 Broadway, (615) 329-1313. The atmosphere is sepulchral, but there is nothing gloomy about the food. Tiny bouchot mussels in a light curry sauce, perfectly roasted quail, and a fruit extravaganza (peach ice cream served in a tuile, alongside delectably ripe peaches on a peach bavarois) all showed solid craftsmanship. The wine list astonishes: 15,000 bottles, from $35 to $5,000, many of them precious old vintages.

Zola, 3001 West End Avenue, (615) 320-7778. Debra Paquette scores some successes, like a stacked salad of yellow and red tomatoes, with herbed goat cheese, avocado, and a topknot of mango chutney, the very definition of vivid midsummer eating. I liked the ice cream flavored with Moroccan spices. But many of the dishes of Greek, Turkish, and Italian inspiration tasted as if every ingredient in the souk had gone into them.

⫸ LOUISVILLE

It all began with the river. As the broad Ohio flows southwest from Pittsburgh toward its merger with the Mississippi, it is interrupted by rapids. In 1778, George Rogers Clark, a young frontiersman from Virginia, paused at that barrier on his trip west and founded a small settlement that evolved into Louisville, the first real city west of the Alleghenies. Clark himself, a brother of Meriwether Lewis's partner, William Clark, pushed on into the wilderness with a meager force of 175 men. Marching through primeval forest and across flooded prairies in a campaign of audacious brilliance, he fought and defeated the better-equipped, more numerous British at isolated villages in the Northwest Territory—Vincennes, Cahokia, and Kaskaskia— securing a vast domain for the fledgling nation.

In 1809, Clark returned to Louisville to spend his final years at his sister's house, Locust Grove. Built in 1790, meticulously restored in 1962, it stands today as a monument to Clark's exploits, which are detailed in a nearby visitors' center. With its Flemish bond brickwork, shellacked ash floors and walnut paneling, its gardens and dependencies, Locust Grove also bears witness to the refined tastes of some of Kentucky's pioneers.

Louisville has preserved other mementos of its earliest years. Farmington, an exceptional small Federal-style plantation house with delicate fanlights and a pair of octagonal rooms, was built to plans drawn up by Thomas Jefferson in 1810. Blue because he feared that his courtship of Mary Todd had failed, Kentucky-born Abraham Lincoln took refuge there for six weeks with his friend Joshua Speed, a scion of the family that owned the plantation. Downtown, the Jefferson County Courthouse, whose pediment is supported by tall, fluted Doric columns, was built a little later, between 1835 and 1860. With a grand cast-iron stairway and balustrade inside a 68-foot rotunda, the design is by Gideon Shryock, a student of William Strickland, the Philadelphia architect who designed the Second Bank of the United States and important buildings in Nashville.

The city, whose inhabitants call it LOO-uh-vul, half swallowing the final two syllables, was named for Louis XVI, the French king who helped the colonies win independence. (Michael Barone's valuable *Almanac of American Politics* notes that only one other American city, St. Paul, Minnesota, was named for a man who was executed.) But ask a native about Louisville and you are likely to hear about more than history or architecture. The Kentucky writers who put together the city's entry in the Depression-era WPA *Guide* to Kentucky said it was "noted for fine whisky, beautiful women and the Kentucky Derby." It still is. "Louisville is too busy making and selling things to have the languor of a town in the Deep South, but it does have its special graces," the guide added. "Its people are friendly and hospitable. Bourbon and water or a cocktail after work is popular; amusement and relaxation are as important as work." After almost sixty-five years, four wars, and several economic upheavals, that description rings as true as ever, right down to the last semicolon.

This is a border city in a border state. Kentucky stayed in the Union during the Civil War, with Kentuckians fighting on both sides, but Louisville lost its heart to the South. Before the war, explained James Holmberg, a curator at the Filson Club, a Louisville historical society, "we were a Western city, but Confederate veterans took over the city and state after the war. Kentucky was the only state to secede after Appomattox."

In 2003, the city and county governments merged into an urban entity with a population of 698,000, but the suburbs now spread into three Kentucky counties and four across the river in Indiana. The metropolitan area has 1.2 million people.

Daniel D. Maye, a Georgia-born executive who came to Louisville by way of Chicago, says it "combines Southern rural charm with Northern urban tolerance." It produced not only Louis D. Brandeis, the first Jewish Supreme Court justice, but also Muhammad Ali, in whose honor the city is completing a $41 million museum and educational center. With interstates and freeways circling and bisecting it, Greater Louisville has developed a big-city feel, yet drivers still gallantly yield to pedestrians and to cars waiting to turn left. Come here during Derby Week, the seven days leading up to the annual Run for the Roses on the first Saturday in May, or the week before that, and the traffic might make you think you're in Manhattan or Los Angeles, even if the nonstop Southern belles and the lawn parties, with lethal mint juleps served in silver stirrup cups, might remind you more of Biloxi or New Orleans.

The city plays host to the world with costume balls, the Pegasus Parade down Broadway, the Great Balloon Race out at the Fairgrounds, and the Great Steamboat Race on the Ohio. Punctuated by calliope toots, it pits the local stern-wheeler, *Belle of Louisville*, against the larger *Delta Queen* from New Orleans. Race day itself might come as an anticlimax if it were not so stirring: the sentimental strains of Stephen Foster's "My Old Kentucky Home," the clang of the starting bell, and the hell-for-leather charge down the stretch, with jockeys' silks flashing, the crowd cheering, and the mighty steeds straining. It is indeed "the most exciting two minutes in sports" (except in 1973, when the great Secretariat won in a record-shattering one minute fifty-nine and two-fifths seconds). It is also a pari-mutuel money-spinner, with $9.1 million bet at the track on the 2003 Derby, and one hell of a good party.

Churchill Downs, where the race has been run since 1875, is open almost every day of the year. Tucked beneath the twin octagonal Edwardian spires, the track's trademark, is a museum celebrating the race, owners, trainers, jockeys, and the horses themselves, from Man O' War, Whirlaway, and Citation to Smarty Jones. A compelling audiovisual presentation of the most recent race is projected onto an oval overhead screen. Or maybe you'd like to collect trivia—this tidbit, for instance: in the old days, women bet candy or gloves.

Louisville has another sporting claim to fame: it is the home of Hillerich & Bradsby, the company that makes Louisville Slugger baseball bats. Lately it has opened a museum, identified by a bat 120 feet tall leaning against the building. Here, too, one can see a film featuring Johnny Bench and Tony Gwynn talking about hitting in such a lively, understandable way that my wife, Betsey, a nonfan, was entranced. You can watch bats being made from wood from fifty-year-old Pennsylvania and New York ash trees, and see sticks used by Babe Ruth and Roger Maris and Barry Bonds (but not Mark McGwire, a Rawlings man).

Down Third Street at the far end of the neighborhood known as Old Louisville stands the Speed Art Museum, one of the city's premier cultural institutions. The Speed owns an eighteenth-century silver tureen by Paul Storr, a beautiful second-century A.D. Roman altar supported by two lions, a Cézanne, a fine early Rembrandt portrait of a woman (the mate of a male portrait in the Norton Simon Museum in Pasadena, California), and a set of folding screens painted in 1911 by Everett Shinn for the interior designer Elsie de Wolfe. An entire reception room from a manor house in Broadhembury, Devon, England, dating from 1619, was removed when the house was pulled down, sold to William Randolph Hearst at the peak of his collecting mania, then resold to a Louisville patron who donated it to the museum. (Odd, the way places catch up to you: that manor house, called the Grange, belonged to a family named Drewe. For years, Betsey and I have been stopping for lunch at a pub in that same speck of a village, on our way from London to visit friends in Devon. The pub is called the Drewe Arms. Snap.)

Some of Louisville's best sculpture, including pieces by Calder, Dubuffet, Tony Smith, Louise Nevelson, and John Chamberlain, is gathered in and around the Kentucky Center for the Arts, a glistening glass box. Its three stages provide homes for Louisville's resident opera, ballet, and symphony orchestra, plus touring musicals and pop concerts.

The Louisville Orchestra, which celebrated its sixty-fifth anniversary in 2002, once had a reputation extending well beyond the region. Beginning in 1953, under its founding conductor, Robert Whitney, it recorded several hundred previously unavailable works by more than 250 composers, including Ginastera, Ives, Villa-Lobos, Piston, and Britten. But in 2003, badly battered by recurrent financial crises, it eased out its music director, the Israeli Uriel Segal. Conceding that "we have an aura of aloofness," the board president, Manning G. Warren III, told the Louisville *Courier-Journal* that the orchestra "will not survive in Louisville unless we can figure out how to reach our community."

A Tony Award–winning regional drama company, the Actors Theater, occupies a three-stage complex on Main Street, part of which dates from 1837, and it recently played its fortieth season. Each winter the company puts on the acclaimed Humana Festival of New American Plays, which has mounted three dramas that won Pulitzer Prizes, including D. L. Coburn's *The Gin Game* (1976), which became a starring vehicle for Jessica Tandy and Hume Cronyn.

Louisville's civic and artistic life has been blessed by a succession of innovative and nationally prominent mayors, among them Wilson W. Wyatt, a founder of Americans for Democratic Action; Harvey Sloane; and the three-term incumbent, Jerry E. Abramson. Much of Louisville's cultural life was underwritten for decades by the Bingham family. Robert Worth Bingham bought the *Courier-Journal* in 1917 from Henry Watterson, one of the greatest of nineteenth-century American editors. In 1933, when he went to London to serve as U.S. ambassador, his son, Barry, took over the paper. Barry Bingham and his wife, Mary, rapidly became a dominant force in Louisville political and artistic affairs; Barry and Wilson Wyatt, boyhood chums, worked in close partnership. But the Binghams' children squabbled over their inheritance, and the paper was sold in 1986. It has lost much of its zest under its less openhanded new owner, the Gannett chain, and many Louisville charities have felt the loss of the Binghams' leadership.

Happily for the city, however, others have stepped in, notably David A. Jones, founder of Humana, the big health care company, and his family. Humana's headquarters, a salmon-pink skyscraper, is one of Louisville's most distinctive modern buildings; its entrance is flanked by Busby Berkeley waterfalls refashioned in Michael Graves's postmodern idiom. Almost next door stands the American office of the Aegon Insurance Group, a good-looking 1992 tower by John Burgee and Philip Johnson whose openwork cap has led the irreverent locals to christen it "the Ban roll-on building."

The nearby waterfront has been redeveloped to great effect,

making it possible to walk for miles along the river. The relatively new Waterfront Park, the bosky centerpiece of the plan, follows in the grand tradition of the master landscape architect Frederick Law Olmsted, who along with successors in his firm designed eighteen parks and six parkways in Louisville between 1891 and 1940. But although the city center has been revitalized to some degree by projects such as the Ali Center and the Glassworks, which includes apartments as well as studios for thirty glass artists, efforts to lure residents to the core neighborhoods have lagged. The city loses a troubling number of young people, and segregation persists; two-thirds of downtown residents are African American.

Humana and other companies in its field are among Louisville's biggest employers; there are more than a dozen hospitals in the city. It is also the global hub for United Parcel Service, which provides 22,300 local jobs, more than any other single company. General Electric makes appliances in Louisville, Brown & Williamson makes tobacco products, and Brown Forman and United Distillers make bourbon. Yum! Brands, the corporate tent for Taco Bell, Kentucky Fried Chicken, and Pizza Hut, has its headquarters here, too.

But if you want to experience the definitive Kentucky fried chicken and explore the Bourbon Belt, the best thing is to head south to Bardstown, one of Kentucky's oldest communities, founded in 1775, the year of Paul Revere's ride in far-off Boston. Its streets are lined with eighteenth- and early-nineteenth-century houses, one of them home to Kurtz's restaurant, where Marilyn "Toogie" Dick serves her glorious fried chicken to hordes of hungry people each weekend, some of whom drive down from Cincinnati. Suitably fortified, you can use Bardstown as a base to study bourbon, the corn-based whisky that, along with Daniel Boone and racehorses, made Kentucky famous. This is the state, as they say, "where the corn is full of kernels and the colonels are full of corn."

WHERE TO STAY

Camberley Brown, 335 West Broadway, (502) 583-1234. Echoes of Derby frolics past resound through the magnificent marble halls of this eighty-year-old, Old Money hotel. Ornate chandeliers, collections of equine paintings and sculptures, and a registration desk concealed behind gilded screens enrich the lobby. The 293 rooms, some of them rather cramped, are nicely appointed, with free high-speed Internet access.

Seelbach Hilton, 500 Fourth Street, (502) 585-3200. F. Scott Fitzgerald set Tom and Daisy Buchanan's lavish wedding reception here in *The Great Gatsby*. Opened in 1905 in the heart of the city, the Seelbach has been restored several times, most recently in 1998, but wrinkles still show. The lobby has fine murals illustrating Kentucky history and the neo-Gothic rathskeller is lined with handsome Rookwood Arts and Crafts tiles.

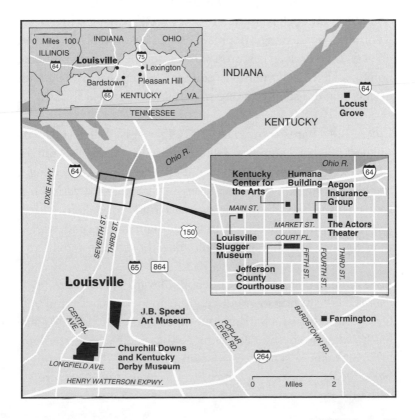

Hyatt Regency, 320 West Jefferson Street, (502) 587-3434. Not exactly a spring chicken either, but it offers the usual chain-hotel amenities, plus a tennis court, a heated indoor pool, and an eighteen-story atrium. A revolving rooftop restaurant overlooks the river, if you go for that sort of thing.

WHERE TO EAT

J. Graham's Cafe, in the Camberley Brown (see above), is just a glorified coffee shop, but it serves an authentic Hot Brown sandwich, a Louisville delicacy invented at the hotel: toast triangles in an ovenproof dish are covered with shaved turkey breast, Mornay sauce, smoky Kentucky bacon, Parmesan, and tomato wedges, then finished under the broiler. The result: a cheese dream with a Ph.D. Open for breakfast and lunch only.

Kurtz's, 418 East Stephen Foster Avenue, Bardstown, (502) 348-8964. Kurtz's has been here since 1937, serving salty, chewy Kentucky ham; magnificently crisp, absolutely greaseless chicken fried in deep cast-iron skillets; soufflélike corn pudding, home-pickled beets, mashed potatoes better than your grandmother's, and biscuit pudding with bourbon sauce. Oh my.

Lilly's, 1147 Bardstown Road, (502) 451-0447. Lilly's served us the best meal of a summer visit to Louisville. "God bless our local farmers!" the menu said; I understood why, after eating a stack of phyllo rounds and ripe tomato slices topped with warm goat cheese. Even better: juicy roast pork tenderloin with a spicy red-brown sauce, cornbread as light as air, and wasabi slaw. Kathy Cary, chef and owner, likes those Asian touches.

Limestone, 10001 Forest Green Boulevard, (502) 426-7477, uses the best Kentucky produce, from spoonfish caviar and buttery Bibb lettuce to Bath County mushrooms. Chef Jim Gerhardt, who lifted the Oakroom at the Seelbach to stardom, brought Adam Seger in to advise on wines, and the list is full of Good Deals. Service can falter, but the malty sour-mash crepes with crabmeat, crawfish, and bay scallops are brilliant.

Lynn's Paradise Cafe, 984 Barret Avenue, (502) 583-3447. Who needs a barrel of monkeys? Nothing could be more fun than Lynn Winter's place, with an eight-foot-tall coffeepot out front, corncob murals, and a funky array of lamps. As a local critic says, it's an 00s wink at 50s style. Thousands of people a week come for gotta-have-'em grits or French toast at breakfast, meat loaf at lunch, and Lynn's warming smile all day long.

The Oakroom, in the Seelbach Hilton (see above), utilizes the whole gamut of Kentucky produce, from smoked spoonfish, Newsom's hams, and limestone Bibb lettuce to mangolike pawpaws, gathered by foragers in Appalachia. The new chef, Walter Leffler, is putting his own spin on "Kentucky Fine Dining" as developed by Gerhardt. Wines and cheeses are skillfully chosen by Jerry Slater, the maître d'hôtel.

Vince Staten's, 9219 U.S. Highway 42, Prospect, (502) 228-7427. Coauthor of a standard guide to the nation's barbecue pits, Vince Staten runs a joint of his own in the suburbs. The decor is plastic, but not the food: succulent ribs and pulled pork sandwiches, first-rate beans and coleslaw. Staten's offers six sauces, culminating in Legal Limit hot.

⫸ ST. LOUIS

In 1904, St. Louis was the fourth largest American city. It was rich, river-rich, thanks to the Mississippi, then the nation's main north-south artery, on whose right bank it is built. Although Chicago had become the dominant railroad hub, St. Louis deemed itself the rightful capital of the Middle West.

So the city staged the Louisiana Purchase Exposition in honor of the centenary of Thomas Jefferson's clever acquisition, the grandest and giddiest, most glorious fair the world had ever seen. It outshone Chicago's Columbian Exposition of 1893—that was the point. It included the first Olympic Games ever held in the United States. It popularized the ice cream cone, Dr. Pepper, and Buster Brown shoes, and showcased the latest scientific wonders, like X-ray machines and incubators for infants. Its biggest hit was a 2,160-seat Ferris wheel. Its palaces and exhibitions spun fantasies of perpetual peace and prosperity. And it taught the country, with a little help forty years later from Judy Garland, a song not soon forgotten:

> Meet me in St. Louie, Louie, meet me at the fair.
> Don't tell me the lights are shining anywhere but there . . .

With attendance exceeding 20 million, that was the apogee. Life in St. Louis has never been as sweet since, and people still murmur wistfully about the magic summer of 1904.

But the lights stayed on for a while. St. Louis prospered for a few decades more, a "solid expanse of bricks and mortar" stretching "into dim, measure-defying distances," as Mark Twain wrote. Though falling behind boomtowns like Detroit and Los

Angeles, St. Louis made money on beer and shoes and built high-caliber cultural and civic institutions that serve it well today. And fate found ways to keep its name on the nation's mind.

W. C. Handy came to town in 1914, sat on the riverbank overlooking the Eads Bridge, an engineering marvel built at the same time as the Brooklyn Bridge, and wrote a tune called "St. Louis Blues." That made two songs about St. Louis that most Americans could hum or whistle or dum-de-dum; how many other cities in the United States can make that claim? Then in 1925 a skinny pilot from Minnesota named Charles A. Lindbergh showed up in St. Louis. After flying airmail to Chicago for a while, he asked a group of local businessmen to finance a plane in which he would make an attempt to fly solo across the Atlantic Ocean. Some thought him a crackpot, but nine of them ponied up the needed $15,000. In gratitude, Lindbergh painted the words "Spirit of St. Louis" on the nose of his frail, silvery Ryan monoplane.

Garrison Keillor, the professional Midwesterner, once said on his radio show that in his part of the country, "We cause them pain, and that makes them the artists they are." He was talking about St. Louis and the distinguished writers who once lived there, like Marianne Moore, Tennessee Williams, and T. S. Eliot. Especially Eliot, who grew up at 2635 Locust Street, the son of a brick manufacturer, but spent his writing life in England.

St. Louis stayed with Eliot. "There is something in having passed one's childhood beside the big river which is incommunicable to those who have not," he wrote. The fog in "The Love Song of J. Alfred Prufrock" is the fog from factory chimneys across the Mississippi, he said, and the urban themes in his poems echo his early fascination with the city's slums.

Other creative spirits, especially musicians, also had something of the city in them, though it was never a jazz or blues capital on the level of New Orleans, Chicago, Kansas City, or New York. Fate Marable's orchestra, with young Louis Armstrong on cornet, played on riverboats that tied up at St. Louis. Chuck Berry, Tina Turner, Miles Davis, Josephine Baker, and Scott Joplin were born here or worked here. Blues clubs like Mike and Min's still dot the old Soulard neighborhood, where a farmers' market has operated since 1838.

The musicians came mostly from a large, vibrant black community, which coexisted, sometimes nervously, with the dominant German Americans. For many years, not entirely by coincidence, St. Louis sent two nationally prominent congressmen to Washington, one black, Bill Clay, and one German American, Richard A. Gephardt. The German painter Max Beckmann, who left his homeland when the Nazis vilified him and his work, gave St. Louis its greatest distinction in the visual arts. After spending 1937 to 1945 in semi-hiding in Amsterdam, the gregarious Beckmann came to St. Louis to accept a teaching job at Washington University. He found not only "trees at last, ground under my feet at last," as he wrote in his diary, but also a generous patron in the person of Morton D. May, the department store magnate. Richer for their friendship, the St. Louis Art Museum, whose gallery by Cass Gilbert is one of two buildings left from the 1904 fair, holds a world-beating Beckmann collection as well as major works by other German Expressionists.

If it is music one seeks, St. Louis is quite well-endowed. Founded in 1879, the St. Louis Symphony is the second oldest in the nation, often listed among the half dozen best. The orchestra plays in Powell Hall, a converted movie palace with stunning acoustics. It developed a habit of spending beyond its means and teetered for a time on the brink of disaster, but it survived thanks to a $40 million infusion from the owners of Enterprise Rent-a-Car and a hard-won spirit of cooperation between management and musicians.

Then, in 2004, it snared David Robertson, one of the most sought-after American conductors of his generation, who built his career in Paris and elsewhere in Europe, as its musical director. In the cloistered world of classical music, it was a coup comparable to the Yankees' signing of Alex Rodriguez, and Robertson promptly declared his intention of strengthening the orchestra's community ties. They are already strong; it has given more than three hundred free performances at schools, churches, and nursing homes in recent years.

Classic musicals are revived every summer at the 12,000-seat amphitheater of the Municipal Theater Association of St. Louis, known to the locals as the Muny. A five-week spring season is offered by the Opera Theater of St. Louis, which shares the stage of the Loretto-Hilton Center, in suburban Webster Groves, with the Repertory Theater of St. Louis. In 2004, the opera presented two rarities, Puccini's *Sister Angelica*, and Cimarosa's *Secret Marriage*, as well as a new children's opera, *Dream of the Pacific*, marking the two hundredth anniversary of the epochal Lewis and Clark expedition.

The Rep is the leading theater company in town, despite its out-of-the-way location. In one recent season it delved into Shakespeare and Arthur Miller and also produced William Nicholson's Chekhovian drama, *Retreat from Moscow*. Then there is the fabulous Fox, another converted movie theater, which houses musicals and concerts in an interior of infinite gaudiness described by the owners as an example of "the Siamese-Byzantine style." Is this a great country or what?

Sometimes it seems as if every second restaurant belongs to an ex-jock. There's Mike Shannon's and Ozzie's and Dierdorf and Hart's. But St. Louis has always been a sports town, as the old-time catchers Yogi Berra and Joe Garagiola, native sons, keep telling us. As late as World War II, St. Louis was one of five cities in the country (along with New York, Chicago, Boston, and Philadelphia) with more than one big-league baseball team. It had the National League Cardinals, of course, a team as popular in the heyday of Dizzy Dean and Stan (the Man) Musial as it has been recently, with the Bunyan-sized Mark McGwire, the home-run king, and the graceful Albert Pujols. With no big-league team west or south of the city, the Cardinals built a huge fan base in those areas. The hapless American League Browns, on the other hand, were for years the butt of a merciless taunt about their city—"First in booze, first in shoes, and last in the American League." Finally, awash in debt, they gave up and decamped to Baltimore in 1954.

By then, St. Louis was struggling, and it has struggled since, with economic change and racial tensions that bred poverty and crime. It pioneered urban redevelopment, seeking to eradicate slums but building new ones instead, like the infamous Pruitt-Igoe project, whose thirty-three towers became gruesome national symbols of good intentions gone wrong. They were demolished in a telegenic cloud of dust in 1973, two decades after opening. What was left behind—much of the midtown area between downtown and the 1,300-acre Forest Park, the site of the fair – turned into a wasteland. Charles Eisendrath, a St. Louis native whose family settled here after the Civil War, calls the area "Hiroshima Flats." The city's population shriveled, from a peak of 857,000 in 1950 to 348,000 in 2000. Clayton, LaDue, University City, Florissant, and other communities ringing the city, meanwhile, attracted not only the well-off but also middle-class and working-class fugitives from the crumbling inner city. More than 2.6 million people now live in this larger metropolitan area.

The area has plenty of big employers. Anheuser-Busch, which dominates the American beer market, has its main office and a century-old brew house, full of gigantic copper kettles, just south of downtown. There are dozens of buildings in the Budweiser complex, with enough crenellations to outfit several medium-size castles. It has been growing ever since Eberhard Anheuser and his son-in-law, Adolphus Busch, got things going in 1861. Mallinckrodt, now a unit of Tyco International, makes drugs and other health-care products, and Monsanto produces herbicides such as Roundup and genetically modified seeds—two intensely controversial classes of products. McDonnell, now part of Boeing, builds aircraft components on the north side, and Emerson Electric and Ralston Purina have headquarters in St. Louis. Trans World Airlines, another pillar of the local economy, was sold in 2001 to American Airlines, and in the ensuing years the city suffered a 50 percent reduction in air service. One of American's piers at Lambert–St. Louis Airport became a ghost town. "It affected every single business in town," a prominent executive told me. "It hurt badly."

When Pope John Paul II visited St. Louis in 1999, *The Washington Post* derided the city as "a hard-knuckle up-South city far removed from the Potemkin village of the Budweiser commercials"—the ones in which the brewery's Clydesdales canter through leafy vales. Quite right, up to a point. But St. Louis has neighborhoods of character, too. Oak-lined gated streets that people here call "private places" are packed with faux châteaus built eighty or ninety years ago and carefully maintained since. The Hill is a spic-and-span square mile of modest frame houses, bocce clubs, salami shops, red-sauce restaurants, and red-white-and-green fire plugs, centered on St. Ambrose Church, a scaled-down red-brick replica of Romanesque cathedrals in Lombardy, where most of the Hill's settlers came from.

St. Louis has the *Post-Dispatch*, flagship of the Pulitzers, not as influential as it once was, maybe, but still many notches above average. Since 2001, the city has also had the Pulitzer Foundation for the Arts, a refined little concrete-slab temple designed by the Japanese Tadeo Ando, open only two days a week and then to a limited number. Someday it may (or may not) house one of the world's finest private collections of modern art, assembled by Joseph Pulitzer Jr. The foundation shares a courtyard with the Contemporary Art Museum St. Louis, another new essay in stark architectural geometry.

St. Louis has Washington University, where twenty Nobel laureates have done research, and St. Louis University, the oldest west of the Mississippi, a Jesuit institution that has taken the lead in reviving the shabby district around its campus. Powered by a relentless, $1 billion–plus fund-raising campaign, Washington U. in 2003 cracked into the charmed top-ten ranks in the widely debated but widely consulted *U.S. News & World Report*'s college ratings.

St. Louis also has a marvelous zoo—with apes and jungle cats, hippos and penguins, and the Flight Cage, a walk-through aviary left over from 1904—and the Missouri Botanical Garden. "If you do nothing else," our friend Tony Bommarito told my wife, Betsey, and me, "go to the Garden," which seemed like bum advice just after a snowstorm. It wasn't. These are pleasure grounds for all seasons. Nowhere in the United States except New York will you find their equal. Even in a frosty Midwestern March, we found a captivating foretaste of spring: camellias and primroses in full bloom in the Linnean House; winter honeysuckles and Ozark witch hazels belying the season with their sweet scents; crocuses and snowdrops pushing bravely through the crusty earth.

It is the majestic curve of Eero Saarinen's Gateway Arch, sleek and graceful as the leap of a salmon, that symbolizes the city's dreams and memories. This flattened catenary arc of stainless steel, 630 feet tall, taller than the Washington Monument, was completed in 1965. It glows gold in the light of a full moon, gleams in sunlight, and turns a dull pewter on overcast days. The arch is a door ever open to Manifest Destiny. It contradicts a commonplace observation made about Missouri: that St. Louis faces east and Kansas City faces west. It was St. Louis, in truth, that bade farewell to Meriwether Lewis and William Clark in May 1804, as they headed up the Missouri River to explore the immense Louisiana Territory. I know of no other contemporary monument of comparable grandeur. Don't just glimpse it from your hotel room or through the window of a taxi. Don't reduce it to a postcard. Give it an hour or two, view it from below and from a few blocks away, take the shuttle to the top, and be sure to visit the excellent Museum of Westward Expansion beneath its base.

Just a few steps from the Arch is one of the city's most historic buildings, the Old Courthouse, with an imposing cast-iron neo-Renaissance dome not unlike that of the Capitol in Washington, sitting atop severely beautiful Greek Revival porticoes. Begun in 1839, completed in 1862, the courthouse was still under construction when the Dred Scott trials of 1847 and 1850 took place there. Those cases led to the monstrous Supreme Court decision in 1857, declaring that slaves were not legally "citizens" and had no right to sue in the federal courts. That decision, in turn, helped to precipitate the Civil War.

A few blocks farther west stands Louis Sullivan's great Wainwright Building (1890–91), a near-twin to his Guaranty Building in Buffalo. Clad in brick and terra-cotta, decorated with botanical motifs of Sullivan's own invention, this is a proto-skyscraper. A steel skeleton holds it up, but you can't see or even sense that. The Wainwright Building is a major landmark in American architectural history, hailed by Frank Lloyd Wright (who didn't hail very much) as the first building with "height triumphant." Almost equally important is the lovely domed tomb in Bellefontaine Cemetery that Sullivan designed for Charlotte Dickson Wainwright, the wife of his client the developer Ellis Wainwright.

WHERE TO STAY

Westin, 811 Spruce Street, (314) 621-2000. Four early-twentieth-century warehouses were turned into this early-twenty-first-century downtown hotel, a short walk from the arch, the river, and Busch Stadium. The 257 guest rooms average 600 square feet, with soaring ceilings, and the upscale Clark Street Grill serves modern American food with Asian accents.

Hyatt Regency St. Louis, St. Louis Union Station, (314) 231-1234. A sixty-five-foot barrel-vaulted lobby covered in seafoam-green Arts and Crafts tiles takes the breath away; there is nothing to match it in any American hotel. Bravo for the Hyatt team, which has added attractive if slightly skimpy rooms and a terrific pool to a brilliant rehab job.

Ritz-Carlton, 100 Carondelet Plaza, Clayton, (314) 863-6300. The Ritz is the city's best hotel by a country mile, and not just because the competition is slight. Fifteen minutes west of down-

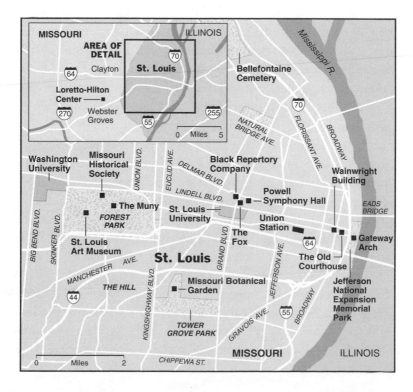

town St. Louis in suburban, swinging (yes, swinging) Clayton, it has a lobby that's ideal for drinks. (Beware the cocktail-hour crush!) Oversized bedrooms and bright marble baths. Try the amazing applewood-smoked Ozark bacon at breakfast.

WHERE TO EAT

Crossing, 7823 Forsyth Avenue, Clayton, (314) 721-7375. Trained at Daniel in New York, Jim Fiala continues to set St. Louis on its conservative ear at this urbane spot. A piece of poached skate that all but melted into a pile of mashed potatoes, giving the effect of a brandade of cod, formed the centerpiece of a compelling meal that began with roasted beets and goat cheese and ended with perfectly simple, simply perfect lemon semifreddo. Equally noteworthy: foie gras in a tart blackberry broth, and well-chosen wines.

Gian-Tony's, 5356 Daggett Avenue, (314) 772-4893. You'll find unreconstructed St. Louis food on the Hill, the close-knit neighborhood where Italians have clustered for a century. At his modest little tavern, Tony Catarinicchia, Sicilian-born, prepares memory-stirring dishes like chicken cacciatore and osso buco and flawless eggplant parmigiana. Deft seasoning and a delicate touch lift his home-style cooking out of the ordinary.

Harvest, 1059 South Big Bend Boulevard, (314) 645-3522. Stephen Gontram is a Wolfgang Puck alumnus, committed to the use of fresh, calendar-honoring ingredients in "rustic American food." Harvest charms with its sand-hued decor, its fairly priced wine list, and its homey Midwestern touches: Ozark ham, for example, pork with apple butter, sweetbreads with pureed parsnips, and a Maytag blue cheese risotto.

Ted Drewes, 6724 Chippewa Street, (314) 481-2652. This white frame building has been dispensing manna, disguised as frozen custard, since 1929. Takeout only; closed in midwinter. Order a cone, a cup, a sundae, or a shake, known here as a "concrete" because it's so thick. No matter what you choose, you'll taste whole eggs, honey, and pure cream.

Tony's, 410 Market Street, (314) 231-7007. There is a bold sign in the kitchen. "Pride," it says, and that quality permeates Vince Bommarito's operation. Subtly lit, a bit old-fashioned, with waiters in dinner jackets transferring food from serving dishes to plates at tableside, this is the city's most cosmopolitan dining room. From carpaccio to cannoli (filled with fresh whipped cream), by way of red-sauced pasta and superlative veal, the menu covers Italian classics plain and fancy. Well-made small dishes at Anthony's Bar.

⫸ KANSAS CITY

The western edge of Missouri was once thought to be the western edge of American civilization, beyond which lay the unknown. The Santa Fe, Oregon, and California Trails all started in Independence and Westport, two small frontier towns that have long since been melded into Greater Kansas City, and in the 1840s brave souls gathered there each spring to begin the arduous journey by Conestoga wagon toward the Golden West. Today Kansas City is the metropolis in the middle: 1,435 miles from Boston on the Atlantic, 1,577 from Los Angeles on the Pacific, 829 from New Orleans to the south, 768 from the Canadian border to the north. The exact geographic and population centers of the nation are both close at hand.

More than geography makes Kansas City the capital of Middle America. There is no such thing as a typical American place, but Kansas City comes close. Old-time wire service reporters were told to write for a mythical "Kansas City milkman," and the novelist John Updike confessed he aimed his words "toward a vague spot a little to the east of Kansas."

Before we go any further, Toto, I should emphasize that the Kansas City we're talking about here is not the one in Kansas. The older, bigger, more vibrant of the two Kansas Cities is in Missouri, east of State Line Road (although a Kansas suburb, Overland Park, captured the gargantuan $700 million world headquarters of the Sprint Corporation, composed of seventeen office buildings spread across a 200-acre campus with its own zip code.)

Kansas City, Missouri, is a plainspoken place, a big-league town with a small-town feel, whose favorite son was Harry S Truman, a president who embodied the sturdy virtues of the common man. He grew up in Independence, rose through Boss Pendergast's Kansas City political organization, an honest cog in a spectacularly crooked machine, and carried the accent and attitudes of the Midwest with him all his life.

Perched on a bluff above the Missouri River, laced with fountains and boulevards, graced by unusually handsome public buildings, this Kansas City survived the vicissitudes of recent decades better than most. It remains an exemplar of the turn-of-the-last-century City Beautiful movement, and it has spent liberally in the last few years to refresh its many beaux arts and Art Deco landmarks and build more modern ones. William Rockhill Nelson, the imperious founder of *The Kansas City Star*, where the young Hemingway honed his craft, did more than anyone to shape his hometown. When Nelson arrived in 1880, it struck him as "incredibly commonplace and ugly," and he resolved that it "must be made over." Such was his wealth and will that when he died in 1915, he left behind a city so transformed that it stupefied country folk who flocked to it.

"Ev'rythin's up to date in Kansas City," they sang in 1943 in *Oklahoma!*, the Rodgers and Hammerstein musical. "They've gone about as fur as they c'n go! They went and built a sky-scraper seven stories high—about as high as a buildin' orta grow." Yet Kansas City still symbolizes the sticks to many Easterners. Asked once by *The Wall Street Journal* why his best steak was called a New York strip and not a Kansas City strip, the manager of the Palm, a Manhattan beef palace, replied huffily, "Do you think we would name our steak after a city with what, three people in it?" A bum steer, that.

It's hard to see how any open-minded visitor to Kansas City could fail to be impressed by the Nelson-Atkins Museum of Art, which has few if any peers west of the Mississippi. Lacking private collections on which to build when construction began in 1930, the trustees had to buy everything, and in the Depression years their dollars went a long way. More important, they had the wit to hire Laurence Sickman, then a twenty-three-year-old graduate student in China, who proved to be one of the greatest American curatorial connoisseurs. Patterning the collection on those in Boston and Cleveland, Sickman assembled trophies of Oriental art, especially Chinese, to rival theirs.

His roomful of graceful rosewood Ming furniture, spare and sensual at the same time, transfixes me. So do the glorious groups of Tang tomb figures, including a posse of polo-playing women; an earthenware Wei orchestra, the only one to survive from the sixth century; and an unmatched collection of landscape paintings from the Northern Sung period (960–1127), which were the models for generations of Chinese artists. But until I toured the collection one day with Marc F. Wilson, the museum's gregarious director, an Oriental specialist, I had never noticed the intricately carved little cages for singing crickets.

Elsewhere at this vast art hangar you will find vivid, realistic and posterlike depictions of regional and mythological subjects by Thomas Hart Benton (great-nephew of a noted Missouri senator), whose *Persephone* (1938) once hung in Billy Rose's Diamond Horseshoe bar in New York; Monet's *Boulevard des Capucines*, from the first Impressionist show in 1874; a pretty courtyard café, and four oversized Claes Oldenburg shuttlecocks on the surrounding lawns—a welcome relief from the building's Greek Revival severity.

Like other metropolitan areas, Kansas City is on a cultural building spree, hoping to persuade more of its 1.8 million residents to live downtown. The New York architect Steven Holl, acclaimed for his Kiasma museum in Helsinki, has designed an addition to the Nelson-Atkins, with buried galleries and glass extrusions above ground that will look like "quartz crystals spilling neatly on the side lawn," in Marc Wilson's words.

Despite a half dozen theater companies, an active chamber music scene, an ambitious ballet company, and a symphony orchestra (whose last musical director departed after only four years), Kansas City has suffered from the lack of an up-to-date performing arts center. By 2010, it hopes to complete a glass-and-concrete hillside showplace designed by the Canadian Moshe Safdie, with a large multipurpose auditorium and a smaller hall. The cost is expected to exceed $300 million. Michael Stern, a son of the legendary Isaac, will take over as the symphony's music director late in 2005 and prepare it for the move into its new home.

But the city's place in performing arts history has already been earned by a galaxy of jazz and blues musicians who first made their mark here, from Joe Turner and Mary Lou Williams to Count Basie and Charlie Parker.

In the 1930s, more than sixty smoky clubs in the black neighborhood around Eighteenth and Vine Streets formed the heartland of American jazz. The film director Robert Altman, a native son, revisited the scene in his 1996 movie *Kansas City*. Virgil Thomson, the composer and critic, who was also born here, reveled in the happy contrast between dry, "moralistic" Kansas City, Kansas, and Kansas City, Missouri, where, thanks to Pendergast's defiance of Prohibition, saloons stood shoulder to shoulder. "Just as Memphis and St. Louis had their Blues," he wrote, "we had our 'Twelfth Street Rag,' proclaiming joyous low life." That era is celebrated in the handsome Kansas City Jazz Museum. Major exhibits are built around four jazz masters: Louis Armstrong, Duke Ellington, Ella Fitzgerald, and Parker, the junkie-genius whose acrylic saxophone, on display along with Ellington's suitcase and Ella's dresses, cost the museum $140,000 in public money. But there is also space for lesser-known local lions like Basie, Turner, the blues shouter Jimmy Rushing, and the band leaders Bennie Moten and Andy Kirk, who called his group the Twelve Clouds of Joy. (If you're looking for live music, you'll find jazz at the Blue Room, part of the museum complex, four nights a week, and blues across town at the Grand Emporium in Westport.)

Fans of the summer game will want to see the adjoining Negro Leagues Baseball Museum, commemorating the Kansas City Monarchs of the old Negro Leagues with balls, uniforms, pennants, scorecards, and a diamond peopled by life-size statues of black stars like Satchel Paige and Josh Gibson. A highlight: the dramatically told tale of the integration of the big leagues by Jackie Robinson of the Brooklyn Dodgers and Larry Doby of the Cleveland Indians.

Jazz, baseball . . . and food. The humorist Calvin Trillin, who is white, made Kansas City's proletarian food famous, but it was blacks traveling up the Mississippi and Missouri Rivers from the South who created it. Trillin has made a trademark of his modest claim that "the best restaurants of the world are, of course, in Kansas City." Maybe only the top four or five, he wrote in *The New Yorker*; maybe only two, I'd say. Winstead's hamburgers, Trillin's hometown favorite, can't compare to Swenson's, the pride of Akron, Ohio, my hometown. Lamar's Do-Nuts don't hold a candle to Krispy Kremes. But Arthur Bryant's barbecue parlor, which Trillin still prefers to Taillevent after four years at Yale and decades of world travel, and Stroud's, whose fried chicken makes the Colonel's taste like oversalted papier-mâché, are every bit as good as he says they are.

Especially Arthur's. For a while, it slipped a little; I attributed the problem to the plastic gloves the health police made the countermen wear when handling the brisket. In those dark days, the flavor lost a little something. But now bare hands are back, slicing a half pound of slow-cooked meat, slapping it between two slices of gummy white Butternut bread, brushing it with the hot, grainy sauce that cures in big jugs in the window, and surrounding it with the Best French Fries in America, cooked in fresh lard. Expensive, sure, as the proprietor once told Trillin, "but if you want to do a job, you do a job."

These days, there are no stockyards in Kansas City. Well, there are, but the last time I looked, the pens between Fourteenth and Sixteenth streets were filled with weeds, not steers. Yet the American Royal Livestock, Horse Show, and Rodeo still takes place every fall, as it has since 1899.

A more citified entertainment, available all year, is a stroll through the central business district, which retains a fine collection of Art Deco buildings. Among the best are the Kansas City Power and Light Building at Fourteenth Street and Baltimore Avenue, particularly impressive when illuminated at night; the Municipal Auditorium on Thirteenth Street, especially its lobby, and the City Hall on Twelfth Street, with strips of recessed windows that lend it a bold verticality. All were built in hard times, between 1931 and 1937, yet all display an unquenchable Midwestern confidence in a streamlined, chrome-plated future. In the preceding decade, that same can-do spirit led Kansas City to build the 217-foot shaft called the Liberty Memorial, also in the Art Deco style, the nation's most prominent monument honoring veterans of World War I (including John J. Pershing, a Missouri native).

On the edge of downtown, spanning an interstate highway, is

the striking 200,000-square-foot Bartle Hall convention center. Its roof is suspended on fifty-six steel cables from four towering concrete pylons. That method of construction yields a pillar-free central exhibition hall; it also represents a vote of confidence in modern engineering from a city deeply embarrassed by the collapse of the roof at Kemper Arena in 1979 and a hotel skywalk in 1981. The skywalk was at the Crown Center, fifteen blocks south of City Hall, which was one of the nation's first mixed-use redevelopment projects. The brainchild of Joyce C. Hall, founder of Hallmark Cards, it replaced abandoned warehouses and tar paper shacks around the Hallmark headquarters with a complex of office buildings, housing, hotels, shops, restaurants, and theaters. The Crown Center now functions as the hub of a mini-downtown, enhanced by a science museum opened in 1999 in Union Station, which was restored at a cost of $234 million. Called "the great gate to the West" by President Woodrow Wilson when he dedicated it in 1914, the station is a monolithic building of enduring grandeur through which half the nation's soldiers passed during World War II. In an infamous gun duel outside the station in 1933, Charles "Pretty Boy" Floyd and his henchman Adam Richetti killed four lawmen.

Still another hub is Country Club Plaza, the nation's first suburban shopping mall when it was built in 1922 by a visionary developer named J. C. Nichols. It is now the heart of a sprawling twenty-square-block retail district along Brush Creek, well within the city limits. Nichols sent his architects to Seville, Spain, and they returned to create beguiling arcades of shops topped with multicolored tile roofs and punctuated by Moorish-style towers modeled on the Giralda. One of the earliest tenants was Fred Wolferman's grocery chain, which gave birth to the habit-forming double-thick English muffins that are still made in the Kansas City area.

A few miles east along Truman Road (what else?) you come to Independence, where there are three main things to see. One is the National Frontier Trails Center, which celebrates the pluck of those who made the trek west. Among the testaments quoted on its walls is that of the historian Francis Parkman, who passed this way right after leaving Harvard: "We knew that more and more, year after year, the trains of emigrant wagons would creep in slow procession toward barbarous Oregon and wild and distant California. But we did not dream how commerce and gold would breed nations along the Pacific."

The other two are devoted to HST: the modest white frame house at 219 North Delaware Street to which the Trumans retired in 1953; and the Truman Library and Museum, where you can see the love letters that Harry wrote to Bess over the course of a long courtship and longer marriage, exhibits tracing his astonishing comeback in the 1948 Presidential election, and the sign from the president's desk proclaiming "The Buck Stops Here." Truman enjoys greater popularity than ever today, at least partly because he epitomizes a saner, simpler era, an era of picket fences, breakfast nooks, and morning constitutionals. With a cozy library and eat-in kitchen, trimmed in 1950s green, the house provides a window on those long-lost days.

I never go there without remembering the former president's exchange with a reporter as he headed back home after the inauguration of Dwight D. Eisenhower. "What's the first thing you plan to do when you get there?" the newsman inquired.

"Carry the grips up to the attic," Truman responded.

WHERE TO STAY

Fairmont, 401 Ward Parkway, (816) 756-1500. It's across Brush Creek from Country Club Plaza, so you won't have to walk far to empty your wallet or purse. This onetime queen of Kansas City hotels, with expansive guest rooms, a marble-clad lobby, and a luxurious pool, is not quite so impeccably run as it was when it was known as The Ritz.

The Raphael, 325 Ward Parkway, (816) 756-3800, gives the Fairmont a brisk run for its money. It counts 88 apartment-like suites among its 123 rooms. The staff is attentive, the food is good, and all in all the place feels like one of those chic but understated hideaways you find in London.

Westin Crown Center, 1 East Pershing Road, (816) 474-4400, has a bustling atmosphere befitting a 725-room behemoth. This is probably the best of the convention hotels, with thirty-one meeting rooms and easy access to the center's two dozen restaurants. An indoor waterfall rescues this establishment from the sterility that plagues chain hotels.

WHERE TO EAT

The American Restaurant, 200 East Twenty-fifth Street, Crown Center, (816) 545-8000, pioneered the use of regional ingredients in updated American classics thirty years ago. Warren Platner's stunning modern decor has been refreshed, and Celina Tio excels in dishes like honey-roasted free-range chicken from Campo Lindo Farm near Lathrop, Missouri, a double pork chop

with an herbed funnel cake, and an Asian American lobster salad that incorporates lime, palm sugar, and hearts of palm.

Arthur Bryant Barbecue, 1727 Brooklyn Avenue, (816) 231-1123. I always prepare myself for the letdown that never comes. For me, this remains the best of Kansas City's eighty barbecue joints. Gates's 'cue is great, but its mood is a bit too buttoned-up. I keep meaning to hit LC's on the East Side, but then I think about Arthur's burnt ends, the crispy beef bits that they throw in if asked, and the car heads for Brooklyn Avenue.

Forty Sardines, 11942 Roe Avenue, Overland Park, Kansas, (913) 451-1040. Michael Smith and Debbie Gold, husband and wife, won a James Beard Award while cooking at the American Restaurant. Now, in the suburbs, they offer unpretentious, satisfying food like cured duck breast, chewy peppered veal flank steak, and, yes, grilled Portuguese sardines. The lemon meringue pie is sublime. The graphics are just as good-looking as the interior design, and there are twenty respectable wines, red and white, for $20. Bravo!

Lidia's Kansas City, 101 West Twenty-second Street, (816) 221-3722. The opening a few years back of Lidia Bastianich's Midwest outpost in a renovated freight house in the reborn, gallery-filled Crossroads district caused such a stir that six hundred requests for opening-night reservations had to be turned down. A New York restaurateur herself, the mother of another (Joseph, an owner of Babbo), and a TV chef (*Lidia's Italian-American Kitchen* on PBS), she champions the lusty cuisine of her native northeastern Italy, like the filled, fried cheese nibble called frico. With the boss far away, quality can be uneven.

Plaza III, 4749 Pennsylvania Avenue, (816) 753-0000, lacks the patina of old-time steak houses like Jess & Jim's, the Hereford House, and the Savoy Grill, which was Harry Truman's favorite. But it serves the best Kansas City strip in town, aged for twenty-one to twenty-eight days in a specially designed cooler.

You choose from a deep list of beef-worthy red wines and eat in a clubby room decorated with photographs of champion cattle.

Stroud's Oak Ridge Manor, 5410 Northeast Oak Ridge Road, approximately at I-35 and Vivian Road, (816) 454-9600. The original Stroud's nestles under a grim overpass on the south side; this branch, an old farmhouse, is more pleasant. You'll have to wait for a table, but that gives you time to sip a first-rate margarita and work up an appetite for the crisp, amber-gold pan-fried chicken, with a skin so succulent it makes you wonder what other cooks do wrong. Great mashed potatoes, peppery cream gravy, and sinful cinnamon rolls; forget the flaccid green beans unless you're from the South.

⫸ CLEVELAND

Cleveland hasn't always had a bad press. At the turn of the last century, under the reform mayor Tom L. Johnson, it was described as "the best-governed city in America," and the local power company used to get some very good mileage out of the smug slogan, "The Best Location in the Nation."

But Henry Miller summed up the prevailing view when he wrote just after World War II that "possessing all the virtues, all the prerequisites for life, growth, blossoming, it remains, nevertheless, a thoroughly dead place—a deadly, dull, dead place." Things weren't helped much, decades later, when the polluted Cuyahoga River, which bisects the city, caught fire, and the hapless mayor at the time, Ralph J. Perk, joined in the revelry by inadvertently applying a blowtorch to his hair.

Then, in 1978, the city defaulted on its debt, the first to do so since the Great Depression. It was bad. Worse than bad. Believe me. I grew up in nearby Akron, and I winced for years at the gibes directed at "the buckle on the Rust Belt" by the rest of the country. But Cleveland has finally begun to reinvent itself in recent years. People called to northeastern Ohio by the exigencies of business or health (the Cleveland Clinic ranks among the world's best) find a great deal more to admire and enjoy than they had expected.

Municipal Stadium, the real Mistake by the Lake, has given way to Jacobs Field, a nifty downtown ballpark popularly known as the Jake, where the once-pitiful Indians played host to World Series games in 1995 and 1997. (They lost both times.) Cleveland Browns Stadium, a new home for a new team with an old name, opened in 1999. (The old Browns—the team that once starred the likes of Otto Graham, Jim Brown, and Lou Groza—had been spirited away to Baltimore in 1996 by its owner, Art Modell, whose name has been mud in Cleveland ever since.) If LeBron James, the high school basketball prodigy from Akron St. Vincent, is to be believed, even happier days lie ahead. Asked by a cynical New York reporter how it felt to be drafted by the lowly Cavaliers in unglamorous Cleveland, he replied: "You come out this season. You'll see how glamorous it is. It's going to be lit up like Las Vegas."

Maybe, maybe not. But the city center already looks less shabby than it did—and not just where sporting facilities are concerned. Five vintage theaters at Playhouse Square, which went dark in the 1960s and nearly disappeared in the 1970s, have been renovated. They offer more than 10,000 seats and entertain more than a million patrons a year at performances of dance, drama, musical comedy, concerts, and opera.

And not far away, right on Lake Erie, stands another symbol of rebirth: the I. M. Pei–designed $84 million Rock-and-Roll Hall of Fame and Museum, open daily, which displays a trove of artifacts including John Lennon's Sergeant Pepper uniform and Elvis Presley's black leather duds. Rotating exhibits celebrate modern groups like U2. Why Cleveland? It was there that a manic disk jockey named Alan Freed coined the phrase "rock and roll" and gave early impetus to the emerging pop form in the late 1950s. An awful lot of hipsters must be coming to check out the Hall. According to the Cleveland Convention and Visitors Bureau, the number of tourist arrivals jumped from 4.4 million in 1994 to 9 million in 2001.

Close to the coal of central Ohio and western Pennsylvania, and linked by the Great Lakes to the iron ore of northern Minnesota, Cleveland developed enormous steel mills and other big factories a century ago, as dark and satanic as any that Blake ever saw in England. Men came from all over Europe to labor in them—Poles, Italians, Serbs, Slovenes, Lithuanians, Croats, Czechs, Slovaks, Romanians, Greeks, and others. Since then, the city's population has slipped sharply. When I was a youngster, it was the sixth largest city in the country; in 2000, with 478,000 residents, it was thirty-third, just behind Las Vegas. But at 2,946,000 in the decennial census, the eight-county metropolitan area, stretching a hundred miles along the south shore of the lake, ranked fifteenth nationally.

Most of the mills have gone dark, but many of the immigrants' descendants remain, and with them a bewildering variety of restaurants, shops, and churches. Especially churches. Cleveland's ethnic neighborhoods (the "cosmo wards") are punctuated by spires, domes, and crosses of every imaginable shape. This is the habitat of kielbasa and Drew Carey and the Polka Hall of Fame. Even in the opening years of the twenty-first century, the city is Ellis Island writ large, especially in places like the venerable West Side Market, one of the largest covered markets in the country, where you can still shop for bread, cheese, and sausage in a dozen languages. Cleveland also has an enormous African American population, the result of black migration from the rural South. Economic and social frustration in the Hough ghetto boiled over in a weeklong riot in 1966, and in 1967 Carl B. Stokes was elected mayor, the first black mayor of a major American city.

Not surprisingly, the mills and other burgeoning businesses made the bosses rich. The most famous of them was John D. Rockefeller, who founded the Standard Oil Company in Cleveland in 1870 and made incalculable fortunes for himself, his brother William, and his partners, including Stephen V. Harkness, Louis H. Severance, and Henry M. Flagler. There were other bosses, too, like Mark Hanna, who built a career as a political mastermind using his mining and shipping wealth; Charles F. Brush, who developed the streetlight; and Jeptha Wade, the creator of the first transcontinental telegraph line. Their nineteenth-century fortunes helped, in turn, to pay for landmarks and institutions that continue to enrich Cleveland (and other places; Harkness money built residential colleges at Harvard and Yale, Flagler money the Florida East Coast Railway and Palm Beach).

Standard Oil dollars were behind the airy, elegant Cleveland Arcade, a shopping mall before its time, with ornate cast-iron balustrades and stairways. Completed in 1890 and beautifully preserved, this five-story glass-roofed gallery, the length of a football field, rivals Milan's famous Galleria Vittorio Emanuele, built just thirteen years earlier. Wade money has nourished the

Cleveland Museum of Art for many decades. The gem of the University Circle area, between downtown and the eastern suburbs, where cultural, medical, and educational institutions are clustered, it has one of the nation's premier collections, housed in a neoclassical building with a modern wing designed in 1970 by Marcel Breuer. (For its first major expansion in thirty years, a $225 million project, the museum has hired Rafael Viñoly, who designed the acclaimed new concert hall in Philadelphia in 2001.) One of the museum's virtues is the system of display, in which decorative objects—furniture, ceramics, textiles—are shown along with paintings and sculpture from the same period. The Asian holdings are superb, matched only in this country, perhaps, by Boston's, thanks to the Oriental scholar Sherman E. Lee, who was the director from 1958 to 1983.

Two items in particular deserve mention: one of America's sporting icons, George Bellows's violent 1907 boxing scene, *Stag at Sharkey's*; and one of the greatest works of art to survive from the early days of the Holy Roman Empire, a glorious portable altar, made about 1040 in Braunschweig (Brunswick) in Lower Saxony, of gold, red porphyry, cloisonné, enamels, niello, gemstones, and pearls. It is part of the Guelph Treasure.

From the museum, it is only a short stroll to Severance Hall (those Rockefeller bucks at work again), which is the home of the Cleveland Orchestra. Improbably, for such a small city, Cleveland rejoices in one of the nation's finest orchestras. It was shaped by the Hungarian-born maestro George Szell (1946–70); on the centennial of his birth in 1997, a BBC commentator said, "You may have no idea where Cleveland is, but if you love music you certainly know of the Cleveland Orchestra, because Szell made it the best in the world." Under Christoph von Dohnányi, his successor, it was merely the best in the country—so said *Time* magazine in 1994. Both at Severance Hall and at its summer home, Blossom Center, south of town, the orchestra strives toward Szell's unattainable ideal: orchestral music as chamber music, four dozen musicians playing with the precision of four. Dohnányi was succeeded in 2002 by the Austrian Franz Welser-Möst, who has yet to convince critics, in Cleveland or elsewhere, that he has the right stuff.

Like other big arts organizations in Cleveland, the orchestra, following a $36.7 million renovation of Severance Hall in 2000 and major improvements at Blossom Center, ran into major budgetary problems. The stock market swan dive hurt the endowments of not only the organizations themselves but also two important local backers of the arts, the Cleveland Foundation and the George Gund Foundation. At the same time, the Ohio Arts Council, under legislative pressure, throttled back its cultural grants across the state.

Peter B. Lewis, a leading local philanthropist who heads the Progressive Corporation, an auto insurance company, locked horns in 2002 with Case Western Reserve University, another of the major institutions in the University Circle area. Seeking to kick-start an improvement in its reputation, the university hired Frank Gehry to build one of his signature buildings, with undulating walls of brick and glass on three sides and a cascade of stainless steel ribbons on the fourth, for its Weatherhead School of Management. Lewis, who has given millions to Princeton University and the Guggenheim Museum as well as to Cleveland causes, agreed to pay for most of the project. But when the cost ballooned from $25 to $61.7 million, he balked, threatening to cut off the university and withhold donations from other regional charities. The cost overrun was the fault of the Case Western Reserve trustees, he argued, and they should resign. They did not, but the building nonetheless opened on time in October 2002, and the Cleveland *Plain Dealer*, hailing it, said it "dares students and faculty to match or outdo, in their own ways, what Gehry has done."

After a decade in the planning, the Cleveland Botanical Garden's new Eleanor Armstrong Smith Glasshouse opened in 2003, bringing tropical Costa Rica and Madagascar to the decidedly untropical north coast of the Midwest. Entire ecosystems have been re-created: from baobab trees to buttercup-yellow flowers, from red rain frogs to blue morpho butterflies. The 18,000-square-foot conservatory houses palms and ferns and vines, birds, even a small stream.

A surprising number of actors were born or brought up in Cleveland, including Bob Hope, Paul Newman, Dorothy Dandridge, and Halle Berry (named for the old Halle Bros.

Department store). Some of them honed their skills at the Cleveland Play House, the nation's longest-running regional theater, which produces classic and contemporary dramas on four stages and maintains a new play development program. Since its founding in 1915, the Play House has mounted world premieres by playwrights of the stature of Tennessee Williams and Arthur Miller. During the regime of Peter Hackett, the artistic director since 1994, several Play House productions have moved to Broadway and off-Broadway. And Karamu House, yet another University Circle cultural landmark, is a nationally important center for the African American arts. It has staged plays by writers like Langston Hughes, August Wilson, and John Henry Redwood, and has trained leading black actors.

Big manufacturers are still based in Cleveland—notably Eaton, which makes auto and aerospace parts; Sherwin-Williams, which makes paints; and Parker-Hannifin, which makes control equipment. But others have left, and the city has yet to replace them (unlike Akron, hollowed out by the departure of big rubber companies, which is now the home to 400 companies in the polymer field with 30,000 employees).

Along with other cities, Cleveland is trying to attract biotechnology start-ups, but it is also betting heavily on the arts. "The arts," reported the *Cleveland Free Press*, a weekly alternative newspaper, "have become the poster child for economic development. Many are talking about the annual $1.3 billion the arts and culture generate, the 4,000 good-paying jobs, the way that the arts have transformed Cleveland's best neighborhoods—Tremont, the Heights, Murray Hill and the Warehouse District."

Cleveland is the largest city in that broad swath of northern Ohio known as the Western Reserve, which the state of Connecticut, its original owner, sold to a group of private investors late in the eighteenth century in a bid to raise money for public schools. The Western Reserve was declared part of the United States in 1800, and Ohio entered the Union three years later as the first state that had never been a colony (like Vermont, Kentucky, and Tennessee) or part of another state.

You can get a glimpse of that era on a day trip east and south of Cleveland, starting at the Kirtland Temple, near Mentor, a stout stone-and-stucco structure, the first permanent church built (1833–36) by the followers of the Mormon prophet Joseph Smith on their way west. South on Route 91 is the leafy village of Hudson, which looks as if it had wandered out of nineteenth-century New England by mistake. It is filled with white Greek and Gothic Revival buildings, including many on the tranquil campus of Western Reserve Academy (where I spent my high school years). Farther south, stop for a moment at the lovely First Congregational Church on the village green in Tallmadge, built in 1821. If you like, you can return to Cleveland by way of Stan Hywet Hall, overlooking the Cuyahoga Valley on the northwest fringe of Akron. A neo-Jacobean mansion built in 1912 for the founder of Goodyear Tire and Rubber, Frank A. Seiberling, it has spectacular gardens, laid out in part by the celebrated designer Ellen Biddle Shipman.

A short drive to the southwest takes you to Oberlin, another academic village, which was a center of abolitionism and a station on the Underground Railway. Oberlin College was the first in the United States to admit students regardless of sex, creed, or color. Today the college is noted for its outstanding musical conservatory and for the Allen Memorial Art Museum, designed by Cass Gilbert and the Philadelphia postmodernists Robert Venturi and Denise Scott Brown, which regularly lends paintings from its comprehensive 11,000-item collection to major exhibitions all over the world. It is considered one of the five best university museums in the country, along with those at Harvard, Yale, Penn, and the Rhode Island School of Design.

WHERE TO STAY

Ritz-Carlton, 1515 West Third Street, (216) 623-1300. This is unquestionably the city's best hotel, luxurious and low-key, with a harpist at afternoon tea. Premium-priced club-level rooms come with a lavish, free cocktail hour. In a city chronically short of good rooms, the Ritz's opening in 1990 gave a powerful signal of commitment to the future.

Renaissance, 24 Public Square, (216) 696-5600. History lovers might like the Renaissance, a Marriott property with magnificent, old-fashioned public spaces, but the 491 rooms vary—some are quite satisfactory, others plain. It's a short walk to corporate headquarters, sports stadia, a shopping mall, and the Rapid Transit train to the airport.

WHERE TO EAT

Johnny's Bar, 3164 Fulton Road, (216) 281-0055. Johnny's is sui generis: old tavern, smart 1920s decor, delicious Italian food

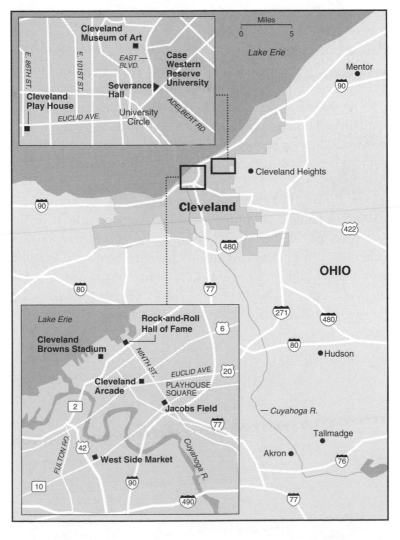

(scallops and shrimp on linguine), great wines, lousy neighbor-hood. It's always crowded with local movers and shakers, who come for the juicy oversized steaks and chops, so it's noisy, but that's part of the joint's charm.

Lola Bistro, 900 Literary Road, (216) 771-5652, is one of the joys of the once-shabby Tremont District, reborn in recent years with the arrival of dozens of art galleries. Michael Symon, a tal-ented cook and "a prolific schmoozer," as Anthony Bourdain called him, specializes in high-wattage dishes with local roots, like walleye with chive spaetzle, and goulash made with lamb shank, beef shortribs, and venison.

Parker's, 2801 Bridge Avenue, Ohio City, (216) 771-7130. This is the city's New American flag-bearer, featuring seasonal Ohio-grown ingredients, often organic, in well-judged dishes like pork tenderloin with rhubarb and braised local mushrooms with herbs. The French-trained chef-owner, Parker Bosley, has in his quiet way been a prime mover in the establishment of a net-work of high-class farmers' markets in northeastern Ohio.

Three Birds, 18515 Detroit Avenue, Lakewood, (216) 221-3500. The name comes from a Bob Marley song title. It seems just right for this bubbly, relatively new bistro in the western suburbs, with its zinc bar, postindustrial decor, and eclectic menu. Chef John Kolar seems to be able to cook anything. He turns out a dandy Thai beef salad and pan-roasts the Midwest's favorite freshwater fish, walleye, napping it with sorrel sauce.

⫸ CINCINNATI

Despite a riverside site of uncommon beauty and a history of uncommon achievement, Cincinnati has always had a reputation as a stick-in-the-mud. Mark Twain suggested that he'd like to go there for the apocalypse because it was always twenty years behind the times, and John Gunther detected "a certain stately and also sleepy quality" in the place. Even Governor Bob Taft of Ohio, a member of the city's (and state's and nation's) longest-lasting political dynasty, told me when I ran into him at a football game that Cincinnati has "an inbred resistance to rapid change." Longfellow, on the other hand, described it as "the Queen City of the West," and in bad times the city clings to that phrase as to a life raft.

A little bit Northern, a little bit Southern, Cincinnati comes close to the national average by a number of standards, including the cost of living and median family income. But there have been major problems lately, particularly in race relations. Racial polarization gutted the downtown in the 1970s and whites fled to the suburbs. In April 2001, after a white police officer (later acquitted) shot a black teenager, Timothy Thomas, who was the fifteenth African American since 1995 to die in such circumstances, three days of riots ensued. Local leaders worked hard to heal the city's wounds, but in December 2003 nerves were rubbed raw again and accusations of brutality renewed when white officers clubbed an African American to death in a parking lot, an act that was caught by video cameras.

Another troubling manifestation of a different kind of social tension in Cincinnati was the indictment in April 1990 of the Contemporary Arts Center and its director on obscenity charges arising from an exhibition of 175 photographs by Robert

Mapplethorpe, a few of which depicted explicitly homoerotic subjects. Those defendants were also acquitted, by a mostly working-class local jury.

But Cincinnati is a city rich in cultural traditions, with a noted musical heritage and a record of innovation in many fields. It had America's first professional baseball team, the Cincinnati Red Stockings, now the Reds, founded in 1869. John and Washington Roebling's sturdy suspension bridge spanning the Ohio River, still in service to this day, opened in 1866, seventeen years before the Brooklyn Bridge. It was in Cincinnati that Rabbi Isaac Mayer Wise of the Plum Street Temple, a liberal intellectual born in Bohemia, shaped modern Reform Judaism, helping to found the Hebrew Union College in 1875, the Central Conference of American Rabbis in 1889, and the Union of American Hebrew Congregations in 1873. The rabbi called his Byzanto-Moorish temple "my Alhambra." Play-Doh was invented in Cincinnati, and Formica, and soap that floats. Dr. Albert Sabin developed his oral polio vaccine while working in the city, and Dr. Henry Heimlich perfected his technique for saving the lives of people who are choking.

Conservative? Provinicial? Well, in recent years, a galaxy of innovative architects, including Frank O. Gehry, Michael Graves, Peter Eisenman, Cesar Pelli, and Harry Cobb, have designed new buildings for several local institutions, notably the University of Cincinnati. Gehry's Vontz Center for Molecular Studies looks like one of those cartoon buildings that are jumping off their foundations, almost ready to burst. The red-brick structure, a vivid if startling gateway to the university, is defined by its bulges.

And it was the Contemporary Arts Center, focus of the Mapplethorpe flap, that gave the London-based Iraqi-born design diva Zaha Hadid her first commission in the United States. When the Lois and Richard Rosenthal Center for Contemporary Art opened in 2003, it struck Herbert Muschamp, the *New York Times* architecture critic, as "the most important American building to be completed since the end of the Cold War." Its stack of concrete and metal cubic and rectangular forms struck me as a Klee magic-square painting in three dimensions.

Before the Civil War, some Cincinnatians with extensive business dealings in the South defended that region's "peculiar institution." But local abolitionists helped thousands of slaves escape across the Ohio River to freedom, defying apostles of the status quo. Lyman Beecher, a fiery Presbyterian preacher, spent the years 1832–50 as president of Lane Theological Seminary here, and his daughter, Harriet Beecher Stowe, drew on her experiences in Ohio and Kentucky in writing her influential anti-slavery novel *Uncle Tom's Cabin* (1852).

That history is celebrated in the new $110 million Underground Railroad Freedom Center—part museum, part think tank—which lured Spencer R. Crow to Cincinnati from his position as director of the National Museum of American History in Washington. The center is a major element in the ongoing reinvention of the riverfront, where the city had its beginnings. A pair of spiffy sports stadia have been built there as well—the Great American Ballpark for the Reds and Paul Brown Stadium for the football Bengals.

Long ago, the Ohio River was one of the main highways west, and that made Cincinnati a boom town in the years after the American Revolution. Founded in 1788, it was given its name by Arthur St. Clair, governor of the Northwest Territory and a veteran officer who had fought at the battles of Trenton and Princeton. St. Clair was a member of the Society of the Cincinnati, an organization of Revolutionary officers founded by George Washington and named for Cincinnatus, the Roman patriot who returned to his farm after saving his city in battle. This city, in turn, was named for the society.

Like the floodwaters that have often plagued it, Cincinnati spread slowly up and out from "the Basin," as the locals call the flatlands along the river, first into the adjoining valleys and later up the steep hillsides. As a Cincinnati Web site (www.insiders. com/cincinnati) puts it, "the steamboat changed Cincinnati almost as much as the apple changed Adam." By the 1840s, it was America's sixth largest city and the center of the young nation's pig-processing industry. People called the city Porkopolis, and visitors complained of the smell. The English novelist Anthony Trollope wrote of "a stench that surpassed in offensiveness anything that my nose had ever hitherto suffered: the odor of hogs going up to the Ohio heavens."

The porkers are gone, but one company founded to make use

of pork by-products like lard lives on as Cincinnati's primary economic engine: Procter & Gamble, the nation's largest producer of household products. P&G's twin postmodern headquarters towers dominate the eastern part of downtown Cincinnati. On a roll lately, the company still reaches into every city, town, and hamlet in America with Tide, Ivory, Pampers, Crest, Old Spice, Crisco, Folger's, and dozens of other brands. Cincinnati is also home base for Federated Department Stores, the retailing leviathan that operates more than 450 stores nationwide, including Macy's and Bloomingdale's in the New York area; Chiquita Brands, the world's biggest banana company (which forced the Cincinnati *Enquirer* to run a front-page apology and pay a $10 million settlement in 1998 after the paper had accused it of illicit operations in Central America); and Kroger, which grew from a single grocery store started in 1883 by Barney Kroger, with $372 of his own money and $350 borrowed from a friend, into one of the nation's biggest grocery retailers. And who could overlook the highly profitable but weirdly named Fifth Third Bank, formed in a 1908 merger between institutions that insisted on retaining their numerical identities? Attracted by good jobs on offer at P&G and outlying manufacturing companies, French, German, and Japanese executives have recently flooded into the city.

But Cincinnati missed what may have been its biggest economic opportunity. At the turn of the last century, it was the world's biggest manufacturer of carriages; when a couple of entrepreneurs named Henry Ford and J. W. Packard came looking for capital to start their auto factories, the local bankers turned them down. So they went to Detroit instead. The main east-west railroads, and eventually the main east-west superhighways, also bypassed Cincinnati. Like people in St. Louis and other older cities in the Midwest, Cincinnatians watched as Chicago became the region's main hub and their city fell into the second tier.

Perhaps because the area reminded them of the Rhineland, Germans had flocked into the Ohio Valley in the 1840s and 1850s, eventually constituting a quarter of Cincinnati's population. German-language newspapers were founded, beer gardens sprang up, and as in so many Midwestern cities, German was taught in the public schools. All that came to a swift end in 1914. Yet the Teutonic flavor lingers. The mostly black neighborhood north of downtown is called Over-the-Rhine. Not by chance, the only Hofbrauhaus in the Americas is across the river in Newport, Kentucky. Graeter's ice cream, dished up in shops around the area, is a toothsome survivor of the city's Germanic past (try the peach). Zoology is a German passion, too, and Cincinnati boasts one of the nation's premier zoos, founded in 1875.

The most important German legacy, however, is the city's love of music. The May Festival, which dates from 1873, grew out of Saengerfests, or songfests, that were given starting in 1849, with up to 2,000 volunteer chorus members. The Music Hall, a sauerbraten Gothic palace that seats 3,400 people, with spectacular chandeliers and a lovely lobby in cream and gold, was completed in 1878 as a home for the festival. It now houses the Cincinnati Symphony Orchestra, Cincinnati Pops, and Cincinnati Summer Opera as well. Early on, distinguished European conductors took charge of the festival, among them Eugene Goossens, Fritz Busch, Max Rudolf, and Josef Krips. In 1906, Sir Edward Elgar traveled to Cincinnati to conduct his oratorio *The Dream of Gerontius*.

Since 1974, Americans have been at the festival helm: Cincinnati-born James Levine until 1979, James Conlon in the years since. Conlon is one of those American musicians who have made their careers largely in Europe, but Cincinnati recognized his exceptional gifts early. Now he is the principal conductor of the Paris Opera and the Cologne Philharmonic, but he nonetheless returns to Ohio each year.

The Cincinnati Symphony, founded in 1895, also has a distinguished history, having had Leopold Stokowski, Fritz Reiner, and Thomas Schippers as conductors; Schippers, who died young, was a great local favorite who also worked at Bayreuth and, notably, at Spoleto, Italy. The Estonian-born Paavo Jarvi is the current music director, and the orchestra, which plays from September to May, remains more adventurous than most. One year recently it offered Glinka, Korngold, Honegger, Nielsen, Griffes, Scriabin, Weill, and Zwilich in addition to more conventional musical fare. The Pops, probably the best known such ensemble after Boston's, has gained an international reputation under Erich Kunzel. It has made no fewer than sixty-five records for Telarc, which have sold more than seven million copies worldwide and consolidated the flamboyant Kunzel's reputation.

The Playhouse in the Park, a professional company with the good fortune to perform in Eden Park, a leafy aerie above the city, presents about ten productions a year, typically ranging from Shakespeare to *Mister Roberts* to *Wit*, Margaret Edson's 1999 Pulitzer Prize winner. The small but enterprising Ensemble Theater performs in a converted bank building in Over-the-Rhine—Edward Albee has directed several of his plays there—and the Cincinnati Opera, the nation's second oldest, mounts four productions a year. In 2005 it will do *Margaret Garner*, an opera about a runaway slave and her daughter, which it jointly commissioned, with Denyse Graves in the lead. It is based on the story of a real-life slave from Cincinnati, which inspired Toni Morrison's novel *Beloved*; Ms. Morrison wrote the opera's libretto.

As for the visual arts, the city has not one but two important museums—the Cincinnati Art Museum and the Taft Museum—both linked with the remarkable Taft family. (That both lent works to the Ingres exhibition in Washington and New York in 1999, a connoisseur's show if ever there was one, suggests the quality of their best holdings.)

It's worth digressing into politics for a moment to sketch in the story of the Tafts. Alphonso Taft was secretary of war and attorney general under Ulysses S. Grant. His son, William Howard Taft, a 350-pounder who had to have a special bathtub installed in the White House, was the twenty-seventh president and subsequently the seventh chief justice of the United States. He focused on the latter role, remarking, "I don't remember that I ever was president."

One of President Taft's sons, Senator Robert A. Taft, a leading isolationist, came close to the Republican presidential nomination in 1952. His son, Robert Taft (with no middle initial) also served in the Senate. And *his* son, Bob Taft, is the current governor of Ohio. The governor likes politics better than his great-grandfather did. How was he getting on in Columbus? I asked. "I love being governor," he replied happily. "I'm having a ball."

Mrs. William Howard Taft was an early supporter of the Cincinnati Art Museum, which has grown into a comprehensive collection housed in a Doric temple in Eden Park, atop Mount Adams. The museum has good modern art, including a splendidly graphic Matisse called *Romanian Blouse* (1937) and a

Warhol portrait of Pete Rose—aka Charlie Hustle, the Reds' tragic hero, who set an all-time record with 4,256 hits, only to be denied admission to the Hall of Fame because he had, as manager, gambled on his own team. But its old masters are its glory. A vast Benjamin West, *Ophelia and Laertes*, was bought in London by Robert Fulton, the steamboat man, not so long after it was painted, then brought to Cincinnati by Nicholas Longworth, founder of another local dynasty, as early as 1828. Closer to our own day, the Emery family enriched the collection with a Mantegna, a small but lustrous Botticelli, and one of the best Bronzinos I know, a cool, austerely beautiful portrait of Eleanor of Toledo and her son.

Thanks to Dr. Nelson Glueck, a Cincinnati archeologist who excavated Petra in Jordan in the 1930s, the art museum also houses the best collection of ancient Nabataean artifacts outside the Middle East.

As for the Taft Museum, quartered in a handsome Federal house downtown, it was bequeathed to the city in 1927 by President Taft's half brother, Charles Phelps Taft. Its leading attractions, for me, are its fine Hals portraits; a brilliantly colored Gainsborough, *Edward and William Tomkinson*; and a great late Turner, *Europa and the Bull*, in which the figures vanish in a shimmer of gold and blue.

Across town, the old Union Terminal, a railway station that looks like a Bakelite Art Deco radio rendered in concrete, has been turned into the Cincinnati Museum Center. A landmark of Deco architecture built in 1933, it continues to evoke the drama of travel in the golden age of rail, while sheltering a local history museum, a children's museum, a museum of natural history and science, and an IMAX movie theater under its soaring half dome. Its ice-cream parlor is sheathed in Rookwood tiles. The Rookwood Pottery, Cincinnati's contribution to the Arts and Crafts movement, was founded by Nicholas Longworth's granddaughter Maria Longworth Nichols. (Her nephew, Nicholas Longworth III, Speaker of the House, married Theodore Roosevelt's sharp-tongued daughter, Alice, in 1906. She called Cincinnati "Cincin nasty.") You can see other, better Rookwood tiles in the Federal courthouse, named for Supreme Court Justice Potter Stewart, a Cincinnati native.

WHERE TO STAY

The Cincinnatian, 601 Vine Street, (513) 381-3000. Designed by the city's favorite fin de siècle architect, Samuel Hannaford, and thoroughly rebuilt in 1987, this is now Cincinnati's preeminent hotel. A period lobby opens into a sunny atrium painted in postmodern colors, Tuscan ocher and pale sky blue. With only 146 rooms to look after (a few of them a little small), the staff has time to provide personal service. Good restaurant.

Westin, Fountain Square, (513) 621-7700. The location is perfect, the tastefully redecorated rooms have lots of elbow room, and the hotel can even claim a footnote in history: the infamous Jerry Springer Show originated from the premises in its early days. But service can be dire. My bags were lost for two hours between curb and room, while undertrained, overcheerful people assured me that they were "on the way up."

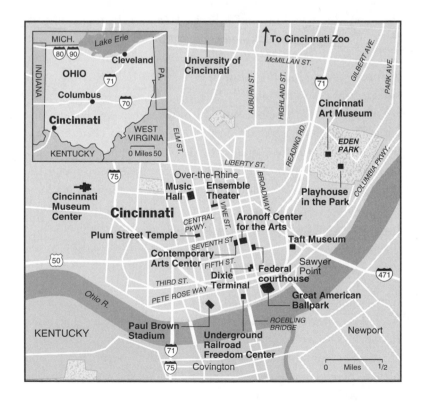

WHERE TO EAT

Camp Washington Chili, 3005 Colerain Avenue, (513) 541-0061. Created in 1922 by a Bulgarian immigrant, Cincinnati-style chili took the town by storm. This improbable passion has never abated, and now there are three chains with 150-odd outlets, plus independents. All serve "three-way" (chili made with cocoa, cinnamon, and allspice, served atop spaghetti, with a crown of grated cheddar); I prefer four-way, with chopped onions, and Camp Washington does it best. Lean over when you eat; the stuff stains.

Jean-Robert at Pigall's, 127 West Fourth Street, (513) 721-1345. A defector from the Maisonette (see below), Jean-Robert de Cavel moved the defunct Pigall's to the head of the class with a lava-stone bar, modern French food (watercress-hazelnut quiche, cranberry ice cream), and a clever prix-fixe policy that includes tax, tip, and valet parking. Vitrines displaying a collection of salt- and pepper shakers add a nice note of whimsy.

Jeff Ruby's, 700 Walnut Street, (513) 784-1200. A brash transplant from New Jersey, Jeff Ruby wore spats to the opening benefit at this addition to his chain of Cincinnati watering holes. Beef and lamb is dry-aged in a glass-walled cooler (cf Gallagher's, New York), and smokers can enjoy steaks, Bibb salads, and cigars in the Toots Shor Room.

Maisonette, 114 East Sixth Street, (513) 721-2260. The Maisonette marked its fifty-fifth birthday in 2004. You, along with the city's famously stodgy movers and shakers, can return to the 1950s in these traditional, formal, softly lighted rooms, ordering things like Dover sole. Don't. Bertrand Bouquin's contemporary creations, some not listed on the menu, like a fresh, lemony crab salad, are more interesting. Superb desserts, wonderful wines.

Pho Paris, 3235 Madison Road, Oakley, (513) 871-1234. Cavel is a partner in this smart-looking Franco-Vietnamese spot in the northern part of town. Silky service, authentic pho (beef noodle soup), sparkling grilled beef with lemongrass, and voila! Another hit for the Cincinatti culinary king.

⫸ DETROIT

I remember Detroit during its days of glory in the late 1940s, when the assembly lines were churning out the cars the country had gone without during the war. It was a proud, prosperous, and self-confident city, the first metropolis of mass production.

My father took me there to watch the Tigers' great left-hander, Hal Newhouser. We tooled down Woodward Avenue, the Champs Élysées of Detroit, shopped for my mother at Hudson's, one of the nation's elite department stores, and ate at Lester Gruber's London Chop House, a clubby restaurant that served better food and wine than any club I know.

All that is gone now, even Hudson's, "rebranded" as a branch of Marshall Field's and moved to the suburbs, like its customers. The rivers of asphalt that Detroit laid down to handle the cars it built—the expressways named for industry titans like Edsel Ford and labor leaders like Walter Reuther—turned out to be exit ramps for most of the city's white population. Detroit was left with a black inner city, its infrastructure rotting, surrounded by well-off suburbs—a true urban nightmare. The *Hideaway Report,* a newsletter aimed at moneyed tourists, reported after a 1996 survey that its readers considered Detroit the world's least appealing travel destination.

Pity. For one thing, cultural riches abound, survivors of those distant days before the 1967 race riots, before the 1973 shock of rising oil prices, and before the invasion of Detroit's turf by foreign cars. The Detroit Institute of Arts is the nation's fifth largest art museum and one of its most comprehensive. An excellent, innovative Museum of African-American History opened eight years ago. The Detroit Symphony Orchestra has one of the most imaginative conductors of the day, Neeme Järvi, as its music director, and the brand-new $60 million Max M. Fisher Music Center as its home (already Detroiters call it the Max). The new facility incorporates the acoustically superb 1919 Orchestra Hall, restored and modernized, as well as space for educational activities and venues for jazz concerts and other events. But the orchestra is wrestling with a $2.2 million cumulative deficit, and Järvi will step down in 2005. In 2004, it had to impose pay outs and unpaid furloughs on musicians and staff members.

Singers of the caliber of Maria Ewing and Ruth Ann Swenson come here to sing with the Michigan Opera Theater at the elaborate Detroit Opera House, built in 1922. And the Cranbrook Academy of Art, which produced avatars of modern American design like Eero Saarinen, Charles and Ray Eames, Harry Bertoia, and Florence Knoll, has been in the city's northern suburbs since 1932.

Detroit was founded in 1701 by a French party under Antoine de la Mothe Cadillac as a trading post. The United States took over in 1796, surrendered the city to the British during the War of 1812, and regained it the next year for keeps. Detroit sits on the north bank of the narrow Detroit River, which along with Lake St. Clair and the St. Clair River links Lake Erie to Lake Huron and divides southeast Michigan from Ontario. Its name means "strait" in French, and French names survive in the city's street grid—Gratiot, Livernois, Beaubien.

Now Detroit is on its fourth or fifth comeback attempt. General Motors has moved its headquarters and 10,000 employees into the once-grim, silo-like Renaissance Center, a relic of failed earlier downtown comebacks. Compuware, a software maker, has brought a workforce of 3,000 in from the suburbs. The football Lions, a perennial doormat, have moved downtown from exurban Pontiac to play in Ford Field, a new stadium that will host the 2006 Super Bowl. It stands next to Comerica Park, the new Tigers ballpark. For the first time in a long time, property values are up. Three casinos meant to make Detroit the Atlantic City of the Midwest are expanding. And billions of dollars have been spent in the last five years sprucing up downtown. "This time it will work," vowed Max Fisher, who has helped to finance Republican campaigns in city, state, and nation for forty years and for whom the music center is named.

Well, maybe. Mayor Kwame M. Kilpatrick, an exuberant, Harley-riding figure often accused of criminal misdeeds, seems determined to make the city cleaner, safer, and prouder. He has demolished thousands of derelict buildings, and there is plenty of loose change out there in the suburbs. A restaurant called Tribute, in Farmington Hills, open only for dinner, Tuesdays through Saturdays, sells $70,000 worth of wine a week.

"Economically, socially, we're moving," said Kilpatrick, who took office at age thirty-one. Many Michigan-built cars now rival Japan's and Germany's best quality. But the cleanup, fix-up job is enormous. Parks and swimming pools have been closed, hundreds of streetlights are dark, and repairing the sewer system will cost further millions. Driving out Cass Avenue, on the western flank of downtown, you pass block after block of empty, weed-infested lots and boarded-up buildings, as bleak as Bucharest.

The old Michigan Central train station is a wasteland of shattered glass, surrounded by a razor-wire fence. The clock on the CPA Building has been stuck at 10:55 for decades.

The crime rate remains intractably high. Drained by the flight of middle-class residents both black and white, Detroit is shrinking. The 2000 census listed its population as 951,000, down from 2 million (!) in 1955. It is more than 81 percent African American. But the metropolitan area, which reaches north to Flint, is still growing. It is the nation's eighth biggest urban complex, with 5.8 million people.

Cars define Detroit. Always have. The nation's first mile of concrete pavement (1909), its first traffic light (1915), and its first urban freeway (1942) were all built in the city. So take a trip to the Henry Ford Museum in the southwestern suburb of Dearborn, which celebrates cars and the culture they spawned. A 1931 Bugatti Royale is on display there; and a gangster's 1929 Packard speedster; Old 16, the Locomobile that in 1908 became the first American car to win a major race; the car in which John F. Kennedy was riding on that dreadful day in Dallas; and the bus on which Rosa Parks was arrested in 1955 in

Montgomery, Alabama. American life on the road is represented by a gas station, a motel, and a highway diner.

The museum also houses other vast collections of Americana—glass, silver, furniture, what-have-you—and the adjacent Greenfield Village groups historical buildings that Henry Ford brought to Dearborn, including the laboratory of Thomas A. Edison and the Wright Brothers' cycle shop. It reopened in 2003 after a major tune-up, carried out to mark the centennial of the Ford Motor Company. (The celebration came at an awkward moment; the big automaker had lost $6.4 billion in the preceding two years, and its young CEO, William Clay Ford Jr., great-grandson of the founder, was struggling to turn it around.)

The Automotive Hall of Fame, just down the road, honors the men who built and led not only Ford but Chrysler and the behemoth of American manufacturing, General Motors. It is worth visiting just to see the orange-and-sunflower-yellow 1931 Cord roadster with white sidewalls, which to these aging eyes has never been matched for raffish glamour.

Almost from the start, Henry Ford paid a revolutionary five dollars a day, and although conditions in the Ford plants were brutal and management resisted unions until 1941, workers came from around the world to earn his wages. (As a direct result, Dearborn has one of the largest Arab populations in the nation.) They came from the South, too, and many were black; one family brought with them a son named Joe Louis Barrow, who dropped his last name and won worldwide acclaim as heavyweight champion. The name of the Joe Louis Arena and the statue of his forearm and fist downtown reinforce his standing as a local icon. (But not to a couple of suburban white men who defaced it with white paint in 2004.)

In the 1960s, a producer named Berry Gordy Jr. created the phenomenally popular Motown sound with the help of performers like the Supremes, the Temptations, and Smokey Robinson. He started his record company in 1959 in a house he called Hitsville, U.S.A., which is now the Motown Historical Museum. In the years since, Detroit has produced its full share of headliners, from Madonna to the radical rockers MC5 to the hip-hopping Eminem, and it also spawned Techno.

The White Stripes are the stars of the moment; they and

other top local groups play every night at clubs like the Magic Stick on Woodward Avenue. Pure D Vinyl in the Fisher Building stocks records solely by Detroit artists, including many that are hard to find. And touring pop music performers of all sorts share the stage at the lavishly restored Fox Theater downtown, the largest surviving movie palace of the 1920s.

Given its huge black population, the city is an ideal site for the 120,000-square-foot Museum of African-American History, which tells its often appalling story soberly and effectively. Powerful exhibits designed by Ralph Applebaum, who created the displays at the Holocaust Museum in Washington, range from slave manacles to a space suit worn by the first black female astronaut. Photographs, recordings of New Orleans jazz and bop, and film of Martin Luther King Jr. and Barbara Jordan in eloquent oratorical form round out the collection.

The Detroit Institute of Arts and the African American collection are only two blocks apart. One is often pictured as white and elitist, the other as black and populist, but in fact they are up to completely different things. One takes an encyclopedic approach to the fine and decorative arts (including works by such leading black artists as Romare Bearden), while the other includes art as but one important element in its story. On a recent Sunday when I was there, the crowd at the institute was predominantly black, while the visitors at the African American museum were mostly white and Asian.

Despite cutbacks in government financing that at one point restricted it to opening only twelve and a half hours a week, and despite the loss of a talented director, the institute has found a way to survive and flourish anew. Daily management was transferred to mostly suburban donors, who opened their wallets to the tune of more than $100 million. Meandering through its rich galleries one day, I was struck by the intensity of the colors in many of its best works, including an icily white Meissen crane by J. J. Kaendler, three glowing predella panels by Sassetta, Brueghel's exuberant *Wedding Dance,* a self-portrait in blue and gold by van Gogh, a view of the Ecuadorean volcano Cotopaxi erupting through a fiery sky by Frederic E. Church, a pulsating scene in the Savoy Ballroom in Harlem by Reginald Marsh, and one of Emil Nolde's many *Sunflowers.*

The great Mexican muralist Diego Rivera supplied the museum's centerpiece, a series of twenty-seven frescoes he painted on the walls of a central courtyard in 1932. Those on the two long walls show a Model-T assembly line and an engine-block plant. They are unabashed hymns to the dignity of workingmen of all races, many of whom are shown wearing fedoras as they toil.

Plenty of out-of-town architectural stars worked in Detroit, too, from H. H. Richardson to Cass Gilbert to Frank Lloyd Wright. But the architect in chief of Detroit's golden age was Albert Kahn, a German-born immigrant (and no relation of Louis I. Kahn, the eminent Philadelphia architect of a later day, who came from Estonia). He built mansions for Michigan industrialists in Grosse Pointe (including a Cotswold-style spread for Edsel Ford at 1100 Lake Shore Road, which is now open to visitors), libraries for the University of Michigan in Ann Arbor, and the immense River Rouge automobile plant for Henry Ford. His Fisher Building, in the midtown district known as the New Center, is an Art Deco masterpiece. An arched hallway three stories high cuts through it, punctuated by eight cylindrical chandeliers.

Kahn also built a house called Cranbrook in Bloomfield Hills, north of the city, for George G. Booth, owner of the *Detroit News,* who turned his estate into an educational complex including schools for boys and girls and an art school. The great Finnish modernist Eliel Saarinen designed the campus and headed the art school. The peristyle, a severe, unornamented sandstone gate with a fountain by the Swedish sculptor Carl Milles, houses a permanent exhibition of works by Saarinen, his son, Eero, and other eminent students. It is a glossary of the best American design, circa 1965, with Eero's pedestal chairs and Charles Eames's bent-plywood jobs. During the warmer months, the house Eliel built for his family on the Cranbrook grounds in a refined Deco vocabulary is open to the public.

A short drive north to Warren brings you to the G.M. Technical Center, among Eero's masterworks (along with the CBS Building in Manhattan and Dulles International Airport near Washington). It is among the projects studied by every would-be architect in the United States. Like the automobile itself, the long, low buildings are constructed primarily of glass, steel, and aluminum, but the end walls are made of glazed bricks in vivid colors—royal blue, yellow, red. They are grouped (at Twelve Mile and Mound Roads in Warren) around a lake in which fountains dance a "ballet" first devised by Alexander Calder. A three-legged stainless steel water tower rises like an exclamation mark above this remarkable ensemble.

WHERE TO STAY

Atheneum Hotel, 1000 Brush Avenue, (313) 962-2323. Much the pleasantest place to stay in the middle of town, at least until the returns are in on General Motors' $100 million remake of the Renaissance Center. Carved from a former seed warehouse in the heart of lively Greektown, the Atheneum is all suites, all the time—174 roomy layouts, with modern decor and huge bathrooms. Close to everything (a bit too close to the casino for peace and quiet), with free limousine service and an indifferent restaurant.

Ritz-Carlton, Fairlane Plaza, 300 Town Center Drive, Dearborn, (313) 441-2000. The top luxury hotel in the Detroit area provides the usual Ritz amenities: chandeliers, antiques, mahogany paneling, showers of flowers, and acres of marble. Rooms are a bit smaller and prices a bit gentler than at most of the group's properties. Despite the sterile surroundings (an office park), the Ritz is a civilized establishment with good food and all-but-flawless service.

Townsend Hotel, 100 Townsend Street, Birmingham, (248) 642-7900. This is my favorite hereabouts, a snug little nook with a wood-burning fireplace in the lobby and 150 charmingly decorated rooms and suites. Tucked into a shopping street in Birmingham, a wealthy suburb north of town, it is not far from the Cranbrook Art School. Newly redone executive suites shine. At full tilt, it sometimes seems just the slightest bit understaffed.

WHERE TO EAT

Cuisine, 670 Lothrop Avenue, (313) 872-5110. Wonder of wonders, a new restaurant in beleaguered downtown Detroit! Chef Paul Grosz, a local lad trained in Chicago and in France, opened Cuisine on a shoestring in 2001 in a 1920s house behind the Fisher Theater, with a pared-down urban flair and classy cooking. Within months the *Detroit Free Press* hailed it as the most exciting addition to the local dining scene in years. Grosz has a passion for luxury ingredients like caviar, wild mushrooms, and quail's eggs; try his foie gras three ways or his four-way lobster tasting (bisque, ravioli, salad, with caviar).

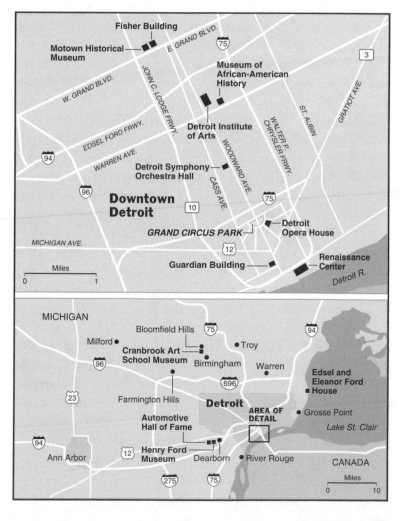

Five Lakes Grill, 424 North Main Street, Milford, (248) 684-7455. Brian Polcyn used to run the Pike Street Grill in Pontiac, but the commute got to him. So he retreated to the picturesque village of Milford, northwest of town, where he and his family have lived for many years, and started the Five Lakes Grill. The furniture is plain, the service down-home sweet, and the cooking deft—sautéed Great Lakes walleye (called pickerel here), fire-grilled chicken breast with ginger aioli, Hungarian-style veal paprikas.

Mon Jin Lau, 1515 East Maple Road, Troy, (248) 689-2332. Local chefs and other venturesome eaters value Marshal Chin's place for its inventive pan-Asian fare, like chili-pepper squid and Mongolian rack of lamb. Situated in Troy, land of K-Mart and used-car lots, it is an excellent choice on Sunday night, when many other top restaurants are closed. Surprisingly good wine list and brisk, knowledgeable service.

Tribute, 31425 West Twelve Mile Road, Farmington Hills, (248) 848-9393. Maybe the best restaurant between New York and Chicago, certainly the finest in this area. In the northwest suburbs, right at a freeway exit, it is the creation of an inventive chef, Takashi Yagihashi, and an ebullient, ponytailed maître d'hôtel, Mickey Bakst, whose subsequent exit saddened many. The eclectic, Asian-influenced menu races from bracingly fresh fluke sashimi to risotto with white truffles to Asian bouillabaisse with kaffir lime foam. The room sparkles with colored glass and the glass-walled wine cellar sparkles with the best of France, Napa, Italy, and Australia. Big Three big shots love it.

Zingerman's, 422 Detroit Street, Ann Arbor, (734) 663-3354, the deli of my dreams, is unmatched outside New York. Ari Weinzweig seduces with whitefish salad on onion rye, pastrami sandwiched between potato pancakes, silky chopped liver, properly cured corned beef, or brisket with schmaltz; eat at tables indoors and out. To go: home-baked breads, mustards, fine oils, jams, pasta, and the very best selection of English farmhouse cheeses this side of Neal's Yard.

⇒ CHICAGO

When friends from abroad come to the United States, I always send them to Chicago, or try to. It is the quintessential American city: muscular, inventive, wonderfully diverse, and as unpretentious as its prairie-flat vowels. "Chicago is American in every chitling and sparerib," H. L. Mencken wrote wickedly in the 1920s, when the city's stockyards, since demolished, were the biggest anywhere. "It is alive from snout to tail."

Reviled in the days of Al Capone and John Dillinger as a haven for hoodlums, Chicago was maligned for years for its cheerful civic corruption and dismissed in the effete East as a hick town. Nelson Algren, one of the writers who knew it best, said that "loving Chicago is like loving a woman with a broken nose." But no longer. Chicago entered the twenty-first century with a growing population of 2,795,186, a prosperous and well-governed model for the country at large.

At the moment, Richard M. Daley does the governing. He won a fourth term as mayor in 2003 without vigorous campaigning, and he and his minions sometimes seemed to be everywhere at once, effacing graffiti, reshaping the schools, and creating new green spaces—like the sixteen-acre $475 million Millennium Park, with a Frank O. Gehry music pavilion, fountains, cafés, sculpture, and more, on the lakefront just north of the Art Institute. But he also encountered budget problems.

Consummate pol that he is, the mayor works hard to maintain links to arts groups, business, labor, blacks, and Hispanics. He bullies his enemies and sometimes acts high-handedly, as when he had Meigs Field, a small lakefront airport downtown, bulldozed under cover of darkness. (Small-plane pilots were infuriated.) He mangles syntax, though not nearly as mercilessly as his father, Richard J. Daley, who spoke unconsciously for all politicians everywhere when he harrumphed, "Together we must rise to ever higher and higher platitudes." The local papers accuse him of cronyisum and corruption, but Richard M.— "Richie" to his constituents—never loses sight of his grand goal: ensuring the city's future by persuading its middle class to stay put. He has made a good deal of headway.

Daley the elder, who ruled Chicago like a pharaoh for twenty-one years, also did a lot to beautify the city. But he is best remembered for flying into a black rage during the 1968 Democratic convention, setting cops on Vietnam War protesters outside the convention hall and on reporters covering them. The ensuing melee, a grim spectacle of swirling tear gas and flailing billy clubs, all but guaranteed the defeat of the party's hapless presidential nominee, Hubert H. Humphrey.

The first president nominated in Chicago was a favorite son named Abraham Lincoln, and a dozen others have been nominated here, too. One was Warren Gamaliel Harding, whose grandiose middle name promised so much more than he ever delivered; he was chosen in the original smoke-filled room, Suite 408-409-410 of the Blackstone Hotel. They must put something into the water in Chicago. Politics—national politics, local politics—never pales here. This is the city that produced not only the Daleys but also Daniel Rostenkowski, a consummate congressional deal-maker from 1958 to 1996, a stout political oak felled by a petty-cash scandal that sent him to jail for seventeen months; aldermen-scoundrels of yore like Bathhouse John Coughlin and Hinky Dink Kenna and Paddy Bauler, who told the world in 1955, "Chicago ain't ready for reform"; and Mayor William Hale Thompson, staunchly pro-German at the beginning of World War I, who threatened to punch King George V of England in the nose if he set foot in the city.

There is nothing Old World about Chicago. Europe seems farther away than it does in Boston, New York or even San Francisco. And yet the genius who did more than anyone to give the city its physical charm—the architect and master builder Daniel H. Burnham, who planned waterfront pleasure parks and scenic drives where other cities have factories and warehouses—did so in the name of transforming Chicago into Paris on the Lake. Lake Michigan, that is, which lies like an ocean at the city's feet, "so huge that you can't see across," as my awed wife, Betsey, said when she saw it for the first time. "Make no little plans, for they have no magic to stir men's blood," said Burnham, who laid out the city that rose from the ruins of the flimsy town consumed in the Great Fire of 1871. He made none, nor have the generations who succeeded him.

Don't ask what Chicago is, a song warns, "unless you've got an hour or two or three." Chicago is many things: the fabulous Frango chocolate mints that they sell at Marshall Field's department store; Oprah Winfrey, queen of television talk shows; Ann Landers, whose syndicated advice to the lovelorn still appears in some newspapers, although she died in 2002; the Chicago River, once a key link between the Great Lakes and the Mississippi River, which is dyed green every St. Patrick's Day; and ever-expanding O'Hare Airport, the kingdom of fallen arches and missed connections used by 70 million passengers a year.

All that plus the Lincoln Park Zoo, which breeds gorillas; the Field Museum of Natural History; the Museum of Science and Industry, the youngsters' favorite, housed in one of the last buildings left from the Columbian Exposition of 1893, which drew an unheard-of 23 million visitors; and the John G. Shedd Aquarium, the world's largest, which my sister, Barbara, calls "the whale jail." It has a 400,000-gallon tank that holds two dozen sharks.

Chicago is good eats, like the frogs' legs at Phil Smidt's in Hammond, Indiana, just across the city line, amid the smokestacks of the old industrial economy, and Italian beef sandwiches and garlicky Chicago hot dogs (hold the ketchup). Fancy stuff, too: Jovan Trboyevic, the fastidious restaurateur who ran the much-mourned Le Perroquet, was once alone in offering proper haute cuisine, but now it's all over town.

Chicago is also a city of tight-knit neighborhoods, so far-flung that the visitor can sample but a few. In the northwest, along gritty Milwaukee and Lincoln Avenues, far from Michigan Avenue's glittering Magnificent Mile, where the affluent and the ambitious shop, immigrants have lived since the nineteenth century: first Germans and Scandinavians, then Poles, Russian Jews, Italians, Ukrainians, Slovaks, and recently Puerto Ricans.

Shop signs in countless languages serve as testaments to the succeeding waves of newcomers. St. Stanislaus Kostka, a neighborhood Polish American church that had the world's biggest Roman Catholic congregation a century ago, was saved from the wrecker's ball by Rostenkowski, who used his legendary clout to divert an expressway around it.

The South Side was America's largest black community for most of the last century. It is home today to Jesse Jackson and Louis Farrakhan, two very different black leaders, and two prominent black members of Congress, Jesse Jackson Jr. and Bobby Rush. Rush was once a Black Panther leader, but now he is a moderate who says, "Most African Americans just want a comfortable middle-class lifestyle." They find it more easily on the South Side than on the West Side, which is nearly as bedraggled today as when the Nobel Prize winner Jane Addams and the women who worked with her at her pioneering settlement, Hull-House, labored there for civic reform and improvements a hundred years ago.

Also to the south is the world-class University of Chicago, founded in 1890 with Rockefeller money. No fewer than seventy-four Nobel Prizes have been awarded to its teachers, students, and researchers. Six are on the current faculty. Among the laureates are Saul Bellow, the novelist, and Milton Friedman, the conservative economist, whose teachings influenced not only his colleagues but also important scholars at the university's law school, like Edward H. Levi, who served as attorney general in the Ford administration.

Beneath the Stagg Field grandstands, the Italian physicist Enrico Fermi and his coworkers achieved the first controlled, self-sustaining nuclear reaction on December 2, 1942, the key step in developing the atomic bomb. The site is marked with a Henry Moore bronze, *Nuclear Energy*. Across the campus, a new Mesopotamian Gallery at the Oriental Institute sheds light on a region of current concern.

Frank Lloyd Wright's prototypical Prairie Style building, the Robie House, stands nearby, echoing the horizontality of the plains in its strip windows, the deep overhang of its eaves, and even in the proportions of his trademark Roman bricks, very long and very skinny. An exterior restoration was completed in 2003.

The house made Wright famous around the world, along with those he built for himself and others in the western suburbs of River Forest and Oak Park, where Ernest Hemingway grew up, amid what he called "wide lawns and narrow minds." Also in Oak Park is Unity Temple, "my little jewel," as Wright termed it, a masterpiece in reinforced concrete, built in 1905 on an awkward site for only $45,000. But the birthplace of modern American architecture, and of the skyscraper, was the Loop, as the central business district is known (after the elevated railroad tracks that encircle it).

Chicago architects capitalized on the fire of 1871, which began in Patrick and Catherine O'Leary's barn on DeKoven Street, much as Christopher Wren capitalized on London's Great Fire of 1666. They were influenced by the great Henry Hobson Richardson's startlingly original Glessner House, a rugged study in rusticated stone (1887) that turned its back to the street, opening instead onto a south-facing courtyard. Louis Sullivan, Richardson's disciple and Wright's teacher, sensed "an intoxicating rawness, a sense of big things to be done," and began with the Auditorium Building in 1889. Its acoustically perfect 4,000-seat theater, spanned by broad, flattened arches, illuminated by thousands of clear, unshaded bulbs, is one of America's great interiors.

At the same time, Burnham & Root were designing the Rookery a few blocks away, organized around a graceful cast-iron light court that Wright reworked in 1905. In 1891 Burnham & Root also built the brooding sixteen-story Monadnock Building, a pioneering skyscraper, and in 1899 Sullivan, in the Carson Pirie Scott & Company store, frankly expressed the revolutionary steel grid in bands of windows that became a Chicago School trademark. Below he applied webs of his luxuriant ornament in cast iron. All of these buildings remain, most of them on or near State Street, "that great street."

Ludwig Mies van der Rohe, the German master who helped found the Bauhaus, came to Chicago in 1938 and reinvigorated its architecture through his teaching at the Illinois Institute of Technology and his own practice. His deceptively simple stripped-down steel-and-concrete designs, like the apartment buildings on North Lake Shore Drive, the Federal Center in the

Loop, and the Illinois Tech campus on the South Side, achieve a rare elegance through the careful calibration of proportion.

From Mies's work grew such landmarks as the John Hancock Tower, the distinctively cross-braced high-rise by Skidmore, Owings & Merrill on the Magnificent Mile; and in reaction to it arose postmodernism, epitomized by the sleek buildings of Helmut Jahn. Recently a $48.2 million campus center has risen at Illinois Tech, an orange-walled extravaganza that gives Americans a look at the genius of the Dutch architect Rem Koolhaas for the first time. In among Chicago's towers stands a fine collection of modern street sculpture: not only Picasso's enigmatic Cor-Ten steel beast outside the Daley Center but also a 100-foot-tall baseball bat by Claes Oldenburg.

But it is for paintings that the Art Institute, a "universal" museum like the Metropolitan and the Louvre, is best known. There is a powerful St. John the Baptist by Guido Reni, admired by Sister Wendy when she visited Chicago, but most of the lures are more modern: Seurat's *La Grande Jatte,* the greatest of Pointillist canvases; *Paris Street: Rainy Day* by Gustave Caillebotte, a magnificent mood piece to which the institute gave pride of place long before the general revival of interest in his work; and two major icons of American isolation, Edward Hopper's *Nighthawks* and Grant Wood's *American Gothic.* In 2004, the institute named James Cuno, who had run the Harvard museums for twelve years and London's Courtauld Institute for one, as its new director.

Farther up Michigan Avenue, the excellent Museum of Contemporary Art showcases its own holdings, which range from Bruce Nauman to Cindy Sherman and well beyond, in a series of barrel-vaulted galleries. The museum looks out across a cityscape typical of this part of Chicago, with wide tree-lined sidewalks and an agreeable little park surrounded on three sides by tall buildings.

Chicago loves its sports. It loves the Cubs and their cozy little park, Wrigley Field, with ivy-covered outfield walls and seldom-used floodlights. (God made baseball to be played under his own light, the team believes.) Forget the fact that the Cubs haven't played in a World Series since 1945 or won one since 1908, despite Sammy Sosa's heroics. Chicago swooned over Da

Bulls and their balletic, clutch-loving, gravity-defying star of stars Michael Jordan. Chicago loved Da Bears in the heyday of Mike Ditka and Walter Payton, but it doesn't know quite what to make of their remodeled home, Soldier Field; one local critic said it looks as if the Starship *Enterprise* had crash-landed on the Lincoln Memorial.

Air Jordan and the Bulls carried the city's name around the globe; so did Sir Georg Solti and the mighty Chicago Symphony Orchestra, which he made one of the finest on earth. At its peak the Chicago was best noted for the sonority of its brass choirs, especially in the late Romantic repertory. Sometimes its Bruckner rang out with the awesome power of the horns of heaven. The orchestra has not quite maintained all of its luster, despite the manifold gifts of its current music director, Daniel Barenboim, who since taking over in 1991 has encouraged subtlety. Today quiet passages are often as impressive as climaxes, though some listeners have detected occasional raggedness. The mighty ensemble faltered financially during the economic troubles of the new millennium, and in 2001 the renowned virtuoso trumpeter Adolph "Bud" Herseth finally yielded his first chair.

Still, Barenboim, who has announced that he will step down in 2006, is a musician of genuine substance as well as a figure of glamour. At Orchestra Hall and on tour in the United States and abroad, conducting and often doubling as a piano soloist, he has kept the orchestra firmly ensconced among the nation's elite musical ensembles.

The biggest recent stir in Chicago music came from the Lyric Opera's heralded premiere of a work it commissioned, William Bolcom's *View from the Bridge,* based on Arthur Miller's play. The critics were kind, and the company liked it so much that it asked Bolcom, a genial University of Michigan professor who likes Gershwin and Youmans as much as Puccini, to produce two more scores for future production.

A general director named Ardis Krainik, one of the rare women in her line of work, propelled the Lyric into the first rank of American opera houses, along with the Metropolitan and San Francisco. (Some would add Houston to the list.) Since she died in 1997, to be succeeded by William Mason, the company has gone from strength to strength. It sold more than

100 percent of its seats for fourteen straight years (subscribers religiously turned in unwanted tickets for resale), an unparalleled accomplishment.

Chicago has also taken the Joffrey Ballet to its heart. Directed by Gerald Arpino, the company moved to Chicago in 1995 from New York because of financial difficulties. It seems to have restored its bank balance and renewed its classical style. Mayor Daley sometimes attends performances.

Big-league drama abounds in the Windy City, which supports nearly two hundred theater companies. Two applauded Broadway productions of recent years originated at the Goodman Theater: revivals of Arthur Miller's *Death of a Salesman,* starring Brian Dennehy, and of Eugene O'Neill's *Moon for the Misbegotten,* starring Cherry Jones and Gabriel Byrne. Lookingglass, another company, took its production of *Metamorphoses* to Broadway, where it won a Tony for its director, Mary Zimmerman. The company has opened a stage in one of Chicago's most imposing landmarks, the castellated Water Works on Michigan Avenue. Steppenwolf helped propel David Mamet and John Malkovich to fame, and Mike Nichols and Elaine May broke in with Compass Players. Its sucessor company, Second City, a mecca for comedy since 1959, launched the careers of John Belushi, Bill Murray, Gilda Radner, and many others. No better riposte could be imagined to the dismissive "Second City" label that A. J. Liebling pasted on the city more than fifty years ago.

The *Chicago Tribune,* still ensconced in its lacy neo-Gothic tower on Michigan Avenue, is today much to be preferred to the wacky, pugnaciously conservative, isolationist sheet full of local puffery and idiosyncratic spelling of which Colonel Robert R. McCormick was the publisher from 1925 until his death in 1955. It also owns the *Los Angeles Times,* the *Baltimore Sun,* and *Newsday* on Long Island, as well as several television stations.

Swift and Armour and the other barons of beef are no more; Chicago is no longer "hog butcher to the world." Only a gate adorned with a bas-relief of a Hereford steer remains of the Union Stockyards, where in 1892 alone 2.5 million cattle and 5 million hogs were slaughtered. Many big Chicago corporations like Walgreen's, United Air Lines, Motorola, and Sears, which abandoned its spectacular skyscraper in the Loop, are now head-quartered in the suburbs. Amoco and Ameritech and a couple of big banks succumbed to takeovers, but others remain, including Quaker Oats, which the city gave $9.75 million in tax breaks to stay. Most of them support the arts with enthusiasm. C. Steven McMillan, the chief executive of Sara Lee, told me, "The arts, politics, and the business community are more heavily comingled in Chicago than in any other American city I know of, to everyone's benefit."

At the foot of La Salle Street, in a splendid Art Deco build-ing with a statue of Ceres on top, is the headquarters of the Chicago Board of Trade, where commodity traders do their in-comprehensible thing. "Few economic institutions," the histo-rian William J. Cronon tells us sternly in *Nature's Metropolis*, "more powerfully affect human communities and natural ecosystems in the modern capitalist world. Even those of us who will never trade wheat or pork bellies on the Chicago futures markets depend upon those markets for our survival." I'll have to take his word for it.

Meanwhile, allow me to shill for a moment for Chicago's other writers: the early reformers and novelists Frank Norris and Upton Sinclair; the overearnest but underrated Theodore Dreiser, whose *Sister Carrie* still moves me; James T. Farrell, whose *Studs Lonigan* is set in one part of the South Side, and Richard Wright, whose *Native Son* is set in another; Ben Hecht and Charles MacArthur, who gave us the greatest of all newspa-per plays, *The Front Page*; and the poet Carl Sandburg, who gave Chicago its overfamiliar nickname, "City of the Big Shoulders." More recently, the city and its ways have been vividly depicted by the late Mike Royko, the irascible columnist; Studs Terkel, the oral historian; the novelist Ward Just; and the short-story virtuoso Stuart Dybek. I particularly like Just's description of Chicago as a city with "its fedora pulled down over one eye."

A moment, too, for the popular arts: the blues that Muddy Waters and other black musicians brought up the Illinois Cen-tral from the Mississippi Delta; the jazz that King Oliver and Louis Armstrong brought to the South Side, echoed by white kids from the suburbs like Benny Goodman and Eddie Condon; and the wacky, wonderful plaster cows (including Ferragamoo, sponsored by the Italian fashion house) that graced the city in the summer of 1999.

It was Sinatra's kind of town, and it is mine, too.

WHERE TO STAY

Burnham, 1 West Washington Street, (312) 782-1111. In a minor miracle of adaptive restoration, D. H. Burnham's Reliance

Building (1891), one of America's first skyscrapers, has been raised from the near-dead and turned into a boutique hotel managed by the Kimpton Group of San Francisco. In the heart of the Loop, it has 103 rooms and 19 suites, a bit below average in size and price. A lot of original detail has been retained.

Four Seasons, 120 East Delaware Place, (312) 280-8800. In city after American city, the Four Seasons is the top-rated hotel, and the Windy City is no exception. The English-country-house-fantasy lobby occupies the seventh floor of a sixty-six-story skyscraper, above a mall full of chic shops (Bloomingdale's, Bendel's). Whatever you want, whenever you want it, it's right there: barber and beauty shop, sauna, indoor pool, and a super restaurant called Seasons.

Peninsula, 108 East Superior Street, (312) 337-2888. High tech (flat-screen TVs) meets opulence (plush beds) in this newcomer among Chicago's grand hotels. Coddling service and a 14,000-square-foot spa including a beautifully equipped gym-with-a-view.

Ritz-Carlton, 160 East Pearson Street, (312) 266-1000. Operated by the Four Seasons chain despite its name, this luxurious lair forms part of the Water Tower Place complex, smack in the middle of the Magnificent Mile. Its expansive lobby, complete with octagonal fountain, is on the twelfth floor. Guest rooms are all anyone could ask, as is Kevin Hickey's cuisine, especially his Sunday brunch, Chicago's most sumptuous.

WHERE TO EAT

Arun's, 4156 North Kedzie Avenue, (773) 539-1909. This may be America's best Thai restaurant, a kitsch-free zone where the food on the plates is as delicate as the ceremonial headdresses adorning the room. Miang kum, the first of twelve stellar dishes at a recent meal, consisted of batons of lime peel, ginger, and coconut, heaped with tiny red peppers and peanuts on betel-nut leaves with tamarind sauce. It would awaken the most jaded palate.

Charlie Trotter's, 816 West Armitage Avenue, (773) 248-6228. One of the nation's two or three premier chefs, Trotter makes gastronomic Fabergé eggs. He bathes foie gras, salmon, and Japanese mushrooms in a warm broth to create a dish that is both rich and refreshing, a rarity. The service is fluent and the wine list mind-blowing.

Everest, 440 South LaSalle Street, (312) 663-8920. The next time someone tells you he never eats on top of skyscrapers, send him to Jean Joho's place, forty floors up. Alsatian-born, Mr. J. blends the cuisine of kings with the cooking of commoners in dishes like creamy sauerkraut soup with caviar. The attention to detail is constant, the tapestry of city lights below stirring, the service urbane, the Alsatian wines the best in the nation.

Frontera Grill and Topolobampo, 445 North Clark Street, (312) 661-1434. You could spend half a lifetime in Oaxaca and know less about Mexican food than you can learn at Rick and Deann Bayless's two restaurants, one casual, the other less so. Both, saturated with vibrant color, serve food prepared from the best ingredients with great care. Every sip or bite is a revelation —margaritas to marlin ceviche to tacos al pastor. A recent menu addition is a sumptuous seafood platter, Yucatan style.

Gibsons, 1028 North Rush Street, (312) 266-8999. Chicago is a steak town from way back. This place, packed with politicians, showbiz headliners, bulky guys in warm-up jackets, and head-turning dolls, epitomizes the city's zest. Order a martini, chopped chicken livers (try them on the house raisin bread), and either a W. R. Cut (a bone-in rib-eye named for the *Tribune's* former food columnist, William Rice) or tender London broil (made with sirloin). Desserts, like strawberry shortcake, are the size of a steamboat.

mk, 868 North Franklin Street, (312) 482-9179. The letters stand for Michael Kornick, the chef, and he stands for modern American cooking with bright flavors. Sweetbreads with caramelized endive, for example, and definitive calf's liver with grilled

Vidalia onions, bacon strips, and a sauce of mustard and pan juices. The decor is terminally chic.

Spiaggia, 980 North Michigan Avenue, (312) 280-2750. The name means "beach," and you can glimpse Lake Michigan from this nifty aerie perched above the Magnificent Mile. But bag the view. Tony Mantuano's thoroughbred Italian cooking, the best between New York and Santa Monica, is the thing to focus on: full-flavored, grown-up, fantasy-free dishes like carpaccio of smoked Sicilian swordfish and gnocchi with rabbit.

Tru, 676 North St. Clair Street, (312) 202-0001. In from the suburbs, Rick Tramonto and Gale Gand are challenging Charlie Trotter and Jean Joho for local supremacy in an airy white room. Tramonto sends out lobster risotto in a miniature copper saucepan and serves amazing savory sorbets (beet, orange pepper) in Parmesan cones. Gand, his former wife, whips up whimsies like pineapple "carpaccio." Well-chosen wines.

⫘➤ MILWAUKEE

Sometimes Milwaukee can fool you. Is this Chicago's twin? There's the same immense Lake Michigan stretching to the horizon, bigger than Massachusetts. There's Wisconsin Avenue, the main stem, which crosses the Milwaukee River on a bridge that looks quite a lot like the one that carries Michigan Avenue across the Chicago River. Both cities have bold, modern trademark buildings with prominent zigzag braces, designed by Skidmore, Owings & Merrill—the Firstar Center in Milwaukee and the John Hancock Center in Chicago. Both nurture old-country traditions, exuberantly celebrated at annual festivals. Both have the Midwestern knack of keeping their feet on the ground.

But Milwaukee, as its visitors' bureau proclaimed in an advertising campaign a few years back, is Chicago several million people ago. It is less crowded, less clogged with traffic, and much less expensive. "It's a big little town, a real family town," said Terry Benske, a real estate agent who makes her living selling houses to people who move north from Chicago after they marry and have children, commuting back to their jobs.

On a gloomy day, when the cold, raw winds are blowing hard, Milwaukee may indeed provide "a gray landscape, drawn with hard lines and great attention to detail," as the English photographer Cecil Beaton wrote after a 1955 visit. But on a bright day with the sun glinting off the lake, downtown is something else: a triumph of civic revival.

The city has saved the best of its past. "Those old Germans," a Milwaukee friend of mine says, "were too frugal to tear anything down, thank God." So Victorian buildings like the imposing Richardsonian Romanesque Pfister Hotel and the flatiron-shaped

City Hall, built in emulation of guild halls in Belgium, stand amid sober neoclassical structures like the headquarters of the Northwestern Mutual Life Insurance Company; Art Deco towers like the Wisconsin Gas Company building, with a neon "flame" on top whose color reflects the weather forecast; and slick modern high-rises by the likes of Helmut Jahn. You can see many of them from the new Riverwalk, a pleasant introduction to the city. From there, it's only a short stroll to the lake or, in the other direction, to Marquette University's campus.

Lately, Milwaukee has been on a building spree. In 1998, the first phase of the postmodern Midwest Airlines Center, a 188,695-square-foot convention facility, opened for business. In 2001, it was joined by $400 million Miller Park, a new ball field in an old idiom, like Baltimore's and Cleveland's, with a seven-panel retractable roof. But the Brewers continued to flounder (2004 was their twelfth straight losing season). The family of baseball commissioner Bud Selig, the team's owners, sold it to a Los Angeles investor in 2004.

The early years of the twenty-first century will be best remembered for the unveiling in 2001 of a stirring $100 million addition to the Milwaukee Art Museum, overlooking Lake Michigan. Designed by Santiago Calatrava, a brilliant Spanish architect on the brink of international superstar status who had never built anything in the United States, it is meant to be, and surely will soon become, a signature structure for the city, comparable to Sydney's Opera House or Bilbao's museum.

Jack L. Goodsitt, a lovable local curmudgeon, complains that Milwaukee has been in decline since the 1930s, when George M. Cohan and Helen Hayes brought touring companies to its theaters, and Eugene's, a waterside restaurant, served "the best food the city has ever seen." Still, he moved back after four years in Palm Beach. "Nothing ever happens here," grouses Goodsitt, a lawyer, "but the one thing we have is people. They do read books, they think, they talk. There's real intellectual ferment. That matters more than the weather. Palm Beach? All they talk about is golf and boats."

Milwaukee's shoulders may not be as big as the Windy City's, but it is no ninety-pound weakling. It is the nation's nineteenth largest city, with a population of 590,000 and an area of ninety-six square miles, and the four-county metropolitan area has a population of 1.7 million. Enough to support the Brewers and the basketball Bucks, enough to sustain a venerable cultural tradition, and enough to consume Rabelaisian quantities of frozen custard—a dense, eggy, creamy freeze worthy of the state that calls itself America's Dairyland. Clad in neon, Leon's is the drive-in custard shrine, opened in 1942. It inspired *Happy Days*. Don't ignore Kopp's, either.

Modern-day Milwaukeeans no longer consider their city a Teutonic stronghold. They don't think of themselves anymore as a pure beer-'n'-brats bunch, however many sausages they may scarf down at Miller Field (or when they head in their thousands up Interstate 43 to Green Bay, a couple of hours north, for a Packers game). President Bill Clinton brought the then German chancellor, Helmut Kohl, to town to give him a taste of home, but look at Serb Hall, the locals say, at our Polish festival, at our Irish festival. Schlitz, "the beer that made Milwaukee famous," is gone—hard to believe in a city where they used to say that kitchens were built with three taps, marked hot, cold, and Schlitz. Only the extensive philanthropies of the Uihlein family, who brewed it, remain as reminders. Blatz is defunct, its old brewery recycled as apartments and offices, and Pabst lives on solely in the elaborate theater Captain Frederick Pabst built in 1895. The Miller Brewing Company prospers (you can tour the brewery on West State Street), joined by a number of thriving microbreweries, notably Sprecher and Lakeside. But everyone knows that St. Louis, another city with roots in Germany, is the big keg now.

Most of Milwaukee's famous German restaurants have seen better days, though there is nothing faded about Fred Usinger, Inc., the king of American wurstmachers (sausage-makers) since 1880. The catalog rests beside me as I write, pure balm for the Hun in me: braunschweiger, beerwurst, thueringer, weisswurst, yachtwurst (ah, yachtwurst).

Milwaukee people, like those in Hamburg, are compulsively orderly; anyone who doesn't keep a neat house and a trim lawn is treated as a menace to society. Few speak German anymore, though a century ago two of three people who read a daily newspaper here read it in that language. The Milwaukee Ger-

mans have assimilated, like the Boston Irish and the Philadelphia Italians, but their German American past has shaped the
city's cosmopolitan present.

The local economy, built upon precision manufacturing,
profited from the skills which the Germans and other immigrants brought with them as well as their Mitteleuropean work
habits. Those traditions live on in industrial companies like
Johnson Controls, A. O. Smith, Briggs & Stratton, Harnisch-
feger, and Rockwell Automation (formerly Allen-Bradley), all
with headquarters in Milwaukee. Harley-Davidson motorcycles
were invented in Milwaukee in 1903, the company is still based
here, and the engines are still made here.

Many immigrants carried progressive political ideals in their
baggage. Milwaukee elected Victor L. Berger, the first Socialist
to sit in Congress, in 1910 and again from 1918 to 1926. Daniel
Webster Hoan, another Socialist, was the city's mayor for twenty-
four years. Socialist ideas had a profound impact on young
Golda Mabovitz, whose family had immigrated to Milwaukee
from the Ukraine. Educated at North Division High School and
Milwaukee Teachers' Training College, she emigrated to Israel
in 1921. As Golda Meir, she rose gradually in the Labor Party
and served from 1969 to 1974 as Israel's premier.

Back in Milwaukee, Socialism eventually died out, to be
succeeded as the city's creed by liberalism, its half brother. For
decades, two German American liberal Democrats held sway
here: Mayor Henry W. Maier, who served seven terms (1960–88),
and Representative Henry S. Reuss (1955–83), a respected
authority on banking. Milwaukee also lent strong support to
Wisconsin political powers like the La Follettes and other Progressives, and to liberal Democrats like Gaylord A. Nelson and
Patrick J. Lucey. Even in a conservative era, the city has contributed thumping majorities to Russell D. Feingold, one of the
most liberal (and least conventional) Democratic senators,
whose father was a part-time Progressive organizer.

Like other cities with a Germanic heritage, like St. Louis
and Cincinnati, Milwaukee has a well-entrenched musical tradition. Yet along with many of them, Milwaukee watched in dis-
may as the finances of its musical mainstay dried up. Starting
in the 1980s, season subscriptions to the Milwaukee Symphony

Orchestra stalled, fund-raising flagged, and labor relations soured, so much that in January 1994 musicians refused to take the stage. Although the refurbishing of Uihlein Hall, part of the Marcus Center for the Performing Arts, and the choice in 1996 of German-born, Juilliard-trained Andreas Delfs as music director sparked a turnaround, hard times in the new century brought a pay freeze and truncated schedule. Still, money was found to bring Yo-Yo Ma and Ute Lemper to town.

Now seventy-one years old, the Florentine Opera Company, which also performs in Uihlein Hall, does "Cav" and "Pag" and other golden oldies, of course. But in 1999 it dipped into unfamiliar repertory, giving the American premiere of Lowell Lieberman's *Picture of Dorian Gray*, based on Oscar Wilde's novel and first performed in Monte Carlo in 1996. A third Uihlein tenant, the Milwaukee Ballet, has been radically reshaped by Michael Pink, who took charge in 2003. He let the contracts of some dancers lapse, promoted many youngsters, and set a hyper-edgy *Giselle* in an eastern European ghetto in 1943.

Alfred Lunt, Milwaukee-born, would be pleased with his hometown. Touring Broadway shows hit town regularly, playing at the 4,100-seat Milwaukee Theater. The Skylight Opera Company, which specializes in musicals and the fizzier operas; the Pabst Theater; the Milwaukee Repertory, which presents works by playwrights ranging from Tennessee Williams to Carlo Goldoni and Steve Martin; and First Stage Milwaukee, which commissioned a new play from the 1992 Pulitzer Prize winner, Robert Schenkkan, all contribute to a brisk theatrical life. Nobody need go to Chicago for brain food. Ten Chimneys, the estate of Lunt and his wife of more than fifty years, Lynn Fontanne, is at Genessee Depot, thirty miles west of town. Each room is dressed as if it were a stage set, executed with the same attention to minute detail as the Lunts' performances.

Facing a near-impossible commission in 1957 to design a combination war memorial and art museum, Eero Saarinen built something boxy that has aged poorly. Its setting, smack on the lakeshore, shared by few other Milwaukee buildings, has always been its trump card. That is now underscored by Calatrava's addition, south of the Saarinen building, which recalls both his celebrated Alamillo Bridge in Seville, a harplike span across the Guadalquivir River, and his Satolas train station at Lyon airport in France. A vaulted 450-foot-long pavilion with galleries for temporary exhibitions forms a link to a 90-foot-high reception hall covered by a movable, louvered sunscreen made of white-painted steel. (Benjamin Forgey of *The Washington Post* compared the opened roof to a soaring sail, a bird in flight, and a matador's cape.)

This new structure is connected to the foot of Wisconsin Avenue, where an orange Mark di Suvero sculpture stands, by a diaphanous suspension footbridge supported by two beautifully inclined masts. Saarinen's building is all right angles; Calatrava's, complementing it, is all curves. The *Milwaukee Journal Sentinel* called the project audacious and congratulated the museum for doing something so "daringly un-Milwaukee."

To my eye, the museum's strengths are a superb assemblage of American folk art, one of the world's best collections of Haitian art, and a fabulous group of German Expressionists—Kirchner, Nolde, Beckmann, et al. (A word of warning: owing to the vagaries of donors' wills, the Expressionists are split into two groups on two different floors.) A major gift in 1997 brought the museum's holdings of works by Georgia O'Keeffe to twenty-one, and it lured David Gordon, former secretary of the Royal Academy in London, as its new director. The decorative arts collection includes objects by Prairie School architects, not only Frank Lloyd Wright but others in his circle, including George Niedecken and George W. Maher.

To get a fuller picture of Wright's genius at work, take a trip to his home, Taliesen, near Spring Green, 110 miles west of Milwaukee, or to Racine, 30 miles south. I would choose Racine, not only because it is closer to Milwaukee but also because there you can visit both the headquarters of the S. C. Johnson Company (guided tours Friday) and Wingspread, the graceful lakeside home of Hibbard Johnson, who was the company's president (self-guided tours Monday through Friday). The architectural historian Henry-Russell Hitchcock said its wings ride the grassy lawn "as if they were floating on waves." The administrative office of the Johnson company is an amazing space, unlike anything built before or since, with skylights of Pyrex tubing and slender dendriform supporting columns. Wright called it "a temple of work, a place you will love to be in." Wright's assistant and acolyte Edgar Tafel dubbed it the architect's Ninth Symphony, and Philip Johnson termed it "the finest room in America."

WHERE TO STAY

Metro, 411 East Mason Street, (414) 272-1937. New not long ago, and knowingly designed to evoke France in the 1920s, with unusually handsome chairs, rugs, and sofas in the lobby. Its sixty-five suites are also well-done, with purest cotton sheets on the beds. The café has tables outdoors and a sinuous, welcoming bar. Service is sometimes slack.

Pfister, 424 East Wisconsin Avenue, (414) 273-8222. "Grande dame" is a cliché for older hotels, but the Pfister lives up to it. The Victorian lobby—painted ceiling, palm court, and paintings of zaftig ladies—bustles all day long, and rooms in the old sec-

1. First Stage Milwaukee
2. Uihlein Hall
3. City Hall
4. Pabst Theater
5. Milwaukee Repertory Theater
6. Midwest Express Center

tion, opening off wide corridors, offer every comfort. Stay there, if you can, rather than the newer tower. The food in the Celia restaurant is well worth a try.

American Club, Highland Drive, Kohler, (920) 457-8000. Built in 1918 to house immigrant workers at the Kohler plumbing-fixture works, this rambling red-brick building has been transformed into a quiet, tasteful resort with courtyard gardens, good food, two Pete Dye golf courses, an elaborate spa featuring an eight-foot cascade, tennis, trout fishing, pheasant hunting, and cross-country skiing. An hour north of Milwaukee.

WHERE TO EAT

Ristorante Bartolotta, 7616 West State Street, (414) 771-7910. A plain, vibrant, yellow-walled room hung with family photos, this trattoria has good bloodlines. Paul Bartolotta used to run Spiaggia, Chicago's best Italian restaurant; here, the family dispenses the Italian comfort food of Chef Juan Urbieta: shrimp with creamy chickpea sauce, pasta quills with duck ragu, sausage and peppers on polenta. Another Bartolotta enterprise, the Lake Park Bistro—3133 East Newberry Boulevard, (414) 962-6300—is much fancier. There, splendid views over Lake Michigan and high-quality china and linens enhance Adam Siegel's French cooking (great *charcuterie*).

Coquette Café, 316 North Milwaukee Street, (414) 291-2655. Sandy D'Amato's cosseting bistro is just the place to defang a blustery Wisconsin evening. Coq au vin with lardons of bacon, perhaps, with a good bottle of Beaujolais, then a grandmotherly floating island, a coffee, and an Armagnac. Andrew Schneider, ex-Sanford, does the cooking.

Eddie Martini's, 8612 Watertown Plank Road, (414) 771-6680. A 1940s throwback ("steaks, chops, seafood," says the sign outside), Martini's is Milwaukee's restaurant du jour, jammed nightly. Great—not just good—strips and porterhouses with appealing sides like sautéed wild mushrooms. There's ono and ahi tuna for carniphobes, plus walleye, the firm, sweet lake fish that has vanished from many Midwestern menus.

Sanford, 1547 North Jackson Street, (414) 276-9608. Sandy D'Amato is a cook of rare virtuosity who can produce a different ethnic menu each night (Hungarian, Greek, Provencal) as well as his regular fare. His wife, Angie, presides winningly over a dining room that was once his grandfather's and father's grocery store. D'Amato's taste combinations are spectacular, fashioned from a flavor arsenal containing sweet figs, pungent pomegranate sauce, foie gras, squab, grilled shrimp, basil oil, and curry noodles.

Three Brothers, 2414 South St. Clair Street, (414) 481-7530. Branko Radicevic, who always wears a black beret, can be as cranky as his Serbian brethren in Belgrade, but he runs a restaurant with very high standards. On simple Formica tables in a Schlitz tavern built in 1897, he serves succulent roast lamb and suckling pig, chicken paprikash, and an amazing, discus-sized phyllo pie called burek, stuffed with spinach and cheese.

MINNEAPOLIS and ST. PAUL

Snow paralyzes some American cities and disheartens others. But Minneapolis and its fraternal twin, St. Paul, do more than cope with it; they positively revel in it. Come here on the morning after a blizzard, and main roads are clear. My wife, Betsey, and I, inured to snow-induced civic inertia in Washington, once watched dumbfounded as a miniature street-sweeping machine brushed snow from downtown sidewalks as it fell.

Drive out to Lake of the Isles, southwest of downtown Minneapolis, on a crisp, cold Saturday, with the skies cerulean blue and the snow heaped eye-high in front of wonderful big Prairie Style houses by gifted acolytes of Frank Lloyd Wright like George Washington Maher and George Grant Elmslie. Youngsters play pickup hockey on the frozen lake, like figures in an Avercamp painting, while more sedate souls glide past on cross-country skis. At such times, "Winter Wonderland" is more than a song title.

No matter how hard the polar winds blow, people here say "You betcha," just as they did in the movie *Fargo*. They smile and urge you to have a nice day so earnestly that you are convinced they mean it. So sincerely that cynics call Minnesota "the Land of the Bland," a dubious epithet for a state with a counterculture that gave the world Bob Dylan and an electorate that chose Jesse Ventura, a bullet-bald former wrestler, as governor.

The Germans and Scandinavians who flocked here in the late nineteenth century were used to cold weather. The Vietnamese, Mexicans, and Somalis who came here in the late twentieth century were not, but they quickly got the hang of it. A good thing, too: from December to March, an average of six inches of snow lies on the ground, and in January midday temperatures struggle to reach the balmy double digits. When the chill gets truly brutal, there is nothing quite like a breakfast of blackberry buttermilk pancakes at Al's, a venerable, fourteen-stool Dinkytown greasy spoon, to toast your bones.

It's not that the Twin Cities are so far north. Seattle and Montreal, London and Paris are nearer the Arctic Circle than Minneapolis and St. Paul, but they're closer to the sea. Stung by *The New York Times*'s assertion in 1885 that Minnesota was an American Siberia, a group of civic boosters founded the St. Paul Winter Carnival, which has evolved over the years into an Arctic Mardi Gras. Every year, with unfailing regularity, Vulcanus Rex, the king of fire, drives wintry King Boreas from his throne, ensuring the return of spring. Seemingly sane men and women run in the world's frostiest half-marathon, and in some years an ice palace is built of 27,000 bathtub-sized blocks of ice.

The humorist Garrison Keillor, the pot-roast poet laureate, whose weekly radio program, *A Prairie Home Companion*, originates from the Fitzgerald Theater in St. Paul, once said that "true Minnesotans have a fondness for storm fronts, a lack of fashion sense, and a belief that there is moral worth in suffering." He could have been talking about John Glotzbach, one of a group of wacky Minnesota Vikings fans who regularly watch the team's games not from comfortable seats inside the relatively sultry Hubert H. Humphrey Metrodome but on portable television sets outside their cars in the parking lot. "I got offered tickets, but I hate the dome," Glotzbach told a reporter from *The Wall Street Journal* with all the righteous zeal of an ice fisherman. "It's way too corporate."

An extreme case, obviously. Less masochistic Twin Cities residents keep frostbite at bay by spending a lot of time indoors. The world's first enclosed shopping mall, Southdale, opened in Edina, a Minneapolis suburb, in 1956. It was soon copied in other suburbs, most grandiosely in the 520-store Mall of America in Bloomington, nine miles south of Minneapolis, which attracts 40 million visitors a year. Alarmed, downtown merchants invented the Skywalk, a system of passageways one story above the street that link buildings and make it possible to reach shops and offices without going outside. Now one hundred buildings in Minneapolis and sixty-five in St. Paul are so linked.

For young cities—Minneapolis was not incorporated until a few years before the Civil War—these two have a surprisingly rich artistic tradition. Philanthropic families like the Pillsburys and Daytons have helped build orchestras, museums, and theaters of national repute.

The Minnesota Orchestra (formerly the Minneapolis Symphony), which celebrated its hundredth birthday in 2002–3, has been led by conductors of the caliber of Eugene Ormandy, Dimitri Mitropoulos, Antal Dorati, and Neville Marriner. Its home is Orchestra Hall in Minneapolis, whose superb acoustics are enhanced by a distinctive "icefall" of white cubes that runs across the ceiling and cascades down the wall behind the players. Hoping to emulate the musical excitement that Esa-Pekka Salonen has generated in Los Angeles, the orchestra passed the baton in 2001 to his fellow Finn, Osmo Vänskä, a development welcomed not only by the state's 100,000 Finnish Americans but also by critics. He promised enough Sibelius and Nielsen to satisfy Scandinavian tastes. The musicians, who earn basic salaries of $90,000, not too much less than their Cleveland and Boston counterparts, have responded enthusiastically to Vänskä's emphasis on detail, precision, and dynamic contrast.

The St. Paul Chamber Orchestra, the closest American counterpart to European groups like the Academy of St. Martin-in-the-Fields, also has an energetic new leader in Andreas Delfs, who added his Minnesota duties to his role as music director in Milwaukee. Music is served as well by the Minnesota Opera, a tireless promoter of new music and of the bel canto tradition, based (as is the chamber group) at the Ordway Center for the Performing Arts in St. Paul, which stages four or five productions annually; by a Viennese Sommerfest, founded by the conductor Leonard Slatkin and now under the artistic direction of Andrew Litton; and by Minnesota Public Radio, a national leader in classical-music programming.

In 1963, an Irish stage genius named Tyrone Guthrie, fresh from triumphs at the Stratford Shakespeare Festival in Canada, gave the Twin Cities a theatrical showplace with an unconventional thrust stage like those of ancient Greece and Elizabethan England. Under its seventh director, another Irishman, Joe Dowling, the Guthrie company is enjoying its greatest successes since the early days, with classics like *A Midsummer Night's Dream*, *Ah, Wilderness!*, and *Who's Afraid of Virginia Woolf?* (with a cast headed by Patrick Stewart and Mercedes Ruehl, so good that theatergoers forgot Richard Burton and Elizabeth Taylor), plus more modern fare like Brian Friel's *Molly Sweeney*. Perhaps the nation's preeminent regional theater, in a metropolitan area that supports the largest number of professional theater troupes outside of New York, including the innovative, Tony Award–winning Children's Theater Company, the Guthrie wants to do much more. A new $125 million Guthrie Theater, containing three auditoriums of various sizes, will open early in 2006 on a plot along the Mississippi River, previously reserved for a baseball stadium. The architect is the widely acclaimed Frenchman Jean Nouvel.

Until then, the theater will carry on in its old quarters at the Walker Art Center, one of the nation's foremost museums of modern art, second only, in some people's thinking, to the Museum of Modern Art in New York. The Walker itself is adding 120,000 square feet to its galleries and gardens in a project designed by the brilliant young Basel-born team of Jacques Herzog and Pierre de Meuron. Herzog says the new building is "conceived like a lantern—a blur between solid, translucent, and transparent." In recent years, the museum has been forced to rotate its collection constantly to make space for special shows, so some of its own iconic pictures, like Franz Marc's *Large Blue Horses*, were often in storage. Now there will be room for most of the best, including sizable holdings of Johns and Judd, Kelly and Rauschenberg.

I certainly hope they can spare a corner for Charles Ray's life-size plastic cast of a wrecked Pontiac—done in 1997 as a comment, I presume, on the fragility of modern life or modern culture or maybe both. And surely the large sculpture garden across from the museum will continue to be dominated by Claes Oldenburg and Coosje van Bruggen's hilarious giant teaspoon, topped with a brilliantly red cherry.

A second major museum, the Minneapolis Institute of Arts, aspires to mini–Metropolitan Museum of Art status, sampling all of world art history. After a ten-year restoration, its collections were reinstalled in 1998, with four thousand objects now on view. Its strengths lie in German Expressionism (lots of Ernst Ludwig Kirchner, a great Max Beckmann triptych, an extraordinary Emil Nolde, all orange and blood red); in Post-Impressionism, including major van Goghs and Gauguins; in Chinese jade; and in American decorative arts. A hall from a Wright masterpiece, the Francis W. Little House on Lake Minnetonka, demolished a number of years ago, is on display here, along with furniture by Wright, Maher, and Elmslie. (Another part of the Little house is in the Met.) The main museum building is a finely detailed beaux arts temple by McKim, Mead & White, the Minneapolis counterpart of St. Paul's great hilltop landmark, the state capitol, designed by Cass Gilbert, a hometown boy. With its marble dome and gilded quadriga by Daniel Chester French, the capitol can hold its own in the company of Boston's (by Bulfinch) and Richmond's (by Jefferson).

Eliel Saarinen and his son, Eero, built a spare Lutheran church in Minneapolis (Christ Church, 1950) that might be in rural Finland. Marcel Breuer built a much-praised, Corbusier-influenced concrete chapel and many other buildings at St. John's University in Collegeville, eighty miles away. But neither dazzles like Frank Gehry's Frederick R. Weisman Art Museum (1993) at the University of Minnesota, a rehearsal for his Bilbao Guggenheim Museum, which changes color with the weather. Clad in brushed steel, its lopsided cubes and irregular cylinders tumble down the east bank of the Mississippi like Marcel Duchamp's *Nude Descending a Staircase* in three dimensions.

The Twin Cities are not river towns in the sense that St. Louis and Memphis are, but the Mississippi, which rises in Lake Itasca, near Bemidji, 220 miles to the northwest, flows right through the middle of the metropolitan area, with Minneapolis mostly but not wholly on the right bank, St. Paul mostly but not wholly on the left. Which is a shame, because it spoils the otherwise telling gibe of Trevor Fishlock, an English journalist, who wrote after spending some time here that the Twin Cities "are divided by the Mississippi River and united by the belief that the inhabitants of the other side of the river are inferior."

Minneapolis is often called a small big city, St. Paul a big small town. Once Minnesota consisted of the Twin Cities, the prairies, and not much else, but in recent years the suburbs have taken over. Today Minneapolis and St. Paul have only about 675,000 people between them, yet there are 3 million in the burgeoning metropolitan area, the fifteenth biggest in the nation. A pioneering Met Council oversees growth in two-hundred-odd local jurisdictions.

The old ethnic order has changed rapidly in the last quarter century. No longer is Minneapolis mostly Swedish and Lutheran and St. Paul mostly German, Irish, and Catholic. After the Vietnam War, Minnesotans opened their arms to boat people and other immigrants from Southeast Asia, notably the Laotian hill people known as the Hmong, who were followed by Latin Americans, Africans, and others. The St. Paul schools teach students from homes where ninety-seven different languages and dialects are spoken. By now, there are 45,000 Hmong in the area, passionate about education. Joua Xiong, a semiliterate health care attendant who grows vegetables for sale in a farmers' market to make ends meet, has six children with university degrees, one of whom is working on a doctorate.

The old economic order has changed, too. The first great fortunes hereabouts were made from flour, timber, and railroads; you can sense how big those fortunes were by visiting the enormous pseudo-Romanesque mansion of James J. Hill on Summit Avenue in St. Paul. It has thirteen bathrooms, twenty-two fireplaces, a pipe organ and a two-story art gallery. When built in 1891, it was the largest house in the Midwest. Hill, a notoriously obstreperous gent, came to St. Paul when it was still named Pig's Eye and built the railroad that linked the Twin Cities to the western wheat fields and to the West Coast.

West of Hill's pile, along a four-mile section of Summit Avenue, his fellow robber barons built Belle Époque houses of their own, most of which have been diligently preserved. In the homely brownstone at 599 Summit Avenue, which he called "a house below average on a street above average," F. Scott Fitzgerald, a St. Paul native, spent the summer of 1919 finishing *This Side of Paradise*, the novel about Princeton that made him famous.

A block south of Summit runs Grand Avenue, capital of the

New Bohemia in the Upper Midwest—young, hip, and brainy. At the corner of Grand and Victoria, you'll find the nexus of the local café culture, chockablock with bookstores and coffeehouses. Café Latte, in an old Studebaker showroom, serves a deservedly famous three-layer turtle cake, dripping chocolate, caramel, and pecans, indescribably rich, improbably light. Betsey spent a half hour trying to figure out how to take one home.

Big business seems far away, but it isn't. The Twin Cities have lost some headquarters lately. Norwest Bank bought Wells Fargo, but its CEO and main office moved to San Francisco, and the new bank took the Wells Fargo name. Honeywell, an old Minneapolis firm, was sold to Allied Signal, and the merged operation moved east. Yet many big names remain, like Northwest Airlines, Target, 3M (Scotch tape, Post-its, and $16 billion in annual sales), and the 150-year-old St. Paul Companies (insurance). Cargill and General Mills (Wheaties, Betty Crocker, Cheerios, and now Pillsbury) make Minneapolis the greatest grain-milling center in the world. The riverside Washburn Crosby Complex, where General Mills was born, has been reshaped into a mixed-use development including the new Mill City Museum. Innovators continue to emerge. The Radisson Hotel chain, based here and once confined to this region, is now international. The Best Buy retail electronics chain has made its founder, Richard Schulze, a billionaire. Medtronic and St. Jude have flourished in the realm of advanced medical technology like heart stents.

The Fitzgerald cult has survived it all, proving to be hardier than Fitzgerald himself. Garrison Keillor campaigned successfully to have a restored St. Paul theater named for him, and there the whimsical Minnesotan and his coconspirators tell tales about a Thanksgiving turkey that fell in love with a dog, and remind us that there is at least one place where "the women are strong, the men are good looking, and all of the children are above average." That place is Lake Wobegon, of course, as important a part of the Minnesota landscape as Lake Minnetonka near Minneapolis and White Bear Lake near St. Paul. Upwards of 2.6 million people listen to the Wobegon news each week on 450 public stations across the nation. But the Twin Cities are progressive, worldly places. They resemble Lake

Wobegon no more than they resemble another North Country stereotype, Sinclair Lewis's *Main Street,* which was based on his proverbially provincial hometown, Sauk Center, Minnesota.

For decades, the Twin Cities sent politicians on to prominent positions in national life. Every four years from 1948 through 1984, with only a few exceptions, a Minnesotan sought the presidency or vice presidency—Harold Stassen, a serious contender before he became a standing joke; Hubert H. Humphrey, Eugene J. McCarthy, Walter F. Mondale. Humphrey, a garrulous, big-hearted electoral warrior, made his national debut at the 1948 Democratic convention. As "the boy mayor of Minneapolis," he had fought segregation in the South, and he exhorted his fellow delegates to step "out of the shadow of states' rights and into the bright sunshine of human rights." Two decades later, Humphrey came agonizingly close to the White House, although as Lyndon B. Johnson's vice president he was hobbled by his support for the hugely unpopular Vietnam War. Not until late on the morning after Election Day, 1968, did he tearfully concede defeat at the old Leamington Hotel. "We had a wonderful political culture," Mondale said over dinner one night. "Clean, progressive, tolerant. Minnesota had a magnificent moderation then."

Former governor Ventura, elected to a single term on the third-party Reform ticket in 1998, was something else. As a wrestler who fought under the nom de guerre Jesse the Body, he wore a feathered boa, and he shed none of his theatricality in office. Yet beneath it all he was a centrist, not an extremist, a libertarian on cultural issues, a conservative on fiscal issues. "His style may be fire-engine red," Steven Schier of Carleton College observed, "but his politics are beige."

WHERE TO STAY

Le Meridien, 601 First Avenue North, Minneapolis, (612) 677-1100. For decades, the parade of world-class hotels passed the Twin Cities by, but now, at last, Minneapolis has a hip, swanky, tech-savvy establishment. Each of 255 rooms in this 21-story downtown tower offers backlit photographs, wall-mounted 42-

inch plasma television screens, and bathrooms with multiple-jet showers and glass washbasins set into limestone counters.

Marquette Hotel, 710 Marquette Avenue, Minneapolis, (612) 333-4545. Built into the IDS skyscraper and now managed by Hilton, the Marquette has a prime location, connected to the Skywalk network. In a city of mammoth hotels, it is manageable in size and individual in character. The oversized rooms on the upper floors have steam baths and attractive views over the city, but there is no valet parking and the staff can be dim.

Nicollet Island Inn, 95 Merriam Street, Minneapolis, (612) 331-1800. Built as a sash-and-door factory in 1893, this modest three-story hotel sits in mid-Mississippi, just upriver from the stone arch bridge that James Hill constructed to carry his

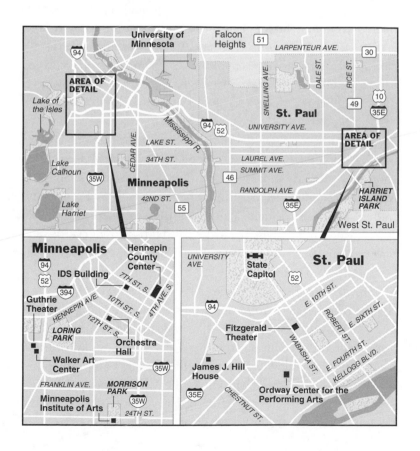

railroad west. Antiques in the lobby and cozy guest rooms give the place a rural feel, and an agreeable restaurant with sweeping river views occupies the glassed-in former loading dock.

St. Paul Hotel, 350 Market Street, St. Paul, (651) 292-9292. If business or pleasure takes you to the smaller of the Twin Cities, make a beeline for the St. Paul, one of the region's best hotels. Built in 1910 and brought up to date seventy-five years later, blessed with a good concierge, it is furnished with a lavish hand (Oriental carpets, exuberant flower displays).

WHERE TO EAT

D'Amico Cucina, 100 North Sixth Street, Minneapolis, (612) 338-2401. J. P. Samuelson has left this urbane establishment to open a promising bistro of his own, but the gutsy culinary style is unchanged under John Occhiato. Quarter-sized smoked trout cakes with horseradish crème fraîche explode with flavor, as do braised oxtails served on pappardelle. Except for the snowdrifts outside in winter, you could be in Piemonte.

La Belle Vie, 312 South Main Street, Stillwater, (651) 430-3545. After a long stint at D'Amico Cucina, Tim McKee set up shop in a picture-book village on the St. Croix River. Spanish, Moroccan, and Portuguese influences, as well as French and Italian ideas, are evident in his brightly seasoned, deeply flavored dishes and imaginative wine list. Harissa, mojo verde, and Serrano ham in a bistro on the American steppes? You betcha.

Levain, 4762 Chicago Avenue, Minneapolis, (612) 823-7111. Steven Brown works wonders with vegetables, turning out visually luscious, delicious dishes like red and golden beets with sweet Gorgonzola. But a bright new idea emerges almost every month in this windowless butter-yellow dining room, which has replaced the shuttered Aquavit as the Cities' hot spot. Other recent successes: salmon with rhubarb sauce and cool, cool cucumbers, and a trio of intense caramel desserts.

Quang, 2719 Nicollet Avenue South, Minneapolis, (612) 870-4739. Take it from someone who learned the hard way, here is real Vietnamese food: a long list of soups, including several kinds of pho, and the best cha gio (spring rolls) I have eaten in the U.S.A.—crisp, greaseless, and flavorful. Sparkling-clean Quang may be the best of the many Asian and Latin eateries, spawned by Twin Cities ethnicization, that stand shoulder-to-shoulder along Nicollet Avenue, aka "Eat Street."

Solera, 900 Hennepin Avenue, Minneapolis, (612) 338-0062. This is another McKee winner, opened in 2002, serving forty-plus hot and cold tapas and three dozen sherries at a curved mosaic bar and in a cavelike dining room. Tempting Spanish dishes—cold-smoked cod, pork ribs with smoky paprika sauce, and an exquisite octopus terrine—are enhanced by an ambitious, endearingly priced, largely Spanish wine list, and what one local critic called "a big-city strut." Do not miss Adrienne Odom's sumptuous desserts, also inspired by Spain.

Tavern on Grand, 656 Grand Avenue, St. Paul, (651) 228-9030. Wall-to-wall walleye, the best anywhere—full of sweet, peppery freshwater flavor, whether served with lemon and tartar sauce or with lettuce, tomatoes, and mayo on a bun—lures people to this simple pub. You can't miss it; there's an eight-foot-long neon fish in the window.

⇒ DALLAS and FORT WORTH

The words and music have stuck in my mind for fifty years, because they seemed so apt. Frank Loesser wrote them for his musical *The Most Happy Fella*, and they stopped the show every time: "You're from Big D, I can guess, by the way you drawl and the way you dress," a big, brassy babe bawled. "You're from Big D, my, oh yes. I mean Big D, little a, double l, a, s. And that spells Dallas, my darlin', darlin' Dallas, where every home's a palace, 'cause the settlers settle for no less."

Big money, big hair, and big talk. Such is the lingering stereotype of Dallas society. Dallas occupies a sizable spot in the national consciousness as the home of "America's Team," the Dallas Cowboys, of J. R. Ewing and Miss Ellie and the gang at Southfork, and of the little guy with the big ears and bigger ambition, H. Ross Perot, a billionaire before he turned forty. And for those old enough to recall the events of November 1963, it occupies an especially melancholy corner of memory, as the accursed place where John F. Kennedy was shot.

Dallas and its smaller sibling, Fort Worth, an unmatched pair if ever there was one, amount to a great deal more than that today. Together with the little cities that cluster around them like pilot fish, they constitute the largest metropolitan area, population 5.2 million, in America's second-largest state (Houston is bigger than Dallas, but its metropolitan area is smaller), boasting the largest collection of major corporate headquarters outside of New York and Chicago.

Dallas is the home of the megastore Neiman Marcus, an emblem of all that is stylish and luxurious—the creation, in large part, of Stanley Marcus, himself an emblem of all that was civilized and sophisticated. (Marcus, who died in 2002 at ninety-six, brought the designer Coco Chanel to Dallas in 1957 for one of his store's fabulous Foreign Fortnights and reported later that he had found her a dull luncheon companion.)

Yet people in Dallas "are tentative, not quite sure who they are supposed to be," as Larry McMurtry wrote in his collection of essays on Texas, *In a Narrow Grave,* whereas its rival "Houston is a boom town, lively, open and violent," where "the common goal is tomorrow's dollar." Harry McPherson grew up in Tyler, a hundred miles east of Dallas, and the big city stayed with him when he went to Washington as an aide to Lyndon B. Johnson. There is much that still rings true about the description of Dallas that he wrote later for *The Atlantic,* including the following words: "Just as you passed the Buckner Orphans' Home—I imagined it full of city kids like Mickey Rooney, presided over by Spencer Tracy—you could see the metropolitan skyline. It floated in the cold autumn sunlight, or trembled in the waves of summer heat. Dallas. Mysterious. Rich. Full of merchants, criminals and transplanted country boys."

Once known as Cowtown, Fort Worth is the home of the Kimbell Art Museum, housed in a masterwork built by Louis I. Kahn in 1972, with an exquisite collection of old masters in its top-lit galleries. At the risk of offending fans of the Frick in New York, the Gardner in Boston, and the Phillips in Washington, I would nominate it as the nation's best small museum.

Hugely wealthy, often eccentric men populate the histories of the two cities: Columbus Marion "Dad" Joiner, who discovered the largest oil field in the world on Daisy Bradford's farm in Rusk County; H. L. Hunt, who bought the leases from him in 1930 for a down payment of $30,000, built an oil empire, and spent his old age as a megarich loony, promoting extreme right-wing causes and theories; and Sid Richardson, a legendary wildcatter whose great-nephews, the Bass brothers, also made a bundle and reshaped downtown Fort Worth.

Dallas took a pasting in the second half of the 1980s. One by one, the overextended big Dallas banks, stuck with worthless real estate and energy paper, were forced to turn to Washington or to out-of-state holding companies for rescue. Finally, not a single locally owned bank was left. Many proud old Dallas families watched their fortunes vanish. There were other shocks as well. Walker L. Railey, minister of the First United Methodist Church, one of the largest in the nation, was accused of choking his wife, leaving her in a permanent vegetative state. He had been the golden boy of the religious community in a city where religion counts for a lot and where a broadcasting network ornaments its offices at Christmas with red tinsel letters spelling out the words "Happy Birthday, Jesus."

And then there was the scandal at Southern Methodist University, another of the city's defining institutions. With its splendid Meadows Museum of Spanish art, it lies at the heart of the enclave, north of downtown, known as Park Cities—Highland Park and University Park. Conservative, wealthy, snobbish, the Park Cities are also known as "the Bubble." The way its residents see things, scandals belong to the messy world outside the Bubble, not the orderly one inside, but it emerged in 1987 that Southern Methodist had been illegally paying its football players. Worse, the board of trustees, led by Governor William P. Clements Jr., had contrived an elaborate cover-up. The National Collegiate Athletic Association imposed tough sanctions, barring Southern Methodist, which had produced gridiron immortals like Doak Walker and Don Meredith, from football for two seasons. As John Steinbeck wrote in *Travels with Charley* (1962), "Football games have the glory and the despair of war, and when a Texas team takes the field against a foreign state, it is an army with banners." In gridiron war, as in other kinds, the rules are often bent, even shattered.

Scattered along the freeways, amid barbecue joints and used-car lots with flags the size of basketball courts, are the headquarters of big companies like Frito-Lay and Exxon, J. C. Penney, American Airlines, Halliburton, Texas Industries, and Electronic Data Systems, and scores of little companies in the computer, software, and communications businesses. Some of the smaller operations went under during the downturn of 2001–3. All suffered. But the region is endlessly inventive and intensely entrepreneurial. Here Herb Kelleher dreamed up Southwest Airlines, with its low prices and hokey style ("Austin Auften," the billboards say). His planes are the Greyhounds of our time. Here a Texas Instruments engineer named Jack Kilby, who had not been with the company long enough to earn a summer vacation, spent July 1958 in the lab and hit upon the idea of the silicon chip, or integrated circuit, launching what has been called the Second Industrial Revolution.

Hard times produced some new and different leaders. At the nadir of the 1980s, with oil prices at rock bottom and the patriarchy in retreat, the city turned to a Democrat, a woman named Annette Strauss (sister-in-law of Robert S. Strauss, the Washington lawyer and politico), as its mayor. Already well-known in the city for her activism, she got dozens of new arts projects moving. Then Dallas, to its own surprise and for the first time in its history, elected a black to succeed her. Ron Kirk served two terms, and in 2002, at another low point, another woman, Laura Miller, moved in to tackle the city's ills.

Like poverty. The Trinity River, *The Economist* once commented, "bisects the city of Dallas as certainly as an ocean." On one bank, Highland Park's whites enjoy average household incomes of more than $200,000 a year; in largely black and Hispanic South Dallas, on the other side of the river, the figure is a measly $11,350. Poor education takes a toll. Latinos will form the majority of the city's workforce by 2010, but only 1 percent of high-tech employees are Latino.

Downtown Dallas is another problem. Banks and law offices—including Bob Strauss's powerhouse firm Akin, Gump, Strauss, Hauer & Feld, with a thousand lawyers worldwide—bring thousands of people into the area by day, but by night the sidewalks have been eerily empty. Still, high-rise apartment blocks have been going up around the center of town lately, and the red Pegasus sign, a landmark since 1934, has been reinstalled atop the renovated Magnolia Hotel. A new arts center may be the key piece of the puzzle when it is finally completed in 2009.

The center's linchpin is the 2,062-seat Morton H. Meyerson Symphony Center, named by its principal donor, Ross Perot, for one of his business colleagues, who sings in the Dallas Symphony Chorus. Designed by I. M. Pei in 1979, it combines the sharp angles of his East Building for the National Gallery in Washington with swelling glass "blisters" that allow the sun to reach its restaurants and lobbies. Both the building and its acoustics have won the affection of the city, as has Andrew Litton, the Dallas Symphony Orchestra's conductor, who has held the job since 1994. New York–born, he reminds me of Leonard Bernstein in his athleticism on the podium and his fondness for dramatic musical effect. The orchestra records regularly, appears every year in Carnegie Hall, and tours Europe—all of the things that the big guys do.

Toward the end of the decade, the Dallas Opera will move into a new home in the arts center, a 2,400-seat, $275 million lyric theater designed by the English architect Norman Foster, winner of the Pritzker Prize in 1999, and leave the barny old Music Hall, a building with all the charm and acoustical subtlety of an airplane hangar. The company mounted a *Ring* cycle there. Its new general manager, Karen Stone, also English, built her career in German and Austrian houses. Also on the drawing boards are a smaller theater by another Pritzker winner, the Dutch master Rem Koolhaas, and a new bridge by the daring Spaniard Santiago Calatrava.

The Dallas Museum of Art is headed by John R. Lane, who earlier put the San Francisco Museum of Modern Art on the cultural map. Its collection, comprehensive in scope but uneven in detail, includes strong pre-Columbian and decorative arts departments and many stellar paintings, among them Mondrians stretching from his early, representational style to the neoplastic masterpiece *Place de la Concorde*; van Gogh's golden *Sheaves of Wheat*; and Hopper's evocative *Lighthouse Hill.* The highlight may well be Frederic E. Church's enormous, chillinducing canvas *The Icebergs,* which was rediscovered in England and purchased in 1979.

Next door is a real jewel, a small museum of Asian art established by Trammell Crow and his wife; his real estate development firm is based in Dallas. The jade, the crystal ball (the world's second biggest, after one in the Smithsonian), and the eighteenth-century sandstone facade of a Rajasthan palace are don't-miss attractions. Installations are immaculate.

Dallas's latest benefactor is Raymond Nasher, a developer whose collection of modern sculpture, widely viewed as the world's best, was courted by major museums from New York to Washington to San Francisco. Instead, he built a $60 million museum and sculpture garden, designed by Renzo Piano, across from the Museum of Art, to house a rotating selection of his Matisses and Ernsts, his Calders and Mirós and Dubuffets. The building's five linked pavilions are topped with shimmering glass barrel vaults that allow natural light to play across the sculptures. Larger pieces by Mark di Suvero and others are displayed in the surrounding museum gardens, where visitors are given folding chairs so they can view the sculptures from whatever angle they choose.

"At the moment," Nasher told me several years before the gala opening in 2003, "Dallas has nothing of real artistic significance, internationally. Perhaps this can be it. This is a nice city, but it's mostly about money. We're hoping to change that a little."

Many come to Dallas to see the grassy knoll near where Kennedy was killed—"allegedly," as an official plaque puts it, by a shot fired by Lee Harvey Oswald. Dallas still has doubts. The Sixth Floor Museum, in the building from which the fatal shots came, shows items such as the camera used by Abraham Zapruder to film the shooting. The late Douglas Kiker, then a reporter for the *New York Herald-Tribune,* who was covering President Kennedy's visit, said after the president was shot: "If I had the power to, I'd call the bombers over this place. How could a thing like this happen?" But of course Dallas did not kill Kennedy any more than Los Angeles killed his brother Robert.

Seven years afterward, a memorial designed by Philip Johnson and paid for by 50,000 people across the country was opened only a few blocks from the knoll. It consists of four thirty-foot concrete walls, with narrow openings on two sides and an unadorned gray granite cenotaph at its center. Some find it moving, while others find it sterile.

Johnson, whose Houston buildings helped define that city's sleek skyline, designed a number of duds in Dallas, including the Bank One tower, a weird neo-Palladian effort, and Crescent Court, which marries lacy New Orleans ironwork to a monstrosity of a mansard roof. Johnson once said (joke?) that he saved his best ideas for Houston. Other well-known architects have misfired here, too, including even Frank Lloyd Wright, whose Dallas Theater Center (completed in 1959) is watered-down Guggenheimery. (This is not to denigrate in the slightest the quality of the dramatic productions that are mounted there. The company, heir to the tradition of Margo Jones, a regional theater pioneer, is ably run by Richard Hamburger, son of Philip, the late *New Yorker* writer.)

Perhaps the most remarkable set of older buildings in Dallas is the twenty-six Art Deco structures on the immense Texas State Fairgrounds, including the Cotton Bowl and the Hall of State celebrating the state's gaudy history. For twenty-four days each fall, tens of thousands of rural folk, and more thousands pretending to be, come to ride the Ferris wheel and see the rodeo.

In Fort Worth, pride of place must go to the Kimbell. Kahn's long, vaulted, refined galleries in oak, travertine, concrete, and stainless steel work as well today as the day they were built (1972). Miraculously, every single picture in the building is worth seeing, or so it seems to me, and almost all of them—the Duccio, the Mantegna, the two Georges de La Tours, the Caspar David Friedrich (the first to enter an American museum), and the magisterial *Cardsharps* of Caravaggio—were acquired over the past three decades. In 2004, the Kimbell bought another gem—Bernini's terra-cotta model for the Fountain of the Moor in the Piazza Navona in Rome.

Two notable Fort Worth museums have recently been rebuilt, with the ubiquitous Philip Johnson doing the honors for the Amon Carter Museum, devoted to American art, completing a facility he began in 1961. The fastidious Japanese architect Tadeo Ando fashioned a magical glass-walled home for the Museum of Modern Art, with an overhanging slab roof of polished concrete supported by strenuous double-Y columns and a two-acre reflecting pool.

Fort Worth was once the southern terminus of the Chisholm Trail, but it has clearly grown well beyond its stockyards, beyond Joe T. Garcia's enchiladas and the gargantuan honky-tonk, Billy Bob's Texas, even beyond its longtime slogan, "Where the West Begins." Fort Worth may be Van Cliburn's hometown, but people call it "Bassville." The Basses have given it a new performance hall, named after their father, Perry, with limestone angels on the facade blowing immense brass trumpets. A pastiche of Secession, beaux arts, and postmodern styles, it is beloved locally, but I agree with a Dallas critic who termed it a romance novel of a building.

WHERE TO STAY

Adolphus Hotel, 1321 Commerce Street, (214) 742-8200. Built in 1912 by the beer baron Adolphus Busch, restored and expanded often since, this dowager is downtown Dallas's best bet. The lobby, a vast, opulent Gilded Age drawing room, is furnished with oversized chairs, ten-foot-tall potted palms, and an antique silver chandelier adorned with Budweiser eagles. Upstairs, the bedrooms are less lavish, but a few are Texas-big, with nice terraces. A formal but unpretentious restaurant (the French Room) has mature, well-priced wines.

Crescent Court Hotel, 400 Crescent Court, (214) 871-3200. Like the Mansion, the newer Crescent Court belongs to Rosewood Hotels, the luxury group developed and partly owned by Caroline Rose Hunt, one of H. L. Hunt's children. A small step behind its stablemate, it offers many of the same amenities, including deluxe bathrooms and sheets soft enough for a princess.

The Mansion on Turtle Creek, 2821 Turtle Creek Boulevard, (214) 559-2100. If this sanctuary north of downtown isn't the

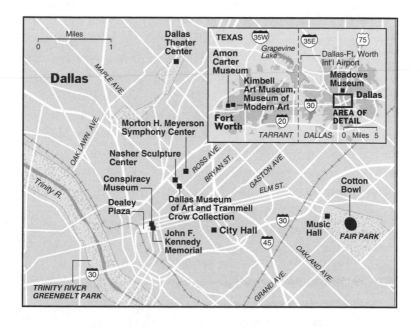

best hotel in the United States, it comes close. The sumptuous flower arrangements alone are worth the price of admission. Magnificent furnishings, of course, including a few old pieces, along with extras like Ethernet facilities. Need a cord for your computer on Thanksgiving Day? No problem: it arrives in six minutes flat.

WHERE TO EAT

Abacus, 4511 McKinney Avenue, (214) 559-3111. Abacus found its niche as soon as it opened. A snappy, geometric modern decor is warmed by potted orchids and autumnal colors on the walls, to say nothing of the Asian-influenced food. Some dishes falter, but several dazzled us: the breads, to start with, lamb pot-stickers with tangerine hoisin sauce, and desserts as jolly as they were tasty, like a scaled-down chocolate malted milk shake.

Citizen, 3858 Oak Lawn Avenue, (214) 522-7253. Chris Ward's food is more pan-Asian, less fusion-formed than Abacus's, more casual, more appealing to young people. Order an assortment of sashimi, and a lovely lacquer tray appears, heaped high with shaved ice and scintillatingly fresh raw fish, some conventional (salmon, yellowtail, tuna), some Texified (tuna marinated in chili oil or studded with jalapeño and cilantro).

The Mansion on Turtle Creek (see above). Spicy house classics, like tortilla soup and lobster tacos, are matched by special-occasion treats like roast turkey with tortilla stuffing and cranberry-jalapeño relish. The team here, headed by Dean Fearing, the chef, has worked together in this elegant spot for years. You can spend thousands on wine; if you're a bit short, ask the help of Kent Rice, a super-sommelier.

Sonny Bryan's, 2202 Inwood Road, (214) 357-7120. At this concrete-block shack, you eat lean, sublimely smoky barbecued brisket of beef at old school desks or off the hood of your BMW. You could slice the atmosphere with a knife; for the beef, you don't need one. Drink Shiner Bock, a dark, malty Texas brew from a long-necked bottle; order a side of thick, moist onion rings and marvel at the clientele: black, white, and brown, tweeds, mink, and bib overalls.

York Street, 6047 Lewis Street, (214) 826-0968. A tiny neighborhood restaurant (twelve tables) with market-driven ambition, modest prices, and nice twists on common dishes—consider the dollop of brandade served with a scallop and corn chowder—and some uncommon vegetables like salsify. Sharon Hage, the chef, used to work at Neiman's.

⫸ HOUSTON

Houston may be the fourth largest city in the United States, if not the fourth largest metropolis (it stood tenth on that list in 2000, with 4,669,571 people), but it is less well-known to most Americans than the Big Three, Los Angeles, New York, and Chicago. It is a steaming, hyper-air-conditioned, boom-bust-boom town that oozes across five hundred relentlessly flat, bayou-laced, mosquito-plagued square miles, the most ethnically and racially diverse, most unionized city in Texas, with aching disparities between rich and poor matched in few other places in the country.

It is the city oil built. Houston was nothing much until the first gusher came in; that was Spindletop, on the Gulf Coast, which blasted Houston and Texas and the whole blessed world into the petroleum era on January 10, 1901. Since then, Houston has been a city of flamboyant oilmen like Glenn McCarthy and Hugh Roy Cullen, a city of big gestures and big spenders, where minimalism is a dirty word and nobody dreams of dressing down. Every so often, the flamboyance gets completely out of control, and you have a scandal on your hands, like the staggering scam in which executives of Enron, once the nation's seventh-largest company, and their allies engaged in massive fraud that destroyed it and cost shareholders billions.

It is the city that a generation remembers for a single radio transmission in 1969, from an astronaut on the moon to NASA's Johnson Space Center southeast of town: "Houston, Tranquillity Base here. The Eagle has landed." The exhilaration faded, though, and Houston suffered even more than the rest of the country when the space shuttle *Columbia* broke up over central Texas in 2003, killing all seven astronauts aboard.

It is the city that gave birth, with Judge Roy Hofheinz's Astrodome, to the startling idea that baseball and football could be played indoors—and, of course, to that emerald-green apotheosis of artifice, Astroturf. It is a city much more Southern than Western, green and not brown, full of magnolias, live oaks, and Spanish moss. The cactus and the tumbleweeds are stored farther west (although Houston's rodeo, which takes place in early March, is the world's biggest).

It is a city that has lent major political figures to the nation. Movers and shakers like the Democrat Jesse H. Jones, who spearheaded the building of the Houston Ship Channel that made Houston a great port, who owned big chunks of the Texas Commerce Bank and the *Houston Chronicle,* and whom Franklin D. Roosevelt summoned to Washington to run the Reconstruction Finance Corporation, which he did so arrogantly that FDR called him "Jesus H. Jones." Republicans like the hard-nosed Tom DeLay, aka The Hammer, the House majority leader beginning in 2002; George Bush, the forty-first president, and his son George W. Bush, the forty-third. Women like Oveta Culp Hobby, the wartime head of the WACs, and the eloquent Barbara Jordan. And lawyers like John B. Connally of Vinson & Elkins and James A. Baker III of Baker & Botts, who held four different high-level positions in three different administrations.

Recently Houston has been taken down a peg. Pummeled in the headlines, Enron ended its lavish backing of the arts, sold off some businesses, and liquidated others. In the wake of 9/11, Houston-based Continental Airlines estimated it would have to cut 12,000 jobs systemwide, but held the final figure below that. The computer maker Compaq ran out of gas, merged with Hewlett-Packard, and shed jobs. To worsen matters, a nasty tropical storm named Allison dumped thirty-eight inches of rain on the city in June 2001, killing twenty-two and causing $5 billion in damage. Hospitals and cultural institutions were hit hard, and 33,000 families sought temporary shelter.

Even in the best of times, Houston is an ugly, sprawling city, unprotected by zoning laws. Block after barren block of weed-infested parking lots and disintegrating houses stand close by upscale shopping centers and lushly landscaped residential Edens like River Oaks. Too many hours are spent in cars on congested but indispensable freeways. "Houston is like my twelve-year-old son, who outgrew his pants three times last year, which is good," said the city's mayor, Bill White, a Democrat who was elected in 2003 on promises to restrain expansion. "But traditionally Houston waits to buy its pants until the old ones are outgrown." Less charitably, a Houston architect, Dan Barnum, lamented in the *Houston Chronicle* at about the same time: "We have no aesthetic roots, no aesthetic foundation, so we don't complain when there is ugly all around us."

Conventions (a $165 million expansion of the George R. Brown Convention Center) and sports (new stadia for the baseball Astros, once owned in part by George W. Bush, and for hockey and basketball) have soaked up a lot of public money. Public enthusiasm was generated by the return of pro football in 2002 in the form of the Houston Texans, replacing the Oilers, who had decamped to Tennessee after the 1996 season. Yet Houston is also a center of art and culture, of distinguished museums and bravura buildings and excellent performing arts organizations. When the English writer J. B. Priestley visited Houston in the 1950s, somebody told him it was "strictly a whisky and trombone town." But that was before the gentling hand of Dominique de Menil took hold.

Mrs. de Menil (pronounced men-EEL), who died in 1997 at the age of eighty-nine, used her large fortune, which came from Schlumberger, her father's celebrated oil-drilling-equipment company, to advance the cause of the arts in Houston. Her monuments are a series of buildings in a neighborhood called Montrose, including the Rothko Chapel, a nondenominational building housing fourteen somber canvases by Mark Rothko, with a Barnett Newman sculpture called *Broken Obelisk* nearby, and the Menil Collection, a private museum comparable to New York's Frick Collection and London's Wallace Collection.

The Menil Collection is housed in one of the best museum buildings erected since World War II—a gray clapboard structure, low-built like the neighborhood surrounding it, with noise-absorbing wooden floors and a clever system of S-shaped light baffles. It is the work of Renzo Piano, co-architect of the Pompidou Center in Paris. Mrs. De Menil had a famously good eye, and the museum is filled with exquisite objects, from a sixth-century Coptic funeral stele depicting a wide-eyed woman, to chiwara antelope sculptures from Mali in West Africa, to icons from Venice and Novgorod and Turkey, to great twentieth-century Surrealist paintings. There is not a clunker in sight.

A few blocks away are the Contemporary Arts Museum, which has no permanent collection, and the Museum of Fine Arts, which does. The MFA, as the locals call it, has an array of superior Impressionist and modern paintings (notably Jasper Johns), plus an excellent sculpture garden and sizable old master holdings. Included among the latter is one of Zurbarán's most touching paintings, showing the Lamb of God trussed for sacrifice, as well as works by Dürer, Bellini, Tiepolo, Van Dyck, and Delacroix.

A second building, designed by the much-honored Spanish architect Rafael Moneo and connected to the first one by an underground tunnel, opened in 2000. It vaulted the museum from thirtieth to sixth place among the country's art museums; it is the largest of its kind in the South and Southwest, though not of the same quality as the Kimbell in Fort Worth, and attracts more than 2.5 million visitors a year. Under Peter C. Marzio, its director, it has made a major effort to involve minority communities in its programs.

The impulse to reach out is also evident on once-a-month family days, with free admission, at the Bayou Bend Collection and Gardens, a splendid property bequeathed to the museum by Ima Hogg, the unfortunately christened daughter of Texas's first native-born governor. Named for the lazy stream that flows through the fourteen-acre property, Bayou Bend, an enormous pale pink house built in 1927, stands amid gardens adorned with statues and fountains and magnificent azaleas. Reached by a suspension bridge crossing the bayou, the house contains 4,800 English and American objects installed in twenty-eight room settings. There is a silver sugar bowl by Paul Revere and a refined lyre-base épergne by an anonymous English craftsman, portraits by Copley and Charles Willson Peale, furniture by Duncan Phyfe and Benjamin H. Latrobe, a cupboard filled with delicate creamware and another with Pennsylvania spatterware.

Hogg, whose brother Will developed River Oaks, was also a founder of the Houston Symphony Orchestra. Once overseen by such notables as Leopold Stokowski and Sir John Barbirolli, it embellished its reputation under Christoph Eschenbach, whose style has been compared to that of the great conductor Wilhelm Furtwängler. He departed (for Paris and Philadelphia) in 1999, and his successor, the Austrian Hans Graf, has yet to make a comparable impact. Much of the orchestra's valuable sheet-music library was lost in the floods, its musicians staged a twenty-two-day strike in 2003 after pay cuts were mooted, and the organization is running a substantial deficit.

Houston is a top theater town. It has a superb resident stage company, the Tony-winning Alley Theater, in business since 1947, which mounts a dozen or so productions a year—two of which went to Broadway in 1999—and opened an innovative Center for Theater Production in 2002; the twin-stage Hobby Center for the Performing Arts, designed by Robert A. M. Stern; a renowned ballet company under the direction of the Australian Stanton Welch; and the Houston Grand Opera, with which the ballet shares the Wortham Theater Center in the revitalized downtown theater district.

In thirty-five years as the opera company's general director, David Gockley has championed modern opera, staged many world premieres, and brought semi-operatic American musicals like *Porgy and Bess* and *Showboat* into the opera house. In 2001, he unveiled plasma television screens to bring close-ups to the balconies. A more recent triumph was the acclaimed inaugural production of an opera based on *The Little Prince,* with music by Rachel Portman and libretto by Nicholas Wright, directed by Francesca Zambello.

For all its banal buildings, Houston has some fine architecture. Long before Piano's eloquently understated building for the Menil Collection went up, there were interesting, mostly modern structures in Houston's three main nodes—downtown, the Galleria complex to the west, and the Rice University/Texas Medical Center area to the south.

The Rice campus, where building began in 1912, is arranged in a series of quadrangles laid out by Ralph Adams Cram (Cesar Pelli has prepared a new master plan). Cram used collegiate Gothic at West Point and Princeton, but for Houston's more semi-tropical climate, he decided that a Mediterranean style would be appropriate. Rice's latest showplace is the Baker Institute for Public Policy, named for George H. W. Bush's secretary of state and headed by Edward P. Djerejian, a former ambassador to Israel and Syria. With state-of-the-art conference facilities, it aspires to take a place alongside similar centers at Harvard and Princeton. Nearby rise the buildings of the medical center, one of the finest in the country, embracing nearly forty hospitals and medical and nursing schools, including the outstanding M. D. Anderson cancer clinic. Two internationally celebrated heart surgeons, Dr. Michael E. DeBakey and Dr. Denton Cooley, helped make Houston medicine world-famous.

Downtown, where Houston was founded in 1836 by its own Romulus and Remus, the brothers Augustus C. and John K. Allen of New York, is a forest of silver and green and terracotta-colored skyscrapers leaping from the flatlands. Among the best are the beautifully proportioned Tenneco building, now known as the El Paso Energy Building, designed by Skidmore, Owings & Merrill, and the seventy-one-story Wells Fargo Plaza, composed of two quarter-round towers clad in dark green glass and offset from one another by only fifteen feet.

But Houston is Philip Johnson country, home to some of his most acclaimed buildings. Pennzoil Place, at 711 Louisiana Street, is the most spectacular of Johnson's local designs, a pair of wedge-shaped towers, tops lopped off at a 45-degree angle, joined at the base by a glassed-in pedestrian gallery filled with trees, flowers, and sunlight. Less successful, if no less distinctive, is the Bank of America Center at 700 Louisiana Street, built of red granite. Drawing upon and greatly magnifying the distinctive stepped gables of sixteenth-century Dutch buildings, it jabs an astonishing silhouette into the Texas sky.

At the feet of these and other buildings is a delightful array of public sculpture by Calder, Oldenburg, Richard Lippold, Henry Moore, Dubuffet, Nevelson (*Frozen Laces*, 1979), and Miró. The Miró, entitled *Personage and Birds* and completed in 1970, is an angular, Tinkertoy-like construction in primary colors that sits below I. M. Pei's fire-sided granite J. P. Morgan Chase Tower (formerly the Texas Commerce Bank Building) at 600 Travis Street. Unfortunately, even that kind of inspired whimsy does not impart much animation to the skyscraper district. However magnificent from afar, at sidewalk level the buildings present almost blank walls of granite and glass, inhibiting—even repelling—street life.

Near the Galleria, the capital of blood-sport shopping, is another must-see Johnson project, designed with John Burgee—the Transco Tower, of which Johnson wrote, "This will always seem like the tallest building in the world." Though only sixty-five stories, it seems taller because it stands above low-rise retail buildings. With its distinctive setbacks, it is reminiscent of the Empire State Building (and some designs in the 1922 Tribune Tower competition in Chicago), executed in mirror glass.

WHERE TO STAY

Four Seasons, 1300 Lamar Street, (713) 650-1300, is not one of the Canadian-owned chain's stars, like its sister in Chicago.

But it's a first-rate business and leisure hotel, with thick carpets, a fabulous pool, and memorably comfortable beds upstairs. The staff tries hard, but they seem overstressed during holiday weekends and conventions.

The Lancaster, 701 Texas Avenue, (713) 228-9500, in the heart of the theater, concert, and opera district, was restored to its 1920s elegance in 1982. With a cheery canary-yellow lobby and gleaming antiques in many of its ninety-three bedrooms, this boutique hotel is one of Houston's gems. Actors and singers love the food in its Bistro and from its twenty-four-hour room service. A Texas-friendly staff provides solicitous care.

St. Regis, 1919 Briar Oaks Lane, (713) 840-7600. The Hotel Formerly Known as Ritz, they might call it. For a time, this elegant hotel, having lost the right to use the Ritz-Carlton name, answered the phone, "Luxury Collection," a clumsy moniker at best. An agreeable new name, the sylvan setting in River Oaks, a lavish use of marble, lush flowers, and a high staff-guest ratio make you feel as if you're staying on a peer's estate.

The Houstonian, 111 North Post Oak Lane, (713) 680-2626, is the most Texan of Houston's top hotels, which may or may not commend it to you. It sits on a woodsy twenty-two-acre site, and the lobby decor resembles that of a laid-back country lodge. Some of the 289 guest rooms are resplendent, some drab. This was George H. W. Bush's voting address when he lived in Washington and where he stayed during trips to Texas.

WHERE TO EAT

Brennan's of Houston, 3300 Smith Street, (713) 522-9711. Houston shares the Gulf of Mexico's humidity with New Orleans, so it is not surprising that the Crescent City's Brennan clan has put down roots here. At the local outpost, Chef Carl Walker adds Texas touches to Creole favorites—shrimp rémoulade with a vinegary corn-jalapeño relish on the side, for example—and creates brilliant new dishes, too, like quail on spinach, paired with a crawfish enchilada. Saturday and Sunday brunch with live New Orleans jazz.

Cafe Annie, 1728 Post Oak Boulevard, (713) 840-1111, is the best restaurant in Houston and maybe the best in Texas, which is saying something. Like many good restaurants here, it's incongruously housed in a strip mall, but inside, the mahogany paneling glows luxuriously. Shy, serious, and bursting with talent, Robert del Grande cooks bold food with roots in both the Mexican and American traditions: coffee-roasted beef, on one hand, and rare tuna with thinly sliced beets and truffle vinaigrette on the other. Mimi, his animated wife, deftly directs the dining room. Do not deny yourself the warm chocolate cake with a beret of coffee meringue on top, or a fine bottle or two.

Goode Co. Then there is Jim Goode, who will show you how to eat well in Houston for a few bucks. At Goode Co. Texas Bar-B-Q (sorry about the orthography), 5109 Kirby Drive, (713) 522-2530, a shed stuffed with buffalo heads and other such nonsense, grab a long-neck Shiner Bock beer and order a beef brisket sandwich (sliced, not chopped) on jalapeño cheese bread. It's the real thing. Around the corner, at Goode Co. Texas Seafood, 2621 Westpark, (713) 523-7154, go for Gulf-fresh shrimp—in a po' boy sandwich, mesquite-grilled with rémoulade sauce or in a campechana, a Mexican-style seafood cocktail, served in a sundae glass with sauce the color of Maureen O'Hara's hair.

Hugo's, 1600 Westheimer Road, (713) 524-7744. Mexico City Mexican, like pork carnitas with grilled onions, served in a dramatic room. You can also sample traditional Tex-Mex at the original Ninfa's, 2704 Navigation Street, (713) 228-1175 (a Bush family favorite), where the skirt-steak fajitas are made with care. Or try Tex-Tex at del Grande's terrific self-service café, Taco Milagro, on Westheimer Road at 2555 Kirby Drive, (713) 522-1999. The margaritas there are unsweetened, the salsas are fresh, and the barbacoa enchiladas with milagro mole sauce will knock your socks off (if you're wearing any).

Mark's, 1658 Westheimer Road, (713) 523-3800. Mark Cox used to cook at Tony's; now he cooks for himself, at Mark's, a crowded, casual spot in a deconsecrated red-brick church. You'll enjoy the pepper-crusted Scottish salmon, the cheesy Mississippi grits, and the nursery desserts—fresh-made strawberry shortcake and an adult version of campfire s'mores, with gooey chocolate and marshmallow cream. Or go for the pasta with boned short ribs of beef, or (remember, you're in longhorn country) the classic rib-eye steaks.

AUSTIN and SAN ANTONIO

In 1836, San Antonio gave Texas its enduring symbol of us-against-them pride and courage, the Alamo. Austin's moment in the sun is today and tomorrow. Its technology boom has generated fortunes that rival the staggering riches earned by the state's early cattle and oil barons.

The two cities are only eighty miles apart, not much more than an hour's drive down I-35 for lead-footed local motorists, and their metropolitan areas are slowly but surely drawing together. They share several things: the equable south-central Texas climate; close proximity to the Hill Country, a region of rustic (though threatened) beauty; an unhurried approach to life; and an unusual ethnic flavor, arising from the interaction of Hispanic culture with that of early settlers from Germany. But no one would confuse them.

Austin is defined first by the enormous University of Texas, with almost 50,000 students on a 350-acre campus, and by the state government—not to slight the big electronic plants just outside the city and one of the country's liveliest, most varied popular music cultures. Willie Nelson lives there, as does Lady Bird Johnson, the farsighted presidential widow, who has enriched Austin and the whole nation with her beautification projects. Ann Richards and Molly Ivins, a pair of bright, witty women, one a former governor, the other a syndicated columnist, find an ample supply of local targets for their barbs.

Austin's population grew by a third and its workforce by almost two-thirds in the 1990s, until the tech bust slowed the economy. But the late George Christian, one of Lyndon B.

Johnson's press secretaries, told me over a lunch of meat loaf, black-eyed peas, and iced tea at Threadgill's, Janis Joplin's old hangout, that the city retained its basic character—"tolerant and laid-back, different from the rest of the state"—despite all the traffic jams and volatile real estate values.

"With the exception of San Antonio, all of our cities are adolescent," the celebrated Texas writer Larry McMurtry observed in an essay called "A Handful of Roses." "San Antonio speaks for itself, and much of its charm is in the way it embodies its past." Already an old community for the Native Americans who first lived along the river there, it became a Spanish mission settlement in 1719. It is a city of fiestas, especially the nine-day Fiesta, an annual spring wingding every bit as flamboyant as, if somewhat less boozy than, Mardi Gras in New Orleans. The city has turned its evident appeal into a significant economic asset, luring dozens of conventions every year. It earns further millions from three big Air Force bases, including Randolph Field, where pilots have been trained since before World War II, and the Army's Fort Sam Houston.

Older than Austin, San Antonio is much poorer and slightly larger, with 1.7 million people living in its metropolitan area, compared with 1.4 million living in Austin's—a margin that is rapidly shrinking. It is also much more heavily Hispanic, in fact the largest Hispanic-majority city in the country, represented in Congress from 1961 until 1998 by Henry B. Gonzalez, a Banking Committee power who brought home plenty of federal bacon, and now by his son Charles. Much of its modern momentum was imparted by another Hispanic politician, Henry G. Cisneros, who was mayor from 1982 to 1990.

Neither San Antonio nor Austin can claim to be even a regional cultural capital, let alone a national one. But scratch the surface a little, and you will discover that Nelson A. Rockefeller's wonderful collection of Latin American art has found a home in San Antonio, and that the University of Texas houses one of the world's greatest troves of twentieth-century manuscripts, including important items by Joyce, Shaw, and Waugh—"sucked into Austin like particles of dust into a vacuum cleaner" (McMurtry again). San Antonio also boasts a stunning new library designed by the Mexican master Roberto Legorreta. A series of boxes piled atop one another, with a breathtaking six-story atrium, it is painted an eye-popping color known to locals as "enchilada red."

Austin's own architectural spectacular, a new building for the university's Jack S. Blanton Museum, was stalled in 1999 when philistine members of the Board of Regents raised so many objections that the architects, Herzog & de Meuron, possibly the hottest firm in the world at the time, threw up their hands and quit. The dean of the architecture school resigned, too. Until a less ambitious replacement can be completed, the Blanton's interesting collection is split between two campus buildings, neither of them adequate. Its most important holdings are the twentieth-century American pictures donated by the author James A. Michener and his wife, Mari (ranging from the Ashcan School through a jaunty yellow oil by Arthur G. Dove called *Good Breeze* to Sam Gilliam and Larry Rivers), and the Suida-Manning collection. It includes works by Poussin and Guercino as well as a Veronese *Annunciation,* some formerly on long-term loan to the Metropolitan Museum of Art.

Conservatism and insularity have done nothing to inhibit the development of dozens of theater companies in Austin. Nor has it slowed the headlong expansion of the popular music scene, which now embraces 810 recording artists and 150 clubs and other stages, featuring everything from rockabilly to Texas swing to Tejano. Every March, journalists and record company executives flock to the South by Southwest Music and Media Conference, known as SXSW, to look for future stars. More than a thousand acts from all over the world show up, each allotted a mere forty minutes to sell itself to the bigwigs.

In San Antonio, a significant effort has been made to build artistic links to Mexico and all of Latin America, as Ron Bechtel, a local architect and food critic, explained to me. The strongest element in this linkage, no doubt, is the Rockefeller Latin American Art Center at the San Antonio Museum of Art. Besides Aztec, Mixtec, and other pre-Columbian art, Spanish colonial silver and altarpieces, and contemporary Latin painting, the Rockefeller center owns a riotously uninhibited collection of Mexican folk art—masks, a crane fashioned from a gourd, and bright ceramic churches, trucks, and trains. A highlight of the museum's other collections is Martin Johnson Heade's tiny *Passion Flowers and Hummingbirds,* which a wall label aptly describes as "a very private vision of the Garden of Eden." He painted it, appropriately enough, in Latin America.

Texas is full of small museums that are little known outside the state, like the Ima Hogg decorative arts collection in Houston and the Trammell Crow Collection of Asian Art in Dallas. In San Antonio, the sleeper is the McNay Art Museum, in a parklike setting on the north side of town, where the Richie Riches of San Antonio live. Among other things, it has a nationally known theater arts collections. (In a special exhibition in that department a few years back, I was amazed to see sketches by Kasimir Malevich made in 1913 for the St. Petersburg production of a largely forgotten futurist opera called *Victory over the Sun.*)

If you happen to be a circus junkie like me, you will enjoy the Hertzberg Circus Museum, which houses the 20,000-object collection of a former state senator from San Antonio. What might be called, in circus-speak, A Peerless Panorama of Posters recalls a more credulous era: images of Frank Buck ("Bring 'em Back Alive"), Gargantua the Great, and P. T. Barnum himself—with no name, just the words "I Am Coming."

A half century ago, Austin was a sleepy town with a couple of enormous buildings—Texas Memorial Stadium, where the Longhorns roam; and the pink granite state capitol, the largest and the most southerly in the United States (except for Hawaii's), with a dome that looks uncannily like the one in Washington. Quite a few one- and two-story cow-town buildings still stand on Congress Avenue and along the streets running off it, but that's not where the action is. The action is out along highways called Loop 360 and Loop 1, at the region's 2,000-odd high-tech companies. Entrepreneur in chief has to be Michael Dell, forty in 2005, the youngest chief executive to lead a company onto the Fortune 500; the tenth richest person in America with $13 billion, according to *Forbes,* perhaps the richest Texan ever. No, that's not a misprint; Dell is richer than the Basses of Fort Worth and richer by far than H. Ross Perot.

He made his money by grafting an old idea to a new business: he eliminated the middleman (and avoided the inventory costs of his rivals) by building computers to order and selling them direct to consumers. That simple scheme made "Dellionaires" of many of Dell's early employees, even secretaries and clerks, and billionaires of some. Aided by federal research dollars funneled into the area by its former congressman the legendary J. J. Pickle, and by the university's talent pool, new companies sprang up like wildflowers after a spring rain.

This represents a sizable change, because Austin was once a stranger to Dallas-sized bankrolls. During the 1960s, it was a counterculture center, Haight-Ashbury with ten-gallon hats, and some of that individualism lingers. "It's a funny, funky, outrageous town," said Molly Ivins. "Where else do they have Spamarama? Or Spam foo-yung, for goodness' sake? Where else do people celebrate Eeyore's birthday? We do." But Austin has no bats in its belfry. It keeps its 1.5 million Mexican free-tailed bats under the Congress Avenue Bridge, or rather they keep themselves there, living beneath the bridge's concrete arches from March until November, streaming out at dusk to eat.

The bridge crosses Town Lake, an idyllic sliver of water formed by a dam on the Colorado River (the Texas Colorado, not the much longer one farther west). Austin climbs from the lake to the university, centered on the 307-foot tower of the Main Building. One of the richest state universities, the lucky owner of extensive oil lands in the Permian Basin, UT, as the students call it, has attracted distinguished faculty members from other campuses. The physicist Steven Weinberg won the Nobel Prize in 1979 and left Harvard for Austin in 1983; "you couldn't blast him out of here with a howitzer," a friend says. "Michigan and Berkeley are the ideals that we all aspire to," said James S. Fishkin, ex-Yale and now a UT professor of government, law, and philosophy, who holds a chair improbably named for Darrell K. Royal, an old Longhorn football coach. "We're already there in several fields of study."

At the edge of the campus stands the Lyndon Baines Johnson Library and Museum, an exemplary institution of its kind, which is just one of many monuments to the former president and his family in the area. Another is the Lady Bird Johnson Wildflower Center, where the magnificent bluebonnets (*Lupinus texensis*) and the Indian paintbrush are ankle-deep in April. A third is the LBJ Ranch, out in the Hill Country near Stonewall, hard by the Pedernales River (which Johnson, in keeping with the local usage, always pronounced "Purdenales").

San Antonio is drenched in history. Its Hispanic past is exemplified by the eighteenth-century missions along the San Antonio River south of the center, notably Concepción, a starkly beautiful twin-towered building (1755) that retains traces of its original frescoes, and San José, with exquisite Churrigueresque ornamentation around its windows and doors. San José gives a good impression of the privations of life for the priests who lived there, having to defend themselves against Apaches and Comanches with gunports and protective walls, and of what must have been, then as now, the pleasures of spring in the Southwest, with feathery mesquite trees and flaming pomegranate blossoms.

San Antonio boosters remind you that theirs is a big-league town; they are proud of the Spurs, who won National Basketball Association championships with a pair of walking skyscrapers, David Robinson and Tim Duncan. Me, I'm pretty excited about the Class AA San Antonio Missions, especially their mascots, the Puffy Taco and Ballapeño, a baseball-headed hot pepper.

For the average visitor, though, San Antonio is synonymous with the Alamo and the Riverwalk. The former, a fort where 189 heroic Texans, including Jim Bowie and Davy Crockett, held off 4,000 Mexicans commanded by Santa Anna for thirteen days before perishing on March 6, 1836, is a shrine to Texas independence, which for many Texans has never ceased to exist. The Alamo itself, which was once a mission church, has a somber dignity that quiets even the hordes of schoolchildren who troop through every day. But the "museum shop" next door is a travesty that sells Alamo butter-spreaders and other equally tasteful goods. The Riverwalk, built with WPA funds during the New Deal, consists of paths along the downtown reaches of the San Antonio River, sparkling at night, overhung with cypresses, crossed by humpbacked footbridges. Hotels, restaurants, and clubs, like the Landing, where the Jim Cullum Jazz Band toots joyously every night, open onto it.

WHERE TO STAY

Driskill, 604 Brazos Street, Austin, (512) 474-5911. A survivor from the old Austin, this was the press headquarters when Lyndon Johnson was president, but old-timers wouldn't recognize it. A skillful restoration effort has wiped away the wens and wrinkles of a century, leaving an 1886 Richardsonian Romanesque landmark for all to admire, with iron columns, beaten-copper

ceilings, stained-glass skylights, and pony-hide sofas. Chef David Bull's imaginative menu (smoked quail, chanterelles three ways) has put the Driskill Grill on the culinary charts.

Four Seasons, 98 San Jacinto Boulevard, Austin, (512) 478-4500. In its way, this shining palace on Town Lake is a perfect symbol of Austin's emergence from small-town torpor into the big time. The decor is chic and Southwestern; the bedrooms come with marble bathrooms and down-soft sheets. Every service imaginable is close at hand here, from a lending library of books by Texas authors to a rental fleet of twenty-four-speed bicycles.

La Mansión Del Rio, 112 College Street, San Antonio, (210) 518-1000. Most hotels along the Riverwalk are cattle cars, and one has more than a thousand rooms. The Mansión is a smaller, much more atmospheric alternative, built into the shell of an old boys' school, with an unusually friendly staff. The best rooms, with small balconies, overlook the river.

Westin Riverwalk, 420 West Market Street, San Antonio, (210) 224-6500, is San Antonio's newest hotel (opened in 1999) and its most luxurious. Only big panes of plate glass separate the marble-floored, flower-filled lobby from the Riverwalk and the river. The 473 "Texas-size" rooms, as the hotel describes them, have large marble-top desks.

WHERE TO EAT

Biga on the Banks, 203 South St. Mary's Street, San Antonio, (210) 225-0722. Bruce Auden, a lean, earnest Englishman, has an expansive new riverside stage on which to perform. His sure hand with seasonings shows in his minced game in radicchio packets and aromatic five-spice-dusted duck breast. On our last visit, the luscious toffee pudding had our fellow diner Tim Zagat, the guidebook man, begging for seconds.

Hilltop Cafe, 10661 Highway 87, Fredericksburg, (830) 997-8922. Who would believe a former gas station, festooned with old license plates, game trophies, and other junk, serving top-notch Greek, Cajun, and cowboy food? C'mon. But there it is, out near the LBJ Ranch. The chicken-fried steak is a cardiologist's nightmare, a glutton's dream, and Miss Gladys's pecan and blueberry pies take the blue ribbon for paper-thin crusts.

Hudson's on the Bend, 3509 Ranch Road 620 North, Austin, (512) 266-1369. Ever-expanding Austin has devoured the countryside in which Hudson's sat a decade ago, but it retains the feeling of a Hill Country ranch house. Jeffrey Blank's menu emphasizes game—elk (smoked and rubbed with cascabel chili), axis venison, boar, quail (stuffed with game chorizo), and pheasant—boisterously but quite expertly cooked and sauced.

Jeffrey's, 1204 West Lynn Street, Austin, (512) 477-5584. Jeffrey's has grown up with Austin, the hippie atmosphere of its youth giving way to smooth service and subtle decor. The accomplished cooking of David Garrido, prized by George and Laura Bush, includes gently fried oysters, foie gras in a puddle of fruity syrup, and a robust beef tenderloin with caramelized-onion horseradish sauce. The lighting is needlessly dim.

Kreuz Market, 619 North Colorado Street, Lockhart, (512) 398-2361. Drive an hour from Austin or San Antonio, order your sausage, brisket (a bit fatty), or shoulder of beef (very lean), barbecued over post oak. They pile it onto a sheet of butcher paper with a stack of white bread. You carry that to one of the big communal tables and pick up pickles, raw onions, and a Shiner bock beer. No fork, no sides, and no sauce. The smoky meat doesn't need it. This may be the state's best 'cue, and locals rip into it like cavemen.

Las Manitas, 211 Congress Avenue, Austin, (512) 472-9357. The food may be better or at least more authentic at Fonda San Miguel, but the smoky, spicy enchiladas rojas and the milder enchiladas verdes at Las Manitas are Tex-Mex classics, and the funky old lefty Austin scene can't be beat. Is that Bobby Ray Inman and Bob Gates, CIA honchos, dining with their wives on Formica in the second booth back? Yep.

El Mirador, 722 South St. Mary's Street, San Antonio, (210) 225-9444. The Trevinos have been here for thirty-two years, and the third generation knows how to do it. The place earned its reputation with meal-in-a-bowl soups like menudo, made with tripe; and chicken cilantro, packed with chunky vegetables. I was dazzled by the supremely tender cabrito (goat), roasted for eight hours and liberally dusted with pepper, and ravishing sweet-potato flan (custard).

Le Rêve, 152 East Pecan Street, San Antonio, (210) 212-2221. Patricia Sharpe of the *Texas Monthly*, no pushover, gives chef-owner Andrew Weissman's establishment three stars and confessed recently that his food "took us from enthusiasm to ecstasy." Who am I to argue? Fish is the strongest suit: bluenose bass paired lustily with braised cabbage and bacon, perhaps, or daurade more delicately enhanced with touches of soy and ginger.

⫸ SANTA FE

Perched on an undulating plateau at 7,000 feet above sea level, Santa Fe inhabits a grandiose landscape with "an austere and planetary look that daunts and challenges the soul," as the adventurous journalist Elizabeth Shepley Sergeant wrote in the 1920s. It is a leafy faux-adobe city, the oldest and highest of the fifty state capitals, built around a core of old adobe buildings—some of them very old, like the Palace of the Governors (1610), the oldest public building in the United States, which during more than four centuries has flown Spanish, Mexican, and American flags. "The City Different," they call it, and that it surely is, a heady blend of Hispanic, Native American, and Anglo cultures, with a brisk topping up, in recent decades, of new money from Texas, California, and New York.

Only 65,000 people live in Santa Fe, only 148,000 in its metropolitan area, "at the base of wrinkled green mountains with bare tops," in Willa Cather's words, yet Santa Fe has a cultural life worthy of a European metropolis. The comprehensive Georgia O'Keeffe Museum, the enthralling Museum of International Folk Art, and a cluster of new arts institutions housed in vivid buildings by Ricardo Legorreta have breathed fresh life into a venerable artistic heritage. So has SITE Santa Fe, with concerts, literary readings, one-man shows and sprawling, far-ranging biennials, all in a converted beer warehouse.

Each summer, the superbly inventive Santa Fe Opera, founded in 1957, playing in a brilliant theater designed by James Stewart Polshek on a hilltop north of town, draws visitors from all over the world. Nancy Zeckendorf, wife of the real estate magnate William Zeckendorf, raised much of the money for the opera house, then moved on to the transformation of a Spanish Revival movie palace, the Lensic, into a showcase for film, music, dance, and theater. Throw in the Chamber Music Festival during July and August, and extensive dance and theater programs, and Santa Fe feels a lot like Salzburg, with margaritas. "Just about everyone comes to Santa Fe, sooner or later," said Sam Ballen, the owner of La Fonda, the city's longest-serving hotel, "and some of them are smart enough to stay."

The Spanish founded La Villa Real de la Santa Fe de San Francisco de Asis, the Royal City of the Holy Faith of St. Francis of Assisi, early in the seventeenth century, just when the English founded Jamestown. In the eighteenth century, conquistadors, clerics, and commoners followed El Camino Real, the Royal Road, north from Mexico City. Early in the nineteenth, wagon trains rolled in from Missouri along the Santa Fe Trail, and late in the nineteenth, the iron horse took over, with settlers arriving on the Atchison, Topeka & Santa Fe. Artists fell in love with the magical Sangre de Cristo Mountains, whose colors change with the passing hours and seasons, and the intense, crystalline light that defines them so sharply at dusk. Tourists fell in love with the artists, with tacos and enchiladas, with the chunky turquoise-studded jewelry made by the Indians, and with the whole "Santa Fe style"—relaxed yet sophisticated, a mix of Chimayo rugs, distressed pine furniture, and tin-framed mirrors. Eventually you could see it in million-dollar houses in Greenwich and Winnetka and taste it almost everywhere, toned down to accommodate timid palates.

Today, though, the soft-edged romance of Santa Fe is confronted with harsher reality. Traffic moves at a burro's pace, with Land Rovers and pickups alike immobilized at rush hour, and in the summertime the central Plaza is colonized by tourists. Pocked with motels and burger joints, Cerrillos Road is as nasty an urban eyesore as any in America. Preservationists have taken to the trenches, battling the developers, and they have slowed if not halted the march of "progress." Santa Fe has only a miniature airport. That and a severe shortage of water (the City Council had to rein in new construction in 2002 and 2003 because of a drought) should help to keep it from turning into another Phoenix. But some locals are already muttering about the Aspenization of their beloved city.

Still, Santa Fe's charm survives. "The fragrance of piñon fills the air. Santa Fe is a town of patios where hollyhocks nod, where towering cottonwoods spatter with shade. Spain is stamped upon the town. The old man who takes his siesta on a bench in the Plaza may count among his ancestors a Spanish don who owned a rancho as big as Delaware. Families still bear names like Delgado, Otero, Ortiz and Seña." Those lines, from the WPA *Guide to New Mexico,* are not so badly out of date today.

The epitome of Santa Fe excess is Canyon Road, two and a half miles packed with cafés and restaurants, interspersed with galleries. Once it belonged to artists; now art fights for its place with schlock and souvenirs. Much of the stuff for sale, said the cartoonist Patrick Oliphant, who spends summers in Santa Fe, "isn't much better than Elvis on velvet." But some of it is. The Gerald Peters Gallery, near the head of the road, sells works by Albert Bierstadt, O'Keeffe, George Rickey, and lesser artists. Equally varied are the wares of the nearby Nedra Matteucci Galleries, which handle California regionalists and the early Taos painters. The Morning Star Gallery sells exquisite old Indian carvings, baskets, pots, and jewelry from many tribes. Downtown, the Andrew Smith Gallery sells photographs by Edward S. Curtis, Ansel Adams, Edward Weston, Paul Strand, Laura Gilpin, and other giants of the silver gelatin print.

Tucked away in the same area, behind high walls and beneath mature apple trees, aspens, and ponderosa pines, hide the handsome adobe houses of some of the local elite. A gem designed in the 1920s by John Gaw Meem, the leading architect of the Santa Fe Pueblo Revival, belongs to Roddey Burdine, a displaced Miamian, who has filled it with superb Native American and Hispanic pieces. In an earlier life, the house was the site of Greer Garson's marriage to Buddy Fogelson, an oilman. The two refugees from Hollywood lived in the city for many years and endowed several buildings at the College of Santa Fe.

For my wife, Betsey, and me, the greatest attraction of the local art scene, the place we always head for first, is the Museum of International Folk Art. It is southeast of town, well outside the center, along with two museums devoted to Indian art and the Museum of Spanish Colonial Art, the latter in another fine Meem house, with a rich collection of furniture, textiles, paintings and carved images of saints, drawn from four continents. Embracing more than 125,000 objects, the folk art museum's collection started with toys but now includes dollhouses, model trains, masks, and colorful pottery from Hungary, India, Senegal, Guatemala, China—everywhere craftsmen without formal tutelage have made objects to entertain or teach or portray, which is to say virtually everywhere.

The collection of Alexander Girard, the architect and designer who created the fondly remembered Fonda del Sol restaurant in Manhattan, forms the museum's backbone, filling a huge gallery. Girard shared with his friend Alexander Calder a childlike love of fun, and the antic spirit of Sandro and Sandy is ever-present in that room. Displayed there and elsewhere in the museum are bits and pieces that will stir the visual memory of anyone who has done much traveling: iron gondola prows from Venice, *matryoshka* nesting dolls from Russia, a Thai spirit house displayed next to a Syrian glass painting of a verse from the Koran, a model nineteenth-century American town, embroidery samplers, and a market scene populated with colorful clay figures from Latin America.

At the Museum of Indian Arts and Culture there is an enormous display of pottery, including black-on-black ware made by Maria Martinez of the San Ildefonso Pueblo, deeply carved vessels by Margaret Tafoya of the Santa Clara Pueblo and charming little figurines from Cochiti. Those and other works are shown within well-explained historical, geographic, and anthropological settings, rather than solely as aesthetic objects. Poetry punctuates the displays, like these words by Luci Tapahonso, a Navajo writer: "We wear the shiny silver of clear water, we wear turquoise made of bright skies."

Downtown, the Museum of Fine Arts, housed in a fine Pueblo Revival building (1917) by the pioneers of the style, Rapp & Rapp of Denver, mixes works by famous visitors (like Robert Henri and Marsden Hartley) with those by artists who came to stay (like Buck Denton and Gustave Baumann). An etching by John Sloan that shows a group of blasé, short-skirted women watching an Indian dance captures the mutual misunderstanding that has often characterized relations among Santa Fe's various communities and the tourists, right up to the present day. Sloan captioned the piece "Knees and Aborigines."

The Georgia O'Keeffe museum, also downtown, owns about a sixth of the 800-plus canvases the artist produced in a lifetime of painting in New York and Maine and at Abiquiu, her last home, which is nearby (tours by appointment). O'Keeffe's near-abstract work appeals to many for whom most twentieth-century art is puzzling, and in its first year the museum attracted 269,000 visitors. Special exhibitions focus on various themes of her art—calla lilies, New Mexico mountains, Manhattan—and that of contemporaries like Arthur Dove and John Marin. "She's been iconicized," said Barbara Buhler Lynes, the curator. "Postage stamps, posters, postcards—but she's more than that. Our job is to show her in an art-historical context."

The O'Keeffe owes its existence to the new Maecenases of the visual arts in Santa Fe, John Marion, the retired chairman of Sotheby's, and his wife, Anne, a Texas heiress. They are also the prime movers behind the Visual Arts Center and the Santa Fe Art Institute on the College of Santa Fe campus. The institute offers intensive study with visiting artists like Wayne Thiebaud and Donald Sultan. Ricardo Legorreta, Mexico's most esteemed architect, created for the two wholly separate institutions a series of arresting buildings reminiscent of I. M. Pei (in the acute angles formed by some walls), Frank Lloyd Wright (in the use of vertical strip windows to control the southwestern sun), and English oasthouses (in the skylight towers). But the sum, enlivened by super-saturated colors, is all Legorreta. Stucco exterior walls are painted iron red; the courtyards are Frida Kahlo blue, Pepto-Bismol pink, clematis purple, and daffodil yellow, the last providing a vibrant contrast with the blue sky above.

The opera house by Polshek, who also designed the acclaimed Rose Center planetarium in New York and President Clinton's library, is every bit as bold and dramatic. Its distinguishing characteristic is an elegant, sweeping curve of a roof, not unlike the one Eero Saarinen designed for Dulles International Airport near Washington. Supported by cable stays hung from masts and lined with wood battens, it has two functions: to protect spectators from the summer cloudbursts that used to drench them, and to reflect the sound. It triumphs on both counts. As in the auditorium it replaced, the sides of the new theater are open, so the stars, the moon, the evening breezes, and the purple mountains' majesty (as well as the occasional moth fluttering over the stage) are all part of the experience.

The Santa Fe Opera is the long shadow of one man, the late John Crosby, who conceived it, brought it to life, and served as its general director and busiest conductor until his retirement after the 2000 season. A champion of Richard Strauss, he presented nine world and twenty-eight American premieres, among them Alban Berg's *Lulu* and six works by Henze, with casts including James Morris, Bryn Terfel, Marilyn Horne, and Kiri Te Kanawa. Under Crosby and his successor, Richard Gaddes, an Englishman, Santa Fe has ranged widely, from a brisk *Idomeneo* starring Jerry Hadley to Handel's early masterpiece, *Agrippina,* to contemporary American composers to an irresistibly sudsy *Countess Maritza,* which made Emmerich Kalman seem almost contemporary. Peter Sellars, John Copley, and Jonathan Miller have headed west to direct. But in the face of crushing economic pressure, more conventional choices crept into the repertory early in the new century.

Spend some time soaking up local color—maybe a coffee, a paper, and a bear claw for breakfast at Downtown Subscription or lunch at funky Harry's Roadhouse, south of town in the lee of the Jemez Mountains, or even a day trip to the artists' village of Taos, seventy miles north. Taos has been almost overrun by tourists and aging hippies, and boutiquity has all but eclipsed its antiquity, true; but the Millicent Rogers Museum, which shows a Standard Oil heiress's collection of prime Indian art objects, including the most spectacular turquoise jewelry I've ever seen, is worth a visit, and so is the world-famous little church at Ranchos de Taos (circa 1800). Photographed by Adams and Strand and a million tourists' Nikons, painted by many, many artists, the church's massively buttressed west end is a true vernacular masterpiece. "One almost shakes in its presence," wrote the architectural historian G. E. Kidder Smith.

The Los Alamos National Laboratory, birthplace of the atomic age, and the Bandelier National Monument—a national park since 1916 that includes mesas, pueblos, and 23,000 acres of wilderness, evocative of a more peaceful day—can be visited on a short journey full of contrasts. At Los Alamos, thirty-five miles from Santa Fe, the Bradbury Science Museum tells the story of the race to develop an atomic bomb during World War II at this once-secret lab, through an excellent movie and several gripping exhibits. The original 1939 letter from Albert Einstein to "F. D. Roosevelt, President of the United States" is there, warning that the construction of "extremely powerful bombs of a new type" might soon be possible, as are casings of early nuclear bombs similar to "Little Boy," dropped on Hiroshima on August 6, 1945, and "Fat Man," dropped on Nagasaki three days later. Each killed 70,000 people; both would have fit easily into the average American living room.

Bandelier—and specifically Frijoles Canyon, which lies within it—was home to the prehistoric Anasazi people, who lived in caves carved from the canyon's tawny tufa walls and in villages on its floor. Paved paths lead to ruined ceremonial kivas, through juniper groves and past numberless tufts of blue-green chamisa and yellow wildflowers. "There are so many chic things in Santa Fe now," said my friend Pat Perini, who comes to town often. "People need to go to Bandelier, listen to the birdsong, and remind themselves that the magic of this spectacular part of the world existed long before any of us arrived."

WHERE TO STAY

Eldorado Hotel, 309 West San Francisco Street, (505) 988-4455. The city's biggest hotel, with 201 rooms and nearby villas, it often has space in high season when others are sold out. On a recent visit, the front of the house was a zoo: driveway clogged, bellmen swamped. But the rooms are stylishly fitted out with regional art and furniture, and the best have terraces, fireplaces and soothing mountain vistas. Good rooftop pool.

Inn at Loretto, 211 Old Santa Fe Trail, (505) 988-5531. This striking adobe building looks like a giant pueblo. Inside are 135 spacious rooms (many with balconies), nicely furnished in the Southwestern style. The spa provides Balinese massages and the restaurant, which is called Baleen, offers temptations like snapper tempura with cabbage.

Inn of the Anasazi, 113 Washington Avenue, (505) 988-3030. The upside of this showplace is a superb location, just off the Plaza, and charming if smallish guest rooms (59 of them), with beamed ceilings and kiva-style fireplaces. A library stocked with titles on the Southwest is a bonus; the in-room humidifiers are another. The downside: views are lacking, and I find the restaurant's food, often needlessly elaborate, much too sweet.

La Posada de Santa Fe, 330 East Palace Avenue, (505) 986-0000. After extensive renovation, this deluxe retreat, with Spanish Colonial artifacts gracing the lobby, opened under Rockresorts management in 1999 with 120 rooms and 38 suites. Adobe buildings, a spa, and a swimming pool are scattered around six acres, shaded by lofty old pine trees.

WHERE TO EAT

Cafe Pasqual's, 121 Don Gaspar Avenue, (505) 983-9340. Resident foodies swear by this gathering place decked with ristras—garlands of dried chili peppers—whose motto is "Panza llena, corazón contento" ("Full stomach, contented heart"). Katharine Kagel's cooking is ambitious, eclectic, and mostly successful: heavenly smoked-trout hash, crunchy vegetable fritters called ghia pakora, and luscious chicken mole, laced with chilies, Mexican chocolate, and cinnamon.

Cafe San Estevan, 428 Agua Fria, (505) 995-1996. I owe this discovery to Margo True, a discerning former editor of mine. Steve Garcia, a onetime monk, worked with John Sedlar, a pioneer of New Southwestern cooking in Los Angeles. In an old house, he serves definitive New Mexican food: a subtly spiced cake of guacamole and corn kernels, old-time tamales packed with shredded pork, enchiladas with red Chimayo chili sauce.

Coyote Café, 132 West Water Street, (505) 983-1615. It is chic in some circles to knock Mark Miller, and I don't much like his Washington operation, Red Sage. But the Coyote is well worth a visit, even if not quite what it once was. Three cheers for the trademark Cowboy Steak (a bone-in rib-eye), aged for three weeks, and the drop-dead-fresh blueberries and peaches served over yogurt sorbet, which gild a summer's night.

Geronimo, 724 Canyon Road, (505) 982-1500. The art crowd passes in review here, drawn by Eric DiStefano's stylish modern cooking. You won't go wrong with the Mexican white prawns with chilies and yuzu-basil aioli, or the juicy mesquite-grilled buffalo burger topped with grilled red onions, provolone cheese, red bell peppers, and ancho mayonnaise. Lowly pork chops get a sexy truffle demi-glace. Eat on the porch.

The Compound, 653 Canyon Road, (505) 982-4353. Mark Kiffin's cooking has resuscitated this adobe old-timer, designed

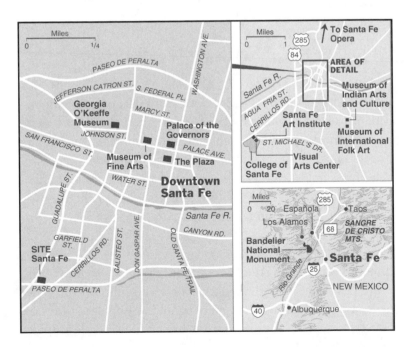

decades ago by Alexander Girard. His midday menus are as good as those at dinner—try veal flank steak on pumpkin polenta—and a good thing, too: this is ground zero for the local ladies who lunch. As for his fig and blackberry tart with rich vanilla-bean ice cream: sprint, don't walk. Terrific wines, too.

⇒ PHOENIX

Phoenix is a city well named. It may not have arisen, like the fabulous bird of Egyptian mythology, from its own ashes, but like the phoenix of old, it sprang to life in a desert. It owes its very existence to modern technology. Without large-scale irrigation and without air-conditioning, Phoenix as it now exists—the dynamic, verdant center of a 200-square-mile metropolitan area of 3.3 million people—would be utterly unthinkable. With temperatures exceeding 100 degrees on more than ninety days a year, with an average high temperature in July of 106 degrees, God's own ungentled climate in the Sonoran Desert is much better suited to cacti and Gila monsters than to human beings.

Not that the year-round warmth in the Salt River Valley, long since rechristened the Valley of the Sun by promoters who found the original name insufficiently poetic, lacks for uses. For starters, it has been good for growing things of value since the Roosevelt Dam, finished in 1911, and other ambitious irrigation projects made commercial cultivation of cotton possible. Lettuce and melons, citrus fruits and dates are produced in quantity as well. Fugitives from the punishing winters and the clamorous cities of the East and Midwest have taken shelter in the valley since the turn of the nineteenth century, when sunseekers put up thirty-odd tents and a half dozen adobe houses in Scottsdale, just east of Phoenix, now a wealthy, self-consciously Southwestern resort- and gallery-filled community of 215,000. In the modern era, the hot, dry conditions have proved ideal for electronic manufacturing. With microchip plants springing up in cotton fields, the Valley of the Sun is turning into Silicon Valley Jr. Genomic engineering firms are also moving in, and tourism has developed into a mighty economic engine, with more than 12 million visitors each year.

Much of the breakneck growth has been unplanned and uncontrolled, and a permissive business culture has left plenty of finagling room for developers and high rollers like Charles H. Keating Jr., the lawyer whose deregulated savings and loan empire went belly up in 1989, setting off a fiscal crisis. (Keating was convicted, but the federal government's bailout of the S&Ls cost the nation's taxpayers billions of dollars). Broad, straight avenues form a grid on the valley floor. Some are lined with orange and grapefruit trees, but more are disfigured by long, sterile parades of strip malls, shopping centers, fast-food joints, motels, and gas stations.

Overreliance on the automobile and the freeway helps to create, on the worst days, a pall of smog that obscures the beauty of the ruddy, jagged mountains girding the valley. But when the air is clean and the sky is blue, or the sun is setting, or the moon is full, it is easy to understand the rhapsodies this landscape evoked in Frank Lloyd Wright in 1932, when he started to build his winter home, Taliesin West, on Maricopa Mesa, twenty miles from downtown Phoenix. It was "a grand garden," the great architect wrote, "the like of which in sheer beauty of space and pattern does not exist, I think, in the world." He worked on his building there for twenty years.

Once upon a time, culturally minded people in Phoenix had to make do with golf, and golf remains a local preoccupation; each year 11 million rounds are played on two-hundred-plus courses in the metropolitan area (or so says the visitors' bureau). But recent decades have brought an ambitious opera company, led for fifteen years until his retirement in 1998 by an ardent Wagnerite, Glynn Ross; new museums, and the new Herberger Theater Center, as well as the restoration of the Orpheum playhouse, a gem of Colonial Revival opulence.

Phoenix has also acquired those other indispensable testimonials to American urban success: professional sports teams. The Phoenix Suns (basketball), the Arizona Cardinals (football), the climate-defying Phoenix Coyotes (hockey), and lately the Arizona Diamondbacks (baseball) have done a lot for civic self-esteem, and taxpayers have poured $700 million into new stadia and arenas in the area since 1990. Peter Eisenman, a brainy, sports-loving architectural theoretician, has designed the most astonishing of these for the hapless Cardinals. When it opens in 2006, it will have a facade made of shiny steel panels, a steel-and-fabric retractable roof, and a remarkable mobile field that will sit outside until game days, when it will slide indoors like a rug on a conveyor belt.

Easy does it is Arizona's style. Men wear string ties and women sport silver jewelry studded with turquoises the size of quail's eggs. Besides golf, people busy themselves with tennis, biking, hiking, and bouncing across the desert in four-wheel-drive vehicles. "The quality of life is what brings people here," said Senator John McCain, who moved to Phoenix soon after his release in 1973 from a prisoner-of-war camp in Vietnam. "A friend of mine got in his car once and drove up to Roosevelt Lake to water-ski, then headed up to Flagstaff to snow-ski. All in a single day."

An unknowing visitor might never notice the desert around him. Pools grace backyards, and front lawns of 20,000 residents are drenched by flood-irrigation systems. Restaurants install misting systems that make it possible to dine outdoors, even in triple-digit heat. A 560-foot jet of water bursts from an artificial lake at Sky Harbor International Airport. "This land was a desert before we got here," said Donald Reigle during a recent drought scare. He is a senior hydrologist with the Salt River Project, which provides water and power for much of Arizona. "It will be a desert when we leave," he added.

Phoenix is a startlingly young place. When Karl Baedeker (or, more likely, one of his minions) passed this way in 1904, he found "a well-built, modern city" of . . . wait for it . . . exactly 5,554 inhabitants. (By that time, Los Angeles, the quintessential Johnny-come-lately among American cities, already had 120,000.) The big boom here began at the end of World War II, with the dawn of the Age of Air-Conditioning. John Gunther came to town in those years and reported, "If you've been in Phoenix a year, you're an old-timer." Now the city ranks as the country's fifth largest, with 1.4 million people—and it is still growing, spreading, annexing. Its population overtook Philadelphia's in 2004.

Phoenix's connections to the Old West are deeply felt. The

Army's struggle against the great Apache warriors Cochise and Geronimo are as lively a folk memory in Phoenix as the exploits of Robert E. Lee and Stonewall Jackson are in Richmond. The cowboy culture lives on in riding stables, rodeos, and parades of horse-drawn vehicles.

Spanish street names and mariachis remind you that the Mexican border is not far away. About a third of Phoenix's residents are of Hispanic descent, many of them illegal immigrants, according to government officials, and two-thirds of the students in the city's high schools are Hispanic. Nine local radio stations broadcast exclusively in Spanish.

Arizona was a lawless territory in the late 1800s. A Harvard geologist named Raphael Pumpelly visited it to work as a mining engineer and wrote later of "a climate of public opinion that blunted all ideas of right and wrong in the minds of newcomers who, suddenly freed from the legal and social restraints of the East, soon learned to justify the taking of life by the most trifling pretexts, or even to destroy it for the sake of bravado." Starting when he was only fifteen years old, and operating with near-impunity, the notorious Billy the Kid roamed through the territory for sixteen years in the 1870s and 1880s until he was shot by Sheriff Pat Garrett in 1891. Two other favorite movie outlaws, Wyatt Earp and Doc Holliday, outfaced the Clanton gang in the gunfight at the OK Corral in Tombstone in 1881.

Statehood arrived a few decades later, in 1912—Arizona was the last of the lower forty-eight to enter the Union—with Phoenix as the capital. One man, a conservative Democrat named Carl Hayden, formed a living political link with the pioneer days for much of a century, serving continuously in Congress, first in the House and then in the Senate, from 1912 until 1969. The state has produced other representatives capable of arousing affection rare in this cynical era, like Senator Barry Goldwater (1953–65), a herald of the new Republican conservatism, who crashed noisily in the 1964 presidential campaign but found himself venerated late in life as a not particularly partisan wise man, and Congressman Morris K. Udall (1961–91), a bright, witty, sweet-natured Democrat who also failed in presidential politics. But the old buccaneering spirit has tainted modern Arizona politics.

Governor Evan Mecham made "enough of a fool of himself," in the words of the author Michael Barone, to be impeached and removed from office in 1988.

Screened by a pretty row of old olive trees, the Heard Museum is Phoenix's premier cultural institution, a treasurehouse of the Native American civilizations that have waxed and waned in the Southwest for at least 15,000 years, as the land turned from grassy savanna to desert. Colorful rugs, basketwork of astonishing delicacy, Navajo and Zuni and Hopi jewelry, and hundreds of kachina dolls, donated by Goldwater and the hotel pioneer Fred Harvey, bear mute witness to the talents of mostly nameless Indian artists. It was the collection of Indian pottery, a particular passion of my wife, Betsey, that drew us to the Heard, and we were not disappointed. The work of the best pueblos—especially Acoma, San Ildefonso, and Santa Clara— is represented in depth, not only the traditional polychrome but also the glossy, often unadorned, highly sophisticated blackware brought to national notice by the work of Maria Martinez. Today Arizona is home to twenty-one Indian tribes, and Phoenix has the largest Native American population of any big city. Gradually, the Heard is easing the long-standing resentments of Indians toward mostly non-Indian custodians of their artistic patrimony.

As the Phoenix Art Museum has expanded, its attendance has increased, too, hitting 290,342 in 2003. ("Perhaps Phoenix will finally begin to put to rest the inferiority complex that has plagued it," *The Arizona Republic* commented.) The museum's main interest for the visitor is its large collection of Western art. This includes not only the obligatory Remingtons and O'Keeffes but also the work of Eastern visitors like Robert Henri and lesser artists like Phimister Proctor, whose panther on the prowl caught our attention, and Lew Davis, whose depictions of early copper camps recall Ben Shahn.

The performing arts have faced tougher going, with several organizations skirting bankruptcy in the 1990s. The Phoenix Symphony narrowly avoided a strike by its musicians, and only lately have its finances moved onto firmer ground. Although famous soloists play with it, the orchestra has never in its fifty years attracted a big-name music director, other than the Mexican Eduardo Mata (1971–77), and it is back in the market.

Under the publicity-loving Glynn Ross, the Arizona Opera mounted full-scale *Ring* cycles at Flagstaff, not far from the Grand Canyon, in the heart of what some German visitors who came to hear them called "der Vildenvest." But the company has pulled in its horns a bit—not so surprisingly, given the red ink the *Ring*s generated. Joel Revzen, a member of the Met's conducting staff, is the new artistic director. In one of his first seasons, the company staged a five-opera, something-for-everyone program, hopping from *The Mikado* to *Sweeney Todd* and *The Pearl Fishers,* in Phoenix and Tucson.

Both the symphony and the opera have headquarters at Symphony Hall, an unwelcoming, fortresslike structure of corrugated concrete now being renovated. It stands at the center of the new downtown, a windblown work in progress consisting of sports arenas, hotels, a science center, a history museum, old Deco towers, vacant lots awaiting development, a gargantuan convention center, and a shopping mall of dubious design and proportion. Across from Symphony Hall stands the resplendent Herberger complex, with two stages that house the Arizona Theater Company, the Actors Theater of Phoenix, the spunky Arizona Jewish Theater Company, and Ballet Arizona, which sent Jock Soto to the New York City Ballet and is directed by Ib Andersen, a longtime mainstay of that troupe.

Out in Tempe, near the Phoenix airport, is Frank Lloyd Wright's vulgar, UFO-like Grady Gammage Memorial Auditorium (1964), and another modern structure that puts it to shame: the Nelson Fine Arts Center, designed in 1990 by Antoine Predock, an Albuquerque architect who reminds me a little of Louis I. Kahn. It is a stucco butte of a building, a pale desert purple, which the architecture critic Paul Goldberger described as "tough, hard-edged and self-assured."

Wright was in far better form, of course, when he built Taliesin West. The great cantilevered drafting room is an epic space assembled from modest materials—local stones embedded in coarse mortar, redwood beams painted Cherokee red, his favorite color, and skylights covered first with canvas and later with translucent plastic. As always with Wright in his prime, the building revels in its relationship to its setting. It snuggles back into the foothills of the McDowell Range, invisible until you are almost upon it, and his simple means echo his appraisal of the surrounding desert: "Nature, driven to economize in materials by hard conditions, generated bare, Spartan forms."

From Taliesin West you can see hundreds of Arizona's trademark cacti, the anthropomorphic saguaros, known to people everywhere from their bit parts in hundreds of westerns. Thousands more wait at the Desert Botanical Garden, in Papago Park, founded in 1939. This amazing place also has 4,000-odd other species of plants, mostly cacti, succulents, and wildflowers. Many of the stately saguaros live for hundreds of years, starting to grow their characteristic upturned "arms" only at seventy-five. The Botanical Garden is rivaled only by the Jardin Exotique in Monte Carlo, and it is far more naturalistic; the cacti here are surrounded by desert, not a Mediterranean city. Along the miles of footpaths southeast of Phoenix, the species are clearly marked: bony-fingered ocatillos and paddle-shaped prickly pears, both green and purple; spiny agaves and aloes, with their spikes of yellow and orange blossoms; barrel cacti and pincushions and organ-pipes and totem poles and candelabras, whose names describe them well; yellow-flowered cassia bushes; penstemons and desert marigolds. It is altogether magical, especially in the flowering season, February to May.

WHERE TO STAY

Arizona Biltmore, 2400 East Missouri Avenue, (602) 955-6600, was designed in 1929 by Frank Lloyd Wright and Albert C. McArthur, one of his former draftsmen. It has been sympathetically renovated since, with sumptuous suites added. Opalescent light fixtures, earthy colors, and Aztec motifs give this 730-room paragon a wholly original personality. Palms, fountains, and eight (!) pools dot the grounds.

The Boulders, 34631 North Tom Darlington Drive, Carefree, (408) 488-9009, is regularly voted one of the nation's top resorts. Sited in tranquil isolation among million-year-old granite rocks, twenty miles from downtown Phoenix, it blends effortlessly into the Sonoran foothills. Pueblo-style casitas with log ceilings and wood-burning fireplaces are furnished with rustic luxury. Smell the cumin-scented air! Watch for the jackrabbits!

Ritz-Carlton Phoenix, 2401 East Camelback Road, (602) 468-0700. An urban hotel rather than a resort, rather formal by laid-back Arizona standards, with European oils and porcelain on display in the public rooms. The 281 bedrooms, each with a marble bathroom, live up to Ritz standards, featuring fine furniture, safes, and deluxe minibars.

Phoenician, 6000 East Camelback Road, Scottsdale, (480) 941-8200. Nestled at the base of Camelback Mountain amid 250 richly landscaped acres, this glittering resort, a monument to 1980s excess, still attracts the Ferrari set. What'll you have? Golf, spa, tennis, hike, swim? All there, at a price, within easy reach of 654 oversized rooms. Chef Bradford Thompson's food at Mary Elaine's restaurant is expensive and extravagant but not ostentatious. Try the butter-braised lobster with fennel, chard, and a hint of star anise.

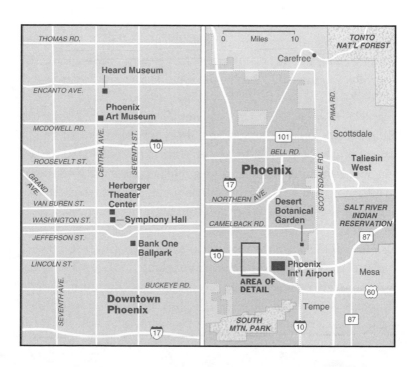

WHERE TO EAT

Christopher's Fermier, 2584 East Camelback Road, (602) 522-2344. Christopher Gross's unbuttoned brasserie fits the city well. Salads, pastas, and comfort food, much of it cooked in a wood oven (truffle-infused sirloin, cassoulet, golden roast chicken), are followed by luxurious tarte tatin or carefully handled cheeses (St. Marcellin, Tête de Moine, four from Egg Farm Dairy in the Hudson Valley). Drinkable wines by the glass.

Los Dos Molinos, 8646 South Central Avenue, (602) 243-9113. On the southern rim of the city sits an old hacienda where the cowboy star Tom Mix once lived. Now a Mexican restaurant of rare quality, festooned with skeins of peppers, it is the site of nightly fiestas. Start with a cheese crisp, a tortilla slathered with melted cheese; go on to torrid, tender adobada ribs and end with sopaipillas, airy, honey-topped pastry pillows.

Hapa, 6204 North Scottsdale Road, Scottsdale, (480) 998-8220. This calm, relaxed spot specializes in Asian American food, by which I don't mean chow mein. I mean cool, fresh shrimp rolls with a citrus dipping sauce good enough to drink; a vegetarian bento box with fine taco-shaped dumplings stuffed with eggplant and avocado; udon with grilled prawns, Chinese vegetables, and a spicy broth; devastating coconut ice cream.

Pizzeria Bianco, 623 East Adams Street, (602) 258-8300. Bronx-born Chris Bianco is the Valley's favorite chef. In an old brick building, too small for the throngs that want in, he makes his own mozzarella, bakes his magnificent pies in a wood-fired brick oven, and tops them with fennel sausages, roasted cremini mushrooms, and other good things.

Sea Saw, 7133 East Stetson Drive, Scottsdale, (480) 481-9463. Nobo Fukuda's Japanese tapas, remarkably fairly priced, cover a huge range: edamame soup, oyster and sea urchin in tomato water, fluke cooked by a drizzle of hot toasted garlic oil, steamed sea bass with green tea soba noodles. Plus offbeat wines from a prodigious cellar.

Vincent Guerithault, 3930 East Camelback Road, (602) 224-0225. This is what happens when an ace chef comes to the Southwest from Lorraine by way of Provence: you eat uncommon delights like smoked salmon quesadillas with horseradish cream and firm, tender sweetbreads coated with blue cornmeal; you drink the world's great wines, Pétrus to Stag's Leap. An old shoe, this long-established restaurant, that wears well.

⦙⦙⦙➡ LAS VEGAS

I'm looking out the window of my hotel room, and the first thing I see is the Eiffel Tower, which has evidently lost its bearings. It's straddling the Louvre and the Palais Garnier. I can also see the Great Pyramid, the Statue of Liberty, and the Bridge of Sighs. As I gawk, I'm sipping a breakfast bracer, described on the room service menu as a Corpse Reviver (no kidding). It contains gin, Pernod, Lillet, Cointreau, and lemon juice. Where am I? Well, it certainly ain't Dubuque, Jack. And it's not Muskogee, either.

It's Las Vegas, of course. Unlike your ordinary city, this is an enterprise built entirely upon excess, where subtlety and understatement are orphans and nothing is quite what it seems. Travel a block or two from the gaudy rialto called the Strip and you come upon dilapidated motels, seedy apartments, and raw, undeveloped land. From that vantage point, you see the hotel-casinos for what they are: gigantic movie sets built in the Nevada desert. Las Vegas sells escapism to ordinary folk who save their pennies for an annual spree of slot machines, hotel buffets (ten bucks or so for all you can eat or, for that matter, lift), and a show or two—"the only entertainment we get all year," as one visitor from rural Iowa told me. The city depends heavily on working people, not plutocrats: 61 percent of visitors, a survey showed, have no college degree.

In the words of J. Terrence Lanni, chairman of MGM-Mirage Inc., which owns several of the city's classier resorts, Las Vegas also appeals to "the guy who's got plenty of money, wants to show it, but can't get into the country club, maybe because he's in the scrap-iron business." And it appeals mightily to the high roller from Dusseldorf or Hong Kong or Hollywood who comes here to do things he feels he cannot do at home. "You can have a great time there," said Philip Treacy, the London milliner who makes the loopy hats women wear to Ascot, "because you never meet anyone you know." The city's latest slogan is "What happens in Vegas stays in Vegas."

Las Vegas is a never-ending party that has gained a new sophistication in the last decade. The trauma of 9/11 drastically but only temporarily slowed the flow of revelers. A twenty-first-century human comedy, the city is thronged by all sorts of people—well dressed, badly dressed, barely dressed, and undressed. If you don't much like gambling, says my wife, Betsey, who doesn't, you can shut out the din and enjoy the many things that it subsidizes. Vegas—not even hayseeds use the "Las"— pulls them in these days with golf, tennis, swimming pools, luxury shopping worthy of Rodeo Drive, and world-class restaurants that move millions of dollars' worth of world-class wine a year. Starting in 1992, top restaurateurs from around the country bought in, although few of them actually moved to Nevada. Todd English from Boston, Mark Miller from Santa Fe, Wolfgang Puck and Piero Selvaggio from Los Angeles, Michael Mina from San Francisco, and Sirio Maccioni from New York were among the first to clone their establishments in the desert. Two more recent arrivals, both highly regarded, are Commander's Palace, Ella Brennan's gumbo showplace from New Orleans, and Bradley Ogden from Marin County, California. Three-star French chefs are on the way, including Alain Ducasse, Joël Robudian, and Guy Savoy. Soon, predicted Sig Rogich, a well-connected Las Vegas public relations man who once worked in the White House, theaters will be built here to house major musicals—and he was proven right in 2004 when it was announced that *Avenue Q,* a Tony winner, would move straight to Las Vegas instead of touring.

Gambling (or "gaming," to use the local euphemism), which once accounted for two-thirds of tourist revenue, now brings in less than half, although 85 percent of people who set foot in Vegas gamble at least a little. Rooms and food, once loss leaders, are now profit centers. Of course, they still build hotels with no chairs in the lobbies, no clocks in the restaurants, no windows in the casinos, and no easy route from the front door to the elevators except past the slot machines. In addition to 37 million visitors a year—"like loading the whole population of Spain onto a plane," as Madrid-born Julian Serrano, the city's reigning chef, remarked wonderingly—Las Vegas also attracts an endless stream of new residents, drawn by low taxes, inexpensive housing, dependable sunshine, and the promise of jobs.

For many, the pot at the end of the rainbow is empty. They can be found living in cinder-block budget motels, where sheets and blankets cost extra, sometimes four to a room. Some give up and move away, but others arrive to take their places.

Nevada has been the nation's fastest-growing state and Las Vegas its fastest-growing city for some years now. The city's population in 1940 was 8,422; by 2000, 1.6 million people lived in the 235-square-mile metropolitan area, about 22 percent of them Hispanic. The newcomers come from everywhere. In a single weekend, I met a bellman from Cranbury, New Jersey, near Princeton, a casino cashier from Shanghai, and a taxi driver from Tulsa, Oklahoma.

"People come to Las Vegas and the slate is clean," said a well-known local television anchor, Paula Francis, in a plain-spoken article in *Las Vegas Life* magazine. "Whether you were high and mighty before, or lowdown and scratching for a living, you come here and start over again. No one looks at your pedigree or your jail record. You start anew." By now, Las Vegas has more than five hundred churches; seven full-fledged hospitals with dozens of doctors specializing in breast augmentation; nascent youth gangs; the highest suicide rate in the nation (18.91 per 100,000 people); one of the busiest airports in the country; a vigorous young symphony orchestra; and the University of Nevada, Las Vegas, which aggressively pursues young men good at putting a basketball into a net.

Las Vegas also affords opportunities for visits to reality. Formed by 726-foot-high Hoover Dam, which took 3.25 million cubic yards of concrete to build, Lake Mead is the largest freshwater reservoir in the world, ideal for boating and fishing—but seventy-five feet less deep after years of drought. The Grand Canyon, not far beyond, can be visited by helicopter. In the other direction, Death Valley beckons, not dead at all but washed with surreal color and platinum-bright light.

Sure, Vegas is the capital of bad taste—gaudy and garish, tacky and trashy, bedizened with gilt and rouge and spangles. It is as cheesy as Gorgonzola. It is so far over the top that it occasionally laughs at itself. In the shopping arcade at Caesars Palace, a casino-hotel with enough ersatz Roman statuary to make J. Paul Getty himself drool with envy, the sign outside the Warner Brothers shop reads, "Warnerius Fraternius Studius Storius." Excess rules. The singer Celine Dion, for whom Caesars Palace built a theater, earns $80,000 a show. The Barbary Coast Casino sells 64-ounce margaritas. Priscilla Presley had her Lincoln Continental flown to Vegas from Beverly Hills for her high school reunion a few years ago.

Some of the best schtick is free: a bride charging through a casino at 2 p.m. in a snow-white wedding dress, with her mother in hot pursuit and her husband, pushing the baby in his stroller, struggling to keep up, or a middle-aged couple soberly discussing the merits of Vegas and Paris as vacation sites and deciding the Jersey Shore is better than either.

As everyone knows, the city's most popular cultural attraction is the Liberace Museum, where the visitor can see his minks, his cars, his pianos, and, of course, his candelabra. As everyone knows, the nightclubs, which once featured the likes of Frank Sinatra and his Rat Pack buddy Sammy Davis Jr., as well as Marlene Dietrich and Noël Coward, now rely on entertainers who are more than a little long in the tooth, like Tony Bennett, Wayne Newton, Jerry Lewis, and (forgive the lapse in gallantry) Debbie Reynolds. Only occasionally do the Stings and Princes of this world show up, and it is said to have cost $10 million to lure Barbra Streisand to the MGM Grand Hotel for a millennium concert. As everyone knows, Las Vegas is also the place where a hard case named Mike Tyson took a bite or two out of the ear of Evander Holyfield, his pugilistic rival. Here, too, a 300-pound white tiger mauled Roy Horn, of the wildly popular act Siegfried and Roy, closing down their show at the Mirage, where they had played to 7 million people.

But high culture is slowly sticking its head above the parapet in Vegas—if you know where to search for it, and providing you're not too fastidious in defining your terms. Take the Las Vegas Philharmonic. When we went on a shopping expedition to the Fashion Show Mall, the strains of Bach's "Sheep May Safely Graze" led us to a string ensemble drawn from the orchestra's ranks. Saks, it turned out, was sponsoring an afternoon concert in the atrium. "Las Vegas has a reputation for having no culture," said Susan Tompkins, one of the five-year-old orchestra's founders, along with Harold Weller, its music director. "We're trying to change that. But most people don't know about us, so we go to them. Besides our regular schedule, we play here and we play in schools."

Or take *O,* the extraordinary show at the Bellagio hotel, which fills 1,800 seats ten times a week. An unlikely combination of circus and ballet, theater and pantomime, with synchronized swimming thrown in, *O* is a production of the prodigious Canadian troupe Cirque du Soleil that is performed in, around, and above an enormous water tank. (*O* equals *eau*—right?) Pucci-like costumes, wondrous stage machinery, and propulsive music lend it the same superb sense of spectacle that *Miss Saigon* brought to Broadway. Only an irredeemable snob could deny that this is a theatrical triumph.

It is no accident that *O* is at the Bellagio. Steve Wynn, the son of an unsuccessful small-time gambler who ran Sunday bingo games in the Washington suburbs, created the Bellagio. A famous talker, he once said he wanted to build things God would have built "if only he'd had the money." Wynn talked with me about Las Vegas, past and present, in his office at the Desert Inn a couple of years ago, with a Warhol portrait of himself on the wall and a German shepherd named Paolo at his side. "This has always been a place where stupid people could make more money than they could make anywhere else," he said. "Thirty percent, easy."

After twenty-two years in Vegas, Wynn set out in 1989 to do something different. He built a hotel called the Mirage, with 3,000 rooms and a fake volcano out front, hoping to capitalize on what he calls "the wonder factor." The idea, he explained, was "the same as the old circus sideshow—something exotic to lure them into the main tent." Having done that, Wynn reinvented Las Vegas in 1998 with the Bellagio, a $1.6 billion extravaganza packed with big-name restaurants. His office had a Rembrandt and a Rothko, among other ornaments, and walls made of the same burled walnut used on Rolls-Royce dashboards. An array of magical fountains is installed in a 254-foot arc in front of the hotel, where the waters swing and sway nightly to the strains of Copland's "Simple Gifts." Wynn installed a $300 million collection of modern paintings, including pieces by van Gogh and Matisse, in an art gallery—a kunsthalle amid the crap tables. But he reached too far. Shares in his company sank, shareholders moaned, and predators pounced. In 2000, the Hollywood financier Kirk Kerkorian bought Wynn out, took over the casinos, and sold most of the pictures, except those that belonged personally to Wynn.

Art and Las Vegas have proved a better match than most anticipated (though perhaps not the architects Robert Venturi and Denise Scott Brown, who argued decades ago that their trade had a lot to learn from Las Vegas, notably its flamboyant neon signs). The Bellagio Gallery of Fine Art now displays traveling exhibitions. (Twenty-six modern masterworks from the Phillips Collection in Washington drew 7,500 visitors a week at twelve dollars each in 2000.) Seeking to one-up the Bellagio, the Venetian Hotel hired Rem Koolhaas, the Dutch master of architectural cool, to design two exhibition spaces where the Guggenheim Museum and the State Hermitage Museum in St. Petersburg, Russia, would show selections from their collections. When severe budget shortfalls forced the Guggenheim to retrench, the larger, 63,000-square-foot space went dark, although the smaller continues to pull in the crowds.

And what of the man who started it all? Almost as soon as he lost the Bellagio, Wynn bought the Desert Inn and most of the 218 acres behind it, pulled it down, and began building Wynn Las Vegas, a newer, grander $2.4 billion hotel—"a place of ideal beauty and comfort," he calls it—with 2,701 rooms, 18 restaurants, and a major Ferrari and Maserati dealership. It is scheduled to open in the summer of 2005.

The hoodlum Bugsy Siegel began the process of turning Las Vegas into a not-so-stately pleasure dome, and an air of moral iniquity clings to it to this day. Other hoods followed Siegel to town, like Moe Dalitz from Cleveland. "A lot of the original casino owners couldn't get driver's licenses in Nevada today, let alone gaming licenses," one current license-holder told me. Things started to change when the eccentric billionaire Howard Hughes arrived at 4 a.m. on November 27, 1966. He rented the eighth and ninth floors of the Desert Inn, and as Christmas approached the management asked him to leave so they could accommodate seasonal high rollers. Instead, he bought the place. Since then, overt mob influence has declined sharply, but it has not disappeared; gangsters were suspected in the mysterious 1999 murder of Ted Binion, a defrocked casino operator, though no one was charged.

Las Vegas remains a place of cheap booze, easy sex, and omnipresent opportunities to be separated from one's dollars in games of "chance" in which the house seldom loses.

Sin sells. Sin is fun. Terry Lanni of MGM-Mirage, a clean-cut professional manager with two degrees from the University of Southern California, told me, "Las Vegas wouldn't be Las Vegas without at least the appearance of sin." Most Americans gamble, one way or another, but many feel a little ashamed of it, which is perhaps why Lanni added, "If my mother had been alive when I came into this business, I probably wouldn't have." A hint of sin is surely what brings foreigners to Las Vegas in droves. Flights land here daily or weekly from Tokyo Narita, London Gatwick, Frankfurt, Paris, and other foreign capitals, even Edmonton, Alberta. But it's easy to overstate this kind of thing. For the most part, what Las Vegas offers is a not especially sinister form of sin, tame enough for grannies in wheelchairs, clutching plastic coin cups at the nickel machines.

Tame enough, furthermore, for more than 2,500 conventions a year, including those of groups conscious of their reputations for probity, including the National League of Cities, the National Association of Attorneys General, and numerous church bodies. Comdex, the information-technology show, attracts 50,000 people each fall, even after the tech bust, and overall 5 million convention visitors spent $6 billion in 2002.

Growth has its darker side—traffic jams, temporarily eased by a new monorail, long lines at the supermarket, crowded schools, and an inadequate tax base. Retirees are the largest group among those moving to the city—some buy million-dollar make-believe Mediterranean villas on 320-acre Lake Las Vegas, a few miles east of the Strip—but having paid their dues in states where they spent their working lives, they are loath to pay more than the bare minimum in property taxes in Nevada.

Then there is water. This is the desert, after all. While there is water beneath the city, Lake Mead no longer offers countless gallons close at hand. Las Vegas is currently confident of adequate supplies only until 2030, and it is already restricting car washes, turning off fountains, and offering to pay people to rip out their lawns.

The city still consumes the stuff with abandon, not only on lawns and in showers but as an integral part of Vegas dazzle. The tank in which the damsels of *O* swim holds 1.5 million gallons, no less. Early on, Vegas flaunted its hot, dry climate with hotels named the Dunes, the Sands, and the Sahara. But the ultimate illusion, perhaps, is bringing the sea to the desert, so now you will find a "rain forest" and several waterfalls at the Mirage (whose name is no accident), a "shark reef" aquarium at Mandalay Bay, a "Grand Canal" at the Venetian, and of course the fountains at the Bellagio. Two new multibillion-dollar projects are on the drawing boards. They like to gamble in Vegas.

WHERE TO STAY

Bellagio, 3600 Las Vegas Boulevard South, (702) 693-7111. This is the epicenter of the Strip and hence of Las Vegas. The 3,005 rooms are furnished in subdued tones of beige (subdued! in Vegas!). The lobby ceiling is an explosion of Dale Chihuly

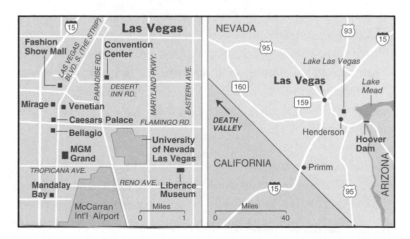

glass. And nothing equals the eight-acre lake and its captivating water-cannon fountains, which shoot spray into the air like rockets and dance as if Busby Berkeley were in charge.

Four Seasons, 3960 Las Vegas Boulevard South, (702) 632-5000. An anomaly in Las Vegas, the Four Seasons has no casino. That eliminates the slog through the gambling hordes to reach your room, which is a blessing. Low-key public areas are in a separate low-rise; the 424 handsome rooms, including number 36101, a princely suite with a matchless nighttime view up the dazzlingly lighted Strip, occupy the top floors of the Mandalay Bay Hotel's adjacent tower. Toasters in the rooms are a nice touch.

Venetian, 3355 Las Vegas Boulevard South, (702) 414-1000. The storied old Sands was bulldozed to make room for this 3,036-suite hotel (1,000 more are on the way). Its frescoes would make Tiepolo weep, and the gondolas plying its faux Grand Canal will make you howl. But the less gaudy rooms are among the town's best, and there is wit at work here: note the copy of Caravaggio's *Cardsharps* above the slots.

WHERE TO EAT

Aureole, Mandalay Bay, 3950 Las Vegas Boulevard South, (702) 632-7401, scores on every count. The peerless Adam Tihany designed it with a swan pond at one end and a 42-foot-high steel-and-glass tower at the other. The tower holds 10,000 bottles of wine, which are fetched by black-clad "wine angels" who fly up, like Peter Pan, to get them. The German and Washington State collections are chosen by sommelier Andrew Bradbury; Chef Phillipe Rispoli's delicate duck pot-au-feu is but one bell ringer among many.

Bradley Ogden, Caesar's Palace, 3570 Las Vegas Boulevard South, (877) 346-4642. Based in the San Francisco Bay area until 2004, Ogden lost his way, but he has recovered his best form here. In the hottest dining room in Vegas at the moment, a refined space with polished wood paneling, he serves Hama

Hama oysters from Washington state in Chinese soupspoons, prepared five ways. After them, perhaps, wood-roasted baby chicken with sage gnocchi and brussels sprouts the size of peas.

Craftsteak, 3799 Las Vegas Boulevard South, (702) 891-1111. In a city awash in steakhouses, this flawlessly managed, unpretentious dining room takes my prize. Grass- and grain-fed beef is selected with care from ranches in the Pacific Northwest and aged in-house. Tom Colicchio, of Gramercy Tavern and Craft in New York, is the owner, and Christopher Albrecht ably mans the ranges. The sides and the wines could not be better.

Emeril's New Orleans Fish House, 3799 Las Vegas Boulevard South, (702) 891-7374. No, fish don't swim in the desert sands, but airplanes bring them to Emeril Lagasse's local outpost six times a week from all points of the compass. Add some tasso ham, some Southern greens, a puddle of grits, and bam! there you are, way down yonder.

Lotus of Siam, 953 East Sahara Avenue, (702) 735-3033. Off the Strip, far from the flash, Chef Saipin Chutima serves the mesmerizing, dramatically seasoned food of her village in northeastern Thailand, which is influenced by China and Burma. Try the earthy pork stew and the sticky rice with ripe mango.

Picasso, Bellagio, 3600 Las Vegas Boulevard South, (702) 693-7223. Julian Serrano, who put Masa's atop the restaurant heap in San Francisco, moved to Las Vegas for keeps in 1987 to cook for this deluxe room, filled with originals by the Catalan master for whom it is named. His vibrant, unforced food shines on the plate: multicolored heirloom tomato salad with tomato sorbet, tartares of three fish, day-boat scallops with jus de veau, and immaculate lamb tenderloin.

Prime, Bellagio, 3600 Las Vegas Boulevard South, (702) 693-7223. Jean-Georges Vongerichten running a steakhouse? Yep. A lavish iced shellfish platter, a zesty watercress-and-red-cabbage salad dressed with ginger vinaigrette, rosy-rare steaks cut from beef hung for twenty-one days, proper bearnaise or bordelaise sauce, crunchy frites, bread pudding—a classic American Saturday-night dinner, as seen through three-star eyes.

Renoir, Mirage, 3400 Las Vegas Boulevard South, (702) 791-7111. Under Alessandro Strata, a protégé of Alain Ducasse, Renoir evokes memories of Paris three-stars with its padded banquettes and walls upholstered in Provençal fabrics. We found the turbot too firm, the sweetbreads not quite firm enough, but the foie gras with pineapple was perfect and the short ribs, with a winy sauce and horseradish scalloped potatoes, were a triumph.

⫸ DENVER

Denver is the Mile-High City, right? Right. Up in the Rocky Mountains, right? Wrong. Denver is 5,280 feet above sea level, without doubt, which is a mile; a brass disk marks that exact altitude on the fifteenth step of the state capitol's staircase. But it isn't in the mountains at all; it lies beneath the Front Range at the western limit of the Great Plains.

Nor is it Blizzard Central, as so many Easterners seem to think. Most years, the sun shines for at least three hundred days (so the Chamber of Commerce swears), the sky is often startlingly blue, and the Rocky Mountains provide a backdrop to daily life so vivid that Albert Bierstadt himself might well have painted it. (Pike's Peak, which is not far away, inspired Katharine Lee Bates to write "America the Beautiful" in 1893.)

Denver burst into being as a mining town after the gold strike of 1858, a put-up-your-dukes, shoot-first-ask-later kind of place. When Horace Greeley of *The New York Herald* spent two weeks here in 1859, on an overland trip from the Atlantic to the Pacific, it was a log city of 150 buildings—not a third of them fit to be inhabited, he wrote. No place of similar size anywhere, Greeley said, had as many brawls, fights, or "pistol shots with criminal intent." After World War II, John Gunther, the dauntless American traveler of that day, judged it "the most self-sufficient, isolated, self-contained and complacent city in the world."

That was a long time ago. Today Denver is a haven of civilized politics, low crime rates, and successful if volatile high-tech and telecommunications businesses, full of baby boomers and other well-educated, healthy people obsessed by the outdoors. They like where they live, and many people who don't live here wish that they could. When the Harris polling organization asked Americans not long ago where they would like to move, only the big retirement states—Florida, Arizona, and California—rivaled Colorado.

Now the twentieth largest metropolitan area in the country, with 2.4 million people, Denver boomed with the 1990s. Its poverty rate dropped by almost 50 percent and its housing values jumped by 120 percent, although inadequate water supplies became a nagging problem. Yet it never feels like a city on the make. It is too laid-back, too comfortable in its close-in neighborhoods packed with unpretentious houses from the 1930s, '40s and '50s, and its smart suburbs. When not at work, all Denver, it seems, bikes, hikes, camps, climbs, hunts, fishes, jogs, skis, and edges perilously close to mountain worship.

Weather permitting, you can cruise by car through Boulder, Rocky Mountain National Park, Granby, and Winter Park, then back to Denver. The ski resorts of Vail, Aspen, and Crested Butte are only commuter flights away, and in summer the charming Victorian mining villages of Leadville (America's highest incorporated town, at 10,152 feet) and Telluride (once the hideout of Butch Cassidy and other rogues) beckon visitors.

No city has everything, not even Paris, and few would anoint Denver as a national cultural capital. Still, this is no philistine cow town, even if some men still wear cowboy boots and the National Western Stock Show draws record crowds each January. It boasts a fine zoo, extensive botanical gardens, and one of America's better natural history museums, and it is rapidly developing into a regional arts center for the Mountain States.

Denver restaurants have achieved a new self-confidence. No longer do elk steak and bulls' testicles (Rocky Mountain oysters) mark the limits of local chefs' imaginations, and no longer, praise the Lord, does every menu in town feature tuna, as if a school of bluefin had just swum up the South Platte River the day before. "The city I grew up in doesn't exist," said Robert B. Yegge, dean emeritus of the University of Denver Law School, whose family has been here for four generations. "The oil boom attracted one group of new people, and the technology boom attracted another one. They're young and well educated, and many bring a taste for the arts with them."

Indeed, more people regularly buy tickets for arts events and other attractions like the zoo than for sports events, even though the football Broncos won the Super Bowl in 1998 and 1999, the hockey Avalanche won the Stanley Cup in 1996 and 2001, and the baseball Rockies bash long balls by the bucketful in Denver's thin air. (All three teams, plus the basketball Nuggets, play in handsome new facilities built in the last half dozen years.) Not many regions tax themselves to support scientific and cultural facilities, but the seven counties of metropolitan Denver do so; more than three hundred organizations have shared in annual grants of $35 million from the levy since 1988.

And not many regions have a cultural center like the twenty-five-year-old, four-square-block Denver Center for the Performing Arts. It includes the Helen Bonfils Theater, designed by Kevin Roche and John Dinkeloo and built in 1975, named for the late owner of *The Denver Post*; the updated Auditorium Theater, opened for the 1908 Democratic National Convention that nominated William Jennings Bryan; the Boettcher Concert Hall by Hardy Holzman Pfeiffer (1978); and a 1,700-space parking garage. The various buildings are linked by a series of towering steel-and-glass arches that form a galleria to keep snow and rain at bay. They house nine theaters with 10,800 seats, second in this country in capacity only to Lincoln Center in New York. The Denver Center Theater Company, an ambitious repertory group, and touring Broadway productions play there, as well as the Colorado Symphony Orchestra, Opera Colorado, and the Colorado Ballet.

Denver's performing arts gem is its rep company, which presents a dozen plays a year on four stages, ranging from Shakespeare, Molière, and O'Neill to Strindberg, Athol Fugard, and Derek Walcott. It won a Tony in 1998 as the best regional theater company. In a large building just across the street, it has what most regional theaters only dream of—rehearsal halls, storage spaces, and shops that fabricate its sets, costumes, and props.

A silver-haired, pink-cheeked North Carolinian named Donald Seawell made it happen. A New York lawyer and Broadway producer (and onetime chairman of the American National Theater and Academy), Seawell collaborated on stage projects with Helen Bonfils. Eventually she made him publisher of the *Post*.

Returning from lunch one day, he said, he decided the area around the auditorium was a perfect site for an arts center. With money from the city and from Bonfils, as well as other donors, the complex was built over three decades starting in the 1970s. Now in his nineties, the courtly Seawell remains active in the Helen G. Bonfils Foundation, which devotes itself to sustaining the theater company.

Founded in 1981 by a pair of displaced New Yorkers, Nathaniel Merrill and his wife, Louise Sherman, Opera Colorado hit a rough patch after Sherman's death in 1998 and Merrill's subsequent resignation. But the arrival of James Robinson as artistic director and Peter Russell as general director in 2001 gave the company new impetus. Under their leadership it has staged not only warhorses but also works like *Fidelio, Ariadne auf Naxos,* and *Eugene Onegin.* Robinson brought with him extensive producing experience in Santa Fe, New York, Dublin, London, Stockholm, and Sydney. Now the company is getting a new home, a 2,400-seat lyric opera house scheduled for completion in 2005. It is to be named for Eleanor Newman Caulkins, a mainstay of the Metropolitan Opera as well as Opera Colorado, who with her family gave $7 million for the project.

The orchestra plays "in the round," with the audience seated around it—as the Berlin Philharmonic does in its home hall. But neither the orchestra, under Marin Alsop, a noted interpreter of Brahms and one of the world's top women conductors, nor the ballet, which wins good notices on New York visits, has yet built a stable long-term financial foundation.

Denver is a young city, but it has grown fast. Within eighteen years of its founding, it was the capital of the nation's thirty-eighth state, with a population of 35,000. Much of the wealth produced in its hinterland enriched other cities—like the smelting millions of Meyer Guggenheim, a Swiss immigrant who struck it rich at Leadville in 1880, and the dry-goods fortune of David May, who started in a tent on Harrison Avenue in Leadville.

In those raucous early days, the performing arts were problematical. Oscar Wilde appeared onstage in Leadville in 1882 in a velvet suit, I learned from the applicable volume of the invaluable *Smithsonian Guide to Historic America,* and read to the miners from the autobiography of Benvenuto Cellini. Asked why he hadn't brought Cellini with him, Wilde replied that Cellini had been dead for quite a while, which elicited the question, "Who shot him?" The year before, one of the mining kings, Horace A. W. Tabor, took offense when the opera house he had built in Denver, with a stage seventy feet wide and fifty feet deep, opened for business. Noting a portrait in the lobby, he summoned his partner and asked who it was.

"That's Shakespeare," the partner is said to have replied.

"Who is Shakespeare?"

"Why, the greatest writer of plays who ever lived!"

"Well, what the hell has he ever done for Colorado?" demanded Tabor, incredulous. "Take his picture down and put mine up there!"

Tabor was also famous for having abandoned his wife for a blue-eyed waitress, Elizabeth "Baby" McCourt Doe, whom he married in Washington in 1883 with President Chester A. Arthur in attendance, inspiring "The Ballad of Baby Doe." His monument in modern Denver is the Tabor Center, a shopping mall that anchors the redeveloped lower downtown or LoDo district. Also in that yeasty neighborhood are Larimer Square, where seventeen Victorian buildings have been converted to shops, and the Sixteenth Street pedestrian promenade.

The Denver Art Museum, largest of its kind between Missouri and California, is housed in a fascinating if forbidding building conceived, late in his career, by the great Milanese architect Gio Ponti. Daniel Libeskind has designed a dramatic addition, due for completion in 2005, with a tangle of glass-and-titanium shards converging on a sunlit atrium. One shard forms a bridge joining the two structures. Though its old master holdings are more limited, the museum has striking collections of pre-Columbian and Spanish colonial art as well as 18,000 American Indian objects, including pots, totem poles, jewelry, and baskets dating back as far as the ninth century. It also holds the personal collection of Herbert Bayer, once a teacher at the Bauhaus, later a leading American industrial and graphic designer who helped to develop Aspen.

A burly, earthy Denver mutual fund tycoon named William M. B. Berger, who died in 1999, assembled a collection of two hundred British paintings and other objects and loaned it to the museum. It includes works by Turner, Holbein, Reynolds, Stubbs, and Joseph Wright of Derby, and a sixteenth-century Nottingham alabaster of a splendor rare even in Britain. Although some critics disagree, the museum's director, Lewis I. Sharp, argues that the collection belongs in the same league as those of the Yale Center for British Art in New Haven and the Huntington Library in San Marino, California. A former curator at the Metropolitan Museum of Art, he told me that many of the Berger works, especially the earlier ones, "are of great beauty and rarity —some of them unique in this country."

The new wing of the Denver Public Library, a postmodern extravaganza by Michael Graves just across the street, houses a collection of books, photographs, and ephemera chronicling the development of the American West. It also displays works by the trinity of American Western art, Bierstadt, Frederic Remington, and Charles Marion Russell. Graves's building, where leaders of the Western world met for a summit conference in 1997, looks as if it had been made from oversized children's blocks—pyramids, cubes, cylinders, and rectangles, piled together to surprisingly good effect and then painted with watercolors. Denver loves it.

But Denver's most discussed building, without a doubt, is the terminal at its $5 billion airport, its second, and much of the discussion is ill tempered. To start with, it is inconveniently located twenty-six miles from downtown. Its "advanced" baggage-handling system, which chewed up luggage for three years, was finally sorted out, but almost a decade after the opening, problems persist with concession-stand contracts, the rental-car setup, employee relations, and airline fees. The building itself has a certain majesty; the main terminal hall is covered with a tent of Teflon-coated fabric. It is meant to echo the Rockies, I guess, but it looks more like a high-tech encampment for a race of Bedouin giants, and I confess that I can't look at it without giggling.

WHERE TO STAY

Brown Palace, 321 Seventeenth Street, (303) 297-3111. Completed in 1892 at the zenith of Colorado's silver boom, to a

Richardsonian design by Frank Edbrooke, a local architect, the Brown Palace is the empress of Denver hotels. A $10 million renovation in the 1990s restored its Gilded Age glow. It has 241 rooms, some a tad skimpy, centered on a sparkling nine-story atrium with a stained-glass skylight and intricate cast-iron balconies. Every president since Calvin Coolidge has stayed here.

Monaco, 1717 Champa Street, (303) 296-1717. You can have a goldfish in your room at this hip new entry from the California-based Kimpton chain, with 189 rooms boldly decorated in vivid blues and reds. Musical memorabilia enliven suites named for Grace Slick, Miles Davis, and John Lennon. Unusually comfortable beds, a terrific Aveda spa, and a location within easy walking distance of downtown are other major selling points.

Oxford, 1600 Seventeenth Street, (303) 628-5400. Opened in October 1891, rescued and reopened in June 1983, this is Denver's oldest hotel. Reasonably priced, comfortable rather than luxurious, it has been skillfully restored and furnished with antiques. The Cruise Room lounge, remodeled in pure Art Deco style in 1933, with hand-carved decorative panels and dramatic cherry-red lighting after dark, is so authentic you expect Fred and Ginger to dance by. The martinis are no less genuine.

Teatro, 1100 Fourteenth Street, (303) 228-1100. This luxury boutique hotel looks as if Giorgio Armani might have had a hand in its design, and it eclipses the local competition. High bedroom ceilings create a sense of space, expansive glass-enclosed showers give you an invigorating drenching, and Frette sheets on the beds make insomnia improbable. As the name suggests, it is located across the street from the performing arts center; the culinary arts are practiced nightly at the hotel's Kevin Taylor restaurant (see below).

Westin Tabor Center, 1672 Lawrence Street, (303) 572-9100. Location, location, location: right on the Sixteenth Street Mall, close to theaters, LoDo restaurants, and downtown offices. The lobby, spartan and blond, features an angular stainless steel fountain. A heated rooftop pool affords a panoramic view of the mountains, and the amply proportioned bedrooms are subtly decorated, mostly in grays. A Palm steakhouse is close at hand.

WHERE TO EAT

Adega, 1700 Wynkoop Street, (303) 534-2222, is built around a glassed-in, 8,000-bottle wine vault (*adega* means "wine cellar" in Portuguese). Kenneth Frederickson, the former owner, assembled a stellar run of vintages, including the usual big names and some unusual little ones. Bryan Moscatello's complex, brassy food looks great on the plate, and sometimes it tastes just as good (toasted star anise soup with a scallop afloat in it), sometimes not (dry pork belly with a distressingly candylike sauce).

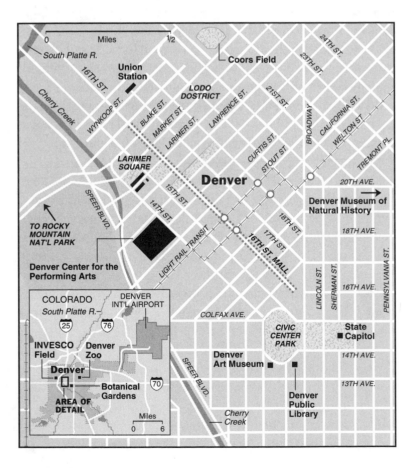

Barolo Grill, 3030 East Sixth Avenue, (303) 393-1040. It doesn't really look very Italian, but Barolo delivers in other respects. The wine list would impress the cognoscenti in Turin with its fifty-odd Piedmontese classics, from Gaja, Ceretto, Einaudi, et al., and the food keeps pace: a superb wine-sauced duck; a mixed fry of scallops, calamari, and baby shrimp, served with a harissa mayonnaise, and perfect gnocchi. Such quality makes it easy to forget silliness like presenting the check inside a mock-up of a Michelin guidebook to Italy.

Kevin Taylor, 1106 Fourteenth Street, (303) 820-2600. Taylor, a pioneer of modern cooking in Denver, dons his toque these days in an urbane environment: color scheme sage and gold, chairs ample, walls paneled, lighting subtle. Ravioli appear in several guises, stuffed one day with crab and lobster, another with porcini and foie gras. At Taylor's last restaurant, the service was often clueless; it's much more knowing here.

Mizuna, 225 East Seventh Avenue, (303) 832-4778. Frank Bonnano, an alumnus of the Culinary Institute of America (the other CIA), Gramercy Tavern in New York, and the French Laundry in California, does things the old-fashioned way. Birds and meat are butchered in-house and stocks are made fresh every night. But the food is twenty-first-century modern—macaroni and cheese made with mascarpone and kicked uptown with lobster chunks; fine Colorado lamb dishes; sea bass poached in green tea. The seating is tight.

Strings, 1700 Humboldt Street, (303) 831-7310. A good-looking spot with a red door, bare maplewood floors, and blocks of Mondrianesque color, Strings has been at it for a long time. On my last visit, the calf's liver and the pasta were hits, the egg roll and the waiter were misses. Noel Cunningham, the Dublin-born chef, is held in high regard by his peers around the country, and Denver's beautiful people flock here.

⫸ PORTLAND, OREGON

My favorite Oregonian, bar none, was Tom McCall, the unortho-
dox scion of an old New England family. Governor from 1966
to 1974, he was such a straight talker that his fellow politicians,
obfuscators all, never admitted him to full membership in their
lodge. Someone called him "a torrent of indiscretion." He drank
a cocktail of his own devising called a hemorrhage: half vodka,
half Clamato juice, the latter presumably chosen to remind him
of his roots. He campaigned tirelessly to keep Oregon within bounds. Visit us, he said in tourist promotion ads, "but for
heaven's sake don't stay."

Oregon is bigger now, and most of the growth has come in
and around Portland. There are 1.9 million people in the metropolitan area, more than half of the statewide total, 540,000 of
them within the city limits. But Portland is still Tom McCall's
monument. Tom McCall Waterfront Park, a ribbon of lawns,
trees and walkways, stretches for two miles along the west bank
of the Willamette River. (Pronounce it will-AM-ette, or they'll
know you're an outlander.) A weekend market takes place there,
and an annual beer festival. Yuppies on their lunch hours min-
gle with Dead Heads and New Agers where not too long ago
trucks roared along a freeway that was demolished.

In Portland, you are meant to use your feet to walk or pedal
a bike, not to press a brake or an accelerator. The city has two
hundred parks and wildlife refuges, innumerable smaller grassy
bits, miles of nature trails, and a strollable downtown that measures a mere thirteen by twenty-six blocks—short blocks, two
hundred feet on a side, that give a lively rhythm to the cityscape.

Perched on gentle hillsides in this area are hotels, some of the best restaurants, and the buildings that house the city's arts institutions, including the Portland Art Museum, the Arlene Schnitzer Concert Hall (a nicely refashioned vaudeville house), the New Theatre Building, housing three stages, the Keller Auditorium, and the Oregon History Center. Some of these face the South Park Blocks, a mall set aside by the city fathers in 1852 as a haven from urban stress, presumably visible at the time only through a microscope. Watch out for the cube-shaped postmodern Portland Building at 1120 Southwest Fifth Avenue, clad in coral, buff, and teal tiles, which was Michael Graves's first big commission (1983); and the twenty sidewalk drinking fountains donated to the city in 1912 by the timber baron Simon Benson in the hope they would keep his workers out of the saloons. They're called "Benson bubblers."

In 1938, the urban-affairs writer Lewis Mumford came to Portland and told its leaders, "You have an opportunity here to do a job of city planning like nowhere else in the world." Latter-day Oregonians, armed with a pioneering land-use law pushed through in 1973 by Governor McCall, took Mumford at his word, creating the nation's only directly elected regional government, known as Metro. It polices the Urban Growth Boundary mandated by the law, confining urban development to a designated 362-square-mile area.

"The city attracts educated, civic-minded, entrepreneurial people," said Steve McCarthy, a local distiller with an abiding interest in politics, who helped develop the successful Portland light-rail system. "They like the scale, they love the outdoors, and they're not going to let anyone spoil it. They're an understated, egalitarian bunch. They don't raise their voices much, and nobody talks about money, although there's pots of it around." Jobs, too, sometimes. In 1999, as computer chip factories and other high-tech employers boomed, everyone in Portland who wanted work found it. But at the start of the new century, the dot-com bust hit hard. The Rose Garden arena, where the Trail Blazers of the National Basketball Association play, went bankrupt, and for a time the metropolitan area had the highest unemployment rate in the country. It has taken time to bounce back, though people keep coming to town, jobs or no.

Portland subsists on four liquids: brew-pub beer, Oregon pinot noir, coffee, and rainwater. It rains a lot, no sense denying that, and there aren't many days when you can see the snowcapped cone of 11,239-foot Mount Hood, the New World Matterhorn fifty miles east of downtown. Most years, the weather bureau says, produce 36 inches of rain and 225 days of clouds. Visitors are warned to keep moving lest they take root in the damp. But the climate is moderate, a lot like England's; and like England, Oregon is a gardener's paradise where roses and rhododendrons flourish with only modest human ministration.

After flowers, food. James Beard, prince of American epicures, grew up in Portland, and it was here, as he wrote in his memoir *Delights and Prejudices,* that he developed his love for food—"the great razor clams, the succulent Dungeness crabs, the salmon, crawfish, mussels and trout of the Oregon coast." Now Portland is one of the West's best restaurant towns, with an avid clientele that feasts on Bartlett pears, raspberries and marionberries, Alsea Acre goat cheese, hazelnuts, wild mushrooms that carpet forest floors, bread from Upper Crust Bakery, and of course Pacific seafood in profusion, including Chinook salmon, petrale sole and superlative Yaquina Bay and Quilcene oysters.

Oregon's rugged, romantic past is echoed in Portlanders' reverence for the environment. Lewis and Clark, sent on their epic transcontinental journey by Thomas Jefferson when the United States was but an infant, reached the Pacific near the mouth of the Columbia in 1805, after shooting the river's fearsome rapids in canoes. Later, agents of John Jacob Astor, then America's richest man, established a fur-trading post nearby, at Astoria. Then, starting in the 1840s, more than 300,000 hardy settlers sold their land, said their farewells and began the eight-month trip from Missouri by wagon train, following the Oregon Trail across plains and mountains. They struggled with cholera and hunger before finally reaching Oregon City and the territory that they called "the land at Eden's gate." Modern-day Portland lies twenty miles farther west.

Splashed across the hillsides west of downtown Portland today, Eden-like, is the green swath of Washington Park, embracing a zoo and three of the Northwest's lushest spaces: the 185-acre Hoyt Arboretum, a forest within a city, full of wild rhodos and enormous ferns, Douglas firs, Sitka spruces, and big-leaf maples; the terraced International Rose Test Gardens, the centerpiece of the annual Rose Festival each June, with discouragingly healthy bushes laid out in formal beds (note that George Burns is planted right next to Gracie Allen); and the stunning Japanese Gardens, perhaps unmatched outside Asia.

A short, exuberant paragraph about the Japanese Gardens, if you will indulge me. If I had a friend who knew little and understood less about Asian aesthetic values, I would send him there, to witness the patience with which moss has been induced to grow over the roof of a gate, the care with which beguilingly shaped boulders have been chosen and placed, and the genius with which cypresses, a pagoda, and a waterfall have been ranged, one in front of the other, so that each emphasizes the other and the sun dapples them all.

Downtown, a classical Chinese garden in the fifteenth-century style of Suzhou, Portland's sister city, opened in 2000 to wide acclaim. Across the river, in the southeastern quadrant of town, bloom the city's most glorious rhododendrons. There, adjacent to the campus of Reed College, a stronghold of the liberal arts and liberal politics, thousands of rhodos—lavender, purple, white, pink, apricot, red, yellow—spread across six acres around Crystal Springs Lake. In Bed E, a group of eight white *Rhododendron loderi* "King George" bushes grown into trees twenty to twenty-five feet tall form an astonishing overhead canopy. Adding to the tranquil delight of the place are mallards, coots, scaups, widgeons, and Canada geese.

To the north, at the river's edge, is the Oregon Museum of Science and Industry, with laser shows, interactive exhibits, and a real-live submarine, the USS *Blueback*. North of there, still on the east bank of the Willamette, is the funky Hawthorne district, filled with Craftsman bungalows, pubs, bistros, shops, and the laid-back folk, young and old, who make Portland Portland.

One bright morning I strolled down Southeast Hawthorne Boulevard, the main stem, sticking my nose into the Cup and Saucer Cafe at No. 3566, a favorite for Sunday brunch; the Hawthorne Street Ale House (No. 3632), run by the BridgePort Brewing Company, oldest of Portland's twenty-eight microbreweries; the Bagdad (sic) Theater (No. 3702), a rococo cinema-cum-pub dating from 1927, which is owned by McMenamins, another of the top local suds houses; Sorel Vintages (No. 3713), a happy jumble of 1950s collectibles and kitsch; and Pasta-works (No. 3735), a mecca for cooks, packed with succulent foodstuffs and the proper pots and pans to cook them in. Its door bears a sign labeling it a "Portable Phone Free Zone." Pow-ell's Books, which calls itself the nation's largest bookstore, has two Hawthorne branches, a general shop at No. 3723 and Pow-ell's Books for Cooks and Gardeners at No. 3747. (The flagship, an erstwhile garage at 1005 Burnside Street housing a million volumes, is back across the river in the Pearl District, a gentri-fied neighborhood of converted warehouses.)

For a small city remote from the nation's main population centers, Portland enjoys a robust cultural life and has done so for more than a hundred years. Start with the Art Museum, the oldest in the Northwest, which has a collection spanning thirty-five centuries. It is housed in buildings (1932; additions and renovations in 1939, 1969, and 2000) by Pietro Belluschi, an important International Style architect who settled in Portland in the 1920s. In 2004, it began a $31.5 million conversion of a nearby Masonic Temple into new galleries for twentieth- and twenty-first-century paintings, including many items from the collection of the controversial New York art critic Clement Greenberg, which it bought in 2001. Other specialties include Oriental art, Northwest Coast Native American art, and art by artists from the region (like Mark Tobey) and others who de-picted it (like Childe Hassam and Albert Bierstadt). The mu-seum also owns a striking black-and-white Maine seascape by Marsden Hartley; a tender little Brancusi *Muse*; and a luminous Bronzino oil, *Madonna and Child with the Infant St. John*. Trav-eling exhibitions stop regularly.

Opposite the museum is the Oregon History Center, whose galleries tell the state's and city's stories with verve. Among other things, you can see the penny that the city's founders, Francis Pettygrove and Asa Lovejoy, flipped in 1845 to choose its name. Lovejoy, who was from Portland, Maine, won; Pettygrove, from Massachusetts, wanted to name the city Boston.

The Oregon Symphony hired Carlos Kalmar, a Viennese con-ductor, as music director in 2003, succeeding James DePreist.

New leaders also arrived at the Oregon State Ballet and the Portland Opera, which tackles offbeat repertory in addition to the standards. (The respected Oregon Shakespeare Festival, with plays by the Bard and modern authors, is five hours away, in Ashland. It runs from February through October.)

If culture palls, rent a car and head east to Mount Hood, then loop back to the city via the Columbia River gorge and the 620-foot Multnomah Falls, one of the highest in the United States. Or head west to the wine country, following route 99W toward Ponzi, Eyrie, and Domaine Drouhin. Most wineries are open (some by appointment only) and signposted, or sample select pinot noirs at Jay McDonald's indispensable Tasting Room in the hamlet of Carlton, near McMinnville, thirty miles from Portland, open from noon until five, Thursdays through Sundays.

WHERE TO STAY

Benson on Broadway, 309 Southwest Broadway, (503) 228-2000, has been around since 1912, and for much of that time it was Portland's leading hotel. Now, lovingly restored, it is once again a pleasure to stay in, with a woody lobby centered on a huge fireplace, a good restaurant (try the Copper River salmon in season), and, it goes almost without saying, a willing staff. The rooms vary, but the place oozes character.

Fifth Avenue Suites Hotel, 506 Southwest Washington Street, (503) 222-0001, is a recent creation of the San Francisco–based Kimpton chain of boutique hotels. Built within the shell of a Gilded Age department store, this jewel has a well-bred feeling from its sunshine-yellow lobby to its bright, amply proportioned rooms. The Red Star Tavern and Roast House occupies the space of the vanished ladies' glove and candy departments.

Lucia, 400 Southwest Broadway, (503) 225-1717. Once the Imperial, this is now Portland's hippest hostelry, with white duvets and pillow-top mattresses on the beds, wood-slat blinds on the windows, and glass and chrome in the bathrooms. A collection of 680 photographs by David Hume Kennerly, who once worked for President Gerald Ford, adorns guest rooms and public spaces. The Thai restaurant, called Typhoon, is okay.

WHERE TO EAT

Heathman, 1001 Southwest Broadway, (503) 790-7752. Philippe Boulot, formerly of the Mark Hotel in Manhattan, imparts a soigné, big-city feeling to this upmarket hotel dining room, but he makes ample use of rustic Oregon ingredients like luscious Hood River peaches, which he serves grilled with magret de canard and roasted with pistachio ice cream. He may well be Portland's most gifted chef, and the Heathman wine list (check the reserve section) is certainly the city's most comprehensive. Boulot's slow-braised leg of lamb is exceptional, as are his veal chop and the salmon hash he serves at breakfast.

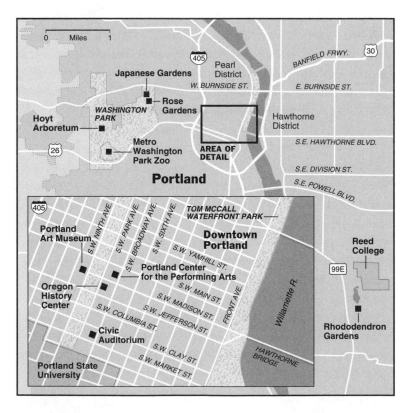

Higgins, 1239 Southwest Broadway, (503) 222-9070. In the judgment of local friends, Greg Higgins's place is the fastest-improving restaurant in town. No pretense, just two plain rooms and a commitment to local, seasonal organic produce. We particularly liked a Breton seafood stew called cotriade, and a calamari ceviche with cumin and hot peppers. Tomato jam sparks up tender Oregon razor clams (of which James Beard was so fond), and sweet Walla Walla onions go into a savory tart that would delight Alsace.

Mother's Bistro, 409 Southwest Second Avenue, (503) 464-1122. Lisa Schroeder, the mom in question, is the real thing all right. But her maternal dishes—mac and cheese, pot roast, chicken and dumplings—show the classical techniques she picked up at Le Cirque 2000 and Lespinasse. Debbie Putnam's coconut cream pies are ambrosial.

Paley's Place, 1204 Northwest Twenty-first Avenue, (503) 243-2403, forms part of a clutch of restaurants in a neighborhood that guidebooks call Nob Hill and locals call Northwest. Russian-born, a former pianist, Vitaly Paley runs this remarkably accomplished bistro in an old Victorian house. He won us over at once with scrambled eggs and morels in an eggshell, garganelli with veal ragú and lamb sausage, a powerhouse roast chicken, and tart-sweet rhubarb sorbet. Captivating service by Kimberly Paley, a former dancer.

Saucebox, 214 Southwest Broadway, (503) 241-3393. Go early to this minimalist den of maximalist Pacific Rim flavors unless you fancy a headache for dinner. With or without the disco thud, Adam Kekahuna's light, bright Vietnamese salad rolls are irresistible, with strips of flavor-boosting mango. Follow them with Hamachi tuna sashimi and avocado, brightened with a snappy ponzu sauce. Excellent desserts.

Wildwood, 1221 Northwest Twenty-first Avenue, (503) 248-9663, is the domain of Cory Schreiber, a local boy made good. The decor is simple: polished floors, Eames-ish bentwood chairs. Go for Sunday brunch, beat the crowds, and try the chunky corned beef hash with spinach, poached eggs, balsamic onions, and free-form biscuits. Or salmon cured in fennel, vodka, and lime. Or sesame-crusted deep-fried oysters. Whatever dish you choose, they have a Pacific Northwest wine that will complement it perfectly. The last time we went (sigh!), the street outside was carpeted with fallen cherry blossoms.

⊪➤ SEATTLE

It is hard to think of a city, other than urban behemoths like New York and Los Angeles, and maybe Washington, that has shaped our everyday lives in the way that Seattle has. Nordstrom, Boeing, Microsoft, Starbucks, Amazon are all important innovators, born here in the Pacific Northwest—off in a corner of the nation, far from the main centers of population—yet they play a central part in daily life across this continent and beyond.

Seattle's man of the millennium is William H. Gates, who created the corporate principality named Microsoft, making powerful enemies in Washington, D.C., Silicon Valley, and Europe in the process. His company, housed in forty-odd X-shaped buildings on a thirty-acre campus in suburban Redmond, was for a time the most valuable in America, and the nerd in chief still commands one of the greatest fortunes in history. Gates and his wife live in another suburb, Medina, in a huge mansion (estimated cost: $97 million) with a wistful quotation from *The Great Gatsby* inscribed on the library's ceiling: "He had come a long way to this blue lawn, and his dream must have seemed so close that he could hardly fail to grasp it."

Although Seattle still has its funky side and revels in its mellow small-town atmosphere, it became an unmistakably rich, high-tech, high-rise, high-expectation metropolis in the dot-com era. However, at the turn of the century, just as the metropolitan area approached a population of 3.5 million, the nation's thirteenth biggest, things started going very wrong. The World Trade Organization's conference in 1999 disintegrated into violence when anti-globalization protesters stormed Seattle's streets, and Mardi Gras 2001 produced another riot. Microsoft ran into serious legal problems on two continents. Boeing laid off workers and moved its headquarters to Chicago. Many of the dot-coms morphed into dot-bombs, and the recession shook the city to its socks. En route to becoming a major international city, eight and a half hours from Tokyo and eight and a half hours from London, it woke up in 2003 to 7.3 percent unemployment.

Like San Francisco, Seattle belongs to the sea; around every corner there is a view of the water. Its streets and its skyscrapers cling to hillsides. It looks to the Orient, and it is obsessed by food and wine. Pike Place Market, the zesty souk on the waterfront— my *Times* colleague Timothy Egan once described it as "the Marrakesh of the Northwest"—was saved from the wrecker's ball in 1973. It lives on as the heart and soul of the city, notable alike for the goofy exuberance of its merchants and for the quality of its fare: Dungeness crabs and Olympia oysters, pale pink stargazer lilies and beaming yellow sunflowers, Rainier cherries and Walla Walla onions. It is the outstanding permanent public market in the United States.

The dreary days of winter may have something to do with Seattle's lust for coffee, which added words like "latte" and "doppio" to the American language through the manic growth of Starbucks. (The name comes from that of the java-loving mate in *Moby-Dick.*) Seattle must have a thousand cafés, and it has shops specializing in espresso-machine repair. Sur La Table stocks enough pots and pans to cook a state dinner.

Fruit is another local passion. A pair of Metropolitan Markets stage an annual Peach-O-Rama, featuring pallet-loads of perfect fruit that has reached a scientifically measured level of sweetness, and the berries from the San Juan Islands are the sweetest I know. But inevitably, there are problems in this food paradise. Jon Rowley, who introduced the ambrosial Copper River salmon from Alaska to the lower forty-eight, told me sadly that the black cod, which he describes as "one of the real aristocrats of the ocean," has all but disappeared from local waters. You can still watch the elegant, silvery salmon swimming up the fish ladder at Ballard Locks, bound with fixated stares in their eyes for the fresh water where they will spawn and die, but every year the runs become smaller.

Seattle is less full of itself than San Francisco, and more

earnest. People worry that they'll be spoiled by success, that they will have to wear neckties, that urban sprawl will get out of hand. But on balance they are optimistic, even about the weather, bravely smiling through the mist. It is all that water that turns buddleias from butterfly bushes into twenty-foot butterfly trees and brings out the flashing crimsons of the fuchsias. (A short ferry ride west across Puget Sound brings you to Bainbridge Island and the remarkable gardens of the 150-acre Bloedel Reserve—a moss garden, a Zen garden, and a noted reflecting pool surrounded by English yews.)

A culture of self-effacement prevails in the city. Some technomillionaires here, worth twenty times as much as New Yorkers with chauffeurs, wear sandals and ride the bus to work. Everyone is pathologically polite, from bank presidents to bellhops. People would rather die than honk, no matter how dense the traffic. Michael Kinsley, a notably mannerly gent himself, who moved west for a while to edit Microsoft's online magazine *Slate,* told my wife, Betsey, and me: "It gets on your nerves. You wonder if you can live up to it."

Seattle makes room for creators. It takes pride in its part in the careers of Quincy Jones, Ray Charles, Kurt Cobain, and Jimi Hendrix, and waxes nostalgic about Pearl Jam. The playwright August Wilson lives close by at Enumclaw. The writer Raymond Carver lived out the last years of his short, hard life at Port Angeles on the Olympic Peninsula, on the far shores of Puget Sound, crafting his terse, claustrophobic stories at the edge of the forest primeval. Gary Larson draws in the Seattle area, and the mystic Mark Tobey painted there. So did the Harlem Renaissance master Jacob Lawrence, who died in 2000. Dale Chihuly, the charismatic glass sculptor, produces his extravagant showpieces, which have been displayed everywhere from Las Vegas to Venice to Jerusalem, in a workshop on Lake Union where the late George Y. Pocock once built the world's finest eight-oared racing shells.

Founded in 1851 on a series of waterside hills then clad with magnificent Douglas firs, Seattle always had noble vistas of the Cascade and Olympic Mountains, weather permitting (as it often didn't and doesn't, especially before the fog lifts at noon). It always had Lake Washington and Lake Union, Elliott

Bay and Puget Sound—all of them crossed these days by floating bridges, steel-arch spans, and fast ferries. By 1900 trade with Asia, timber, and the financial backwash from the Klondike gold rush had put big bucks in local pockets. Still, visitors from more cosmopolitan cities weren't much impressed. Several decades ago Sir Thomas Beecham, the conductor, who waggled his baton for a few seasons in these parts, called Seattle "an aesthetic dustbin." His countryman Alistair Cooke called it "a rain-soaked fishing village halfway between San Francisco and Alaska." But that was before the World's Fair of 1962, with its monorail and its Space Needle (recently given a $20 million face-lift), and the forty-year population explosion that followed it.

As the United States rediscovered its outdoors, it discovered Seattle, a city whose residents can sail among the orca whales in the San Juan Islands, with bald eagles cruising overhead, and climb snow-capped Mount Rainier in the same week. With its mild if legendarily rainy climate, the place was made for skiing, cycling, running, rowing, sailing, hydroplane racing, and a dozen other sports. Eddie Bauer, originally a Seattle outfitter for mountaineers, grew into a national sporting-goods powerhouse. The Recreational Equipment flagship superstore, a co-op to which almost one of three people in the region belong, has a 65-foot artificial indoor peak where young studs practice rock climbing.

Starting about 1975, a half dozen books and magazines, including *Harper's* and *Money*, rated Seattle as the nation's most livable city. It got a bold new art museum, cunningly slotted into the streetscape downtown by Robert Venturi in 1991, and a heralded new home for the Seattle Symphony, Benaroya Hall, opened in 1998. A new ballpark for the Seattle Mariners, Safeco Field, was unveiled in 1999 to replace the hated Kingdome, which was demolished in only 16.8 seconds. The new park, with a retractable roof, cost $517 million (gulp!), financed mainly by taxes; it is the nation's most costly sports center.

A $250 million rock-and-roll museum known as the Experience Music Project opened in 2000. Designed by Frank O. Gehry, it houses 80,000 artifacts inside a furiously billowing aluminum-and-stainless-steel shell decked out in gold, silver, red, powder blue, and iridescent purple. Tickets cost too much ($19.95

each), attendance quickly sagged, and key staff members quit. Susan Nielsen, a local columnist, wrote that "the whole inside of the building is like a guy trying so hard to be hip that the muscles stand out on his neck." Paul G. Allen, Gates's compadre in founding Microsoft, financed this museum and helped to underwrite a $430 million high-tech stadium (gulp again!) for his Seattle Seahawks football team—now a vestigial monument of Seattle's gilded age in the high-speed 1990s.

Steven Holl's poetic little St. Ignatius Chapel at Seattle University (1997) proves again that buildings need not be grandiose to be great. Holl, who grew up in nearby Bremerton, described his complex creation in simple terms, as "a stone box containing seven bottles of light." In the way it filters sun through colored lenses, it was clearly influenced by Le Corbusier's iconic pilgrimage chapel at Ronchamp in eastern France.

Despite civic and corporate financial reversals, the building boom rolls on, attracting world-renowned architects like the Dutch master Rem Koolhaas (a new glass-sheathed public library lauded by one eastern critic as "a blazing chandelier to swing your dreams upon"), Terry Farrell, the British postmodernist (a new aquarium), and Canada's Arthur Erickson (a shimmering Museum of Glass in Tacoma, Chihuly's hometown). All this activity unsettles the old guard, which is attached to the city's comfy beaux arts look, typified by the terra-cotta walrus heads that decorate the Arctic Building on Third Avenue. A sleek new hotel, W, prompted locals to ask, "It's nice, but is it Seattle?" Many people harbor similar doubts about the Venturi and Gehry buildings. Phyllis Hayes, who has deep local roots, summed up the attitude this way: "Wonderful things are happening, but they're happening too fast, and they cost so much."

Angst has never been Seattle's style, but it earned a reputation for radicalism early on. Anna Louise Strong, a charismatic Marxist, was the sole woman elected to the school board in 1916, but she was thrown off because of her support of the Industrial Workers of the World (the Wobblies), a pioneering hard-left union that was active in the Seattle general strike of 1919 (the only general strike in the nation's history). Seattle was idled again in 1934 by a maritime stoppage.

At the same time, Seattle has always been marked by an emotional reticence, perhaps a legacy from its Scandinavian settlers. Walt Crowley, a historian who runs a crackerjack local Web site (historylink.org), talks of this as "a city with a split personality, a yin side and a yang side." Two of its top politicians, both Democrats, both senators, exemplified the split. Henry M. Jackson, "the senator from Boeing," concentrated on national security issues (1953–81); he was an understated paragon of probity, while Warren G. Magnuson (1944–81), a prime mover on civil rights and environmental law, was far more rambunctious, and he fancied a drink or two.

The art museum, whose dramatic main staircase is a late-twentieth-century version of the Louvre's, houses a few choice old masters, including a Paolo Uccello illustrating episodes from the *Aeneid,* and rich holdings of African tribal art and Northwest Coast Native American art. It has a fine Asian collection, shown in an Art Deco building in Volunteer Park. One day it will have much more, and an expansion is planned. More than $250 million was spent on art by area collectors one year recently, and the museum aspires to the splendid Barney A. Ebsworth collection of modern American art that it has already shown. It includes Edward Hopper's melancholy masterpiece *Chop Suey.*

The symphony, ensconced in a new hall adorned with a pair of arresting white clusters by Chihuly and major works by Mark di Suvero and Robert Rauschenberg, also aims high. The intense and proficient Gerard Schwarz, its music director since 1985, has taken it on the road, performed Deems Taylor's neglected opera *Peter Ibbetson,* and explored the music of the Pacific Rim. But it has accumulated deficits of $1.16 million.

Seattle is awash in theater. The Intiman Theater, a national leader, staged *The Kentucky Cycle* by Robert Schenkkan in 1991; the play won a Pulitzer Prize in 1992, before it opened in New York. The Seattle Repertory Theater has a long-standing relationship with Wendy Wasserstein dating from the days when it was run by the director Dan Sullivan. In 2000 ACT—the letters stand for A Contemporary Theater—commissioned a new Philip Glass opera, *In the Penal Colony,* based on a Kafka story, with sets by John Conklin. Each of the three has a budget exceeding $3 million a year and thousands of subscribers.

But opera is easily the city's cultural long suit, thanks mainly to Glynn Ross, who brought Wagner to the Northwest, and Speight Jenkins, his successor at the Seattle Opera. A lean, fervent man, once a New York reporter and critic, Jenkins has been at the helm for two decades. In 1975 Seattle staged the *Ring of the Nibelungen*—the first time the whole cycle had been produced within a week's time, as originally prescribed, anywhere in the United States aside from the Metropolitan. New York took notice, as did London and Bayreuth. Other cycles followed. In 2001, Jane Eaglen, the premier Wagnerian soprano of her day, sang Brünnhilde, and still another is scheduled for 2005 in McCaw Hall, completely rebuilt with vastly improved acoustics at a cost of $127 million. The 2001 *Ring* sold out early to Wagnerians all over the world. Why Seattle? Earlier Jenkins productions had sometimes been booed, even pelted with fruit, but they came to be seen as classics. He pushed the company far into the red but lifted it out again. "We became the thing in town," he said, "and then people from elsewhere came here out of curiosity."

WHERE TO STAY

Alexis, 1007 First Avenue, (206) 624-4844. A graceful century-old 109-room classic, this is a member of the boutique hotel chain assembled by the California hotelier Bill Kimpton. The public spaces are filled with the work of regional artists (including several Dale Chihuly glass sculptures), and the big bedrooms are decorated with cheerful fabrics. No view, but you awaken to the sound of seagulls and foghorns. Terrific Aveda spa.

Fairmont Olympic, 411 University Street, (206) 621-1700. Grand with a capital G: a lobby straight from a Renaissance palace, a shopping arcade where you can buy a ball gown or an antique candelabrum, and a windowed rooftop pool. This dowager, built in the 1920s but very well preserved, used to be a Four Seasons. Even small rooms have duvets and luxurious bathrooms. Need a shine, a notary public, or a car wash? Just ask.

Inn at the Market, 86 Pine Street, (206) 443-3600. Understated, enlivened with touches of Asia and Provence, this is a
discreetly distinguished little hotel—especially if you can snag
a room like 514, a suite that overlooks the Pike Place Market
and Elliott Bay and the peaks of the Olympic Peninsula beyond
it. Fax machines, kitchenettes, and even orchids in the bedrooms. Betsey and I wish there were one of these in every city.

W, 1112 Fourth Avenue, (206) 264-6000. Hard-edged, high-
tech decor, soft-edged service from a black-clad staff—an apt
combination for Seattle. The lobby is small, crowded and noisy,
too hip by half, but the 428 guest rooms are quiet and comfortable, with 250-count sheets and CD libraries. Drew Nieporent's
"Earth and Ocean" is right on the premises, but the coveted silver "W" yo-yos are available only through the catalog.

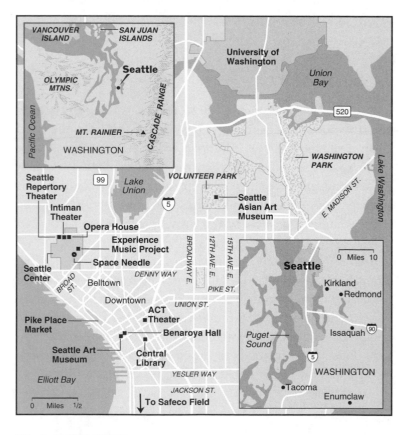

WHERE TO EAT

Canlis, 2576 Aurora Avenue, (206) 283-3313. Soon to be fifty-five years old, a classic room in stone and redwood cantilevered over Lake Union, Canlis was revitalized by an astute chef, Greg Atkinson. He has moved on, but the menu still dances to seasonal and regional rhythms, with lime-seasoned raw Alaskan scallops and Frog Hollow Farm peaches, not to mention steak tartare of Wagyu beef fit for King Bill Gates. Remarkably graceful service, and the wine list runs to fifteen hundred selections.

Dahlia Lounge, 2001 Fourth Avenue, (206) 682-4142. Tom Douglas is Seattle's premier restaurateur, and this is his premier restaurant. Japanese lanterns, red walls, and music from the forties and fifties cast a casual glow over the delicious Asian-accented food. Six fishy bites (for example, albacore with ponzu sauce) come nestled in ice; a slab of grilled Alaska king salmon rests on a chowder of tart sorrel and sweet corn. Ethereal triple coconut cream pie to conclude with. No wonder they shot a scene for *Sleepless in Seattle* here.

Mistral, 113 Blanchard Street, (206) 770-7799. Formed as a chef in the kitchen of David Bouley, William Belickis opened his bright white Belltown restaurant in 2000 and frog-marched it to the head of the local dining class. His enthusiasm and perfectionism are written all over a repertoire of miraculously pure, intense flavors that includes the inventive (lemon-marinated tuna with blood-orange jelly) and the conventional (breast of guinea hen with roast carrot puree). Unhappily, the service is straight off a used-car lot.

Le Pichet, 1933 First Avenue, Seattle, (206) 256-1499. Tiny room, zinc bar, slate-top tables, interesting wines by the glass, and accomplished, unaffected cooking define this cozy café. Welcome to France. Try the charcuterie (a hunk of velvety chicken liver pâté, maybe) followed by a Breton casserole of shellfish and poached eggs in lobster sauce. Jim Drohman steers a steady course north of bistro banality, south of nouvelle nonsense, and Seattle loves him for it.

Ray's Boathouse, 6049 Seaview Avenue Northwest, (206) 789-3770. Ray's seafood is never less than impeccably fresh, and on a fine summer's day what could be more enthralling than sitting on the deck, watching the boats, with a breeze mussing your hair? Order something simple for lunch, say manila clams steamed with beer, dill, and butter, or sesame-crusted halibut with sticky rice, and choose from 177 white wines. I counted.

Shiro, 2401 Second Avenue, (206) 443-9844. This is the plain Jane among Seattle's top restaurants, a stark little place with plastic chairs and paper napkins. No matter; the sushi is superb. We especially liked the shiro roll, made with mackerel, shiso, and ginger, and sea urchin roe (uni), so soft and creamy it barely clung to the rice. Shiro Kashiba grinds his own wasabi, and in October he makes magic with matsutake mushrooms.

Wild Ginger, 1401 Third Avenue, (206) 623-4450. Another of Seattle's favorites, Rick Yoder's pan-Asian brasserie now inhabits multimillion-dollar quarters across from Benaroya Hall. It was jammed from the instant it opened. Japanese screens, origami lampshades, and rattan chairs set the right tone for a wide variety of satays, each served with a different sauce, authentically spicy Malaysian laksa, and baby bok choy to die for.

⫸ VANCOUVER

Conspire to arrive by ship if you possibly can. Like Naples, like New York and Cape Town, Vancouver looks its best from the water, with its shiny glass towers rising like Xanadu against a backdrop of indigo peaks whose foothills dip their toes in the harbor. Jan Morris, who has seen a city or two in her day, wrote that Vancouver's setting, at the southwest corner of Canada, "is better than San Francisco's, because of the greenness, better than Sydney's, because of the mountains all around, rivaled perhaps only by Rio and Hong Kong."

More than 40,000 newcomers take up residence each year, and the metropolitan area now boasts a population of nearly 2 million, third largest in Canada. One in five people who live here are ethnic Chinese, according to the 2001 census. Clean, leafy, blessed with a temperate climate marred only by rainy winters, Vancouver seems to have it all. It is relatively crime-free; Vicky Gabereau, the host of a nationally televised talk show based here, says proudly, "There's no place in town I wouldn't walk, day or night, unless I was wearing a big diamond ring or planning to take my shirt off."

Geographically Vancouver may be isolated, but it is nevertheless as cosmopolitan a city as any boulevardier could hope for. A friend of mine who lives in Seattle, three hours' drive to the south, remarked that Vancouver "has a sexy beat, a kind of skirt-swinging glamour" she finds missing from her hometown. "Everyone wants to live here," Mike Harcourt, a former mayor and provincial premier, told me, and he was exaggerating only a little. John Nichol, a onetime senator in Ottawa, said that when he left Vancouver he missed "the tang of the sea in my nostrils, the sense that everything beyond is Asia." The city's other special quality, he added, is its newness. "Everyone in Vancouver is just out of the bush, or almost," he said. "There was nothing here to speak of just eighty or ninety years ago."

If Canada as a whole is markedly calmer than the United States—Kim Campbell, a former prime minister, once described her countrymen as "decaffeinated Americans"—Vancouver is even more laid-back. In summer the workweek tends to start about noon on Mondays and end about noon on Fridays. Canadians who live elsewhere call this region Lotusland. That implies a degree of disengagement from the serious business of life, and it is true that Vancouver is full of distraction: sailing in the sheltered waters that stretch from here to Vancouver Island, skiing in Whistler, just seventy-five miles up the Sea-to-Sky Highway, or simply gazing at the magnificent panoramas outside one's office or apartment window. No point in fighting all that, so in summer performing arts groups move outdoors, offering Shakespeare in a waterside park and Mozart in the mountains. (More distraction: in 2010 the city, with Whistler, will play host to the Winter Olympics.)

Downtown Vancouver is situated on a thumb-shaped peninsula on the eastern shore of English Bay, with water on three sides. At the peninsula's tip is one of the city's most remarkable features, Stanley Park, a thousand-acre reserve, much of it dense natural forest, a fifteen-minute walk from downtown. Vancouver folk defend it as fiercely as New Yorkers defend Central Park, resisting any incursion into their "wilderness." Astonishingly, the park is only slightly younger than Vancouver itself. As they began rebuilding after a disastrous fire in 1886, the city fathers persuaded Ottawa to give them the land, once a military reservation, as an urban oasis.

If you want to see how the city lives, join the crowds who visit the park on weekends. Amid bronze-leaved Japanese maples and ancient cedars whose corded trunks reach straight and tall to the sky, Mr. and Mrs. Vancouver and their kids throng Stanley Park on foot, in horse-drawn carriages, on bicycles, on in-line skates. Waiting there for them are rugby fields, a cricket pitch, tennis courts, three beaches, a pool, a lake, a lagoon, a restaurant, a fish-and-chips stand, a pitch-and-putt golf course, angling piers, yacht basins, a rowing club, a lawn-bowling club, an aquarium with no fewer than eight thousand marine creatures, a zoo, cormorants and seals posing on the rocks at low tide, and not a single scrap of litter. My wife, Betsey, noticed the motto on the license plate of a parked car. "Beautiful British Columbia," it said. "They don't lie," Betsey said.

Waves of immigrants from Japan, India, Vietnam, and especially Hong Kong have given the city an Asian flavor. The great recent surge in Chinese immigration was caused by political uncertainty in Hong Kong in the 1980s and early 1990s. Some wealthy Chinese hedged their bets, staying on in Hong Kong and building houses in Vancouver as investments (and possible future refuges), though the successful handover of the colony to Beijing calmed a lot of nerves. People no longer talk as much about Hong Kouver.

Still, Vancouver supports three fiercely competitive Chinese-language daily newspapers, a Chinese-language radio station, two Chinese-language cable television channels, and malls doing business exclusively in Cantonese and Mandarin. It eats dim sum—excellent dim sum—the way New York eats pastrami. Exotic fruits like mangosteen, longan, and rambutan, rare or unavailable in the United States, are sold by every greengrocer in town. The city's Chinese population has grown so much that it now fills four Chinatowns; you want to visit the original one, which stretches along Pender Street. One building there bears the date 1889. But Nathan Fong, a writer who strolled through the crowded street markets with us—pointing out unfamiliar items like whole lotus roots, and one or two that even he did not recognize, like a globular fruit called santol—said that Pender Street had changed drastically. "When I used to walk here with my parents and grandparents twenty-five years ago," he remarked, "we always saw people we knew. But not anymore." Near Main and Pender, the Times Square of this Chinatown, are dozens of restaurants. Small shops like Dollar Meat that sell uncooked as well as barbecued ducks and pork reminded me of similar places in Causeway Bay in Hong Kong, except that these are spotlessly clean, bereft of the flies and mangy dogs that you always encounter in Asia.

Vancouver is named for Captain George Vancouver of the

British Navy, who explored what is now called Burrard Inlet in 1792. But it was the coming of the Canadian Pacific Railway, which decided in 1884 to make this its transcontinental terminus, that ensured the city's future. Shipping is a major business here; looking across to Asia, Vancouver is Canada's principal port. Trade in timber from the heavily wooded hinterland started during Vancouver's earliest days, and so did the exportation of grain grown on Canada's broad prairies.

New lines of work have developed recently. Tourism is one, stimulated by Vancouver's beauty, superlative food (especially in the Asian restaurants, which may be unmatched in North America), and convenience as a jumping-off place for Alaskan cruises. High-tech manufacturing plants and environmental research labs generate thousands of jobs.

On Granville Island in the center of the city you can see the creativity of Vancouver at work. Shabby warehouses and derelict factories there have been converted into studios for glassblowers, potters, weavers, quilters, and the like; only the best, chosen by a jury, are granted space. A rope factory has been transformed into a public market selling everything from French stocks to Korean sweet-potato noodles to dolmas to fish, fish, and more fish. The island is now one of the city's favorite stops.

Perhaps more surprisingly, Vancouver has become a film capital. Hollywood producers as well as homegrown auteurs have made movies a billion-dollar-a-year business in Vancouver, and the white trailers of the crews are a familiar sight on the city's streets. Robert Altman was one of the first directors to discover the low costs, high skills, and photogenic local land- and cityscapes; he made *McCabe and Mrs. Miller* in Vancouver in 1970, and dozens of other movie and TV productions followed, including *The X-Files* and *Smallville*. "In Canada when you don't fit in where you grew up, you come to Vancouver," said Tom Rowe, a partner in the film-producing Sextant Entertainment Group. "There is tolerance and freedom here, which has an impact in the film business and other things."

Like writing. Douglas Coupland, a local novelist, coined the expression "Generation X" in his 1991 novel of that name, and William Gibson gave the word "cyberspace" to the language in his 1982 short story "Burning Chrome." W. P. Kinsella wrote a novel called *Shoeless Joe*, about a game they play across the border; it became *Field of Dreams*.

And the counterculture. Vancouver was full of hippies forty years ago, and quite a few are still around, grayer if not wiser. You see far more sandals here, summer and winter, than in most cities. Sophie's Cosmic Café in Kitsilano is a relic of the time when that area, now gentrified, was the hipsters' hangout. Weed, known locally as "B.C. Bud," remains a staple. The British Columbia Marijuana Party Bookstore caters to users in one neighborhood, and the British Columbia Compassion Club provides a lounge for those who smoke for medical reasons. Nobody protests; indeed, former prime minister Jean Chrétien said shortly before retiring that he might smoke some pot.

Having helped to block the building of a proposed waterfront freeway, as well as the bulldozing of old, characterful neighborhoods, and hoping to limit the paving-over of farmland, former mayor Harcourt became an apostle of rapid transit, green zones, and wilderness reserves. One consequence has been increasing urban density, typified by a forest of steel-and-glass skyscraper apartment blocks along False Creek in central Vancouver. But congestion, especially traffic congestion, remains a problem, and officials here and across the border are working on a comprehensive growth-control strategy for the basin stretching hundreds of miles from Vancouver to Olympia, Washington.

Arthur C. Erickson is Vancouver's big architectural kahuna, one of a triad of Canadian stars, along with Israeli-born Moshe Safdie (designer of Vancouver's elliptical, up-to-the-minute, hugely popular library, which draws 8,000 visitors a day), and Frank O. Gehry, based in California. An apostle of Le Corbusier, Erickson designed the handsome Canadian Embassy on Pennsylvania Avenue in Washington, near the Capitol. For his hometown Erickson, now eighty, has produced a Sikh temple, office buildings, most of Simon Fraser University in nearby Burnaby, and the focal point of downtown Vancouver, Robson Square, where he reworked an old courthouse. Now the Vancouver Art Gallery augments its small collection of Canadian art with traveling shows. Ferragamo, Vuitton, Dunhill, and other chic-eries cluster around Erickson's three-block-long mall.

At the far end of the mall, landscaped by Cornelia Hahn

Oberdorfer, another internationally known Vancouver artist, Erickson placed the Law Courts, one of his key works. Conceived as the antithesis of traditional court buildings, which are often dark and forbidding, it is dominated by a vast, airy, welcoming atrium covered by a sloping glass-and-tubular-steel roof and heavily planted with vines and shrubs. Justice, it says, is for all.

Another must-see Erickson building is off to the west (on the West Side of town, that is, not to be confused with the West End or West Vancouver). At the University of British Columbia he adapted the post-and-beam construction methods of the aboriginal Indians for a Museum of Anthropology displaying a compelling collection of their evocative art. Baskets, textiles, jewelry, and wooden sculptures of ravens, otters, and bears are included in the collection. Its high point is the largest grouping anywhere of totem poles, those magical towering objects carved for thousands of years by the coastal tribes. They stand in a Great Hall, formed by a series of enormous reinforced-concrete trusses and glassed-in on one side, overlooking the Straits of Georgia.

The performing arts have established a solid beachhead in Vancouver. Less than ten years old, Ballet British Columbia has developed rapidly under the leadership of John Alleyne. The Vancouver Opera suffered a big setback in 1988 when poor attendance at some of its arcane offerings, like works by Leos Janáček, caused the Briton Brian McMaster to quit as general director. But it recovered, and although it has not since ventured into anything quite as recondite as Janáček, it produced Carlisle Floyd's *Of Mice and Men* in 2002. Founded in 1919, the Vancouver Symphony was dealt an even harder blow in 1988; out of money, it was forced to suspend operations. But Romanian-born Sergiu Comissiona rebuilt it during a nine-year stint as music director; he was succeeded in 2000 by Bramwell Tovey, an Englishman identified with choral works, new music, and young audiences.

Bill Millerd has run the highly respected Arts Club Theater Company, based on Granville Island, for more than thirty years. It stages seven, eight, or more Canadian and foreign plays each year. To the irritation of some chauvinists, the Vancouver Playhouse does fewer Canadian plays. Next door, the Queen Elizabeth Theater plays host to touring musicals, pop and rock concerts, and television events as well as the opera and the ballet. But perhaps the most successful of Vancouver's theatrical efforts is Bard on the Beach, an annual festival in a red-and-white tent in Vanier Park that stages Shakespeare against the ever-stirring backdrop of water and mountains. It began in 1990 with one play and a budget of only $25,000. In the summer of 2004, its fifteenth anniversary season, it drew 80,000-plus spectators to more than two hundred performances of three plays, including *Macbeth*. "We've touched a nerve, I guess," said Christopher Gaze, an Anglo-Canadian actor who founded the company and still leads it. "We've played to 96 percent capacity several summers recently. We're affordable, accessible, and out of doors, which is what this city wants. We struggled a little, but then the support came—whumpf!—like a forest fire."

Given good weather, the call of the wild can be irresistible in Vancouver, even for sedentary souls like Betsey and me, and you don't have to rent an ocean kayak or a mountain bike to explore the city's glorious surroundings. One easy way to do it is by steam train, the antique Royal Hudson, which puffs forty miles up the coast to the logging town of Squamish in the summertime, snaking past waterfalls and mammoth Douglas firs, clinging at times to cliffs one hundred feet above the sea. The return trip by boat is no less spectacular.

A scenic ninety-minute ferry ride across the Straits of Georgia, winding through the rocky, conifer-shrouded Gulf Islands, will deposit you (and your rental car, which is well-nigh indispensable) on 350-mile-long Vancouver Island, which shields the city from the Pacific. Victoria, the trim little provincial capital, is the best place to alight first.

Not long ago, I'm told, Victoria was pure, provincial Victoriana. The Canadian-born CBS correspondent Morley Safer recalls arriving at the Empress Hotel one afternoon in the 1960s and stumbling into a thé dansant, with music by Billy Tinkle and his orchestra. But modern Victoria is much less sedate. Betsey and I spent a Sunday morning in one of the many hotels that circle its landlocked harbor, reading the newspapers, eating breakfast, and watching the tiny local ferries scuttle back and forth like cockleshells, dwarfed by the big Seattle boat. Seaplanes came and went, kayaks slid silently past, and handsome yawls heeled in the wind. Best of all, it happened to be the day of the Chinese dragon boat races, with twenty oars flailing away on each canoe and a drum booming a steady cadence.

Brilliant summer flowers filled every pot, every hanging basket and every bed around the harbor, all as carefully tended as a dowager's coiffure. But the truly amazing displays are at Butchart Gardens, a half hour north. There, in and around an old limestone quarry, bloom millions of roses, billions of dahlias, trillions of tuberous begonias, some as big as a softball, and zillions of Japanese and Chinese tourists. I exaggerate, of course, but not much. Every spring the gardens import 135,000 flower bulbs from the Netherlands, and every summer evening bushes and blossoms are lit by thousands of lights linked by eleven miles of hidden wiring. It is a show worth crossing a continent to see.

WHERE TO STAY

Four Seasons, 791 West Georgia Street, (604) 689-9333. Canada is justly proud of this Toronto-based chain, and Vancouver has no more prestigious address. Guests can avail themselves of an indoor-outdoor pool and a 165-shop mall that leads off the swanky lobby (with Birger Christensen and Prada as bait for the unwary). From the upper floors broad vistas open across the harbor to the mountains, but the bedrooms are a bit dowdy.

Metropolitan, 645 Howe Street, (604) 687-1122. Built as a Mandarin hotel, the Metropolitan retains that group's understated elegance, and in Diva, it has one of the city's better dining rooms. Blond wood, ribbed silk, and chrysanthemum prints evoke Asian tradition; business-class rooms with safes, ergonomic chairs, and computer printers plant the Met in the twenty-first century. The staff knows your name before you check in.

Pan Pacific, Suite 300-999 Canada Place, (604) 662-8111. Part of Canada Place, where the big cruise ships dock, the 504-room Pan Pacific juts into the harbor beside the five white sails that have become the city's architectural trademark. Glass walls in the three-story lobby take full advantage of the site; guest rooms, trimly furnished in bird's-eye maple, offer hypnotic views.

Squash courts, running track, expensive and worth every penny.

Sutton Place, 845 Burrard Street, (604) 682-5511. The choice of many a worldly traveler, this was once the property of the French-owned Meridien chain, and it still feels more French than North American. Guests are greeted by antiques, marble floors, lavish floral displays, and a friendly front-desk team, and the 397 rooms show a similar attention to detail. An adjacent connected building offers condominiums for rent by the week.

WHERE TO EAT

Bishop's, 2183 West Fourth Avenue, (604) 738-2025. John Bishop chases no fads and turns no somersaults. His food is simple and straightforward, marked by clear flavors, bright colors, and combinations that work—grilled salmon with a ginger glaze; seared scallops in red pepper and chive bisque, topped with a potato galette; halibut on a warm potato salad. The service is suave and personal. This is a restaurant that will run and run.

C, Suite 2-1600 Howe Street, (604) 681-1164. The C stands for contemporary and for sea, which nicely sums up this glass-and-steel pavilion hard by False Creek, just across from Granville Island. In winter it's best at night; in summer go at midday, sit on the terrace, and watch the world go by—in kayaks, on in-line skates, and on bicycles built for two. Robert Clark's octopus confit grilled over maple chips has become a local classic. His Taster Box includes several delicate morsels like wild sockeye cured in quince syrup.

Le Crocodile, 100-909 Burrard Street, (604) 669-4298. Michel Jacob named his place for a restaurant in his hometown, Strasbourg, and there are always Alsatian dishes on the menu, like onion tart and pheasant on sauerkraut. They are impeccably cooked, like everything here, including liver with onions and sweetbreads with Calvados. This is a place to savor fondly remembered flavors of yesteryear. Proust would have adored it.

Kirin Mandarin, 1166 Alberini Street, (604) 682-8833, turns out superb northern Chinese food, served by uncommonly gracious waiters in a postmodern room. Among the dim sum, try the deep-fried prawn and yellow chive roll; among the larger dishes, half a Peking duck, served in two courses—thrillingly crisp skin with scallions, pancakes, and a very light hoisin sauce, followed by duck meat steamed with cabbage and mushrooms.

Lumière, 2551 West Broadway, (604) 739-8185. Rob Feenie is Vancouver's culinary phenom, its Thomas Keller or Jean-Georges Vongerichten, and his welcoming restaurant is usually cited as the city's best. A signature offering is red kuri squash ravioli with truffle butter; typical summer fare is tiny slices of lightly seared salmon, served cold atop a granita confected from celery juice, ponzu, and shiso. Four tasting menus are offered, or you can order single courses at the no-fuss, no-reservations Tasting Bar.

Piccolo Mondo, 850 Thurlow Street, (604) 688-1633. A small, serene realm of Old World courtesy, this is one of the city's hidden treasures. George Baugh and Michele Geris, husband and wife, soft-spoken and able, serve zephyr-light pastas and definitive, mahogany-dark osso buco. With which, praise the Lord, one can drink judiciously priced ten-year-old red wines from Bruno Ceretto and Monte Vertine. Try that in New York.

Sun Sui Wah, 3888 Main Street, (604) 872-8822. Dim Sum equal to Hong Kong's best and more in a squeaky-clean room designed by Bing Thom, a Vancouver architect. The gentle flavors of the best Cantonese cooking prevail here, and the XO sauce is as delicious as any I've tasted. Ask Allan Yung, the savvy manager, for guidance; but don't miss the tripe, squab, or ham sui gok (deep-fried, pork-stuffed sticky-rice dumplings).

Tojo's, 202-777 West Broadway, (604) 872-8050. Reserve a counter seat; watching Hidekazu Tojo work, seeking his counsel, and laughing at his (bad) jokes is integral to the experience. The B.C. roll ("inside out" salmon skin) is the trademark, but the seasonal specials are better. Sablefish in broth with sliced pine mushrooms, served in a bowl covered with parchment, amazed us. So did halibut cheeks and citrus-cured albacore.

Vij's, 1480 West Eleventh Avenue, (604) 736-6664. On the menu at Vikram Vij's animated, artistic restaurant, tucked behind a magnificent teak door just off Broadway, it says "curry art," and that's what he and his wife, Meeru, practice. They choose sweet, peak-of-season mangoes and combine them with acidic tomatoes in a Gujarati sauce spiked with cumin. Slimline lamb chops ("popsicles" in Vij-speak) are bathed in a red curry cream, rich in fenugreek. Even the rice (basmati) is noteworthy, as is Vij's keen attention to his clients.

⇒ SAN FRANCISCO

More than any other, San Francisco is the city Americans fantasize about. No one sings about leaving his heart in Chattanooga. No one calls Baltimore Baghdad by the Bay, as Herb Caen, San Francisco's six-day-a-week prose laureate for more than fifty years, called his town. For me San Francisco has always been a paradox: a thoroughly worldly place, yet remote from and indifferent to world capitals like New York and London; in other words, rather smug. The always upbeat Caen, who before his death in 1997 did for San Francisco what Samuel Pepys did for long-ago London, once quoted a local citizen who, upon arriving in heaven, reported back to his friends at home that "it's nice, but it isn't San Francisco."

San Francisco looms large in the imagination of all who know it, myself decidedly included. Like Paris and Venice, it is a polity without peer, a city of myth and magic. For myself, I can't think of it without thinking of sourdough bread and Alice Waters, who reinvented American cooking in Berkeley, across the bay; Joe DiMaggio, a fisherman's son, and A. P. Giannini, another Italian American, who built the world's largest bank here; Alcatraz and San Quentin prisons; Turk Murphy and San Francisco jazz; the hairpin bends on Lombard Street and the clanging cable cars; Joe Montana and Jerry Rice, Willie Mays and Barry Bonds, he of the bulging biceps.

The weather I could do without. Fog veils San Francisco so often that a local radio station has adopted the call letters KFOG. Fog bleaches the color from the perky paint jobs on the Victorian frame houses that march up and down the city's hills.

When the fog finally lifts, when everything sparkles in the sun, it is an occasion for celebration. Yes!—a five-bridge day, with all the spans clearly visible.

But fog has its uses. Years ago, crossing the Bay Bridge from Oakland to San Francisco at dawn, my wife, Betsey, and I watched bug-eyed as the Transamerica pyramid and the city's other towers rose bronzed and beautiful from their cloudy bed. Nothing, in truth, not fog or rain or fire or quake, ever quite masks San Francisco's beauty or quenches its ebullience. Its setting rivals Rio de Janeiro's. Its charm compares with Boston's. Its joie de vivre nearly matches that of New Orleans, lacking only the last Latin measure of heedlessness. Real-life characters from Nob Hill and Telegraph Hill, Chinatown and the Tenderloin have walked straight into the pages of Bret Harte, Jack London, Frank Norris, Dashiell Hammett, Tom Wolfe, who found the essential San Francisco experience in "roaring up hills or down hills, sliding on and off the cable-car tracks," and John Steinbeck, a romantic who described the city as "a golden handcuff with the key thrown away."

Hemmed in by bay and ocean at the tip of a narrow peninsula, San Francisco is relatively small. It ranked only thirteenth on the list of American cities in 2000, with a population of 780,000; Los Angeles, San Diego, and even San Jose were all bigger. But the nine-county metropolitan area that surrounds the bay, with 7 million people, is the nation's fifth largest. The San Andreas Fault, where two sections of the earth's crust (known as plates) come together, runs through this area. Shifts in the plates caused the great earthquake and fire in San Francisco in 1906, in which three thousand people were killed, and a 1989 quake that took sixty-six lives and precipitated the collapse of Oakland's Cypress Freeway. Scientists consider more (and more severe) earthquakes inevitable but cannot predict when they will occur.

The city's early prosperity was based on the construction of the transcontinental railroads, on Comstock Lode silver, and on shipping. San Francisco's port was where Harry Bridges and his militant longshoremen organized the nation's first successful union for dockworkers in the 1930s.

George Hearst struck it rich in the mines. His son, William

Randolph Hearst, struck it richer in yellow journalism, which he helped to invent; a great-granddaughter, Patty, was kidnapped in 1974 by the Symbionese Liberation Army, a radical group led by criminals, but she survived. The circulation of Hearst's flagship, the *San Francisco Examiner,* whose logo proclaimed it "Monarch of the Dailies," slowly shriveled, but it swallowed its much larger rival, the *San Francisco Chronicle,* whose proprietorial families took lessons from the Hatfields and the McCoys. W. R. Hearst was satirized by Orson Welles in *Citizen Kane,* and the men who built the Central Pacific, mostly on the back of Chinese coolies and the largesse of Washington, were reviled as profiteers in their own time and afterward. They were called the Big Four: Leland Stanford, Collis P. Huntington, Charles Crocker, and Mark Hopkins. Their wealth and political power soon became legendary.

For years, San Francisco seemed to get by on beauty, charm, and the spending of strangers, but all that changed at the end of the twentieth century. The area had a history of technological innovation, and high technology, in the form of the computer revolution, generated unimaginable fortunes here in the 1990s. Intel, Hewlett-Packard, and thousands of smaller, less-known companies—hardware companies, software companies, dot-com companies—created something called Silicon Valley, near the southern end of the Bay. A third of all the venture capital invested in America flowed into the valley. Five of the twenty best places to earn a living in the United States, a survey by *Forbes* magazine found in 1999, were within an hour and a half's drive of downtown San Francisco. No wonder people wanted to live here. No wonder the median price for a single-family house in the region rose past $460,000. (In Atherton, a tony suburb, it hit $2.5 million.)

It was too good to last, and it didn't. The dot-com bubble burst in 2000, inflicting deep wounds on San Francisco and the communities around it, and the pain was sharpened by the general economic downturn that followed 9/11. Tourism sagged, hotels slashed their prices, tens of thousands were laid off—10 percent of the Silicon Valley workforce in one year, 5 percent in another—and "For Rent" signs went up in windows all over town.

Biotechnology and medical-device manufacturing eventually took up some of the slack, but not before California was plunged into a fiscal crisis, some of whose causes stretched back several decades. The lackluster governor at the time, Gray Davis, was driven from office in a referendum, to be succeeded by Arnold Schwarzenegger, the iron-pumping, Harley-riding, cigar-loving film star. "It's the most difficult I've made in my entire life," he said of his decision to run, "except the one I made in 1978 when I decided to get a bikini wax."

Meanwhile, San Francisco's omnipresent homeless population swelled by 18 percent to 8,640 one night in October, 2002. Untouched by Silicon Valley's orgasm of prosperity, they continued to beg for money at freeway off-ramps by day, rolling out their sleeping bags by night in the doorways of expensive stores and other buildings, hoping that the police would pretend not to notice. If the police did move in, some of them whipped out their cellular phones and called up television stations to ask them to film the action. Generous welfare policies, broad public tolerance, and ineffectual leadership all contributed to the problem.

The economy notwithstanding, San Francisco went on a cultural tear, cementing its position as the West Coast's arts capital, although Los Angeles is by no means the pothole full of philistines many San Franciscans see when (if) they head south. Inevitably, budgetary woes set in, especially at the San Francisco Opera, the nation's second largest after the Met. With the highest overhead of any West Coast arts organization, it has occupied a privileged position in the city's social life for more than a century, but in fiscal 2002 it ran a $7.6 million deficit, cut two productions and slashed costs by a quarter.

An old autocrat named Kurt Herbert Adler had built the opera's reputation in the 1950s and 1960s, bringing singers like Tebaldi, Schwarzkopf, and Fassbaender to the United States for the first time. Pamela Rosenberg, the general director since 2001, launched an enterprising program centered on broad themes such as the Faust legend, including a staging of Busoni's *Faust,* and seminal works of modern opera, including a production of György Ligeti's *Le Grand Macabre.* The company has never shied away from the little-known, and invited Valery Gergiev to conduct three Prokofiev operas, for instance, including *War and Peace.* In 1999, just before the bust, the opera offered four cycles of

Wagner's immense *Ring of the Nibelungen* at the War Memorial Opera House (the place where the United Nations Charter was signed on June 26, 1945, by representatives of fifty nations). Jane Eaglen, Deborah Voigt, and James Morris were among the gods, demigods, and giants onstage.

Not to be outdone, the city's symphony orchestra mounted an ambitious Stravinsky festival that same year, exploring the composer's work in Russia, Paris, and Los Angeles (where its music director, Michael Tilson Thomas, then in his twenties, knew Stravinsky at the end of his hugely productive career). Successor to luminaries like Monteux and Krips, the lean, adventurous Maestro Thomas is one of only three American-born music directors of major American orchestras (along with Leonard Slatkin in Washington and Andrew Litton in Dallas). MTT, as the local papers like to call him, is one of San Francisco's genuine celebrities these days, a Pied Piper leading the young back into the concert hall. Even a Vienna audience would have been impressed, I think, by a powerful but never bombastic Bruckner Ninth I heard him conduct in Davies Symphony Hall. A protégé of Leonard Bernstein, he is identified, like his mentor, with Gustav Mahler and with contemporary American composers such as John Thow, William Kraft, and John Adams.

The San Francisco Ballet is in the hands of a New York City Ballet alumnus, Helgi Tomasson, who has transformed a regional troupe into a fine classical company since taking over as artistic director in 1985. It's enough to quote Anna Kisselgoff of the *Times,* who proclaimed the troupe "world-class."

All three companies perform in the Civic Center, whose centerpiece is the grandly restored City Hall, with an enormous, echoing rotunda, impressive even to those usually left as cold as a musher's nose in midwinter by civic grandeur. Nearby stand the new public library and the even newer Asian Art Museum, in the old library building. Natural light floods into the museum through angled skylights installed during the adaptation by Gae Aulenti, the Italian wizard who turned a Paris train station into the Musée d'Orsay.

Comparisons are odious, if entertaining, but I would argue that the Asian is Aulenti's best work and San Francisco's best museum. Built around the collection of Avery Brundage, one-time Olympic czar, it contains Japanese, Korean, and Indian works, but the Chinese material is supreme. When the Chinese leader Jiang Zemin visited the museum, he was dazzled by a gilded image of the Buddha from A.D. 338. I'll bet you will be dazzled too, but also intrigued by three twelve-panel painted screens from twelfth- to sixteenth-century Japan, a gloriously embroidered bridal robe from Korea, and a Bollywood-ish throne from nineteenth-century India.

For the moment, the M. H. de Young Museum occupies a quake-weakened, obtrusively buttressed building in Golden Gate Park, but it is constructing a new $135 million home designed by Herzog & de Meuron, the avant-garde architects responsible for the Bankside Tate Modern in London. Paths cutting into the museum, set to open in 2006, will enable visitors to weave in and out of its galleries. The de Young excels in American paintings, from George Caleb Bingham's *Boatmen on the Missouri* to Frederic E. Church's *Rainy Season in the Tropics* to Grant Wood's *Dinner for Threshers*, a plain-faced group portrait that outshines the so over-familiar *American Gothic*. (Many of the best pictures came from Mr. and Mrs. John D. Rockefeller III.)

Founded by the flamboyant Alma de Bretteville Spreckels, whose rich, indulgent husband, Adolph, inherited a sugar fortune, the rebuilt California Palace of the Legion of Honor, the de Young's sister museum, reopened in 1995. It occupies a picturesque site in Lincoln Park overlooking the mighty rust-red pylons of the Golden Gate Bridge, the iconic structure that embodies San Francisco's spirit the way the Statue of Liberty embodies New York's. Its collection centers on European art, mainly French, including a moody *Old Woman* by Georges de la Tour, a powerful off-center portrait by Degas, *The Impresario*, a Monet *Waterlilies*, and some seventy Rodins.

Another vibrant arts district has sprung into being in the redeveloped area south of Market Street, known as SoMa. At its core is the Yerba Buena Center, designed for the many small-scale arts organizations in the Bay Area. It includes galleries by the 1993 Pritzker Prize–winning architect Fumihiko Maki, sheathed in corrugated-aluminum siding yet somehow delicate, and a theater designed by James Stewart Polshek, dark and angular on the inside but more like a jaunty piece of de Stijl sculpture outside. Around the perimeter are a children's entertainment and education center, complete with carousel; the shiny $85 million Metreon, Sony's urban version of a Disney theme park, with an "environment" by Maurice Sendak, visited by 6 million customers a year; the Ansel Adams Center for Photography; and the San Francisco Museum of Modern Art. Scheduled for completion soon are a new Jewish Museum designed by Daniel Libeskind, who created a brilliant one in Berlin, and a new Mexican Museum designed by Ricardo Legorreta.

The big cheese, of course, is the Museum of Modern Art, which has been around since 1935 and is now housed in Mario Botta's landmark building of 1995, with its distinctive truncated cylindrical tower. A bequest from Elise Haas, of the Levi Strauss family, brought it several pictures once owned by Sarah Stein, the sister-in-law of Gertrude, including a breathtaking Matisse, *Femme au Chapeau*. The late Phyllis Wattis, the San Francisco cultural world's chief benefactor (and a great-granddaughter of Brigham Young), gave millions to help buy important pictures by Mondrian, Magritte, Rauschenberg, Ellsworth Kelly, and Brice Marden. But because of the need to rotate pictures, major San Francisco area artists like Richard Diebenkorn and Sam Francis are sometimes underrepresented on the museum's walls.

Frank Lloyd Wright also left his unmistakable mark on the city, with his jewel-like building on Maiden Lane, now the Circle Gallery, a precursor of the Guggenheim in its use of a spiral ramp, and his Buck Rogers–style civic center in suburban Marin County. Architecture buffs will also want to see something of Bernard Maybeck, the individualist who foreshadowed the California Arts and Crafts movement. (The temple-like Palace of Fine Arts near the Golden Gate, left over from the 1915 Panama-Pacific Exposition, and the First Church of Christ, Scientist in Berkeley are his masterworks.) A glacier-white Richard Neutra house, cantilevered over a cliff overlooking the Bay Bridge, is at 56 Calhoun Terrace. And the excess of San Francisco's Gilded Age is vividly displayed in Alma Spreckels's twenty-six-bathroom beaux arts mansion on Pacific Heights. It now belongs to Danielle Steel.

San Francisco has an established social order and lots of Old Money, even a mini–Wall Street. It has a fondness for clubs— the Olympic; the Bohemian, with its grove on the Russian River north of town; and the Pacific Union, whose brown sandstone clubhouse atop Nob Hill once belonged to the silver millionaire James Flood. It is bracketed by two universities of international stature—the University of California at Berkeley, east of the bay, and Stanford University at Palo Alto, south of the city.

As early as 1883, Robert Louis Stevenson remarked on the city's cosmopolitan character, detecting "the airs of Marseilles and Peking" in its streets. Writing in the same vein fifty years later, a later traveler, John Gunther, described San Francisco as "brilliant, polyglot and sophisticated," and said it "will tolerate everything, including the intolerable." It has always embraced rule-breakers. From its very beginnings as an R&R stop for gold rush pioneers, through the wide-open era of Barbary Coast sa- loons to the heyday of North Beach topless bars, featuring the silicone-boosted charms of Carol Doda, San Francisco has been a good-time town, prepared to live and let live.

No one benefited more from San Francisco's forbearance than Willie L. Brown Jr., a black boulevardier who started life as a sharecropper's son, a man with the charm of Cary Grant, the audacity of a jewel thief, and plenty of political smarts. Willie, as they say in San Francisco, seldom specifying his last name, "is a piece of work." Some people bridled at his girl- friends, Italian suits, and flashy cars, but he built an empire in Sacramento during a record fifteen-year tenure as Speaker of the Assembly (1980–95), then won two terms as mayor (1996–2004). He would often attend a half dozen political functions before meeting friends for dinner at a restaurant, then stand at midnight on the street outside, greeting and teasing a few of the tourists who pour into his city (14 million in 2002).

Countercultures have flourished by the bay since World War II. In the 1950s, Columbus Avenue nurtured the Beat Generation and its bards, Jack Kerouac and Allen Ginsberg. In the 1960s came the hippies of Haight-Ashbury, preaching Flower Power, dreaming multicolored dreams, and packing Bill Graham's uproarious rock concerts, and the student rebels of Berkeley, led by Mario Savo. Then, in the 1970s, Huey Newton, from

Oakland, made the Black Panthers the militant voice for the dispossessed of the nation's ghettos. Gay men and lesbians were given an honored place in San Francisco when they were still locked inside the closet in other places. It was inevitable, perhaps, that the American AIDS epidemic hit first and hardest here, but it was still horrifyingly unexpected when the gay activist Harvey Milk, whose election as a supervisor in 1977 had thrilled San Franciscans, was assassinated the next year along with the city's mayor, George R. Moscone. Gavin Newsom, Brown's successor as mayor—young, straight, a hunk—opened the gates of City Hall to same-sex marriages in 2004, triggering a national storm; before California's supreme court barred the practice, 4,037 couples were wed.

As a result of its tolerance, San Francisco attracted a considerable colony of zanies. In 1891, the English novelist Rudyard Kipling characterized it as "a mad city—inhabited for the most part by perfectly insane people, whose women are of remarkable beauty." Maybe Kipling was thinking of Joshua Norton, who proclaimed himself emperor of the United States in 1859 (and advanced the obviously loony notion of a bridge connecting San Francisco and Oakland). I saw one of his spiritual descendants a few springs ago, a portly fellow with full beard and flowing hair, dressed in overalls and railroad engineer's cap, ambling happily along a street in the financial district, blowing soap bubbles from a little pipe.

WHERE TO STAY

Campton Place, 340 Stockton Street, (415) 781-5555. A polished little diamond of a hotel, ideally situated just off Union Square, marred only by a few overly snug bedrooms. The multinational, multilingual staff will jump through hoops to make you comfortable. Several of San Francisco's best chefs have presided in turn in the dining room.

Four Seasons, 757 Market Street, (415) 633-3000. This is the city's premier hotel, a worthy successor to the grandes dames of the past like the St. Francis, the Clift (which went bankrupt under Ian Schrager), and the Fairmont. Located on the edge of SoMa, it offers all the usual Season-al luxuries and facilities—plus superlative service, thanks to the management of Stan Bromley, probably the nation's most accomplished hotelier.

Mandarin Oriental, 222 Sansome Street, (415) 276-9888. In the heart of the financial district yet close to Union Square, Chinatown, and SoMa, this is a spectacular sibling of one of Hong Kong's finest hotels. It occupies floors thirty-eight to forty-eight of a skyscraper, furnished in a svelte Asian style. We stayed once in an amazing suite whose bedroom and bathroom afforded views over both the Bay Bridge and the Golden Gate.

Ritz-Carlton, 600 Stockton Street, (415) 296-7465. As ritzy as they come, perched on the side of Nob Hill, this classic, cos-

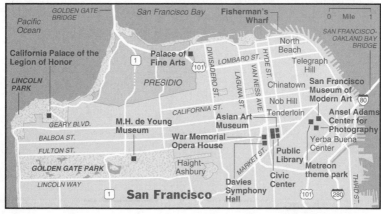

seting hotel is fairly stuffed with marble, crystal, and brocade, and the bedrooms are luxurious in dimension as well as decor. Our family ate an impeccable Thanksgiving dinner one year in Sylvain Portay's elegant dining room, and many San Franciscans consider his everyday meals the best French food in the city.

WHERE TO EAT

Chez Panisse, 1517 Shattuck Avenue, Berkeley, (510) 548-5525. What to say? Alice Waters only gets better in the restaurant she founded in 1971, buying superlative ingredients from small farmers and handling them with reverence. Every night, a balanced, seasonal, six-course set menu is served in an old Craftsman house half hidden by trees. In the final week of May, menus might emphasize fava beans, morels, king salmon, and asparagus. The atmosphere is sometimes a little worshipful, but you can eat nearly as well in the more secular café upstairs.

Fifth Floor, 12 Fourth Street, (415) 348-1555. Laurent Gras is a superstar aborning. Just taste his slow-poached pork belly, an echo of his years with Alain Ducasse in Paris, and his homage to the Pacific—a wafer of toro (tuna belly) seasoned with Hawaiian sea salt, daikon, and lime juice, and topped with Iranian osetra caviar. Notice the absence of cream, the ascension of flavor. Keith Fergel, the sommelier, dispenses great wines.

Gary Danko, 800 North Point Street, (415) 749-2060. Long ago, San Francisco was known for luxurious dens like Ernie's and the Blue Fox. Now it has Gary Danko, chef extraordinaire, pampering his loyalists with pancetta-wrapped frogs' legs and juniper-crusted venison. The range of ripe artisanal cheeses, mostly from California, is unmatched.

Masa's, 648 Bush Street, (415) 989-7154. Masa's has been an institution downtown for decades, and Ron Siegel, a conqueror of the Iron Chef, maintains the tradition with his haute-cuisine menus studded with foie gras and truffles. I love the duck breast with port-soaked dates. Formal service strikes some as overbearing, others as exemplary; classy wines are cleverly paired with each course. If only the tabs were as minimal as the decor!

Oliveto, 5655 College Avenue, Oakland, (510) 547-5356. Close your eyes, and Paul Bertolli will whisk you to the Umbrian countryside. He marries peasant heartiness with city-slicker lightness: house-made salumi, fresh noodles with delicate sand dabs, gnocchi with sage and brown butter, and roast pork bathed in pan juices with fleshy white beans on the side. A friend of ours called the dense chocolate tartufo "heroin on a plate."

Slanted Door, Ferry Building, Market Street at the Embarcadero, (415) 861-8032. You will find no better Vietnamese food anywhere in the United States (or, I daresay, in Vietnam). Relocated to the new culinary crossroads of San Francisco, Charles Phan continues to produce dishes like spring rolls and caramelized shrimp with the finesse of Thomas Keller. The spicy squid and the crab with cellophane noodles aren't so bad, either.

Tadich Grill, 240 California Street, (415) 391-1849. Born with the gold rush, Tadich's turned 150 in 1999. Fabulously fresh local fish, simply prepared, is the Buich family's forte: sand dabs and petrale sole, grilled or pan-fried; the tomato-based seafood stew called cioppino, and peerless Dungeness crab in the shell, in a cocktail, or in a salad. Go for lunch, late, and sit at the king-size, horseshoe-shaped bar or in a curtained booth.

Yank Sing, 101 Spear Street, (415) 957-9300. It's a toss-up between this place and Ton Kiang in the city's dim sum sweepstakes. I tip my hat to Yak Sing because it is cleaner, quieter, and more central. On offer here daily are sixty tasty morsels, including Peking-duck buns and superb, translucent-skinned dumplings filled with lobster, shrimp, or pea shoots. Questions? Ask the waitresses, who are models of cheerful efficiency.

Zuni Cafe, 1658 Market Street, (415) 552-2522. A friend of mine calls Judy Rodgers's Spartan café, with copper bar and roaring wood oven, "the soul of San Francisco." So it is, in its delicious simplicity, whether you order a pristine martini and a plate of oysters at the bar, or a Caesar salad fit for a Caesar, or, if you go late, an unlisted treat: a princely hamburger made from house-brined beef, ground only after you order and served on a focaccia bun.

⟫ LOS ANGELES

My earliest memories of Los Angeles are the wisecracks of radio comedians. Fred Allen, as I recall, described the city as "a nice place to live, if you happen to be an orange." Oscar Levant said that when you stripped away its tinsel, you found more tinsel. I formed an indelible picture of L.A. noir from Bogart and Bacall in *The Big Sleep*, Howard Hawks's sardonic, hard-boiled tale of spoiled rich girls, con men, gunmen, and other rogues, which William Faulkner and others adapted from Raymond Chandler's novel. Later, on television, I was fascinated by Jack Webb as the curt Sergeant Joe Friday in *Dragnet*.

More than anywhere else, Los Angeles has defined itself by popular culture—by the entertainment industry, which is based, after all, in Hollywood. Most of us, Americans and foreigners alike, carry show-business images of Southern California around in our heads. But they are sweepings of reality, snippets of grainy black-and-white or gaudy Technicolor; splicing them together into an accurate picture is a tall order.

One might begin with the idea of the place. For several generations Los Angeles was a twentieth-century Eden, a garden at the continent's edge where almost anything seemed possible. Today much of it is a paradise defiled, spoiled by sprawl, smog, and selfishness. Fires and mud slides, riots and earthquakes have scarred landscapes and psyches. Six days of rioting in 1965 in Watts, a largely black neighborhood on the south side of town, claimed thirty-four lives and caused an estimated $100 million in damage. In 1991, policemen beat Rodney King, a black man, and the incident was captured on videotape, but four officers, all white, were acquitted by a white jury drawn from the suburbs. This time, riots exploded in several parts of Los Angeles County, and state and federal troops were called in. Again, the trouble lasted for six days; when order was finally restored, 54 people were dead, 13,212 had been arrested, and damage was estimated at $700 million. And that was not the end of the troubles. In 1994, an earthquake shook the region, centered in Northridge, twenty miles northwest of downtown in the San Fernando Valley. Highways buckled, several commercial buildings collapsed, and fifty-seven people were killed.

Splendors remain—and not just the chicks on Melrose Avenue and the biceps boys on the beach at Venice. Contemplate the Santa Monica Mountains at dusk, wade into the surf at Malibu, glide through the tunnel of lavender-blue jacaranda blossoms on Palm Drive in Beverly Hills in June, or walk along the placid residential streets of Pasadena, past glorious Arts and Crafts houses by the brothers Charles and Henry Greene, set on broad lawns maintained only by heroic irrigation and the sweat of Mexican gardeners. Then you will understand the lasting allure of this vast, inchoate metropolis by the Pacific. There are days when hibiscus, jasmine, and oleander scent the air, and you imagine yourself in Grasse, the perfume town on the Riviera, as my wife, Betsey, did on our last visit. There are also days when the air is so acrid with exhaust fumes that your eyes sting. On those days, I think of a comment by the novelist John Gregory Dunne: "None of the merry-go-rounds seem to work anymore."

Los Angeles has always traded heavily in glamour and illusion, ephemeral merchandise that is here today and gone tomorrow, like movie sets and the sex appeal of leading ladies. "The back lot was thirty acres of fairyland," wrote F. Scott Fitzgerald in *The Last Tycoon*, "not because the locations really looked like African jungles and French châteaux and schooners at anchor and Broadway at night, but because they looked like the torn picture books of childhood, like fragments of stories dancing in an open fire." Yes, this is a fairyland, the home of hype and hyperbole, but it was also the home of two of the most important presidents of the last century, Richard M. Nixon and Ronald Reagan. Their libraries are nearby—Nixon's in Yorba Linda, where he was born, Reagan's in Simi Valley.

Colonized as El Pueblo de Nuestra Señora la Reina de los

Angeles de Porciuncula in 1781, Los Angeles had but 102,479 people in 1900. Fifty years later, it had 1,970,358, and by 2003 the city and the satellites that surround it had more than 16 million, spilling across 34,000 square miles, over mountains and into the desert. By 2025, demographers say, the region will grow by another 6 million, twice the present population of Chicago.

Explosive growth is creating a radically different society. While the area's black and non-Hispanic white populations remain relatively stable, its Asian (12.6 percent of the total) and Hispanic populations (44.6 percent) are skyrocketing. Drive down the streets in the center of Los Angeles—yes, ye skeptics, there is one—and you see signs written in a Babel of languages and alphabets: Korean and Hindi, Lao and Japanese, Thai and Vietnamese, Russian, Spanish, and Portuguese. As did immigrants in New York in the twentieth century, newcomers give Los Angeles much of its kinetic energy. But they present tremendous challenges. For the foreseeable future, the region will need to build 25,000 new housing units a year, and partly because of the city's seemingly endless expansion, the state needs 300,000 new teachers in short order. The Los Angeles Unified School District is the nation's second biggest, after New York's, with 750,000 pupils; for 42 percent of them English is a second or third language, if they speak it at all. Inevitably, Mayor Richard J. Riordan (1993–2001) made education his top priority. He gained control of the school board in 1999, but acute problems remained when he handed over to Jim Hahn in 2001, and the dropout rate in the district far exceeds the statewide average.

Tom Bradley, an earlier five-term mayor (1973–93), once remarked that Southern California provided people with "a place where they can be free, where they can do things they can't do anywhere else"—things like nude sunbathing, wearing purple hair, or founding oddball sects, both religious (like Aimee Semple McPherson's) and political (like the John Birch Society). People cut themselves loose from the restraints of tradition, obligation, even family. For every fabulous fortune there are graveyards full of shattered dreams. So people don't hold back. If you have a body, you flaunt it; if you have money, you spend it. Buy a Bentley (and take it over to the Bel Air or the Peninsula for lunch so people can see it) and build a narcissist's castle.

Angelenos create and they innovate. They launch fads. Eccentricity reigns, as the poet Ogden Nash observed: "Yes, it is true, Los Angeles is not only erratic, not only erotic, Los Angeles is crotchety, centrifugal, vertiginous, esoteric and exotic." Carey McWilliams, the radical writer and editor of *The Nation*, who knew the place well, described it as "a circus without a tent." The zaniest zaniness of all is the city's love-hate relationship with its cars. "Hand wash" shops are everywhere. People drive two blocks to buy a loaf of bread. They go slowly, exquisitely mad in freeway traffic jams. Hertz sternly warns those who rent its vehicles here, "Unfortunately, many Californians are in a hurry and usually ignore yellow lights (and sometimes red lights)." In *L.A. Story*, Steve Martin had a hilarious go at the car culture, putting pedestrians in gas masks. He lampooned the city's mania for decaf, diets, and nose jobs, its compulsive consumption and its linguistic primitivism. He heard even the traffic signals speaking Valley: "Uh, Like, Don't Walk."

But with so many people from somewhere else panning for gold in Los Angeles, it suffers from a severe identity crisis. It is not so much a city as a concatenation of cities, from Anaheim to Azusa and Cucamonga, as they said on Jack Benny's show. Now more than ever, under the pressure of demographic and economic change, Los Angeles is hard to unify.

The oil and aircraft industries have all but disappeared as bulwarks of the regional economy, and most of the formerly influential banks have been merged into out-of-town institutions. Even *The Los Angeles Times*, once a pillar of the city's civic architecture under the stewardship of the Chandler family, was sold in 2001 to the Tribune Company, the Chicago media conglomerate. These seismic shifts have weakened the city's power structure. Barry Munitz, president of the J. Paul Getty Museum, a preeminent local cultural institution, compared Los Angeles to a ball poised at the top of an incline—stuck up there because of "a lack of enough educational, artistic, civic, economic, and social leaders ready to shoulder the burdens."

The Los Angeles Police Department, with its reputation in tatters, is struggling to eradicate rampant corruption. Already battered by evidence of officers' planting evidence, lying in court, and shooting unarmed suspects, Chief Bernard C. Parks suffered a further humiliation in 2002 when his granddaughter was murdered. William J. Bratton, imported from the East later that year after successful stints as police chief in New York and Boston, has taken up the fight.

Some say that the vernacular architecture, indeed the only architecture, of Los Angeles is the ticky-tacky bungalow. But in fact this is a place packed with architectural fascination, ranging from things that look exactly like what they are—the Tail o' the Pup hot dog stand, an oversized stucco-and-sheet-metal wiener, and the Capitol Records tower, shaped like a stack of 45s—to things that evoke a never-never world, like Mann's (formerly Grauman's) ornate Chinese Theater, whose like never graced the streets of Old Cathay.

In the old downtown, along Broadway, as animated as the new downtown is sterile, stand the Bradbury Building (1896), chaste tan brick on the outside, lacy metalwork and skylighted sparkle inside, and the Grand Central Market (1917), a survival of the city's past, where the ethnic stew of its present simmers. Lawyers and construction workers, African and Mexican and Asian Americans, crowd the aisles, buying tin toys and purslane and chop suey and (if they're smart) following the crowds to Roast to Go, which has been dispensing the city's best tacos since 1952—soft tortillas filled with hand-chopped pork (or hog maw or tripe, your choice) with spicy red sauce.

The Gamble House in Pasadena (1908), a private house that is now a museum, with hand-finished woodwork of unmatched elegance, is the Arts and Crafts masterwork of Charles and Henry Greene, brothers and celebrated architects. Art Deco landmarks stand along Wilshire Boulevard, including the zigzag Moderne tower of the old Bullocks department store (1928). For the main public library downtown (1930), topped with a gilded hand holding aloft the torch of truth, Bertram G. Goodhue adopted a more pared-down if richly allusive Deco style, and in the Textile District, Robert Derrah built a streamlined Moderne icon for Coca-Cola (1937), a bottling plant masquerading as a cream-and-scarlet ocean liner, complete with portholes, gangways, and a flying bridge.

Frank Lloyd Wright wrought some of his marvels in the hills and canyons on the north side of town. Most of them are private, but two are open episodically to the public: the decaying Hollyhock House (1920), containing much of its original furniture, and the Ennis-Brown House (1924), a cliffside "Mayan" temple in patterned concrete block.

A pair of Vienna-born architects, Richard Neutra and Rudolph Schindler, created what we know as the California style. Neutra's Lovell House (1929), near the Ennis-Brown House, is a stack of gray-and-white steel-and-stucco planes jutting from a hillside, perhaps as good a modern building as California has. It remains a private residence, but the innovative, Japanese-influenced little house that Schindler designed for himself in Hollywood in 1922, a set of rooms using utilitarian materials (glass, redwood, concrete, and canvas), with sliding walls that open onto gardens, has been made into a museum. The British architectural historian Reyner Banham wrote that the house is so original it looks "as if there had never been houses before." Yet a hungry developer has jeopardized its leafy setting by proposing to build a condominium right in its shadow.

Frank O. Gehry, the architect of the moment, triumphant in Bilbao, planning great things all over the world, lives in Los Angeles and has done some of his best work there, starting with a minimalist Hollywood studio for Lou Danziger (1964) and continuing with the Dutch-gabled cottage in Santa Monica that he rebuilt starting in 1978 (what must the neighbors have thought?), using plywood and chain-link fencing. Showy though he often is, Gehry can also work almost anonymously. He turned a dingy police department garage into the Geffen Contemporary, a successful branch of the Museum of Contemporary Art, with a simple series of baffles and platforms, and he opened the formerly dark and disorganized Norton Simon Museum into a light, free-flowing series of galleries.

The stainless steel spinnakers that shape the Walt Disney Concert Hall may well mark the apex of Gehry's career. The epic ten-year struggle to build it certainly illustrates the disconnect between high culture and pop culture in Los Angeles. When it opened in 2003, with the Los Angeles Philharmonic in residence, it won almost universal, perhaps excessive praise for its looks and its acoustics (aided by a timbered auditorium). One gushing critic said the building shows that "the values of modern democracy can be translated into modern form." Others predict it will come to symbolize L.A. as the Opera House symbolizes Sydney. But except for the Walt Disney Company, none of Hollywood's studios, whose executives make millions of dollars, and very few of their stars contributed a dime. Without the exertions of the city's number one supporter of the arts, Eli Broad, who heads the SunAmerica company, the fund-raising drive might have foundered. Broad (the name rhymes with "road") made his money on annuities, not movies.

Gehry's masterpiece is the latest attempt to make downtown's heart beat again, along with the massive, dignified Los Angeles Cathedral, designed by the Spaniard José Rafael Moneo, an asymmetrical study in ocher that has drawn standing-room-only crowds to its Spanish-language masses since opening in 2002. The resuscitation began with the $375 million Staples Center, a multipurpose arena built in 1999 that has played host to the Los Angeles Lakers, the Rolling Stones, and the 2000 Democratic National Convention. Perhaps most important, vacant factories, banks, and office buildings have been turned into lofts, 4,000 of them, raising hopes that L.A. will finally have a viable, twenty-four-hour core. Restaurants and hotels are opening, and people have actually begun walking.

Locals decry the city's lack of a professional football team, and they complain about the teams the city does have, which (except for the Lakers) lose so often that sports columnists rant and rave about Loss Angeles. Of course there is always Hollywood. The city's most visible industry is film, generating more than $31 billion a year. From D. W. Griffith to Marilyn Monroe to Steven Spielberg, film has carried Hollywood's melodramatic values around the globe. Television joins in the pop culture wars, portraying an unreal world filled with youth, beauty, and virility. Legions of gawkers flock to Hollywood Boulevard, hoping, like the hicks in Nathanael West's memorable Hollywood novel, *The Day of the Locust*, to catch a glimpse of a celebrity—any celebrity. Against all expectations, Hollywood has also functioned as a kind of political farm system, nurturing Ronald Reagan, George Murphy, a hoofer turned senator, and Arnold Schwarzenegger, a muscle-builder, an actor, and now the governor.

But the city need make no apology for its intellectual and

artistic life, even if New Yorkers and San Franciscans often talk as if culture in Southern California were confined to yogurt. Two major local universities, the University of Southern California and the University of California at Los Angeles—the Trojans and the Bruins—compete with each other both academically and athletically, and both have a number of strong departments. Faculty members and graduates of the renowned California Institute of Technology in nearby Pasadena, known as Cal Tech, have won twenty-nine Nobel prizes, among them the witty physicist Richard Feynman and the idealistic chemist Linus Pauling, who won twice. The Claremont Colleges, thirty-five miles east of Los Angeles near the San Gabriel Mountains, are regularly ranked among the nation's top small liberal-arts institutions.

Conducted by the hip, vibrant young Finn Esa-Pekka Salonen and managed by the highly regarded Deborah Borda, who resigned from the New York Philharmonic to move west, the Philharmonic plays not only in downtown Los Angeles but also under the stars in the Hollywood Bowl, which got a magnificent new concert shell in 2004. It ranks among the nation's best orchestras, a peer of the traditional Big Five bands in Boston, Philadelphia, New York, Cleveland, and Chicago, with a budget second only to Boston's. The city's musical life deepened greatly during the war years and afterward, when both Igor Stravinsky and Arnold Schoenberg lived here, as well as many great performers, like Jascha Heifetz.

The orchestra has had a long series of outstanding conductors, among them Otto Klemperer, Zubin Mehta, and Carlo Maria Giulini, but none achieved as much as Salonen. He chose Mahler, Haydn, and Lutaslowski for the orchestra's first season in the new hall and did them all proud. Its endowment is slim, but the orchestra operates in the black.

Hollywood actors and directors do not often lend their talents to the legitimate stage in Los Angeles; many limit their work to the movies, and some prefer the London or New York theater; but there are significant exceptions. In recent years, stars like Donald Sutherland, Al Pacino, Piper Laurie, and Frances Sternhagen were seen at the Mark Taper Forum and Ahmanson Theater. The Taper specializes in premieres of new works by important playwrights like August Wilson and Tony Kushner.

Not until the arrival in 1984 of Peter Hemmings, a gentlemanly English arts administrator, did the Los Angeles Opera spring to life. The great Spanish tenor Plácido Domingo is its artistic director (he holds the same title in Washington), and Kent Nagano, a respected young American with extensive European experience (Lyon, Salzburg), will continue as its music director until 2006, when James Conlon, who has a similar background, is to succeed him. Domingo sings and conducts as well as running the operation.

On a limited budget—$20 million versus San Francisco's $50 million and the Met's $170 million—Hemmings nurtured the company through adolescence and lured some big Tinseltown talents to the Chandler Pavilion as designers and directors, including the painter David Hockney and the director Herb Ross. Hockney's designs for Strauss's *Die Frau ohne Schatten* and Robert Wilson's setting of *Madama Butterfly* won international acclaim, and Domingo has doubled the budget to $48 million in his first five years at the helm and brought in Garry Marshall and William Friedkin to direct.

All Los Angeles wants to see Richard Meier's Getty Center, a series of interconnected travertine and enameled aluminum pavilions built in 1997 on an isolated hilltop near the western end of Sunset Boulevard. From afar, it looks like a village on a Greek island; up close, it feels like a multidecked ocean liner. The center was built to house J. Paul Getty's collection, once in a museum in Malibu, and also as a research and conference center. About 1.3 million people a year visit the Getty Museum, many of them just to see the gardens and the views. It is chic in certain circles in Los Angeles to say that the collection isn't up to the building, but not everyone agrees. Not people who like Masaccio and Mantegna, or F. X. Winterhalter, the sadly underesteemed portraitist of European empire. Surely not students of Rembrandt, who is represented here by two of his most vibrant portraits. As for van Gogh's *Irises*, it could seduce a stone.

In Pasadena, the great names march with equal if not greater majesty through the halls of the Norton Simon Museum: Giovanni di Paolo, Bellini, van Gogh again (his best *Mulberry Tree*), Cézanne, Klee; reaching a climax in Zurbarán's exquisite little *Still Life with Lemons, Orange and a Rose*. It is one of the world's choice small collections. A mile or so away, in manicured San Marino, the Huntington Library offers great manuscripts, a recently acquired Greene and Greene collection, a William Morris collection, thousands of roses and camellias, and Gainsborough's famous *Blue Boy*.

The biggest museum in town, the Los Angeles County Museum of Art, is a work in progress, with a major building and reorganization program incomplete. Only thirty-six years old, it has put together an encyclopedic collection of some 150,000 works of art, including an extensive group of German Expressionist paintings, but it cannot match the Getty's staggering financial resources. The Museum of Contemporary Art, whose red sandstone building was the Japanese architect Arata Isozaki's first American commission (1987), has acquired hundreds of works recently in a bid to keep pace with its rival, the San Francisco Museum of Modern Art, which spent $125 million in two years.

"There are fine high-culture facilities here," said Tom Werner, who produced, with his partner Marcy Carsey, successful situation comedies in the 1990s. "But it isn't really that sort of place. When I was growing up in Manhattan, when it rained on Saturday, my mother took me to the Metropolitan Museum. When it rained on Sunday, she dragged me to hear Leonard Bernstein's concerts. Here, it never rains on weekends."

WHERE TO STAY

Bel Air, 701 Stone Canyon Road, Bel Air, (310) 472-1211. Britain's *Tatler* magazine chose this as its Hotel of the Millennium, which is not far off the mark. The Bel Air never, ever lapses into Hollywood-style ostentation, creating instead the illusion that you're staying with rich, very relaxed friends. Gardenias and birds-of-paradise bloom in twelve lush acres of gardens. Superb food on a terrace overlooking a swan-filled pond.

Casa Del Mar, 1910 Ocean Way, Santa Monica, (310) 581-5533. Built in 1926, this was a favorite playpen of the stars in Hollywood's heyday. Flawlessly restored, it faces the Pacific across a broad beach near the Santa Monica Pier. Nothing is commonplace. The 129 guest rooms, decorated in pale, sherbety tones, are outfitted with wood-slatted venetian blinds, and rubber duckies wait beside Jacuzzi tubs to soothe the road-weary.

Raffles L'Ermitage, 9291 Burton Way, Beverly Hills, (310) 278-3344. Tucked into a residential neighborhood, L'Ermitage is sleek, serene, and stylish. Guest rooms have three phone lines, plus a cell phone, 40-inch television set, DVD player, and bar with free soft drinks; sycamore panels slide shut to divide sleeping areas from dressing rooms.

Peninsula, 9882 South Santa Monica Boulevard, Beverly Hills, (310) 551-2888. Bentleys and Ferraris crowd the courtyard,

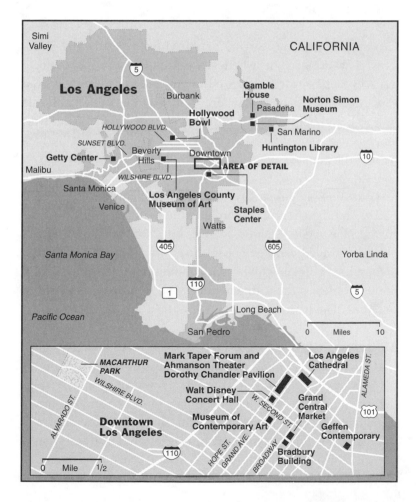

and weird and wonderful people populate the lobby; this is a prime showbiz port of call. But even the lowly get Frette sheets on their beds, oversized towels, fresh-fruit still lifes, and breakfast served on Limoges china.

WHERE TO EAT

Bastide, 8475 Melrose Place, (323) 651-5950. A new star, this, with Provence-tinged French cooking by Ludovic Lefebvre, an alumnus of the admired L'Orangerie. Sea scallops are perfumed with fennel, Pernod, and lemon; a veal daube, as wine-dark as Homer's sea, is rustic, cool-day food. Decor by Andrée Putman.

Chinois, 2709 Main Street, Santa Monica, (310) 392-9025. This is where I embellished my reputation as a pop-culture guru by failing to recognize either Gwyneth Paltrow or Brad Pitt. More important, it is where Wolfgang Puck put California in a wok and begat delightful dishes like Shanghai lobster with ginger curry sauce. After twenty years, the gold-faced Buddha behind the bar still surveys a noisy, well-fed crowd nightly.

Lucques, 8474 Melrose Avenue, West Hollywood, (323) 655-6277. An offshoot of Campanile, which is itself enjoying a deserved new vogue, Lucques is hot, hot, hot. In Harold Lloyd's old brick-walled carriage house, Suzanne Goin whips up lusty dishes like a Technicolor salad of heirloom tomatoes and a bone-in rib-eye steak with pan juices and a gratin of thinly sliced potatoes. The barmen mix the town's best dry martinis.

Matsuhisa, 129 North La Cienega Boulevard, Beverly Hills, (310) 659-9639. From this unprepossessing little place grew Nobu Matsuhisa's worldwide empire. The sushi approaches perfection; notice the marbling of the pale pink toro and the subtle crunch of the fried soft-shell crab roll. But also try the black cod marinated for three days in miso, or the fabulous fried oysters bathed in a spicy, garlicky sauce. Best at the bar at off-hours.

Philippe, 1001 North Alameda Street, Los Angeles, (213) 628-3781. Philippe (say fill-EEP-ay) sells a million French dip sandwiches a year to a motley cast of customers. The sandwich was invented here in 1918. Stand in line, shuffle your feet in the sawdust on the floor, order a twice-dipped beef with coleslaw and potato salad, both delicious, on the side. Then slather the sandwich with the house's hot mustard and dig in.

Spago Beverly Hills, 176 North Canon Drive, Beverly Hills, (310) 385-0880. Wolfgang Puck's surprisingly unsnobby, unshowbizzy flagship has no weaknesses. Lee Hefter has shaped a winning menu ranging from authentic Wiener schnitzel to sweet-corn agnolotti. Sherry Yard prowls farmers' markets for fruit in peak form for her succulently simple desserts (boysenberries and sugar-lipped peaches on our last visit). Great wines.

Valentino, 3115 Pico Boulevard, Santa Monica, (310) 829-4313. Like my friend David Shaw of *The Los Angeles Times*, I know no better Italian restaurant in the United States, nor any better wine list. Forget about the menu; put yourself in the hands of Piero Selvaggio, the suave, warmhearted Sicilian-born owner. He will give you a taste of this and a sip of that: for instance, subtler bresaola and richer Chianti than you ever imagined.

ⓘⓘⓘ▶ SAN DIEGO

San Diego is a hard city to squeeze into a phrase. For starters, it has been a Navy and Marine Corps base since 1846. Capitalizing on one of the Pacific Coast's best harbors, rivaled only by San Francisco's and Seattle's, the armed services have made the San Diego area the world's biggest military complex, home to 108,000 sailors and marines, 128,000 family members, 21,000 civilian employees, and 59,000 retirees. Tom Cruise and the other jet-jocks in *Top Gun* flew out of San Diego's Miramar Naval Air Station.

It is an island of prosperity little blemished by California's fiscal crisis, a tourist town with a Victorian Gaslamp District beloved of vacationing families and conventiongoers. Long outclassed as a lure for food lovers by Los Angeles and San Francisco, it has developed a vibrant roster of restaurants. Its innovative, world-class zoo and remarkable 1,800-acre Wild Animal Park, thirty miles northeast, draw throngs every day. So does Sea World, a marine park whose painfully hokey style never fazes fans of Shamu, the whale. And Mexico—Tijuana, Baja California, and the rest—begins a few minutes from San Diego's southern boundary.

It is also a university town. The University of California at San Diego, only forty-five years old, has built a global reputation in such diverse fields as bioengineering, genetics, oceanography, and neuroscience, spinning off science-based businesses along the way; Qualcomm, a world leader in wireless technology, is perhaps the best known. UCSD has eleven Nobel laureates on its faculty, and seven others have taught there in the past. The university has been designated as one of the two national supercomputer centers.

It is a mecca for sportsmen, with swimming, surfing and tennis; hang gliding above the cliffs at La Jolla; golf at championship courses like Torrey Pines and La Costa, using gear made by companies like Callaway, Taylor Made, Cobra, Titleist, and Lynx, all based at Carlsbad, just up the coast; and sailing out of America's Cup Harbor, made famous by Dennis Conner. What makes much of this possible is the benign climate, and people who live here talk constantly about their climatic blessings. "The weather is the main thing that shapes this place," said James L. Bowers, a philanthropic consultant who moved to San Diego from New York. "In three decades as a San Diegan, I've never worn a coat, summer or winter." Another transplant, Professor Samuel Popkin of UCSD, added this: "The five minutes of sun you get every day walking to your car in winter adds up. San Diego mothers look as healthy as Washington daughters."

People used to look upon San Diego as urban vanilla pudding or white bread, more Midwestern than the Midwest. Its newspapers, owned by the Copley family, uncritically boosted the city and backed conservative politicians and values. One of their editors was Herbert G. Klein, a strategist and spokesman for Richard M. Nixon. If San Diego was bland, La Jolla, the gilded enclave north of downtown, was blander still. The mystery writer Raymond Chandler, who spent the last thirteen years of his life here, called it "a town of arthritic billionaires and barren old women." He said he longed to stand naked at high noon on the main drag, Girard Avenue, and shout four-letter words, but he never did it (and La Jolla, to tell the truth, has more to offer than he recognized).

Before World War II, San Diego had a population of only 150,000. During the war, a single Consolidated Vultee Aircraft factory employed 48,000 workers, and the naval bases were swollen with troops on their way to the Pacific Theater of Operations. Those who stayed on after the war were mostly white people escaping dead-end jobs, cold winters, and moribund older cities. They joined retired naval officers, who congregated on Coronado, an almost-island connected to the mainland by a sandspit.

But the city is yeastier now. A funny thing happened to it on its way to a population of 1.3 million (2.8 million in San Diego County): Asian and Hispanic migrants arrived in quantity. Along with eggheads attracted by new high-tech ventures, they helped to give the region a vastly more cosmopolitan atmosphere. As of 2003, 27 percent of the city's population was Hispanic and 14 percent was Asian American. You can eat Thai, Chinese, Vietnamese, Korean, and Singaporean on Convoy Street.

At about the same time, San Diego became something of a magnet, like other California urban areas before it, for wackos and weirdos. In 1997, the country glimpsed a far more lurid side of life here with the mass suicide of thirty-nine members of a cult that called itself Heaven's Gate, in Rancho Santa Fe, previously known only as an elite resort and residential community.

For better and for worse, San Diego has taken its place among the nation's biggest cities, ranking seventh in population (but seventeenth among metropolitan areas). A new ballpark and new high-rise hotels grace the skyline, and superb if overcrowded freeways link homes, shops, offices, and seventy-plus miles of sandy, unsullied beaches. The city is young, though, still in the throes of becoming. Many profoundly regret its rapid growth, just as many did when it was much smaller.

And with big-city status came big-city woes: in 2003, the indictment of three councilmen for taking bribes; and in 2004, a burgeoning city pension-fund scandal so dire that *The New York Times* labeled San Diego Enron-by-the-Sea.

Neil Morgan of the *San Diego Union-Tribune* has spent years reminding San Diego that it is no longer a cozy little corner of the country. He wrote in one column that the time had arrived for the people of San Diego "to decide finally who we'd really like to be when we grow up." Still prodding away, Morgan recently complained that governments "work and plan just as they did for the middle-size, middle-class city we always thought we were. We have not yet understood our new identity."

If anything epitomizes San Diego, it is Balboa Park, a verdant 1,200-acre enclave only a few blocks from downtown. Locals treasure it and vociferously defend it, and why not? It houses not only the zoo but also a fistful of first-rate museums; one of the city's best theaters, the Old Globe, a replica of the similarly named house in Shakespeare's London, and a magnificent outdoor organ with 4,518 pipes (donated by the Spreckels family, one of the city's wealthiest, which made its first millions in sugar). All that plus miles of flower beds and trails, punctuated by lovely fountains and grand, century-old shade trees. The park dates from 1915, when San Diego held a yearlong world fair, the Panama-California Exposition, to mark the opening of the Panama Canal. Bertram D. Goodhue, an Easterner, was chosen as the architect. Although he built Nebraska's capitol in a vaguely Art Deco style and the chapel at West Point along neo-Gothic lines, he chose something altogether different for San Diego—a hybrid of Spanish Renaissance and Mexican colonial styles, heavily encrusted with stonework as ornate as the finest lace. For decades thereafter, what Goodhue created in Balboa Park reigned as the Spanish Colonial Revival style, adapted for tens of thousands of houses across the nation.

Space, railroad, sports, photography, and folk art museums count among the park's gems. When I was last there, the latter, called the Mingei International Museum, was graced by seven of Niki de Saint Phalle's oversized, Seussian creatures, whose mirrored and enameled surfaces glistened appealingly in the sun. Two museums concentrate primarily on paintings and sculpture. The San Diego Museum of Art has a collection strong in Spanish, Italian, and American works (notice the three exquisite little depictions of peaches by Raphaelle Peale and one of Morgan Russell's rare Synchronist studies). John Singleton Copley's masterpiece, *Mrs. Thomas Gage*, a portrait of an aristocratic Englishwoman with liquid brown eyes, hangs at the smaller Timken Museum of Art.

The zoo, which draws 3.2 million visitors a year, is San Diego's premier attraction. Largely supported by private funds, it has pioneered the use of landscaped habitats, with moats replacing cages, and in 1975 began a program to reproduce endangered species like the giant panda. (Four pandas, including Mei Sheng, a male cub, are currently in residence.) Unlike many, this zoo, which houses more than 800 kinds of animals, pays as much attention to flora as fauna, maintaining a collection of 6,500 botanical species. On many days the Polar Bear Plunge presents a captivating sight as one of the gigantic carnivores frolics on and underneath a white plastic "ice floe" in the moat.

Serious music has had a harder time. The opera company,

though not of national stature, attracts good audiences to varied, ambitious programs. Australian-born Ian Campbell, the general director for two decades, mounts works like *Katya Kabanova* and *The Pearl Fishers* as well as the Italian standards. But dance is a bit of a stranger, and the San Diego Symphony went bust in 1996, returning only in 1998. All that changed in January 2002, when Irwin Jacobs, the erstwhile computer science professor who founded Qualcomm, gave the orchestra $120 million—the largest donation ever made to a symphony orchestra, which put the ensemble on the musical map; the appointment of Jahja Ling as music director underlined the point. Born in Jakarta, of Chinese descent, Ling is a protégé of the celebrated maestro Christoph von Dohnányi.

The highlight of the performing arts scene may well be chamber music, particularly the intimate, warmly collegial La Jolla Summerfest each August, put on by the same organization that presents big-league concerts in La Jolla and San Diego. The young Taiwanese American violinist Cho-Liang Lin heads the festival, which regularly attracts musicians of the caliber of Yefim Bronfman, Gil Shaham, and Ralph Kirshbaum.

But it is the sea, not high culture, that brings people to San Diego, and there is no better way to savor the area than to wander south along the coast from Del Mar (where Bing Crosby once owned a piece of the racetrack) to Point Loma, the most southwesterly point in the continental United States. You could pause at Torrey Pines State Reserve, an unspoiled seaside tract of rugged ravines and sandstone cliffs, which glow red in the setting sun and lurk menacingly in the frequent fogs. Most of the world's remaining Torrey pines, fewer than 5,000 of them, are concentrated there—beautiful, wind-contorted trees that bear needles in clusters of five.

Ellen Browning Scripps, the philanthropic sister of the publisher E. W. Scripps, bought and saved these trees for posterity. Her dollars also shaped La Jolla, endowing the Scripps Institution of Oceanography, whose new Birch Aquarium opened in 1992, the Scripps Clinic, and the Scripps Memorial Hospital. Miss Scripps was the principal patron of the trailblazing architect Irving J. Gill, whose elegantly minimalist buildings, on which cornices and window moldings and pediments are all discarded in favor of unembellished surfaces and simple yet memorably graceful arches, dominate a whole section of La Jolla. Gill's work is astonishingly similar to that of Adolph Loos in Vienna, although the two appear to have known little if anything of each other. His buildings are not widely known today, yet the art historian Henry-Russell Hitchcock writes that "his best houses extend very notably the range of achievement of the first generation of modern architects."

Three buildings—the Bishop's School, the beautiful La Jolla Women's Club (1912–14) and Ellen Browning Scripps's own house, converted by Robert Venturi for San Diego's Museum of Contemporary Art—are within easy walking distance of one another. Downtown, the early Marston House, near Balboa Park, and the remarkably restored First Church of Christ, Scientist, at the corner of Second Avenue and Laurel Street, can both be visited. The museum that Venturi fashioned from Scripps's house is a tour de force of adaptive restoration, and its collection includes a fine assembly of present-day art, including works by Californians like Ed Ruscha, John Baldessari, and Bruce Nauman.

La Jolla offers other seaside pleasures as well, including the La Jolla Playhouse, founded by Gregory Peck and some of his Hollywood pals. One of San Diego's main stages, along with the Old Globe and San Diego Repertory Theater downtown, the playhouse produces many plays that go on to New York.

Then there is the campus of the Salk Institute, the research center founded by Dr. Jonas Salk, the conqueror of polio. Designed by Louis I. Kahn, it is composed of two mirror-image six-story buildings, built of teak, glass, and unfinished concrete, facing each other across a travertine plaza bisected by a narrow canal. The angled facades of the buildings set up a powerful rhythm, seeming to recede into infinity, like some renaissance study of perspective, and the little waterway appears to empty into the Pacific beyond.

To pass instantly from high culture to pop culture, all you need do, dude, is head a few miles south to the point where Garnet Avenue reaches the sea. There stand two local institutions, the Crystal Pier Hotel, a motel built on a pier over the ocean, and Kono's Café, with a perpetual queue of customers waiting for egg burritos. On the boardwalk that runs along the sand (a concrete walk, actually, but why quibble?), a Pacific Beach world passes in review each morning, crying out for a twenty-first-century Brueghel to immortalize it. There are joggers and skateboarders, bicyclists and riders of a kind of stand-up tricycle known as a California Chariot; there are bums smoking nasty butts and mothers pushing or pulling three-wheeled prams and hundreds of Rollerbladers, some gliding as if they had been born on the things, others wobbling as if they had been born to fall down. In a few moments one fine August morning, my wife, Betsey, and I saw an aging hippie with a ponytail and a Colonel Sanders beard, and numberless ancient women who had clearly spent a lifetime ignoring American Cancer Society warnings about too much sun, and inevitably, I suppose, a burly man with a green macaw perched on his shoulder.

Finally to Point Loma, where both San Diego and modern California got their starts. On September 28, 1542, the explorer Juan Rodríguez Cabrillo sailed past this rocky promontory and into the bay of what is now San Diego. Standing today near the old lighthouse, looking down at jets taking off from the airport, skyscrapers clustered downtown, and tens of thousands of sailboat masts rising from marinas, I found it hard to imagine the virginal landscape that greeted him.

To get any real understanding of the isolation of the Spaniards who explored this territory, you have to head back inland, eight miles up the San Diego River. There in 1774 Father Junípero Serra built the Mission of San Diego de Alcala, the first of a chain of twenty-one missions along the coast. This is a neighborhood of freeways and subdivisions now, but as you visit the little cell where Father Serra lived, and stand in the garden beneath the pristine facade of the mission's bell tower, you may be able to conjure up a picture, if only barely, of how limitless this new continent must have looked to him and how distant Madrid must have seemed.

WHERE TO STAY

Del Coronado, 1500 Orange Avenue, (619) 435-6611. Very few hotels offer as much history with a night's rest as this turreted Victorian landmark, built in 1888 of white clapboard and red shingles and regularly updated since, with evident TLC. Wallis Simpson and the Prince of Wales may have met at the Del; Monroe & company cavorted there in *Some Like It Hot*. It boasts 688 rooms (ask for a junior suite in the original building), eight posh oceanfront cottages, a beach, two pools, and unforgettable sunsets.

La Valencia, 1132 Prospect Street, La Jolla, (858) 454-0771, is a cluster of pink buildings overlooking the Pacific, offering a taste of yesteryear in downtown La Jolla. A friend of mine recalls seeing Gregory Peck and his wife climbing out of a convertible and sweeping into the lobby, which seems perfect for this classic establishment, built in 1926. Some of the rooms are small, but none lack charm, and the service is flawless.

Lodge at Torrey Pines, 11480 North Torrey Pines Road, La Jolla, (858) 453-4420. Built in the Craftsman style, just off the eighteenth fairway of a championship golf course between La Jolla and Del Mar, the Lodge is the area's Latest Big Thing. Among many attractions are a bluff-top site above the ocean, guaranteed tee-times, rooms that average an ample 520 square feet, six acres of grounds, and a first-class restaurant (see below).

Rancho Valencia, 5921 Valencia Circle, Rancho Santa Fe, (858) 756-1123. This breathtaking hideaway, a half hour north of San Diego, is the California dream writ large. Tucked into luxuriant vegetation and surrounded by tropical flowers, casita suites of rustic refinement offer every comfort, including dressing rooms and freshly squeezed orange juice delivered with your morning paper. The tennis facilities (eighteen hard courts in a garden setting) are exemplary, as is the croquet lawn. Bountiful brunches on Sunday.

W, 421 West B Street, (619) 231-8220. Hip, hot, and happening, in a most un–San Diego way, with black-clad desk clerks and 261 sleek, tech-equipped rooms, the new W is the talk of the town. Successful? It reportedly sells $100,000 worth of liquor each weekend. Beach, the rooftop bar, has a heated sand floor, and Rice, the top-of-the-line dining room, serves Pacific Rim extravaganzas like miso-glazed swordfish with mango-cilantro rice.

Westgate, 1055 Second Avenue, (619) 238-1818. This is San Diego's premier downtown hotel, a courtly, traditional establishment with crystal chandeliers and Oriental rugs, housed in a 1970s tower. Spectacular views over the bay from the guest rooms on the upper floors, which are distinguished by absolute quiet and generous proportions.

WHERE TO EAT

A. R. Valentien, in the Lodge at Torrey Pines (see above), (858) 777-6635. Named for a noted San Diego plein air painter, this is the domain of a talented, beret-wearing young chef named Jeff Jackson, who is obsessed with ingredients at the peak of their seasons (not so hard to find with the celebrated Chino Farms just up the road). His cooking is deliciously pared-down, as exemplified by his line-caught king salmon with morels and green garlic, and his voluptuously juicy roast chicken served on leeks melted in butter.

Cien Anos, Sanchez Taboada 10451, Tijuana, 011-52 (664) 686-6679. No tacos in sight here. This dramatic multilevel restaurant, not far south of the border, both delights and enlightens with its sophisticated Mexican food, mostly prepared from century-old recipes: octopus stewed with chilies and herbs, crepes stuffed with the hauntingly flavored corn fungus called huitlacoche, and grilled chicken in tangy tamarind sauce.

George's at the Cove, 1250 Prospect Street, La Jolla, (858) 454-4244, has been lifted into a whole new league by Trey Foshee. Forget about the ocean view and pay attention to your plate. If you're lucky, you might get to sample Foshee's sea urchin bruschetta, an inspired juxtaposition of creamy, salty roe with crisp, peppery radish slices, or his red-fleshed strawberry figs with goat cheese and balsamic vinegar. Pow!

Laurel, 505 Laurel Street, (619) 239-2222. Laurel is a kind of San Diego agora, a handsome, relaxing space busy with business lunches, pre-theater dinners, and late-night suppers. Amy DiBiase has proved a capable successor to Douglas Organ, the founding chef, turning out winners like a Roquefort and onion tart, Moroccan-spiced lamb with an eggplant-and-tomato tagine, Kobe beef beneath a sheet of Hudson Valley foie gras (twenty-first-century tournedos Rossini), and butterscotch pot de crème. Knowledgeably chosen wines.

Parallel 33, 741 West Washington Street, (619) 260-0033. I first encountered tiny Amiko Gubbins at the exuberant Café Japengo. Now she has her own stylish restaurant, based on the fact that San Diego, Japan, China, Morocco, and other culinar-

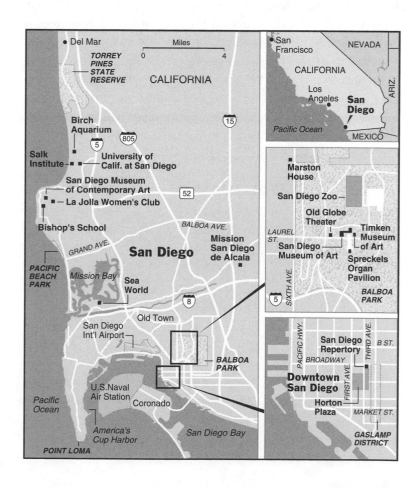

ily intriguing places lie at roughly the same latitude. She dances deftly from cuisine to cuisine, from Moroccan b'stilla to striped bass with yuzu sauce to Shanghai noodles dressed with crab.

Point Loma Seafoods, 2805 Emerson Street, (619) 223-1109. San Diego is not the greatest town for formal dining, but its casual spots are dandy—like this lively waterfront market and carryout whose cases hold a wealth of fresh and smoked fish. They make the definitive tuna sandwich from sourdough bread and freshly caught, home-baked albacore. Also shellfish salads, premium chowders, and San Diego's fast food of choice, the fish taco— fried pollock, shredded cabbage, and sauces, wrapped in a tortilla.

Tapenade, 7612 Fay Avenue, La Jolla, (858) 551-7500. This is that rare and elusive bird, a real French bistro with real French food, cooked by a real Frenchman, Jean-Michel Diot, who grew up near Lyon (where else?). Service can be shaky if Sylvie Diot is off for the night, but there's nothing problematic about the food, whether traditional (an ethereal puff-pastry tomato tart with basil oil, serious steak frites, full-flavored Scottish red partridge and hare) or innovative (tuna carpaccio with ginger).

⫸ HONOLULU

The mythic, exotic Honolulu of grass skirts and towering palms has been familiar to Americans for generations. In 1866 Mark Twain came to Hawaii as a special correspondent for *The Sacramento Union*, extolling the beauty of "the dusky native women" in his dispatches and marveling at "a summer calm as tranquil as dawn in the garden of Eden." A century later, the biographer Leon Edel found "a beatitude of the leisure life," with fallen hibiscus and plumeria blossoms carpeting his lawn.

Our grandfathers listened to Webley Edwards and his long-running radio show, *Hawaii Calls*. They heard Bing Crosby crooning "Sweet Leilani." Some of them sailed west on the luxurious Matson liner *Lurline* and discovered the charms of the ukulele, the lei, and the muumuu, as well as the then-unfamiliar flavors of fresh coconut and pineapple. The handsome Duke Kahanamoku won Olympic gold medals in swimming both in 1912 and 1920 and later introduced the world to surfing, which he learned on the beach at Waikiki. In bronze, he stands there today. Statehood and jumbo jets brought later generations to a more worldly city, made increasingly famous by celluloid images: Burt Lancaster and Deborah Kerr making love, or so we assumed, on a deserted beach; Elvis Presley singing "Can't Help Falling in Love" in *Blue Hawaii*; and, on the small screen, Jack Lord in *Hawaii Five-O*. In 1931 Ellery J. Chun, a Yale-educated tailor, gave Honolulu one of its enduring emblems, the luridly colored aloha shirt, a classic of kitsch couture. During World War II, GIs bought thousands of them. Harry S Truman often wore them, and so did Elvis.

But there is another, less carefree Honolulu, invisible to the hordes who populate the high-rises on the brutally overdeveloped, relentlessly commercial Waikiki. For all the grandeur of rocky Diamond Head, rising from the sea southwest of Waikiki, the voluptuous beauty of orchids and bougainvillea and flame trees, the seduction of sun and sea and trade winds, the city faces big challenges. Far too heavily dependent on tourism now that industrial cultivation of pineapple and sugarcane, which made it rich, has ended, Honolulu's economy rises and falls with that of Japan, which supplies many of its visitors. And with Japan mired in recession, Honolulu missed the mainland boom of the 1990s. Its population stagnated, investment and inflation-adjusted incomes fell, bankruptcies rose, unemployment and poverty increased. Hawaii labored to diversify, but more than 100,000 people left the state for the mainland.

Honolulu, like Hawaii as a whole, is burdened by a sclerotic state government, greedy unions, and an overblown benefits system. State income taxes are among the nation's highest, and *Forbes* magazine gave the city its booby prize for economic development. For decades, dominance by a single party, the Democrats, inhibited change—and on occasion fostered corruption. Alarmed by indications that Hawaii voted at the lowest rate of any state in 2000, *The Honolulu Advertiser* mourned a "democratic system left to rot through indifference or even hostility." But two years later, Linda Lingle, a onetime journalist, surprised the chattering classes by capturing the statehouse for the Republicans for the first time in forty years.

Honolulu remains a place of boundless tolerance, where most babies are born of mixed ethnic stock, and prejudice is viewed with disdain. A local woman whose forebears came from Germany, Spain, Korea, Japan, and the Philippines gaily told my wife, Betsey, and me that she was "real chop suey." People of Japanese origin eat fried rice and Peking duck; people of Chinese origin eat sushi. McDonald's serves noodles as well as burgers. There can be few more exuberant neighborhoods in the United States than Honolulu's Chinatown on Saturday morning, market day. Sidewalks and aisles of food markets are jammed not just with Chinese speakers but with Thai and Lao and Samoan and English speakers, all darting in and out of noodle factories, lei shops (try Lin's at 1017A Maunakea Street), curio dealers, chop suey joints, hairdressers, benevolent societies, duck-to-go dealers (try Nam Fong at 1029 Maunakea Street), jewelry stores, acupuncture clinics, herbalists, and hole-in-the-wall restaurants, all the while taking care to avoid basket weavers squatting at the curb and graphic artists with their wares on the pavement.

"Honolulu has become a Eurasian experience in my lifetime," said Jay Fidell, a lawyer who came here in the 1960s from Queens. "The business community is completely polyglot. I know of no place in the world where race means less, although there is a divide between those who were born in Hawaii and those who have moved here."

As best we know, the first settlers reached Hawaii 1,500 years ago, sailing across immense reaches of the Pacific from the Marquesas Islands in twin-hulled canoes. It was a stupendous feat of navigation, using only the stars and the currents, matched about 500 years later by a group of Tahitians, who probably conquered the Marquesans. Both groups were Polynesians, like the Maori tribesmen of New Zealand. When Captain James Cook arrived in 1778, naming the islands in honor of the Earl of Sandwich, his patron, he found that his Maori interpreter could understand what the locals said.

Over the three decades ending with his death in 1819, the great King Kamehameha I, based in Honolulu, united all the islands under his rule. After he was gone, missionaries came, sailing from New England around treacherous Cape Horn in handsome schooners. Hiram Bingham of Bennington, Vermont, preached the first sermon in Hawaii in 1820 and began the five-year task of building Kawaiahao Church in 1837. The church still stands, not far from the state capitol in the center of Honolulu, an enlarged copy in coral blocks, hand-hewn from local reefs, of a village Congregational church in New England, with a broad central aisle, pews for 1,500, and an old Boston clock.

Whaling ships followed, and their sailors transmitted venereal diseases to Hawaiian women, who died by the tens of thousands. But the missionaries persevered, banning alcohol and the hula, the mesmerizing dance through which the Hawaiians celebrated their culture, and devising the shapeless muumuu to disguise womanly curves. The missionaries' story is told just across the street at the Mission Houses Museum, installed in three unadorned buildings where the stiff-necked New Englanders kept their stores, developed a written form of the Hawaiian language, and printed the Bible in it.

"They came to do good and stayed to do well," Hawaiians say about the missionaries. That is not quite true. It was the children and grandchildren of the missionaries—like the descendants of Amos and Juliette Cooke, of whom more later—who grew rich. By 1862, *haole* (foreigners) owned 75 percent of Hawaii's land, and a handful of *haole* companies still own much of it. Hawaiians and part-Hawaiians constitute a largely landless minority in their own islands, outnumbered by the descendants of the Japanese, Chinese, Portuguese, Filipinos, and mainlanders who made their way here.

Sugar barons from North America played a crucial role in deposing the last Hawaiian queen, Liliuokalani, in 1893. The American president at the time, Grover Cleveland, called this a disgrace, but in 1898 the United States, egged on by Theodore Roosevelt, annexed the islands, which became the fiftieth state in 1959, with Honolulu as the capital. Iolani Palace, a frothy confection of Corinthian columns and New Orleans–style cast iron, with a Grand Hall full of gleaming woodwork and an equally grand Throne Room, stands as a forlorn if well-kept reminder of the vanished monarchy.

The Bishop Museum, too little visited by tourists, contains convincing evidence of the artistic gifts of the early native islanders. Among its treasures are a newly restored six-man outrigger racing canoe of highly varnished wood, which even on dry land embodies the very idea of speed; a life-size wooden image of the war god Ku, scowling fiercely, knees bent and teeth bared, one of only three to have survived; and a group of fabulous helmets and cloaks, fashioned from red, yellow, and black feathers of tens of thousands of birds.

Anna Rice Cooke, a wealthy descendant of missionaries and married to another, gave Honolulu its Academy of Arts, designed by Bertram G. Goodhue in 1927, which sits beneath a mighty monkeypod tree. On its doorstep during our last visit, we ran into Barney A. Ebsworth, a St. Louis art collector who maintains a house in Honolulu. "This is the best general art museum anywhere in the tropics," he said, which sounded like hyperbole to me until I toured the galleries. In fact, Honolulu's is a jewel among smaller American art museums. Not surprisingly, it has a comprehensive collection of early views of Hawaii, as seen through the eyes of nineteenth-century British and French visitors. Not surprisingly, it has a choice selection of objects that vividly illustrate the mingling of Eastern and Western artistic traditions in porcelain, textiles, ivory, silver, and other media. For us, the highlights included large detailed watercolor illustrations of a mango and a pineapple, done in Canton in 1865, and a room lined with French panoramic wallpaper, titled *Natives of the Pacific*, from 1804.

But something wholly unexpected lurks in this handsome group of single-story pavilions, grouped around a series of six courtyards: a collection of modern masterworks, many of them bought in the 1920s by Anna Rice Cooke. Sitting in mid-Pacific, she developed a taste for Gauguin, van Gogh, and Pissarro at the same time as the most sophisticated collectors in Paris and in St. Petersburg. Then, in 1925, she built a house high on Makiki Heights, overlooking the city, leaving it later to her daughter, Alice. In 1988 it became the city's Contemporary Museum, notable for a multiroom installation by the English painter David Hockney, evoking his wide-eyed, childlike sets for Ravel's opera *L'Enfant and les Sortilèges*, and for a pair of George Rickey sculptures made wildly kinetic by the breezy site.

Limited public tours ($25) of another house, Shangri-La, a five-acre Oriental fantasy built by the reclusive Doris Duke in 1938, leave from the academy. Its bedroom suite was modeled on the Taj Mahal, and it houses a priceless 3,500-piece collection of Islamic art—ceramics, textiles, furniture, architectural fragments, manuscripts, and rugs.

Music and dance have been important in Hawaiian life from the start; Don Ho did not spring from a musical desert. As Matt Catingub, the young conductor of the Honolulu Symphony Pops, gently reminded me, choral music has a proud tradition throughout Polynesia, especially in Fiji and New Zealand (birthplace of the great part-Maori soprano Kiri Te Kanawa). Over the years, the islands have developed a special affinity for ukuleles, adapted from the four-stringed braguinha brought here in 1879 by immigrants from the Portuguese island of Madeira; for slack-key guitars, tuned lower by Hawaiian cowboys decades ago to give a more "tropical" tone and to make them easier to play; and for the Hawaiian steel guitar, a horizontal instrument with a singing tone created by a sliding steel fret. New life has been breathed into traditional Hawaiian music and into the hula of late by younger musicians like Keilii Reichel, an instrumentalist, singer, and hula master. The visitor can now find performances of the real stuff as well as the hokum of years gone by.

The musical revival mirrors a growing Hawaiian sovereignty movement. Although fewer than 1 percent of Hawaii residents are of pure Hawaiian ancestry, about 20 percent have classified themselves as wholly or partly native in recent surveys. The centennnials of the overthrow of Queen Liliuokalani in 1993 and of American annexation in 1998 inspired demonstrations, sanctioned to some degree by the governor at the time, John D. Waihee, the first of native Hawaiian descent to hold the job. Since then, the movement has gained wide acceptance across ethnic lines here, but there is no agreement on specific goals. Do the Hawaiians want true independence? A commonwealth? Nation-within-nation status?

Samuel P. King, a senior federal judge in Honolulu, told me that "a broad majority thinks these people got a raw deal and deserve something." Still, the whole idea bothers him. "I have three-sixteenths Hawaiian blood," he said. "My grandson—the one in that sky-diving picture on the wall—he has three sixty-fourths. Everyone here marries outside their group. It's one of the triumphs of this place, or so I've always thought. I'd hate to think our values are changing."

For years, native Hawaiians took great pride in the Bishop Trust. Founded by the last lineal descendant of Kamehameha I and devoted to the maintenance of schools for children of at least partly Hawaiian descent, its wealth now totals more than $6 billion. At one time it owned 10 percent of the New York investment firm Goldman Sachs, as well as a bank, a shopping center, and an aluminum plant in China. But the five trustees were forced out in 1999 for failing to perform their duties while paying themselves $1 million a year each. Then, in 2002, the

Kamehameha Schools for the first time admitted a student without any Hawaiian ancestors, exciting shouts of "betrayal!" from native Hawaiian activists.

Politicians of many ethnic backgrounds have succeeded in Hawaiian politics, but nobody doubts that Japanese Americans have run the show since statehood. Their leading figure, Senator Daniel J. Inouye, remains the state's dominant politician. Wounded in World War II as a member of the storied 442nd Regimental Combat Team, the most highly decorated unit in American history, he has held high public office since 1954.

With three-quarters of Hawaii's people, Honolulu bestrides its state. It is a smallish city, with a metropolitan population of 876,156, about the same as Greater Albany, and it is remarkable in its isolation. Tokyo is 3,860 miles away, Los Angeles 2,553 miles away. Solitary though it may be, the city stands at the crossroads of the Pacific, and on one day in its history it grasped the nation's consciousness as few other cities of its size ever have. That day was December 7, 1941, the fateful day of the Japanese sneak attack on Honolulu and its great naval anchorage at Pearl Harbor, the day Franklin D. Roosevelt vowed would "live in infamy," the day the United States was brusquely plunged into World War II.

Honolulu remains a military town. Big installations lie all around its periphery—the Army at Schofield Barracks, the Air Force at Hickam Field, the Navy at Pearl Harbor, and the Pacific Command at Camp H. M. "Howlin' Mad" Smith. Above the city, in a volcanic crater known as the Punchbowl, 33,230 servicemen and women from World War II, the Korean War, and the Vietnam War are buried on grassy slopes. One of them is the most famous American war correspondent, Ernie Pyle.

But even the Punchbowl cannot match the emotional wallop delivered by the USS *Arizona* Memorial—a simple structure built athwart the hulk of one of the battleships sunk in 1942 by Japanese dive-bombers and torpedo planes as they lay at anchor off Ford's Island in Pearl Harbor, long known as "the Gibraltar of the Pacific." Shattered by a 1,760-pound Japanese armor-piercing bomb that ignited the forward ammunition store, the *Arizona* went down in a mere nine minutes, with the loss of 1,177 crewmen, including the captain. Roughly 1.5 million people visit this site every year, and most days some are Japanese. At a visitor center on shore, operated by the National Park Service, a remarkably unjingoistic film, narrated by the actress Stockard Channing, supplies historical context.

Transported to the memorial by launch, the visitor sees an American flag flying from a pole attached to a rusty strut that once supported one of the ship's tripod towers. The base of a gun turret and other bits of corroded metal protrude from the water, and fuel oil, leaking slowly from a ruptured tank below, forms a kaleidoscopic slick on the surface. Only a few hundred yards away, another battleship, the USS *Missouri*, rides at anchor. Japan surrendered on the *Missouri*'s deck on September 2, 1945, in Tokyo Bay. Beginning and end join at Pearl Harbor.

Names of the *Arizona* crew members whose war ended in its first hour are inscribed on a marble wall at the memorial. Among them, I found to my amazement—to my horror, really—is my own. My head spun and my eyes must have bugged when I saw it up there: R. W. Apple. Who was he?

His name, a helpful park service historian told me, was not really identical to mine; he was Robert William, and I am Raymond Walter. He was from Illinois, a fireman first class, meaning he tended the ship's huge boilers. No relative, as far as I know, yet Apple is not a common name, and I feel linked to him all the same. In the past, I always thought of my father when someone mentioned Pearl Harbor because I was driving around with him when word of the attack came over the radio on that Sunday afternoon long ago. From now on I also think of this other R. W. Apple, perishing on the *Arizona*.

WHERE TO STAY

Halekulani, 2199 Kalia Road, (808) 923-2311. This is the premier hotel in the islands and one of the finest in the United States, an oasis of taste in tacky Waikiki, with 700 employees for 456 rooms. Order freshly squeezed pineapple juice for breakfast in your handsome beige or off-white bedroom, gaze out to sea, and glow. Two of Hawaii's top restaurants are downstairs, plus chic shops and a pool with the famous orchid logo.

Kahala Mandarin Oriental, 5000 Kahala Avenue, (808) 739-8888. Tucked between a golf course and the sea, out beyond Diamond Head but still only fifteen minutes from downtown, the Kahala is the antithesis of Waikiki. Dolphins cavort in a man-made lagoon, palms sway above a broad beach, and torches light the tropical gardens at night. Orchids, mahogany, and teak play leading roles in the restrained, refined Asian decor.

Royal Hawaiian, 2259 Kalakaua Avenue, (808) 923-7311. A survivor from the Lurline era, "the Pink Palace of the Pacific" was built in 1927. With flowered rugs, pink ceilings, and period

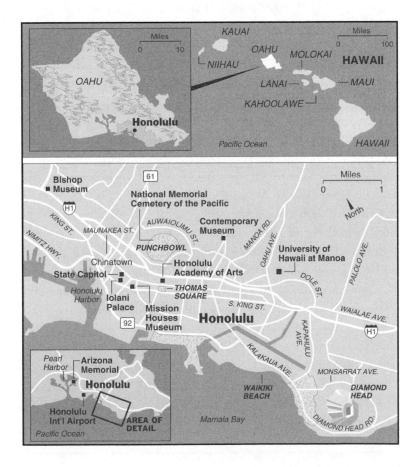

furniture, the Royal remains true to its time, but careful updating and a modern tower cater to contemporary tastes. The old girl still has the broadest beach on Waikiki, and the beach-side bar serves the best mai tai in town, if you're feeling frisky.

WHERE TO EAT

Alan Wong's, 1857 South King Street, (808) 949-2526. They do magic tricks in Alan Wong's open kitchen, producing food that is complex but never fussy. Ingredients and ideas come from everywhere. A bag of steamed clams, pork, and shiitakes has its roots in Portugal, and beautiful, barely cooked Atlantic scallops are combined with Japanese edamame beans and tiny Italian gnocchi. On busy nights in busy seasons, service sags.

Chef Mavro, 1969 South King Street, (808) 944-4714. George Mavrothalassitis cooks serious food for serious people. Born in Marseille, he has a cutting-edge style that shows Greek, Provençal, and Pacific influences. Poached and roasted chicken is finished not with cream but with a ginger, egg, and lemon infusion, light and bright and entirely appropriate. Eating it, you can't help recalling avgolemeno, the iconic Greek soup.

Hoku, 5000 Kahala Avenue, (808) 739-8779. In the Kahala Mandarin's showplace restaurant, Wayne Hirabayashi turns out nimble mid-Pacific variations on European standards. An oxtail consommé gets a lift from julienned Chinese cabbage and star anise; Niçoise salad is embellished with grilled ahi tuna, sweet Maui onions, and quail eggs. Exquisitely aromatic sorbets have Asian accents as well: guava, mango, and lemongrass.

La Mer, 2199 Kalia Road, (808) 923-2311. The more formal of the Halekulani's two restaurants, La Mer eschews the fusion cooking so popular in Honolulu. Hewing instead to the precepts of French classicism, it produces ravishing food. The chef, Yves Garnier, makes brilliant use of prime local fish (yellowtail, for example, topped with crushed pistachios), but Oriental spices are few and far between. Superb wines, superbly served.

Roy's, 6600 Kalanianaole Highway, (808) 396-7697. Roy Yamaguchi has outposts everywhere—Maui, Guam, New York, Pebble Beach—but this is his original restaurant, opened in 1988, and on it sails. Just a bite or two here will make you forget any disappointments elsewhere in the Kingdom of Roy: a peppery snapper fillet with green beans, Japanese eggplant, and savory sticky rice, perhaps, or a moist, earthy pot roast of pork with a ginger sauce, colorfully arrayed on the plate with carrots and broccoli. Ace service, too.

Sam Choy's Diamond Head, 449 Kapahulu Avenue, (808) 732-8645. Sam Choy, a big man with a bigger heart, is the sole Hawaiian superchef who was born in the islands. So he keeps traditional items like poke (cured raw fish) and the kind of reef fish he caught as a boy on the menu, along with more innovative dishes. Portions are daunting.

INDEX